D1492648

1/8/06

Clinical Governance in Mental Health and Learning Disability Services

A Practical Guide

Edited by
Adrian James, Adrian Worrall
& Tim Kendall

Gaskell

Gaskell is an imprint of the Royal College of Psychiatrists,
17 Belgrave Square, London SW1X 8PG
http://www.rcpsych.ac.uk

British Library Cataloguing-in-Publication Data
A catalogue record for this book is available from the British Library.
ISBN 1-904671-12-8

Distributed in North America
by Balogh International, Inc.

This publication is dedicated to Sarah, Lucy, Alice and Jasper, to Rex and to Rosa, Sam,
Mimi and Kitty. We thank Jim and Mary James for support, encouragement and editorial
advice and Margaret Allen and Lesley Hocking for secretarial help and expertise.

Printed in Great Britain by Cromwell Press Ltd, Trowbridge.

Contents

Figures

Tables

Boxes

Contributors

Tim Amos, Senior Lecturer in Forensic Psychiatry, University of Bristol, and Consultant Forensic Psychiatrist, Fromeside Clinic, Bristol

Martin Briscoe, Consultant Psychiatrist, Wonford House Hospital, Dryden Road, Exeter EX2 5AF

Errol Cocks, PhD, Professor of Psychology & Human Services, Zayed University, PO Box 19282, Dubai, United Arab Emirates

Paddy Cooney, Director, National Institute of Mental Health (England), 2 Tower Lane, Taunton, Somerset TA1 4AR

Jenny Firth-Cozens, Special Advisor on Modernisation, London Deanery of Postgraduate Medical and Dental Education, 20 Guilford Street, London WC1V 4DZ

John Geddes, Professor in Psychiatric Epidemiology, Department of Psychiatry, University of Oxford, Warneford Hospital, Oxford OX3 7JX, UK

Kim L. Goddard, Assistant Director Governance, Springfield University Hospital, 61 Glenburnie Road, London SW17 7DJ

Pearl Hettiaratchy, Consultant Psychiatrist, Robin's Hill, 2 Oliver's Battery Road North, Winchester, Hampshire SO22 4JA

Adrian James, Consultant Forensic Psychiatrist, Langdon Hospital, Exeter Road, Dawlish, Devon EX7 0NR, CHI Reviewer and former Medical Director, Devon Partnership NHS Trust

Cornelius Katona, Dean, Institute of Medicine and Health Sciences, University of Kent at Canterbury, Kent CT2 7PD

Robert F. Kehoe, Consultant Psychiatrist and Medical Director, Cygnet Hospital at Wyke, Lower Wyke, Bradford BD12 8LR

Katy Kendall, Lead Clinician, Specialist Mental Health Services, and Consultant Psychiatrist, Sheffield Care Trust

Tim Kendall, Deputy Director, College Research Unit, Co-Director, National Collaborating Centre for Mental Health, and Medical Director and Consultant Psychiatrist, Sheffield Care Trust, Fulwood House, Old Fulwood Road, Sheffield S10 3TH

Gillian Leng, Programme Director of Clinical Guidelines, National Institute for Clinical Excellence, 71 High Holborn, London WC1V 6NA

Mary Lindsey, West Resource Centre, The Kernow Building, Wilson Way, Pool, Redruth, Cornwall TR15 3QE

Peter Littlejohns, Clinical Director, National Institute for Clinical Excellence, 71 High Holborn, London WC1V 6NA

Carole Longson, PhD, Programme Director of Technology Appraisals, National Institute for Clinical Excellence, 71 High Holborn, London WC1V 6NA

Sheila Mann, Consultant Psychiatrist and Medical Director, North Essex Mental Health NHS Partnership Trust, Trust Headquarters, Cuton Hall Lane, Springfield, Chelmsford CM2 5PX

Claire Palmer, Clinical Effectiveness Manager, Kings College Hospital NHS Trust, London

Clare Perkins, Specialist in Public Health, Cheshire

Rachel E. Perkins, Clinical Director and Consultant Clinical Psychologist, South West London and St George's Hospital Mental Health NHS Trust, 61 Glenburnie Road, London SW17 7DJ

David Roy, Medical Director, South London and Maudsley NHS Trust, 9th Floor, Tower Building, 11 York Road, London SE1 7NX

John J. Sandford, Consultant Forensic Psychiatrist, Llanarth Court Hospital, Llanarth, Raglan, Usk NP15 2YD

Gabriel Scally, Regional Director of Public Health, South West England, Monmouthshire

Pete Snowden, Clinical Director, Personality Disorder Service, Ashworth Hospital, Parkbourn, Maghull, Liverpool L31 1HW

Lesley Stevens, Hampshire Partnership NHS Trust, Adult Mental Health Directorate, Winchester Community Mental Health Team, Connaught House, Romsey Road, Winchester, Hampshire SO22 5GE

Martin F. Ward, Independent Nurse Consultant, MW Professional Development Limited, 2 The Elms, Gloucester Street, Faringdon, Oxfordshire SN7 7HY, formerly Director, Mental Health, Royal College of Nursing

Barry Wilson, Independent Consultant in Social Care

Melba Wilson, Chair, Wandsworth Primary Care Trust, Teak Tower, Springfield University Hospital, 61 Glenburnie Road, London SW17 7DJ

Adrian Worrall, Programme Manager, Royal College of Psychiatrists' Research Unit, 4th Floor, 21 Mansell Street, London E1 8AA

Foreword

When it was introduced, the concept of clinical governance was new, challenging and prone to confront traditional cultures and attitudes. There were even clinicians who thought that *The New NHS: Modern and Dependable* (1997) had given birth to the Spanish Inquisition, before which the faithful would be sacrificed to the rules of an era they neither liked nor understood. Some were reassured by the distinction made between an individual's clinical appraisal and the clinical governance of services whose shortcomings might be due more to a shortage of resources or their mismanagement than to its clinician's failings.

Gradually, clinicians have become engaged in the process, many with great enthusiasm. Clinical governance has settled to what it always promised to be – an opportunity for clinicians, managers, patients and their carers to work together to improve services for the common good, and to ensure that they have the means to implement what that entails. Through it, clinicians may come to trust the expertise of patients in their own treatment and patients may come to trust that clinicians will be acting in their best interests.

In such a mutual partnership, it should be possible for both to accept that, in exceptional circumstances, each may have to accede to the better judgement of the other. Patients with mental illness may defer to clinicians the responsibility for decisions they have temporarily lost the capacity to make for themselves. Clinicians under 360° appraisal may appreciate that patients can sometimes point out ways in which performance can be improved that they cannot see from the inside.

But life is not always as simple as this. Anyone who has worked or been treated in the National Health Service will know that in practice it has to balance competing priorities. Rapid service for the maximum number of patients has to be balanced against the quality of care that can be safely given; the right of patients to choose their treatment has to be balanced against what can be economically offered in a world of finite resources. The confidentiality on which the doctor–patient relationship is founded has to be balanced against sharing of the information that carers need to look after the patient properly; the freedom of the individual has to be balanced against the public's right to protection.

Such balances are enshrined in every National Service Framework; and they are there in clinical governance too. All clinicians are required to practise evidence-based medicine and there is plenty of research to show what that might be for any illness and its treatment. But what of narrative evidence – what the individual patient feels like on the end of it rather than what science says groups of such patients ought to feel? Patients need proof that clinicians are up-to-date with the latest techniques and practising them to the best of their ability. But what happens if rigid guidelines stifle innovation for fear that straying from them may be construed as a departure from good professional practice? Patients may wish to hold clinicians to account, and punish them when things go wrong. But clinicians can learn from mistakes only when they are able to examine procedures openly in an atmosphere free from blame.

To make matters even more complicated, in the field of care covered by this book, many of the qualities that clinical governance is designed to improve are difficult to assess. It is relatively easy to monitor a patient's response to medication, but holistic 'packages' of social care – jobs, housing and friendships – are far less tangible. Ill-health is clearly definable but well-being and self-esteem are not easy to pin down. Examinations can test the content of a trainee's knowledge, but how do we assess the processes that patients value most – the ability to listen to the patient's story or break bad news with sensitivity; to carry the anxieties of those in crisis and make clear decisions in the midst of it all; to work alongside others in the team while offering firm leadership; to form opinions of one's own while empowering those who may disagree.

Attitudes to clinical governance are now very positive, but it remains a concept which needs much skill and commitment to implement. What is needed is a clear and comprehensive handbook for clinicians, managers and patients to find their way around. This is it. The authors are to be congratulated on a truly practical guide that is both informative and readable, and not a rack, a thumbscrew or a bonfire in sight!

Sir Liam Donaldson
Chief Medical Officer
Department of Health

Mike Shooter,
President,
Royal College of Psychiatrists

Preface

Rachel E. Perkins

To the uninitiated, mental health services involve an often incomprehensible array of structures, personnel and procedures. Most people never encounter the care plans, care coordinators, case conferences and ward rounds, or the bewildering array of associated therapies and therapists. Neither are they subject to the impenetrable jargon with which mental health services are replete. Now we have yet another process to contend with: 'clinical governance'. If we ask what it actually means, it becomes clear that this clinical governance simply cannot be done without the involvement of service users.

Within a policy agenda that requires health services to be 'modernised' to meet public expectations, the National Health Service (NHS) Plan (Department of Health, 2000) requires a reshaping of the NHS from the patient's point of view. A seamless range of easily accessible services is described, shaped around the needs, wishes, preferences and convenience of the different individuals and groups who require them. These are services in which patients are treated with the dignity and respect that is their right, and are provided with the full information they need to inform their decisions; they are services that staff continuously work to improve.

At its core, clinical governance is no more or less than the processes by which NHS organisations and their staff are accountable for, and continually improve, the quality of what they offer, and learn from the things that went wrong in order to decrease the chance of them happening again. If services are to be designed around the people who use them, then it is not possible to think about processes to improve their quality without the involvement of their users. Service users must be involved at all levels: in the design of the treatment and support they receive; in giving feedback about the operation of services they receive, in order to improve the extent to which these meet their wishes and expectations; and in the planning and development of services, in order to ensure that the necessary range and quality of provision are available to meet their requirements. In addition, users need to be provided with enough information about the range of options available to make informed choices about what they would prefer, and their choices must be respected by those who provide the assistance. And when they are not happy with what goes on, users' complaints must be taken seriously and addressed. As the NHS Plan (p. 92) states:

'The NHS needs to be seen to say sorry where things go wrong, rather than taking a defensive attitude, and to learn from complaints so the same problems do not recur.'

User involvement is required by all national policy and guidance relating to mental health services (Department of Health, 1998, 1999a,b, 2000, 2001). But real user involvement requires more than the expression of good intentions. It cannot be achieved by simple expedients like a signature on a care plan or the inclusion of a token user or two on committees. If services are to be reshaped from a users' point of view, this will involve more than a simple 'add-on' to existing ways of working.

Traditional beliefs and practices which implicitly assume that mental health professionals have access to a specialised body of knowledge that is not accessible to, and cannot be understood by, non-professionals, prevent any meaningful user involvement. If this is the case, then 'involving service users' is reduced to persuading them that the professional knows best. Professionals do have expertise and access to information, but meaningful user involvement requires that these are made available to those who receive services, so that they can make informed decisions about what they want. Professionals must also be humble enough to recognise that they do not have a monopoly on relevant information and expertise.

Those who have mental health problems have experience and expertise that most mental health professionals lack: a knowledge of what it is like to live with mental health difficulties and what different treatments and services feel like from the receiving end. And different service users experience these things differently. Users are not an undifferentiated 'lump' within which the views and experiences of one can be taken as a proxy for all. Research evidence can tell us only about the average response of groups of people. But there is no psychiatric intervention that has the same effect on everyone who receives it; therefore, the individual's experience is critical. Similarly, mental health problems are not experienced in a vacuum: they occur in the context of the whole of that person's life – a life apart from the mental health arena that is so often forgotten by services. Different people have different preferences, aspirations and goals; they come from different communities and cultures; they occupy different roles, relationships and social networks – and all of these influence how different types of treatment and support are experienced and what most enhances their quality of life.

A fundamental culture change is required on the part of providers: a major shift in assumptions, attitudes and practices - a move away from traditional perspectives, in which the professional is seen as the sole expert who must therefore determine what patients need, to one in which the expertise of personal experience is respected and heeded. User involvement in services will be no more than tokenism if those providing services lack a commitment to listen to those on the receiving end of their ministrations. Providers must take seriously what is said and act upon it if possible – even when this runs contrary to what they consider to be 'best' for the person.

Clinical governance is about improving the quality of services. Quality is not restricted to the clinical aspects of care, but includes quality of life and the entire patient experience (Department of Health, 2000). Clinical governance therefore involves tapping this experience centrally: it cannot be effective in achieving its goal of service improvement without meaningful user involvement.

References

Department of Health (1998) *Modernising Mental Health Services: Safe, Sound and Supportive*. London: Department of Health.

Department of Health (1999a) *National Service Framework for Mental Health*. London: Department of Health.

Department of Health (1999b) *Clinical Governance: Quality in the New NHS*, HSC 1999/065. London: Department of Health.

Department of Health (2000) *The NHS Plan: A Plan for Investment, a Plan for Reform*, cm 4818-I. London: TSO.

Department of Health (2001) *Modern Mental Health Policy Implementation Guide*. London: Department of Health.

Part I

Setting the scene

CHAPTER 1

Introduction

Adrian James and Adrian Worrall

The wording of the title of this book was chosen because the editors set out to provide a guide and were determined that it would be practical. Their own experience and the comments of colleagues suggested that the term 'clinical governance' had crept into the vocabulary almost unexplained and settled down in a nest of buzzwords like 'accountability', 'audit', 'assessment' and 'appraisal', to say nothing of the other letters of the alphabet. The concepts were not entirely unfamiliar and resonated with the experience of clinicians and managers, but this time a coherent pattern was emerging. The diverse practitioners of the multi-skilled enterprise that is the National Health Service (NHS) were beginning to find common ground. Since this process started, sufficient experience has been accumulated to map that common ground and identify the fundamental features of the landscape.

The number of people who need to become familiar with the territory has increased significantly. Most need to be able to find the sites that are of particular relevance to them, but their understanding of the lie of the land will be enhanced if they appreciate the perspectives of colleagues with other needs. So the contents of this book are offered to the community of mental health and learning disability practitioners. Psychiatrists, medical directors, managers, clinical governance leads and members of trust boards will have their own wide interests but in a multidisciplinary team nurses, psychologists, occupational therapists, social workers, users and carers will find material that accords with their needs. In addition, more broadly based policy-makers will find insights that should help them to appreciate how clinical governance relates to a specialised service. The lived experience of our writers offers a wealth of practical wisdom and the range of disciplines from which they are drawn gives promise that this guide is both well informed and comprehensive. This introductory chapter provides an overview to help the busy practitioner to use the text to best advantage.

What is clinical governance?

Definitions and descriptions of clinical governance abound. The concept was introduced in *The New NHS: Modern, Dependable* (Department of Health, 1997) and further developed in *A First Class Service* (Department of Health, 1998) and *Clinical Governance: Quality in the New NHS* (Department of Health, 1999). Obscurities still remain, however. Two basic descriptions may prove helpful:

'a framework through which NHS organisations are accountable for continuously improving the quality of their services and safeguarding high standards of care by creating an environment in which excellence in clinical care will flourish.' (Donaldson & Scally, 1998)

'the system of steps and procedures adopted by the NHS to ensure that patients receive the highest possible quality of care. It includes: a patient centred approach; an accountability for quality; ensuring high standards and safety and improvement in patient services and care.' (Commission for Health Improvement, 2001)

It will soon become apparent that clarity of thinking will be maintained only if, as in the above descriptions, clinical governance is distinguished from its components. Clinical audit, clinical risk management, education and training, patient involvement, the delivery of information and evidenced-based practice are discrete issues (we prefer not to adopt the term 'service governance': it has arisen, understandably, where integrated trusts are involved in 'best value' arrangements with local authorities out of concern for sensitivities associated with the word 'clinical').

The process of keeping minds clear has been helped considerably by documentation from three sources. *Clinical Governance: Quality in the New NHS* (Department of Health, 1999) has already been mentioned: it identifies a series of clinical governance components. The Royal College of Psychiatrists (2004) has set out clinical governance responsibilities in its guidelines for professional practice. Finally, members of the Royal College of Psychiatrists Clinical Governance Support Service have developed clinical governance standards for mental health and learning disability services. These are reprinted in Appendices 1 and 2 and the key sections attached to these standards are listed in Box 1.1. This list should prove useful to readers seeking to identify the issues that apply to their service. It also provides a lead into discussion of the issues and outcomes that are still open to debate.

Each of these sections typically includes suggestions about procedures, representation, strategies and reporting arrangements, and then proceeds to matters more specific to the topic area. Examples are given in Box 1.2.

In the final analysis, judgement of the effectiveness of the clinical governance measures now being introduced will depend on outcomes,

---

Box 1.1 Key elements of clinical governance

- Clinical governance structures and accountabilities
- Service user and carer involvement
- Clinical audit
- Clinical risk management
- Evidence-based practice
- Staffing and staff management
- Education and training
- Information management.

Box 1.2 Examples of clinical governance activity

- Participation in clinical audit of the prescribed doses of antipsychotics
- Using information from critical incident reviews to develop action plans
- Providing written information for service users and carers
- Agreeing personal development plans for all staff
- Dissemination of locally relevant clinical guidelines.

---

particularly as they impinge on cost and patient experience. Performance will need to be measured and procedures established to ensure that this measurement is both accurate and presented helpfully. These issues are discussed in Chapter 18. This is also an opportune point at which to encourage our readers to e-mail any comment on the content and presentation of this book to enquiries@cru.rcpsych.ac.uk. While policy, practice and organisation are on the march, continual review is essential.

Mental health and learning disability services: some special features

Before we move on to summarise the chapters it would be as well to draw attention to issues, dealt with in more detail by our contributors, that have special relevance to mental health and learning disability services: the interests of these two linked services seldom diverge. Evidence-based practice is a case in point. The widely held view that mental health services can offer less evidence of outcomes is not borne out by the facts. It is access to information and appraisal procedures that calls for careful treatment. Risk assessment and management and the training of staff to cope with violence, the risk of homicide and parasuicide are of particular relevance in these fields. The services engage a more varied staff than many others and this calls for well-honed skills in team-building and management, and for the meshing of personnel with widely varying levels of professional expertise, training needs and job expectations. These differences enrich the services but present their own problems, especially when cultural values appear to diverge, as might be the case between, for example, health, social services and criminal justice; assessment and performance measurement might also prove especially problematic. Above all, user and carer involvement calls for special insights. Patients and carers are often vulnerable and misunderstood: the protection of their rights calls for special skills of advocacy and communication. The use and monitoring of care programmes are of particular relevance, as is patient involvement in the procedures of the Mental Health Act Commission and the mental health review tribunals. Professionals may legitimately be in open disagreement, for example in reports to courts regarding risk or treatment against a patient's expressed wish. All these matters are taken up in the chapters that follow.

The lie of the land

The material in this book falls into four parts:
- Setting the scene (Chapters 1 and 2)
- Foundations and organisational structure (Chapters 3–8)
- Building blocks/key elements (Chapters 9–16)
- Translating clinical governance into the clinical context (Chapters 17–22).

Part I: Setting the scene

In Chapter 2, 'Background, history and philosophy: the origins of clinical governance', Clare Perkins and Gabriel Scally describe how various and apparently disparate elements coalesced over time into a pattern now recognised by the term 'clinical governance'. Gabriel Scally, as one of those instrumental in assembling the building blocks, is especially well placed to guide us through this process.

The introduction of the internal market in 1989 did not address matters of quality improvement. It took the introduction of patient charters and Confidential Inquiries to move the standards agenda forward; the establishment of the Cochrane Centre in Oxford was a key factor. High-profile cases in Bristol (paediatric cardiac surgery), Exeter (breast cancer screening) and Kent (cervical screening) prompted moves towards significant change. In 1997 *The New NHS: Modern, Dependable* firmed up the agenda by introducing national standards and guidelines (National Service Frameworks) for use in clinical governance and placed a statutory duty for quality assurance on NHS trusts. The National Institute for Clinical Excellence (NICE) played a pivotal part in producing authoritative national guidelines for the achievement and measurement of effective clinical and cost procedures, and the Commission for Health

Improvement (CHI) emerged as the guarantor of high-quality clinical services. Medical staff became a particular focus with the introduction of compulsory annual appraisal and the role of the National Clinical Assessment Authority in operating a rapid referral service for performance assessment is described.

Chapter 2 brings early coherence into what might otherwise appear to be the bewildering proliferation of agencies, authorities, instruments and procedures which are the themes for Part II of the book. What is referred to as a sea change in the approach to quality assurance in the NHS is seen to be as relevant to the mental health and learning disabilty services as it is elsewhere.

Part II: Foundations and organisational structure

Part II examines the elements of sound foundation-building and the agencies that exist to assist, support and validate the process.

In Chapter 3, 'How to structure clinical governance', Adrian James sets out the importance of establishing a clear and shared understanding of the objectives of clinical governance procedures, and he emphasises the importance of ensuring that the many and disparate partners in the enterprise are brought into all stages of the process, from ownership to evaluation. The preferred approach is through directorates, whose function and remit are covered in detail, together with suggestions for the effective measurement of performance.

Trust boards must be involved in this process. In Chapter 4, 'The role of trust boards in clinical governance', Claire Palmer and Tim Kendall describe the disappointing outcome of research into board involvement. Clinical governance was well behind financial management in the preoccupations of the boards and its principles were seldom in evidence in the consideration of quality assurance. The authors suggest the creation of clinical governance departments charged with the delivery of quality across the fields of mental health and social care, to ensure that trust boards put in place systems that combine delivery with evaluation in a format that is accessible and understood not only by the provider but also by users and carers.

We now move on to the agencies whose purpose is to enable these processes to move forward in an informed way. John Sandford in Chapter 5, 'Health care inspectorates', outlines the evolution and effects of inspection. He provides us with an account of the structure of the Commission for Health Improvement (CHI) and a five-point guide to its functions and the six principles that underpin its procedures. These procedures are described as they happen at unit level so that the many partners to the process can know what and who are involved. Investig-ations can occasionally arise from evidence of persistent service failure, as can the intervention of the Secretary of State. The CHI has an extended role in its new incarnation as the Healthcare Commission (its statutory name is the Commission for Healthcare Audit and Inspection)Finally, Chapter 5 acknowledges that while the CHI has bred good practice, there are tensions in its operation still to be resolved.

Chapter 6, 'The mental health guidance programmes of the National Institute for Clinical Excellence', provides an opportunity for Peter Littlejohns, the Clinical Director of NICE, to give us his insights into the role and working of the agency, which was established in 1999 as a Special Health Authority and is acknowledged to be a key player in the government's strategy for quality improvement. Its small team works closely with partners and stakeholders, trusts and clinical governance professionals to provide guidance on the effectiveness of clinical interventions. In the course of this process it assesses new and existing technologies and develops clinical guidelines and audit criteria which take into account the effect of treatments on the quality of life and the alleviation of pain and disability. The role of NICE in the work of the National Confidential Inquiry into Suicide and Homicide by People with Mental Illness is described. Professor Littlejohn concludes by indicating how services can use the findings and processes of NICE, which are easily accessible on the agency's website, as guidelines in the routine assessment of their own work.

In Chapter 7, 'National support for clinical governance', Adrian Worrall summarises the key stages in clinical governance, then helpfully throws light on the reasons why managers find implementation difficult; he then goes on to describe models of national support and the benefits of peer review. This brings him to the work, programmes and publications of the Clinical Governance Support Service and an outline of the standards that it advocates. He concludes with information on organisations that support and facilitate clinical governance and notes on evaluation.

Part II of the book concludes with Chapter 8, 'Clinical governance and the National Service Framework for Mental Health', by Melba Wilson, who draws on her experience as both policy director of MIND and non-executive director of a large mental health trust in London. In particular, she is concerned to relate the procedures of clinical governance and the National Service Framework to mental health issues and to this end gives clear, practical guidance. This is a chapter that knits together many of the themes presented by preceding authors and by taking readers systematically through the issues she takes the mystique out of what might otherwise appear to be a welter of confusing detail and organisational overlay. The trick is to identify those areas within each directorate in which clinical intervention leads to demonstrable improvement recognised across the disciplines and service delivery areas. Finally, the author spices her optimism with realism in suggesting that, to be thorough, the entire process might span 10 years.

Part III: Building blocks/key elements

Part III is a detailed exploration of the key elements in the structure of clinical governance as we would expect it to operate in a trust that provides mental health and learning disability services. Issues and objectives for managers and practitioners are identified and the authors flesh out the issues implicit in the clinical governance standards reproduced in Appendix 1.

In Chapter 9, 'Involving service users and their relatives', Rachel Perkins establishes that users and carers have a special expertise derived from experience. Professional staff need to recognise the value of this expertise but are likely to need training to make best use of this valuable resource. Well presented information can encourage users and carers to be involved in all the stages of clinical governance, from early planning to evaluation. Chapter 9 covers the process in detail.

John Geddes, Director of the Centre for Evidence Based Mental Health, recognises the problems faced by many clinicians in Chapter 10, 'Evidence-based practice'. Pressures of time and opportunity and the inadequacies of earlier training may mean that initially clinicians are poorly equipped to conduct research and then to assess and interpret the findings. He takes the reader through the stages of this process and highlights clinical epidemiology and information technology skills as areas where remedial training might prove most useful.

If evidence-based practice is to be successful, the considerations raised by Mary Lindsey in Chapter 11, 'Evidence-based policies, guidelines, procedures and protocols', must be addressed. In areas such as mental health and learning disability services, which span health and social care authorities, clear policies and procedures can come only from jointly produced strategies that cover all stages, from introduction and development to their application in day-to-day practice. There need be no tension between national policy guidelines, trust involvement and local schemes of implementation if stakeholders – from the workforce to users – feel empowered and know that they are involved in the enterprise from the moment of adequate induction to the evaluated outcome.

We now come, in Chapter 12, 'Risk management', to considerations that apply in a very particular way to mental health and learning disability services. Tim Amos and Peter Snowden are consultant forensic psychiatrists who deal with risk in their everyday practice. For them, quite simply, risk management procedures, from recognition through assessment to containment, are strategies for the reduction of risk events. Against the backdrop of national concerns (such as those involving CHI, the Clinical Negligence Scheme for Trusts and the National Confidential Inquiries) the authors deal with the assessment of individual patients using assessment scales in conjunction with patient histories and clinical examination. They also deal with the responsibility of trusts to offer process guidance to clinicians. Deaths linked to mental illness led to recommendations based on the National Confidential Inquiries and these are outlined in some detail. Elsewhere in the chapter we are offered the reflection that adverse events will usually happen as a result of a series of failures rather than one incident.

At the start of this chapter we identified appraisal as one of the buzzwords and that is the subject of Chapter 13. Sheila Mann and Cornelius Katona draw on their experience with the Royal College of Psychiatrists to take us through the appraisal process in some detail. In describing its role in the improvement of standards of care and team effectiveness they demonstrate its value to the appraisee in terms of education, personal and professional development and career progression. They then move on to discuss the role of the components of appraisal in the processes of revalidation and the remedying of poor performance.

From appraisal to the concerns of Chapter 14. 'Education and training', is a short step. Lesley Stevens and Pearl Hettiaratchy link developments in staff training and skills enhancement to the concerns of appraisal, revalidation and continuing professional development. In effect, they demonstrate how many of the issues dealt with in previous chapters have to be integrated into the training and development strategies of each NHS trust: training in evidence-based practice and its outcomes is a case in point.

From education and training to the subject of Chapter 15, 'Clinical audit', is but another small step. Robert Kehoe is an assistant medical director who presents the processes and benefits of clinical audit with enthusiasm, and demonstrates its relevance and effectiveness in areas apparently as diverse as clinical performance, risk assessment, dealing with complaints and professional development. He also analyses the reasons why procedures may fail and audit is different from research.

In Chapter 16, 'Multi-agency working', Paddy Cooney and Brian Wilson provide material which fills out another of our recurring themes, cooperative working between agencies and authorities in the planning and delivery of mental health and learning disability services. These call for partnerships across health, social services, education, housing and criminal justice. The implications for both structure and investment are analysed and the need for clear communication across disciplines and cultures is stressed. There are instructive comparisons of hierarchical and cooperative management systems, and the authors draw attention to the accountability that local authorities have to their electorates. This chapter might be summarised by the reflection that the providers of mental health and learning disability services may need to negotiate more and direct less.

Part IV: Translating clinical governance into the clinical context

Part III talked of building blocks but in practice it is the way that they are assembled that gives meaning to the structure. This section selects key areas of this process for more detailed examination. The importance of information systems and the monitoring of performnce are singled out, as are the roles of lead clinicians and nurses. Finally, emphasis is placed on the management of change and, fittingly, Part IV concludes with the needs of those in our care who are the most vulnerable.

Information that is reliable and accessible underpins the delivery of an effective treatment and care service. In Chapter 17, 'Clinical information systems', Martin Briscoe stresses the need for clinicians to be conversant with information technology and actively engaged in its adaptation to the special needs of our services. Given the flood of information that is available, educated judgement and discrimination are necessary and service providers need also to be aware that users and carers should have access to information geared to their needs and suitably presented.

In Chapter 18, 'Monitoring and improving performance', David Roy outlines the different approaches to monitoring and their uses in helping both clinicians and managers to be more accountable. The development of clear and transparent standards accessible to trusts, teams and individuals is the key to an understanding of performance and the measurement of change. But quantitative evaluation needs to be filled out with the insights of clinical supervision and appraisal if performance is to be improved and shortcomings identified and remedied.

In the wealth of material on process and practice presented up to this point of the book, few key players are identified. However, in Chapter 19, 'Clinical governance and the role of the lead clinician', Tim and Katy Kendall clarify the responsibilities of one. Hitherto, these responsibilities have often been poorly appreciated by trusts (and sometimes by the clinicians themselves). Lead clinicians and their teams need to be located at the centre of multidisciplinary clinical and social care services. The authors, in support of colleagues who bear these responsibilities, draw attention to the need for them to develop special competencies, and to enjoy the support and resources that match the demands.

Effective nurse leadership is another key element in the delivery of clinical governance. In Chapter 20, 'Clinical governance and nurse leadership', Martin Ward describes the centrality of the nursing profession not only to effective care but also to the development of a comprehensive service. This calls for a renewed understanding of the need for adequate support and resources to be available to nurses within the team. The author goes on to describe in detail how nurses have a special contribution to make to an evidence-based service, as well as the function and skills of the nurse consultant. It should go without saying that ease of communication and shared expectations across the disciplines will facilitate good practice.

Implicit in the contributions of the authors of this book is the acknowledgement that the development of clinical governance is relatively recent. In Chapter 21, 'Managing change in mental health services', Jenny Firth-Cozens stresses the need for staff development programmes to encourage an openness that accepts that mistakes and misjudgements can occur and that recording and reporting are parts of a learning process that will lead to job satisfaction. Developments along these lines are not easy and call for the setting of goals that are realistic and capable of being managed.

Finally, in Chapter 22, 'Vulnerable people in care: person-centred values and clinical governance', Errol Cocks shifts the emphasis from the teams that provide to the particular needs of vulnerable people with learning difficulties who are in care. They are especially susceptible to concern about change and any service problems that they experience, and they are therefore in need of special safeguards. These considerations may take providers into new territory, where considerations of personal and social needs are as important as health, and new flexibilities may be needed. The issues elaborated in this chapter return us to our earlier concern to site the needs of the user and carer firmly at the heart of clinical governance.

The way forward

Most of the concerns that have been addressed by our authors have centred on the needs of people, be they users and carers or staff with their many and varied responsibilities. Earlier, we referred to the community of mental health and learning disability practitioners, a community, if we may borrow a phrase, with its own special needs. Unfortunately, the resources allocated, whether they be of finance, personnel or the provision of training and support, often reflects outmoded attitudes to those who need our care. The introduction of clinical governance has provided us with a renewed opportunity to demonstrate, by the measures we adopt, that our services need better support if an integrated health care system is to prosper.

References

Department of Health (1997) *The New NHS: Modern, Dependable*, cm 3807. London: TSO.
Department of Health (1998) *A First Class Service: Quality in the New NHS*. London: Department of Health.

Department of Health (1999) *Clinical Governance: Quality in the New NHS*, HSC 1999/ 065. London: Department of Health.

Royal College of Psychiatrists (2004) *Good Psychiatric Practice* (2nd edn). Council Report CR125. London: Royal College of Psychiatrists.

Background, history and philosophy: the origins of clinical governance

Clare Perkins and Gabriel Scally

- In the early years of the NHS, there was no discernible comprehensive approach to the assessment and improvement of quality
- The mid-/late 1990s saw a number of highly publicised cases that underlined the problems of existing quality mechanisms and which were in danger of undermining public confidence in the NHS
- Case studies from mental health inquiries demonstrate the need for robust quality improvement and assurance mechanisms
- In 1997 the government outlined the first comprehensive quality framework for the NHS
- The implementation of clinical governance in the NHS marks a sea change in the approach to quality.

The history of quality management in the National Health Service

In the early years of the National Health Service (NHS), from its foundation in 1948, there was no discernible comprehensive approach to the assessment and improvement of quality in health care. Quality was seen as inherent in the system, sustained by the ethos, training and skills of the health professionals working within it (Donaldson & Gray, 1988). Quality of care, if it was considered at all, was the domain of the clinical professions.

Exploration in the USA in the 1960s of the quality of health care began to stimulate debate on the concept of quality of health care in Britain. Over time, it became recognised that defining and measuring quality in health care was more complex than in other fields, such as industry. The North American Avedis Donabedian developed one of the most important and widely respected classifications of quality in health care, in which there are three aspects: structure, process and outcome (Donabedian, 1996).

Public attention was perhaps first drawn to issues of poor-quality care in the NHS in the 1960s, with publication of allegations of low standards of service provision and the ill-treatment of elderly patients at a number of hospitals in different parts of the UK. This was followed by the report of the official committee that inquired into Ely Mental Handicap Hospital, Cardiff. The inquiry found that there had been staff cruelty to patients and it made recommendations for improving conditions and preventing similar problems in other hospitals. Additional resources were allocated for mental handicap hospitals and services for those with a mental illness and for elderly people, and the Hospital Advisory Service was set up to visit and report on conditions in these hospitals. Despite these initiatives, the Ely Hospital inquiry was followed by reports on poor conditions in other long-stay hospitals, such as South Ockendon and Normansfield, which demonstrated that significant and systematic improvement was difficult to achieve. It was not until the mid-1980s that the attention of policy-makers became focused on the improvement of quality throughout the NHS.

From its beginning, the NHS was an administered rather than managed system. During the 1950s and 1960s there were rapid pharmacological, immunological and technological advances in health care. These, coupled with an ageing population and rising patient expectations, resulted in major funding pressures on the NHS and increasing difficulty in delivering evidence-based, cost-effective health care. In the early 1980s the main focus of government policy was on how to make the NHS more business-like and efficient (Ham, 1991).

Roy Griffiths was asked to give advice to the government on the effective use of the workforce and related resources in the NHS. Griffiths (1983) described a lack of clarity in accountability at local level and stated that managers should replace administrators, be given clear performance targets and be held to account. The report also stated that hospital doctors should become members of management teams and participate fully in decisions about priorities, and this introduced an element of personal responsibility for the use of NHS resources. The report was endorsed by the government and resulted in the replacement of the system of consensus management, in which team agreement was necessary for decisions to be made, with general management. Power and responsibility were now concentrated in the hands of a general manager. Hospitals became managed organisations with a more explicit approach to setting targets and evaluating services. However, the targets concentrated on the non-clinical aspects of quality, such as cost per case or operations completed.

The White Paper *Working for Patients*, published in January 1989, announced huge changes in the approach to the delivery of health services. The changes were intended to create competition between hospitals and other service providers through the separation of purchaser and provider responsibilities. The theory was that the creation of an internal market in health care would create competition between health care providers and that purchasers would demand and get higher-quality provision. However, a study by Gray & Donaldson (1996) that reviewed purchaser–provider contracts as a means of addressing quality issues found little evidence of a systematic approach to quality improvement. The White Paper also placed on hospital doctors a responsibility to participate in regular clinical audit.

By the mid-1990s a number of separate mechanisms for improving quality were evident in the NHS, including accreditation schemes, patient charter standards, a complaints process, clinical audit and the Confidential Inquiries, independent inquiries and professional performance procedures. The establishment of the Cochrane Centre in Oxford and the York Centre for Reviews and Dissemination was an important contribution to the thrust for more evidence-based practice. However, there remained a fragmented approach to quality, with little connection between management and professionally based initiatives.

High-profile clinical incidents and public confidence in the NHS

The mid- and late 1990s saw a number of highly publicised problems in the provision of services that underlined the problems of existing quality mechanisms and which also were in danger of undermining public confidence in the NHS as a whole. Of these problems perhaps that relating to death rates in paediatric cardiac surgery in Bristol had the highest profile. This case saw three doctors found guilty of serious professional misconduct by the General Medical Council (GMC). Although two of the doctors were surgeons directly involved in the surgery on babies and young children with serious heart conditions, the other was the former Chief Executive of the United Bristol Hospitals NHS Trust. The setting up by the government of a public inquiry into the events in Bristol underlined both their importance and the need to establish systems in the NHS where concern about the quality of clinical services is at the centre of its operation.

Two other major failings in the NHS helped move clinical quality to centre stage. The NHS has run two major national screening programmes aimed at improving women's health – for breast and cervical cancer. Serious problems in the quality of screening in breast cancer in Exeter and in cervical screening in Kent were revealed and investigated. These failures, which were serious in their own right, were doubly concerning because the screening programmes were supposed to be highly organised and to have a thorough quality assurance mechanism.

The conclusions drawn from these and other high-profile examples were clear. The quality of the clinical care provided to patients was not a universal nor a central concern of either NHS organisations or indeed some clinical professionals. Existing mechanisms were not systematic in their approach, not preventative in their effect and not universal in their application.

The need for clinical governance: case studies from mental health inquiries

A landmark case in the mental health field was that of a London patient, Christopher Clunis, who was involved in the death of Jonathan Zito. The report of the inquiry established by the North East Thames and South East Thames Regional Health Authorities into the care and treatment of Christopher Clunis was published in February 1994. It revealed very serious deficiencies in the provision of care to this very ill and vulnerable man (Ritchie, 1994). One of the outcomes of this process was that independent inquiries following all homicides committed by people with mental illnesses were required (Department of Health, 1994).

The three following case studies are taken from the reports of inquiries arising from incidents within one region of England in 1997. They demonstrate recurring themes, such as poor record-keeping, poor communication and multidisciplinary working, poor assessment processes and a lack of adequate staff training, which contributed to the poor quality of care received from the NHS by these individuals.

David Edward Roberts

David Edward Roberts, described by health professionals as 'not a real patient', pleaded guilty to the manslaughter of Joseph Osmond on 2 December 1998. He had accessed mental health services on two occasions during 1997, once as an in-patient for assessment under section 35 of the Mental Health Act, and the other time for assessment for detention. In his first period of care, the inquiry found that clinical practice and staffing levels fell below normally acceptable standards, and that the clinical environment did little to assist his care. On neither occasion was David Edward Roberts treated for a psychiatric disorder. In hindsight, the inquiry team concluded that he should have been. The recommendations of the internal inquiry encompassed clinical record-keeping, continuing professional development for clinical staff on the assessment and treatment of personality disorder, a review of the staff skill mix, improved ward security measures, and maintenance of good practice for assessment under section 35 (Wiltshire Health Authority, 1999).

Justine Cummings

In May 1998 Justine Cummings was convicted of the manslaughter of her fiancé, Peter Lewis. Justine Cummings suffered profound and enduring mental health problems from an early age. The inquiry found that although the death of Peter Lewis could not have been anticipated or prevented, there were a number of areas of poor practice in mental health services in Somerset that needed to be addressed. The inquiry was particularly concerned about fragmentation of services, people in different disciplines working in isolation, poor assessment and assembling of information, poor application of the care programme approach, poor record-keeping, and weak personnel and management practices (Somerset Health Authority, 2000).

Shane David Bath

In May 1998 Shane David Bath was convicted of the murder of Ayse Sullivan. He was diagnosed as having a severe personality disorder and had a long history of contact with services in Dorset over a period of almost 20 years, from when he entered local authority care. The inquiry identified some recurring themes, which started in hospital with a failure to gather information about Shane David Bath; this led to poor assessments, including risk assessments by health and social services. There was limited inter-agency communication and multidisciplinary working. There were no Mental Health Act assessments for compulsory admission to hospital, the care programme approach and discharge planning were poorly performed, he was never allocated to a community mental health team in Dorset, and follow-up by the community psychiatric nurse was ineffective. The inquiry made numerous recommendations for services in Dorset, which encompassed assessment, treatment and follow-up care, including ensuring compliance with the Mental Health Act in relation to the use of electroconvulsive therapy, and ensuring evidence-based practice in the prescription and administration of neuroleptic drugs for patients under the age of 18 years (Dorset Health Authority *et al*, 2000).

The cases highlighted the need for genuine improvement in mental health service provision and public reassurance. This could be achieved only through a comprehensive quality framework for the NHS, with clearly defined and audited standards of care.

The first comprehensive quality framework for the NHS

In 1997, the government set out its vision for a modernised NHS in England in *The New NHS: Modern, Dependable*, in which it announced the replacement of the internal market with integrated care and an approach that would combine efficiency and quality (Department of Health, 1997). It stated:

'There have been some serious lapses in quality. When they have occurred they have harmed individual patients and dented public confidence.'

This White Paper set out three areas for action to drive quality into all parts of the NHS:

- national standards and guidelines for services and treatments
- local measures to enable NHS staff to take responsibility for improving quality, including a new system of clinical governance, backed by a statutory duty for quality in NHS trusts
- a new organisation to address shortcomings.

The origin of the term 'clinical governance' can confidently be attributed to Liam Donaldson, a public health physician who at that time was a Regional Director of Public Health. Its genesis lies in the business world, where the importance of corporate governance was highlighted by the Cadbury Committee (Scally & Donaldson, 1998).

Details of the new framework for quality in the NHS in England were outlined in *A First Class Service: Quality in the New NHS* (Department of Health, 1998):

Setting quality standards

The National Institute for Clinical Excellence was to be established as a Special Health Authority by early 1999 to produce authoritative national guidance on the clinical and cost-effectiveness of new and existing treatments and services. National Service Frameworks would be produced for major care areas and disease groups as part of the overall approach to achieving consistent clinical standards across the NHS. Mental health and coronary heart disease were to be the subject of the first two National Service Frameworks, which would draw on the experience of the implementation of the recommendations of the Calman–Hine report on cancer services (Department of Health, 1995).

Delivering quality standards

A system of clinical governance, as part of an overall NHS governance framework, would ensure:

- a comprehensive programme of quality improvement and monitoring activity
- clear policies aimed at managing risk
- clear lines of responsibility and accountability for the overall quality of clinical care.

Lifelong learning and strengthened professional self-regulation would support clinical governance. Further guidance on clinical governance was issued in the document *Clinical Governance: Quality in the New NHS* (Department of Health, 1999a). The responsibilities of NHS trusts were to be reinforced by a statutory duty for quality.

Monitoring quality standards

'The government, the NHS and the public need to know whether services really are delivering the high quality care that patients have a right to expect.' (Department of Health, 1998)

The absence of an external guarantor of high-quality clinical services was one of the most notable driving forces in the new approach to quality. Although individual specialties could be reviewed, there was no mechanism for achieving an overview of all services within a trust. The government planned to address the need for monitoring of quality standards by establishing a new statutory body (under the Health Act 1999), the Commission for Health Improvement (CHI), to provide independent scrutiny of local clinical governance arrangements in England and Wales and to help address serious problems. Also part of the package of measures was a National Performance Framework, and a new National Survey of Patient and User Experience, introduced to provide systematic and comparable information on the experiences of patients and other service users.

The government then turned its attention to two specific quality problems: the need for a new approach to dealing with poor clinical performance in the NHS, and the need to learn systematically from adverse clinical events. The GMC had introduced its own professional performance procedures in 1997. However, the growing number of cases of poor clinical performance hitting the headlines, such as the case of the Bristol paediatric heart surgeons, demonstrated that there were no effective mechanisms throughout the NHS for the identification and addressing of poor performance at an early stage.

The consultation paper *Supporting Doctors, Protecting Patients* (Department of Health, 1999b) proposed a number of changes to NHS procedures for dealing with poor medical practice, intended to provide a clear interface with professional self-regulation. These included the introduction of appraisal for doctors, strengthening pre-employment checks, the introduction of credentialling and the concept of a performance assessment and support service, with assessment and support centres.

In The NHS Plan (Department of Health, 2000a) the government announced its intention that all doctors employed in or under contract to the NHS would, as a condition of contract, be required to participate in annual appraisal and clinical audit from 2001. This would contribute to the GMC's 5-yearly mandatory revalidation process for all doctors.

The NHS Plan also announced the establishment of the National Clinical Assessment Authority (NCAA), which would operate as a new performance assessment and support service, to which a doctor could be rapidly referred, where any concerns about a doctor's practice would be promptly assessed and an appropriate solution devised. The intention was to see an end to lengthy, expensive suspensions, multiple investigations of the same problem, variable local approaches and delay in acting to protect patients. Details of the NCAA and other mechanisms implementing *Supporting Doctors, Protecting Patients* were outlined in *Assuring the Quality of Medical Practice* (Department of Health, 2001a).

In June 2000 a report of an expert group on learning from adverse events in the NHS, entitled *An Organisation with a Memory*, was published (Department of Health, 2000b). The report cited numerous examples of tragedies which could have been avoided had the lessons of past experience been properly learned. For example, under the heading 'Suicides by mental health inpatients', the report stated:

'For some years it has been recognised that a major means of suicide among inpatients in mental health units is hanging from curtain or shower rails. A paper first drawing attention to this was published in 1971. These events can be prevented by fitting collapsible rails that give way under the weight of a person. On at least one occasion, a collapsible curtain rail that had given way, preventing a hanging, was incorrectly repaired. When another patient later attempted to hang himself from the same rail it failed to collapse and the patient died.'

Its recommendations, which have been accepted by ministers, include the creation of a new national system for reporting and analysing adverse health care events, to make sure that the NHS does learn the lessons when things go wrong.

Building a Safer NHS for Patients (Department of Health, 2001b) outlines details of the new national reporting system and the setting up of the National Patient Safety Agency to implement and operate it.

There has been recent debate about the value of independent homicide inquiries, given the potential harmful impact on patients, mental health staff and the public in general (Szmukler, 2000). The Parliamentary Health Select Committee (2000), in its Fourth Report, *Provision of Mental Health Services*, recommended that there should continue to be public inquiries into homicides committed by people with mental illnesses, but that they should be carried out on a systematic national basis. The government in its response to that report (Department of Health, 2000c) stated that a balance needs to be struck between learning the lessons from events where mistakes have been made, maintaining public confidence in services, and supporting families and staff. The government advised that, following the acceptance by ministers of the recommendations of *An Organisation with a Memory*, work would begin on improving mental health inquiries, with a focus on their conduct, the products of implementation and follow-up of recommendations, and a systematic mechanism for sharing more widely the learning from individual inquiries.

Most health professionals have welcomed the new quality framework for the NHS in England and subsequent additional components. A challenging timetable for implementation was set and the framework is now firmly established and evolving in the NHS. There is recognition that the framework is part of a 10-year modernisation programme for the NHS and that the significant cultural change that is needed will not happen overnight.

Conclusion

The introduction of clinical governance to the NHS marks a sea change in the approach to quality improvement. Although many of the driving forces have arisen within the acute hospital sector, serious failures of care in mental health services have added to the case for a rethink. What is clear is that more attention than ever before is being paid to how the NHS identifies and responds to the deficiencies in care that are inevitable in a health care organisation of its size and complexity. There remain many unanswered questions as to how health professionals will respond to the many challenges that clinical governance systems will inevitably produce, and, more importantly, how the NHS will respond to the many issues that will be raised by clinicians during a thorough examination of quality of care.

References

Department of Health (1994) *Guidance on the Discharge of Mentally Disordered People and Their Continuing Care in the Community*, HSG(94)27. London: HMSO.

Department of Health (1995) *A Policy Framework for Commissioning Cancer Services: A Report by the Expert Advisory Group on Cancer to the Chief Medical Officers of England and Wales*, EK(95)SI. London: HMSO.

Department of Health (1997) *The New NHS: Modern, Dependable*, cm 3807. London: TSO.

Department of Health (1998) *A First Class Service: Quality in the New NHS*. London: Department of Health.

Department of Health (1999a) *Clinical Governance: Quality in the New NHS*, HSC 1999/065. London: Department of Health.

Department of Health (1999b) *Supporting Doctors, Protecting Patients*. London: Department of Health.

Department of Health (2000a) *The NHS Plan: A Plan for Investment, a Plan for Reform*, cm 4818-I. London: TSO.

Department of Health (2000b) *An Organisation with a Memory: Report of the Expert Group on Learning from Adverse Events in the NHS*. London: TSO.

Department of Health (2000c) *The Government's Response to the Health Select Committee's Report into Mental Health Services*, cm 4888. London: HMSO.

Department of Health (2001a) *Assuring the Quality of Medical Practice*. London: Department of Health.

Department of Health (2001*b*) *Building a Safer NHS for Patients*. London: Department of Health.

Donabedian, A. (1996) Evaluating the quality of medical care. *Milbank Memorial Fund Quarterly*, **4**, 166–206.

Donaldson, L. J. & Gray, J. A. M. (1988) Clinical governance: a quality duty for health organisations. *Quality in Healthcare*, **7** (suppl.), 37–44.

Dorset Health Authority, Bournemouth Social Services & Dorset Social Services (2000) *Report of the Independent Inquiry into the Care and Treatment of Shane David Bath. Chair: A. Weereratne.*

Gray, J. D. & Donaldson, L. J. (1996) Improving the quality of healthcare through contracting: a study of health authority practice. *Quality in Healthcare*, **5**, 201–205.

Griffiths, R. (1983) *NHS Management Enquiry*. London: Department of Health and Social Security.

Ham, C. (1991) *Health Policy in Britain*. London: Macmillan.

Parliamentary Health Select Committee (2000) *Provision of Mental Health Service*. London: Hansard.

Ritchie, J. (1994) *Report of the Inquiry into the Care and Treatment of Christopher Clunis*. London: HMSO.

Scally, G. & Donaldson, L. J. (1998) Clinical governance and the drive for quality improvement in the new NHS in England. *BMJ*, **317**, 61–65.

Select Committee on Health (2000) *Provision of Mental Health Services* (Fourth Report). London: TSO.

Somerset Health Authority (2000) *Report of the Independent Inquiry into the Care and Treatment of Ms Justine Cummings. Taunton, Chair: H. Laming.*

Szmukler, G. (2000) Homicide inquiries: what sense do they make? *Psychiatric Bulletin*, **4**, 6–10.

Wiltshire Health Authority (1999) *Report of the Independent Inquiry into the Care and Treatment of David Edward Roberts. Devises, Chair: G. Halliday.*

Part II

Foundations and organisational structure

CHAPTER 3

How to structure clinical governance

Adrian James

This chapter will identify:

- the fundamental purpose of clinical governance
- the key issues to be tackled
- a structure for implementing clinical governance at a service directorate level
- barriers to implementation and how to overcome them
- future developments.

The purpose and structure of clinical governance

The fundamental purpose of clinical governance is to ensure the best possible quality of patient care. This has to be delivered within a framework of accountability that links all levels of operation and service within the organisation; final accountability rests with the chief executive officer, who is ultimately responsible for clinical care in a National Health Service (NHS) trust. The focus of all elements of such a structure is on continuous quality improvement (Scally & Donaldson, 1998). It must raise the awareness and profile of quality within all parts of an organisation and demonstrate to those outside the organisation that quality is of the utmost importance. Leadership and accountability must be transparent and the structure must ensure coverage of the main elements of clinical governance and facilitate the convergence of the managerial and clinical agenda (Oyebode et al, 1999). It must also establish easy links with outside agencies, such as the Commission for Healthcare Audit and Inspection (Healthcare Commission), National Institute for Clinical Excellence (NICE), local health improvement programmes, Royal Colleges and professional regulatory bodies. Engagement with users and carers in quality assurance is crucial (Department of Health, 1998). It must facilitate the incorporation of established good practice, set standards and monitor achievement. Remedies for poor performance must be found and risk management encompassed. Ultimately a structure must bring order to otherwise confusing and daunting tasks and convey a sense of purpose and priority. The first 20 clinical governance reviews of mental health trusts indicated that many still lack the infrastructure to support effective clinical governance (Commission for Health Improvement, 2003*a*).

Key issues

Philosophy

A healthy quality improvement environment will require a culture that is open and positive, and that promotes continuous learning. The strategy must be owned by all parts of the organisation, involve users, and be user centred. If patient care is not improving, then there is no purpose in clinical governance. Ultimately, change will occur only if multidisciplinary functioning and team evaluation are targeted.

Strengthening foundations

Quality improvement programmes need to use existing mechanisms, and individuals with an interest in quality improvement should be targeted and brought into the new strategy. Wattis & McGinnis (1998) suggest that quality improvement programmes require the development of three types of capital:

- human capital, by workforce training for example
- structural capital, by investment in such things as information systems
- customer capital, through relationships with the users and commissioners of services.

The foundations of clinical governance are listed in Box 3.1.

Box 3.1 The foundations of clinical governance

- Existing mechanisms for user involvement, such as patients' council/advocacy schemes
- Trust risk management committee
- Libraries
- Information technology
- Clinical audit
- Existing team meetings – making them more focused on evidence
- Links with universities and academic departments – with an emphasis on service-based research
- Mechanisms for continuing professional development and personal development plans
- Appraisal mechanisms – making them more structured and open, and gathering information from a variety of sources.

Coordination

Responsibility must be devolved to a point as near to the delivery of care as possible. Implementation on a sub-specialty basis is preferable, although there should be some cross-over between specialties so that good practice in one area can be used in another. For some small specialties or units, links will need to be made with similar units in other organisations, such as mother and baby units and eating disorder services. Leadership and accountability need to be established at all points within a structure. Strategies can fail because accountability procedures are remote from the point where clinical governance procedures should be delivered. Leadership can be divided between the various tasks of clinical governance as long as boundaries are made clear.

Task coverage

Any number of structures can be developed but it is important that the key tasks of clinical governance are identified and related to one another in a programme. A number of functional groups need to be developed around the components of clinical governance set out by the Commission for Health Improvement (2003b), and these are discussed in the next section. Each group needs an identified leader, so that the clinical governance programme has representation from a spread of disciplines across functions. Leaders should be selected on the basis of their enthusiasm and skills in a particular area and their proven ability to take up new ideas and carry things through. Each group should have approximately ten members, with a spread of disciplines and grades, and meet for no more than 1½ hours quarterly. Meetings need to be structured, focused and properly minuted.

Culture

It has been argued in other areas that a no-blame culture is essential. However, if real progress is to be made, an 'acceptance of fault' culture needs to be established, where mistakes are recognised and responded to. This can often be facilitated by those seen as the most senior colleagues admitting their own mistakes in a positive way, and if clear steps are taken to facilitate improvement. For too long complaints or criticisms have been viewed negatively and there is a need to move towards open dialogue with those who use services.

A suggested clinical governance structure

Box 3.2 outlines one possible structure of groups to implement the clinical governance programme.

> **Box 3.2** Functional subdivisions of clinical governance
> (after Commission for Health Improvement, 2003*a*)
>
> - Clinical audit
> - Risk management
> - User, carer and public involvement
> - Clinical effectiveness
> - Education, training and continuing personal development
> - Information management
> - Staffing and staff management.

Clinical audit group

The clinical audit group should coordinate multidisciplinary clinical audit and measure performance against agreed standards and performance targets. Topics covered must be central to the functioning of each unit and not dictated by the need to present at a meeting. The emphasis should be on completion of the audit cycle: that is, the results of the audit must be used to change policy and procedures, to drive up standards, in an outcome-based approach; real change should then be evident in subsequent re-audit. A key area for consideration would be accessibility of services to users and carers, which has received much attention in the National Service Framework for Mental Health (Department of Health, 1999) and the NHS Plan (Department of Health, 2000). Topics could include:

- clinical notes
- Mental Health Act documentation
- prescription patterns, in comparison with agreed standards
- seclusion policy and procedure
- assessment response times
- attendance at case conferences by outside agencies
- critical incident review
- adverse events monitoring
- implementation of guidance from NICE.

Risk management group

The risk management group would monitor and develop risk-reduction strategies in identified high-risk areas for users, carers, staff and the general public. This could include the development of an adverse events team (James, 1999) to provide a quick local response by senior clinicians and managers to an immediate problem, such as a serious violent incident. This group should take a lead in ensuring that standard VII of the National Service Framework (preventing suicide) is met (Department of Health, 1999).

Areas of work for the group should include:

- deliberate self-harm
- patient and staff safety
- violence
- absconding
- treatment side-effects.

User, carer and public involvement group

Ideally, this group would be chaired by a user with appropriate training and support. Alternatively, the group could be co-led with a senior member of the multidisciplinary team.

The group's main purpose would be to empower users and carers so that they can play a full part in improving service provision in order to create a positive treatment environment. The group could also promote user participation in the other groups and ultimately could be seen as being redundant if users and carers are brought into the mainstream of all processes. It should play a key role in the implementation of the NHS Plan, for example in establishing a patients' forum in every NHS trust (as is required by the Plan). It should canvas the views of patients and carers on the quality of service provision and publish a new patient prospectus, as well as an annual account of views received and action taken.

Areas of work for the group could include:

- user satisfaction surveys
- user suggestion surveys
- patient advocacy services.

Clinical effectiveness group

The clinical effectiveness group would aim to bring evidence-based practice from local and national sources into local service provision. Research and national guidelines would need to be reviewed and their local applicability explored and agreed. Dissemination of such material to the right people, and at the right time, would be a major task. The group should coordinate the research and development elements of everyday practice and should also coordinate library activities. The new NHS Modernisation Agency has led a drive towards protocol-based care in the NHS and is working towards a 2004 target for the majority of NHS staff to be working under agreed protocols (Department of Health, 2000). A particularly neglected area is that of health promotion within psychiatric practice and this will require a special focus (standard I of the National Service Framework).

This group should focus on the development of:

- protocols
- guidelines
- integrated care pathways
- local service-based research
- implementation of NICE guidance.

Education, training and personal development group

This group should aim to promulgate a philosophy of lifelong learning among all staff, to identify educational gaps and attempt to fill them through local education opportunities or outside sources. There is a particular need to pick up the training requirements arising from developments in service provision highlighted by the other groups. A rolling programme of training needs must be developed and prioritised. Every member of staff needs a personal educational development plan. A particular area of work would involve the multi-skilling arrangements and nurse consultant developments suggested in the NHS Plan.

Thus, key areas dealt with by this group should include:

- mandatory training
- service-based training needs
- continuing professional development
- personal development plans
- leadership skills
- multi-skilling
- team-building
- occupational standards for non-professional staff
- management of individual learning accounts.

Information management group

Effective clinical governance is underpinned by comprehensive information management systems. This group should be the servant of the other groups, and should ensure that information informs clinical governance activities and allows for appropriate performance management and the dissemination of good practice and lessons learnt (see Chapter 17).

Key areas of work would include:

- reporting and monitoring of targets and achievements
- involvement of patients in identifying information needs
- development of a health care records system
- Caldicott Guardian and confidentiality issues
- training and support for information management.

Staffing and staff management

This group should develop a strategy to ensure the highest possible standards of clinical practice, to monitor professional performance and to deal with poorly performing clinical colleagues. The sensitive, high-profile nature of this group may mean that it comprises a smaller number of senior managers and clinicians, and it is likely to be chaired by the clinical director or service leader and have senior representatives from other professional groups. The group would take an overview of performance and develop structures and policies which may then be implemented by others. For example, if there is concern about the performance of a consultant psychiatrist, then it is likely that this will be explored initially by the clinical director, pursued further by the medical director of the trust and lead to the formation of a professional advisory panel of senior medical colleagues.

Links should be established with the National Clinical Assessment Authority and UK Council of Health Regulators under the NHS Plan.

The main work of the group would involve the development of policies and procedures and review mechanisms for:

- performance portfolios
- induction
- appraisal
- adherence (for psychiatrists) to the guidelines of *Good Psychiatric Practice* (Royal College of Psychiatrists, 2001)
- team performance
- clinical supervision
- staff feedback.

Implementation points

The key to implementation is the identification of clinical leaders and multidisciplinary involvement. It is better to develop a full structure (see below), and modify it later, rather than a prolonged process of trying to develop the perfect structure at the outset. A developmental approach must therefore be adopted and the structure reviewed regularly, particularly if concurrent organisational change occurs. A good spread of staff is necessary across all disciplines and grades and, ideally, all members of a clinical team should be involved at some level in order to ensure ownership and to spread workloads. Topics covered must be key to the objectives of the organisation and be patient focused rather than those that appeal to a small number, possibly on the basis of some obscure interest.

Each of the clinical governance groups within a directorate maps onto the relevant topic area. The issues covered within each of these areas –

Box 3.3 Key points for the implementation of a clinical governance programme

- A shared vision
- Sponsorship by the top team
- A culture that promotes continuous learning
- The use of existing building blocks
- Administrative support
- Leadership in all parts of the structure
- Multidisciplinary involvement across all grades
- Partnership with external organisations
- Short, structured meetings
- Implementation close to the point of service delivery
- Delegation where appropriate
- A focus on outcomes
- A developmental approach, combined with structural review
- Assimilation of quality issues raised in central initiatives such as the National Service Frameworks and Healthcare Commission reviews.

---

such as strategy, resources, committee structure, involvement of users in each area and examples of quality improvement in the particular area – can be used as a basis for the terms of reference for each of these groups and used to structure agendas. This will ensure that there are no gaps or surprises when the Healthcare Commission makes a visit.

Key implementation points are summarised in Box 3.3.

Clinical governance presentations

A meeting needs to be established at which the various clinical governance groups, outlined above, can present their findings for examination by the wider group of staff and at which members of a clinical specialty can debate issues and agree a way forward. This ensures effective multidisciplinary and service-wide ownership of decisions and gives the groups an opportunity to have their own work acknowledged and to receive feedback. A rolling programme of clinical governance afternoons has proved effective in some areas (Gralton *et al*, 2000), with ten meetings a year (every month except August and December). Meetings should be open to all staff and attendance at them monitored through individual performance reviews. The presence and involvement of service users in such meetings need facilitation and can provide real benefits in maintaining a patient focus and ensuring that decisions are owned and implementable.

Time must be given within meetings for discussion and attempts made to achieve consensus. The meetings must be made attractive, for example through the provision of a nice lunch or even the award of a prize for the best contribution (either a presentation or a question). It is important that senior members of the team are seen to value the meetings and to present and contribute, but that the meeting should not be seen as being dominated by the top team. The problem of nurses attending can be overcome through rostering nurses specifically for attendance at the meeting. Each of the groups described above should have particular slots timetabled a year ahead and members of the group should decide which topics to present. Some of the slots can be used for comparisons with outside groups and to invite outside speakers to talk about a particular area of expertise, such as evidence-based practice.

A chair will be necessary to provide some focus and to ensure the meetings relate directly to outcomes. Meetings need to be minuted to provide a full transcript of questions, answers and solutions. The minutes need to be disseminated widely within the organisation and particularly to the heads of the clinical governance groups, members of the clinical governance committee, and to heads of professional departments.

Table 3.1 shows a suggested meeting structure.

The key points are:

- subgroups must present findings to wider staff group
- there must be service-wide ownership of findings
- there must be regular planned meetings.

Setting up

Key members of the psychiatric sub-specialty must agree the need for a clinical governance structure that is then 'sponsored' by them. The directorate management team, or clinical specialty management team, needs to own the process and share the vision with users. Structures must be developed in partnership with other organisations, such as

Table 3.1 Suggested format of a clinical governance afternoon session for a clinical governance committee that meets ten times per year (every month except August and December)

Time	Subject
12.30–1.00	Lunch
1.00–1.45	Clinical effectiveness
1.45–2.30	Risk management alternating with clinical audit
2.30–2.45	Tea/coffee
2.45–3.30	Use of information alternating with user/carer involvement
3.30–4.15	Education and training alternating with staffing and staff management
4.20	Finish

Chair: chair of directorate.
Minutes: clinical governance administrator.
Discussion record sent to heads of clinical governance groups.

primary care trusts and social services, so that processes are seen to be 'joined up'.

The suggested clinical governance structure should operate easily in a specialty with a staff number of 50 to 75; groups of up to 250 members of staff would improve its viability. This spreads the load and responsibility and allows greater diversity of opinion. Where teams have too few staff they can link up with other similar teams, either within their own organisation or outside. For example, a forensic unit may be ideal if it has 80 beds and 200 members of staff, as may a general adult service with 100 beds, 6 community teams and 400 members of staff, but a child and adolescent service with only 20 members of staff in a community team would need to link up with another service to develop clinical governance networks.

It is important to make people feel that a load has been taken away from them and that a structure has been developed to deal with issues with which they are grappling. This makes it less overwhelming and more helpful rather than another burden.

Organisational arrangements

The structures within each sub-specialty or directorate must interface with wider trust or organisational arrangements. The latter will depend upon the type of organisation the specialty sits within and different arrangements will be necessary for primary care trusts, community trusts, mental health and learning disability trusts. Organisations that are integrated with the local authority will need to work with 'best value' arrangements (see Chapter 16). Managing the interface between the various partner organisations will need particular attention, in order to avoid duplication and ensure a common purpose and seamless clinical governance arrangements across primary, secondary and tertiary care and particularly with social services. At the very least, there should be communication but preferably cooperation, coordination and, in some cases, merger of arrangements.

Within the trust structure there need to be clear lines of account-ability and responsibility, leading up to the chief executive and trust board. Fig. 3.1 shows a suggested structure from clinical directorate to trust board level. The clinical governance groups at executive and board level will be involved in coordination rather than implementation. Fig. 3.2 shows a suggested structure within a directorate or clinical specialty. These structures should not be seen as rigid and can easily be modified according to the needs of the organisation, so that form can follow function.

A task-orientated subdivision helps to bring order and clarify respon-sibility. Effective multidisciplinary leadership of each group will enhance ownership and partnership working, and create the necessary culture for

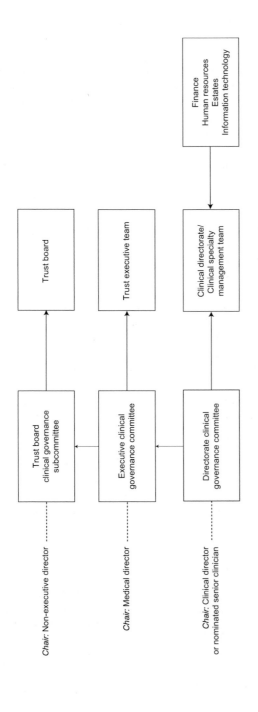

Figure 3.1 A suggested trust structure for clinical governance.

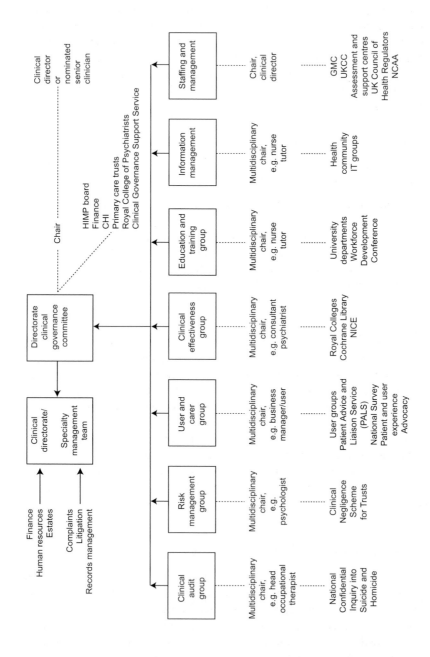

Figure 3.2 A suggested structure for directorate/clinical specialty clinical governance.

real change. Such leaders will need to be inspirational communicators, empower others, be accessible, draw others together with a shared vision, and promote a development culture (Alimo-Metcalfe & Alban-Metcalfe, 2000). It is essential that each subgroup develops links with outside agencies that are pertinent to the work of the group. These are also shown within Fig. 3.2 – for example, the clinical audit group links with the National Confidential Inquiry into Suicide and Homicide, and the risk management group links with the Clinical Negligence Scheme for Trusts.

Required elements of the structure

The document *A First Class Service* (Department of Health, 1998) identifies a number of 'musts' within any structure:

- the chief executive officer must have ultimate responsibility for quality assurance
- there must be an annual assurance statement
- there must be a named senior clinical lead
- an annual report on clinical governance is required
- there must be a clinical governance subcommittee of the trust board.

Overcoming barriers

In any process of change, a number of barriers will be identified and a clear strategy needs to be developed to overcome these. Some are potential barriers, others are real and some may never be fully dealt with. Table 3.2 identifies a number of barriers and presents suggestions as to how to overcome them.

It is essential that clinical governance is supported and underpinned. Appropriate administration is necessary to ensure that meetings are minuted, discussions during presentations recorded and suggestions disseminated appropriately. The programme will need additional financing, and suggestions for change will have fiscal consequences. There will be a need for reward and sanction and for time to be made available.

Links with other trust/directorate areas

Links will need to be established with personnel departments so that integrated workforce planning can be carried out. Finance departments need to be driven by clinical excellence and a crucial element of best practice will include evidence of cost-effectiveness. With the advent of the Healthcare Commission, which has picked up the Commission for Health Improvement's former functions but also the Audit Commission's Value for Money Studies in Health, robust links will

Table 3.2 Barriers and how to overcome them

Barrier	Means of overcoming barrier
Lack of clinical leadership	Identify leaders and training needs
Lack of infrastructure (e.g. information technology)	Investment (e.g. in clinically relevant information technology)
Lack of evidence-based guidelines	Access sources such as the Cochrane database
Apathy	Stress new opportunities and non optional approach
Scarce clinical time	Use clinical governance to gain more resources
Fear of loss of clinical freedom	Use clinical governance to regain control
Tension in team learning (as opposed to uni-professional learning)	Stress need for continued uni-professional learning and clinical governance at directorate level, generally on a team basis
Enthusiasm not sustained	Demonstrate that real change has occurred
Cultural inertia	Enlist culture carriers
Fear of external control	Stimulate need for local systems and control to avoid imposition
Concerns about criticism and blame	Provide a more stimulating professional environment in which conflict is brought into the open and dealt with
Concerns about workload	Structure reduces anxiety and panic, and spreads the workload

need to be established with performance management arrangements within trusts (see Chapter 5). Clinical governance must influence information technology departments and systems to ensure that they have a clinical focus and enable performance to be reliably monitored and that they make data available in the public domain where appropriate. Above all, clinical governance will need to form a major part of the agenda of both the trust board and executive to keep the focus on excellence of clinical care.

Future developments

Clinical governance structures must have built-in mechanisms for reviewing outcomes and proving their own effectiveness. Data on structural implementation already exist (Latham *et al*, 1999) and point towards some success in production of strategies, the establishment of committees and the appointment of leads, but there is as yet little evidence of cultural change or a real difference at the clinical workface.

> **Box 3.4** Ways of monitoring performance
>
> - User feedback
> - Outcome measures specified and reviewed 'what difference is this making' approach
> - Specific objectives with attached performance measures
> - Reflection sessions to review the effectiveness of the programme
> - Brain storming sessions to identify new topics and assess the programme
> - Meetings with other units to review systems and objectives
> - Outside facilitators.

In its report *Getting Better? A Report on the NHS*, the CHI (2003c) concludes that the NHS as a whole is improving and that such signs are evident in areas of the NHS where people have raised concerns. The evaluation and evidence of improvements in patient care is what really matters. Ways of monitoring the performance of a clinical governance programme are suggested in Box 3.4.

Conclusions

An effective clinical governance structure will facilitate the development of high-quality mental health services that are user led and focused (Appleby, 2000). Such a development can be used to implement and monitor adherence to National Service Framework standards at a local level (Table 3.3).

The key points are as follows:

- Users should be involved in the planning and monitoring of all areas of clinical governance where confidentiality is not an issue
- Coherent performance measures need to be developed
- All recommendations should be accompanied by clear statements of their resource implications
- A member of staff should be identified who will coordinate effectiveness measures (an 'effectiveness tsar', perhaps a psychology assistant)
- Similar structures should be developed in partner organisations, so that guidelines can be compared across services and implications for those organisations understood
- There need to be sophisticated mechanisms for translating research into practice
- Research needs to be conducted into the effectiveness of clinical governance itself.

Table 3.3 Clinical governance groups and National Service Framework (NSF) responsibility

NSF standard	Clinical governance group
I Health promotion	Clinical effectiveness
II Primary care	Education and training
III Access to services	Clinical audit
IV Severe mental illness Protocols/guidelines Assertive outreach	Clinical effectiveness
V Severe mental illness Waiting times/access Care plan	Clinical audit
VI Carers	Users and carer
VII Suicide prevention	Risk management

A successful structure will contribute to addressing the five challenges set by the Prime Minister and reiterated in the NHS Plan:

- partnership working
- improving performance
- enhancing skills of professionals and the wider workforce
- focusing on the needs of patients
- preventing ill-health wherever possible.

It is a challenge to set up a well-organised system of clinical governance. It is necessary to address the key areas of culture, leadership and responsibility both when setting up the system and, more importantly, once the system has been set up. Clinical governance can offer real change for patients, and this will justify the time and effort by all those involved. This will be addressed in succeeding chapters.

References

Alimo-Metcalfe, B. & Alban-Metcalfe, R. (2000) Leadership. Heaven can wait. *Health Service Journal*, **110**, 26–29.

Appleby, L. (2000) A new mental health service: high quality and user-led. *British Journal of Psychiatry*, **177**, 290–291.

Commission for Health Improvement (2003a) *Emerging Themes from Mental Health Trust Reviews*. Available at www.chi.nhs.uk/eng/about/publications/emerging_themes/emerging_themes_mh.pdf.

Commission for Health Improvement (2003c) *Getting Better? A Report on the NHS*. London: CHI.

Department of Health (1998) *A First Class Service: Quality in the New NHS*. London: Department of Health.

Department of Health (1999) *National Service Framework for Mental Health*. London: Department of Health.

Department of Health (2000) *The NHS Plan: A Plan for Investment, a Plan for Reform*, cm 4818-I. London: TSO.

Gralton, E. J., James, A. J. B. & Oxborrow, S. (2000) Clinical governance: six months of a functional programme in a forensic service. *Psychiatric Bulletin*, **24**, 444–447.

James, A. J. B. (1999) Clinical governance and mental health: a system for change. *Clinician in Management*, **8**, 92–100.

Latham, L., Freeman, T., Walshe, K., *et al* (1999) *The Early Development of Clinical Governance: A Survey of NHS Trusts in the West Midlands*. Birmingham: Health Services Management Centre, Birmingham University.

Oyebode, F., Brown, N. & Patty, E. (1999) Clinical governance: application to psychiatry. *Psychiatric Bulletin*, **23**, 7–10.

Royal College of Psychiatrists (2001) *Good Psychiatric Practice*, CR90. London: Royal College of Psychiatrists. Available at www.rcpsych.ac.uk/publications/cr/cr90.htm.

Scally, G. & Donaldson, L. J. (1998) Clinical governance and the drive for quality improvement in the new NHS in England. *BMJ*, **317**, 61–65.

Wattis, J. & McGinnis, P. (1998) Clinical governance: making it work. *Clinician in Management*, **8**, 12–18.

CHAPTER 4

The role of trust boards in clinical governance

Tim Kendall and Claire Palmer

- This chapter examines the response of trust boards to their new role of accountablity for clinical governance
- It also reconsiders the role and function of the trust board in the light of current experience.

Introduction

'The content of the Board's agenda will send a powerful signal to the whole organisation, to the local media, the public, and to the health organisation's partners. The more substantial and searching the issues the Board discusses, the more it will be concluded that the organisation has a clear sense of direction on clinical governance and is taking it very seriously.' (Department of Health, 1999: para. 35)

Clinical governance is New Labour's mechanism to ensure continuous quality improvement throughout the National Health Service (NHS). It is not voluntary and, for the first time, chief executives and trust boards are accountable for the quality of clinical care in their trust. Trust boards must now alter their roles and priorities, to elevate their responsibility for clinical quality to the same status as their responsibility for financial matters. They need to set a tight timetable to implement these changes, which should have begun immediately following the publication of the landmark White Papers (Department of Health, 1997; Scottish Office Department of Health 1997; Department of Health and Social Services, Northern Ireland, 1998; Welsh Office, 1998).

Making non-clinical chief executives and their trust boards accountable for the quality of clinical care is clearly a major innovation, one with which trust boards have had no previous experience. Until this time responsibility for clinical matters lay firmly with clinicians, and most obviously with the medical consultant, whereas financial and organisational management responsibility resided in the management infrastructure all the way up to the trust board, a situation often perceived by

> **Box 4.1** The new role of trust boards (Department of Health, 1999)
>
> - To assume responsibility for assuring the quality of services
> - To appoint a senior clinician as clinical governance lead
> - To establish a clinical governance committee
> - To ensure that boards receive regular reports regarding the quality of clinical care, and that these are given the same status as financial reports
> - To produce an annual report on clinical governance.

clinicians as divisive. In part, clinical governance directly addresses this problem by extending the responsibility for clinical quality to include the trust board. It also requires the trust board to assume new roles consistent with its new responsibilities (Box 4.1). These changes were, nevertheless, intended as the first steps in a 10-year programme that would directly link the trust boards' activity and influence to the delivery of clinical and social care by teams, so as to ensure continuous quality improvement, to reduce variation in the delivery of care and to transform trusts into modern 'learning organisations' (Department of Health, 2000*a*), able to learn from both their mistakes and their successes.

These are truly radical aims, especially for an organisation built in the early post-war period with a command and control structure (Irvine, 2001), and all too often, little direct connection between the activity of the trust board and clinical activity. In this new and unfamiliar role, the trust board would now give out a 'powerful signal' through the trust board's agenda and discussions with all its local constituents and partners that it had a 'clear sense of direction' in leading these changes.

In this chapter, we first present some empirical research examining the response of trust boards to their new role over the 18 months following the publication of *The New NHS* (Department of Health, 1997). We then discuss the results and reconsider the role and function of trust boards in the implementation of clinical governance, in the light of 4 years of experience of working to develop the necessary structures and changes to modernise mental health and learning disability services.

Participants, methods and results

We invited 84 trusts that were already subscribing members of the Clinical Governance Support Service (CGSS) of the Royal College of Psychiatrists' Research Unit (a subscription service specifically aimed at supporting mental health and learning disability trusts in the delivery of clinical governance) to participate in a confidential study of trusts' board minutes from January 1998 to June 1999. Fifty-one trusts (a response rate of 61%) submitted a total of 603 minutes, an average of 12 sets of minutes (range 2–18) for the whole 18 months.

Minutes were subjected to a quantitative content analysis (Bowling, 1997). This identified the clinical governance issues discussed, when issues were first raised, their frequency of discussion, and the frequency of their occurrence as formal agenda items. Issues and items identified included finance, clinical governance and other quality-related initiatives. Data were analysed using Microsoft Access. No attempt was made to determine the quality of recorded discussions.

The 51 trusts came from all counties/regions of the UK. Fifty trust boards (98%) had discussed clinical governance at least once during the study period, just over 50% having started discussions before July 1998 (i.e. in the first 6-month period). There were no consistent differences detected between regions or counties.

Clinical governance was discussed at 210 of the 603 (35%) trust board meetings for which minutes were received, that is, at an average of four board meetings (range 0–11) for each trust over the period of study. Eighteen (36%) trusts were responsible for 131 (62%) of all the sets of minutes in which discussion of clinical governance was recorded. From January to June 1998, discussion of clinical governance was recorded 0.25 times per set of minutes (i.e. at 1 in 4 trust board meetings) on average; from January to June 1999 the average increased to 0.5 times per set of minutes (i.e. at 1 in 2 trust board meetings).

The minutes of 39 trusts (76%) recorded the decision to establish a clinical governance committee, the majority (22 trusts) having done so between January and June 1999. Twenty-one trusts (42%) had no record of deciding to establish their committee before 1 April 1999, the date set by the government as the deadline for mandatory formation of a clinical governance committee. Moreover, only 11 (22%) trust boards recorded discussion of reporting arrangements for clinical governance (Box 4.2).

A range of quality-related activities were identified from the White Papers and the number of times each was recorded in trust board minutes is shown in Fig. 4.1. Of all the quality-related activities

---

Box 4.2 Key findings of the study

- Forty-two per cent of trust boards had no record of establishing a clinical governance committee by 1 April 1999
- Clinical governance appeared as an agenda item in only 17% of all trust board minutes over the first 18 months of the implementation of clinical governance
- Only 11 trusts (22%) recorded discussion of clinical governance, reporting arrangements by July 1999
- One trust board (out of 51) had no record of having discussed clinical governance over the first 18 months of its implementation.

discussed in 18 months, complaints, risk management and monitoring of waiting lists were recorded far more frequently than all others.

The frequencies with which trust board minutes recorded finance, activity and a number of quality-related issues as formal agenda items are shown in Table 4.1, which shows that 93% of trust board minutes had finance as an agenda item, with very little variation between each 6-month period. Clinical governance appeared as an agenda item in 17% of trust board minutes throughout the 18-month study, but with gradually increasing frequency, from 4%, to 17%, to 31% in each of the respective 6-month periods. If the rise over the last period of the study continued at

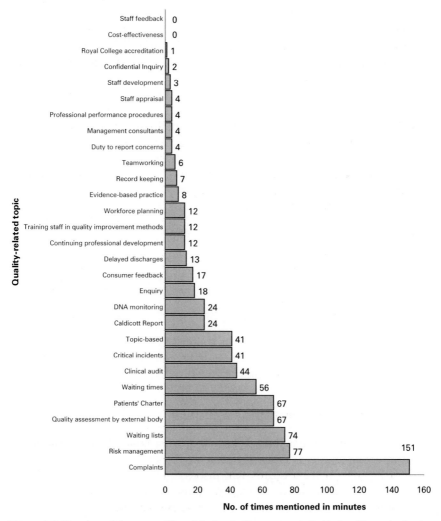

Figure 4.1 Number of times quality-related activities are recorded in trust board minutes.

Table 4.1 Number of times different agenda items appear in the trust board minutes

Item	Jan–Jun 1998 n (%)	Jul–Dec 1998 n (%)	Jan–Jun 1999 n (%)
Finances	186 (94)	189 (95)	187 (90)
Activity	68 (35)	70 (35)	58 (28)
Quality	51 (26)	51 (26)	42 (20)
Complaints	48 (24)	35 (18)	47 (23)
Clinical governance	8 (4)	33 (17)	65 (31)
Clinical audit/effectiveness	9 (5)	15 (8)	15 (7)
Total number of minutes returned	197	199	208

the same pace, clinical governance would have reached equality with finance as an agenda item at trust board meetings by September 2001 at the earliest.

The NHS Executive (Department of Health, 1998) outlined four key strategic areas for clinical governance:

- clear lines of responsibility and accountability for the overall quality of clinical care
- a comprehensive programme of quality-improvement activities
- clear policies aimed at managing risks
- procedures for professional groups to identify and remedy poor performance.

The minutes of only 11 trusts (22%) explicitly related clinical governance to these areas.

Effective leadership is a central element in the implementation of clinical governance, perhaps nowhere more so than at trust board level. To assess the extent to which trust boards show evidence of leadership, we adapted criteria from the 'excellence model' (Greenhalgh & Eversley, 1999) to clinical governance, and identified the number of trust board minutes that showed evidence of the criteria for leadership. Table 4.2 shows the number of trusts that could be identified from the minutes as having conformed to the predetermined criteria for leadership.

What does this research suggest?

This study was designed to explore what trust boards 'say' about clinical governance and to examine the records of matters reported to the trust boards. Clearly, trust boards will discuss matters that are not released for scrutiny or are not recorded: we are therefore seeing matters the trust boards would want to be seen to have discussed. This is highly likely to include matters relating to clinical governance. As this was a quantitative

Table 4.2 Number of trust boards that could be identified from their minutes as having met criteria for leadership in relation to the implementation of clinical governance

Criterion	Number of trusts	Percentage of all trusts (n = 51)
Board's responsibilities clearly identified/stated	8	16
Members attended national events	5	10
Board organised local events/workshops.	17	33
Board allocated, or discussed the allocation of, resources	4	8
Board ensured staff-time could be freed up for participation	2	4
Board formally communicated with staff	11	22
Board communicated with service users	9	18
Board communicated with general practitioners	2	4
Board implemented systems for recognising and rewarding individuals	10	20

study, we can say little about the quality of discussion; but we can comment on the topics discussed and their frequency of appearance. Also, this is not an analysis of what trusts had achieved or what trusts said they had achieved in response to questionnaires. Moreover, the trusts involved, as subscribing members of the CGSS, were arguably more likely than other trusts to be actively engaging clinical governance. These factors limit the generalisability of the following conclusions.

According to their formal records, the majority of the mental health and learning disability services' trust boards in this study had responded slowly and variably to the advent of clinical governance, despite mandatory government deadlines. For example, by June 1999 clinical governance still did not appear as an agenda item in the majority of trust board minutes and over a third of trust boards had no record of setting up their clinical governance committee. At this rather slow pace of change, it is likely to take the majority of trust boards a number of years for clinical governance to reach the same status as finance.

The minutes also suggested that a large majority of trust boards were not explicitly using clinical governance as the organising framework for their discussion of quality-related issues. When quality issues were raised, the topics most often discussed were those that were most likely to expose the trust board to criticism, such as complaints and risk, which indicates a predominantly defensive approach to issues of quality – what has been described as a method for checking the barrel for 'bad apples' rather than systems to increase the number of 'good apples' (Irvine, 2001). Moreover, clinical governance appears to have been 'added on' to the trust board agenda, rather than being integrated as the organising conceptual and practical framework for all quality-related matters.

This view is supported by the results of the leadership analysis. Few trusts board minutes recorded board discussion of matters related to clinical governance that would suggest they were leading their trust into a new culture of continual (clinical) quality improvement. Only a handful of trust boards recorded that they had directly addressed their roles and responsibilities, formally communicated with staff about clinical governance, discussed the new changes with service users or general practitioners or allocated specific resources to clinical governance.

Taken together, these finding suggest that many trust boards, certainly at June 1999, did not properly understand clinical governance or their leading part in it. This lack of leadership and poor understanding of clinical governance by trust boards may be part of a more widespread ignorance (including ignorance on the part of clinicians). Whether it is or not, too long a period of poor leadership at trust board level during a time of supposedly radical change will further divide clinicians from managers and lead to accusations of 'yet another top-down exercise' that will do little to improve the lot of patients. That said, we need to consider whether or not the government's timetable may be too tight for an organisation as large and diverse as the NHS.

Implementing clinical governance

In the introduction to this chapter we asked whether trust boards were equipped and able to lead the implementation of clinical governance, improving the clinical outcomes of health care. The results of our study suggest that for many trust boards, clinical governance has been an add-on, a 'tick-box' exercise or a search for 'bad apples'. Setting up new committees and re-labelling individuals, although necessary, are not sufficient to make real changes in the delivery of care to patients. Although at the time of writing we are now 4 years on from the period of this study, it is our impression that trust boards are still struggling to understand the relationship between their role in the implementation of clinical governance and the delivery of care to patients.

'The primary focus of clinical governance is the delivery of care to patients.' (Department of Health, 1999)

To understand the role of trust boards in clinical governance, it is necessary to examine the role of mental health and social care teams within the overall organisation, and how the trust board might best discharge its key role in influencing teams to deliver high-quality care to service users and carers. Trusts also have a responsibility to work in partnership with other health organisations to coordinate and jointly plan improvements in health care delivery, and to improve the integration of health care.

The focus on teams

Teams deliver care for patients and carers. Trust boards, clinical govern- ance committees and audit departments do not. Although individual clinicians do provide care to patients and carers, no one individual has the range of skills necessary to address the diversity of patients' and carers' needs within mental health. Teams are also the best placed to deal with serious untoward incidents, complaints, poor performance and indeed the bulk of what falls within the remit of 'clinical governance' (see also Chapter 21). This includes our response to risk, workforce issues, how a team manages knowledge and information, and the development of effective multidisciplinary working. In other words, the practice of multidisciplinary clinical and social care teams of analysing and assessing the quality of their services and seeking ways to improve them *is* the practice of clinical governance at service level (Department of Health, 1999). Clinical and social care teams are the indivisible and fundamental unit for the implementation and development of clinical governance.

This view suggests a radical re-think of the organisational changes needed to enhance the implementation of the modernisation agenda, with clinical and social care teams at the heart of these changes. Trust boards need to start asking how any change, at whatever level of the organisation, will affect the functioning of their teams and the quality of treatment and care they deliver. This means that the trust board must have a grasp of the performance of teams, including regular reports on the outcomes of mental health and social care by team (see Chapter 19). This focus on teams has important implications for the way in which the trust board organises the departments and the clinical governance committee.

Reorganising the role of departments

If the primary focus of clinical governance is the quality of treatment and care provided by teams to service users and carers, then the trust board will need to ensure that this is reflected in the function and organisation of departments, such as human resources, training, information technol- ogy, clinical audit, clinical effectiveness and research and development. They, too, will need to organise their activity to support the needs of teams, re-focusing their work to assist teams in the implementation of clinical governance. For example, teams need assistance in developing tailor-made clinical information systems consistent with their specific clinical role, as well as the mental health information strategy (Depart- ment of Health, 2001); they need help in collecting information for audits designed specifically for the situation in which they work; they need methods for monitoring team and individual functioning, and ways of monitoring performance; they need access to up-to-date evidence-based clinical practice guidelines and protocols. The expertise to plan and implement these sorts of initiatives lies predominantly within a trust's departments.

It is, therefore, centrally important that trust boards ensure that departments work alongside teams, and that they are willing and able to suit the particular day-to-day needs of each team. This cannot be done 'at a distance': teams need to genuinely know the departments who come to work with them. A close working relationship between departments and teams should also allow earlier identification of problems and declining team performance. An effective use of the clinical governance committee can be to provide a common meeting point for team and service managers and departmental leads. In addition, 'sectorising' departments to ensure regular face-to-face meeting between teams and known members of departments may help.

Just as teams directly serve patients and carers, so the trust departments now need to directly serve teams.

Care programming and inter-agency working

Although teams, supported by departments, are the prime focus for the implementation of clinical governance, it must be remembered that patients and carers often have more than one team involved in their care, and sometimes more than one agency. There are mechanisms in place in mental health and social care to ensure continuity of care between teams, services and agencies, most importantly the care programme approach (CPA). Again, the clinical governance committee can act as a means of planning and integrating CPA work by teams, services and agencies. This work must be quality assured, adequately resourced and openly supported by the trust board. However, problems about cross-agency and multi-service working continue to result from a clash of cultures and different systems of quality monitoring, most obviously between mental health (which uses clinical governance) and social services (which undertake 'best value' reviews). At the time of writing, trusts integrating with social services organisations appear unable to bridge the conceptual gaps betwen their difference approaches to quality improvement. The development and coordination of seamless services and good inter-agency working is directly an issue for trust boards.

Trust boards, service users and the outside world

We have made the case that to achieve real improvements in the quality of healthcare, a trust's departments and organisational structures need to support teams, monitor the performance of teams, and feed relevant

---

Box 4.3 First steps for trust boards

- To ensure a demonstrable presence in reviewing the work of multidisciplinary teams by monitoring the functioning and effectiveness of teamwork using accurate outcome information
- To ensure the reorganisation of trust departments and organisational structures so that they directly support teams
- To ensure the implementation and monitoring of the care programme approach and inter-agency working
- To ensure integrated planning of services to match the measured needs of the local population
- To ensure that service users and carers have a genuine and demonstrable influence upon the workings of the trust (e.g. service users reviewing services)
- To routinely measure their own success by the success of teams in improving the outcomes and experience of mental health and social care.

---

and factually based information not only upwards, but also back down to the teams. To develop and coordinate this is the responsibility of the trust board and its clinical governance committee. The trust board also needs to ensure the equitable distribution of resources to teams, and to receive regular reports on the work of teams and how departments effectively support this. To achieve these ends the trust board, with the lead clinician and the clinical governance committee, must ensure an effective and functional integration of the activities of departments, teams, managers and other agencies (Box 4.3).

Trust boards also have broader functions. For example, they are financially accountable, they must generate a number of reports and they must respond to external review and inspection, most notably by the Commission for Health Improvement. In this regard, it is of interest that the Commission for Health Improvement appears to be taking an organisational development view of trusts, valuing proper integration of systems and structures as they influence the delivery of care by teams to the service user. In addition, the trust board must develop local policies and ensure the generation and implementation of a range of local protocols and directives in response to the National Institute for Clinical Excellence, the Department of Health, the regional NHS Executive and health authorities, and now strategic health authorities. The extent to which the trust board delegates these functions to the clinical governance committee will depend upon a range of factors such as the size of the trust, the experience and quality of its staff, the type of trust, and the trust board's style of management.

To promote effective working across different organisations, trust boards need to build partnerships with local primary care trusts, and with other local health organisations. Developing working partnerships between mental health trusts, primary care trusts and social services is essential for the joint monitoring of the overall care service users and carers receive both within and between different agencies. These partnerships are also necessary to plan changes in a 'joined-up' way. There is also a good case for mental health and learning disability trust boards forming joint boards with other health organisations, especially those in primary care and social services.

For all the above reasons, the trust board is also responsible for the strategic planning for the overall organisation. This depends upon the trust board working closely with other local health organisations, service users and carers, and with the public. It also requires accurate and up-to-date information on the mental health and social care needs of the population, and the extent to which teams can or cannot meet these needs. The need for accurate information is probably one of the major challenges for all health and social care organisations over the next 3–4 years.

Finally, for a trust board to remain focused upon the delivery of health and social care by teams to service users and carers, as is required by clinical governance, it needs regular feedback from both. For the teams, direct trust board feedback about performance, with periodic service review with enough time to hear the views of the teams, is probably sufficient. For service users and carers, the trust board needs a different kind of relationship, with service users and carers having an important role in, and genuine influence upon, the working of the trust. The trust board must be – and be seen to be – quickly responsive to the concerns of service users and carers, and must ensure transparency in the process and outcomes of care, and in the workings of the organisation. Indeed, the trust boards' success needs to be measured by their ability to influence positively the experience and outcomes of the care their teams deliver. It means putting service users and their carers, and the teams that provide their care, permanently at the heart of clinical governance.

Summary

Many mental health and learning disability trust boards have been slow to respond to the advent of clinical governance and the publication of *The New NHS*. Many trust boards seem unclear about their roles and responsibilities regarding clinical governance, most obviously with respect to the organisational integration of the activities of teams, departments and the wider trust. We have made a number of suggestions about reorganising the internal relationships within trusts and have identified the necessary external relationships for the trust board to assist in the implementation of clinical governance and to match the delivery of mental health and social care to the needs of the population. In so doing we have identified a number of roles that a trust board might consider for adoption. However trust boards might conceptualise and operationalise their role, we have proposed that they need to recognise that a health service centred on the patient and carer is also a health service centred on the team that delivers their care.

- Many trusts are not clear about their roles and responsibilities regarding clinical governance, nor about the practicalities of implementation
- Trust boards must place the delivery of care by teams to service users and carers, and the outcomes and experience of care by service users, at the heart of their strategy to implement and monitor clinical governance
- Trust boards must develop services on the basis of the known needs of the local population
- Trust boards must engage service users and carers in the review of services
- Trust boards might benefit from taking an organisational development approach to the inner workings of the trust and how this influences the process and delivery of care.

References

Bowling, A. (1997) *Research Methods in Health: Investigating Health and Health Services.* Buckingham: Open University Press.

Department of Health (1997) *The New NHS: Modern, Dependable,* cm 3807. London: TSO.

Department of Health (1998) *A First Class Service: Quality in the New NHS.* London: Department of Health.

Department of Health (1999) *Clinical Governance: Quality in the New NHS,* HSC 1999/065. London: Department of Health.

Department of Health (2000a) *An Organisation with a Memory: Report of the Expert Group on Learning from Adverse Events in the NHS.* London: TSO.

Department of Health (2000b) *The NHS Plan: A Plan for Investment, a Plan for Reform,* cm 4818-I. London: TSO.

Department of Health (2001) Mental Health Information Strategy. London: Department of Health.

Department of Health and Social Services, Northern Ireland (1998) *Fit for the Future.* Belfast: Department of Health and Social Services.

Greenhalgh, T. & Eversley, J. (1999) *Quality in General Practice.* London: King's Fund.

Irvine, D. (2001) The changing relationship between the public and the medical profession. *Journal of the Royal Society of Medicine,* **94**, 162–169.

Scottish Office Department of Health (1997) *Designed to Care: Renewing the NHS in Scotland.* Edinburgh: Scottish Office.

Welsh Office (1998) *NHS Wales: Putting Patients First.* Cardiff: Welsh Office.

CHAPTER 5

Healthcare inspectorates

John J. Sandford

This chapter will:

- outline the evolution of healthcare inspectorates
- outline the principles and functions of the Commission for Health Improvement (1999–2004) and the Commission for Healthcare Audit and Inspection (2004 onwards)
- discuss the benefits and drawbacks of healthcare inspection
- discuss the effect of inspectorates and service rating on future clinical practice.

The history and evolution of inspectorates

Inspectorates have been around for a long time and are a well-recognised feature of modern governance in both the public and private sectors. Governments have long promoted audit and inspection in order to ensure quality and 'democratic accountability', and to enforce political change. In modern liberal democracies inspectorates are credited with a number of roles, including ensuring standardisation, evaluating quality, evaluating efficiency (cost-effectiveness) and exposing corruption and bad practice.

Inspection and inspectorates within healthcare have a very long historical pedigree. Their role can be seen as the setting of standards and expectations in the furtherance of public health. The first governmental interventions in public health inspection were the 1225 Acts of Parliament that ordered the repair and inspection of sewerage systems in London.

Psychiatric services are arguably second only to infection control in being deemed suitable for inspection, standardisation and monitoring. It was a 1763 House of Commons Select Committee that first recommended the licensing and inspection of private madhouses. Since then there has been a continuous and ever-changing pattern of legislation to oversee the care of people with a mental disorder, in both private and public institutions. Many health professionals express concern about the rapid changes in the structure of healthcare inspections, but examination of the historical record (Table 5.1) shows that this is not a new phenomenon.

Historically, inspectors and inspectorates have been seen as progressive forces, working to raise standards in the public interest. Many inspectorates and commissions would appear to conform to the ideal of repeat inspection prompting rising standards that in turn lead to an improvement in the public good. Her Majesty's Inspectorate (HMI) of Prisons, HMI of Constabulary, environmental health officers and the licensing of nursing homes would all generally be viewed as positive and in the public interest.

Alongside their interest in quality, the role of inspectorates in encouraging efficiency is also long-standing but arguably less benign. In the 1920s, Neville Chamberlain revamped the District Audit Service as part of a clear agenda of limiting council spending under the guise of efficiency. It is this aspect of inspectorates, along with the issue of independence, that has always caused both professionals and the public understandable and sometimes legitimate concerns.

In the past 20 years the role of inspectorates has been brought to the centre of the political stage because of the expansion in their numbers and roles. In the 1980s, the Conservative government created the Audit Commission, with wide-ranging powers to appoint auditors to all manner of public bodies. It also introduced Ofsted, the Office for Standards in Education. This introduced the two core features of the modern inspectorate: external validation of performance; and the collation of national statistics and the creation of league tables.

Following the change of government in 1997 the new Labour administration continued the Tory zeal for inspectorates. In addition to increasing the number of inspectorates and inspectors, it also introduced a third element: the promotion of a specific programme of targets. For example, the Audit Commission was tasked with providing and measuring 'best value' markers for councils. These included specific guidance on targets, for example how long it should take a borough engineer to improve a broken paving stone! The Labour government also introduced, perhaps most controversially, a fourth element to inspection: to encourage changes in public sector organisations in order to make them more efficient and effective – the so-called 'modernisation agenda'. It was the Labour administration that set up the Commission for Health Improvement (CHI) along with related inspectorates for social services and housing.

The CHI was the first external regulator or inspectorate of state-run general healthcare providers, although by no means the first inspectorate of mental healthcare providers. Its role quickly expanded from what it was at foundation – to assess 'corporate responsibility' for the provision

Table 5.1 Pre-20th-century mental healthcare inspectorates

Year	Act/report	Provisions
1763	Report of the Select Committee of the House of Commons	Recommends the licensing of private madhouses in London and a Commission of Inspection (its members to be elected by the Royal College of Physicians)
1774	Act for the Regulation of Private Madhouses	Implements the recommendations of the 1763 report
1808	County Asylum Act	Sets up the county asylums
1828	County Asylum Act	Consolidates previous legislation and introduces standardised records concerning the activity of asylums collected by the justices of the peace and forwarded to the Home Office. The Secretary of State for Health acquires power to send inspectors into any county asylum
1828	Care and treatment of Insane Persons Act (the Madhouse Act)	Sets up the Metropolitan Commission in Lunacy. The Commissioners are given a duty of inspecting asylums in London and are no longer elected by the Royal College of Physicians but are appointed
1832	Insane Persons and Asylum Act	Transfers responsibility for supervising the inspection of asylums in London to the Lord Chancellor, who oversees the Metropolitan Commission in Lunacy. The Secretary of State retains inspectorial role for county asylums
1842	Lunatic Asylums Act	Gives power to the Metropolitan Commissioners, under the Lord Chancellor, to inspect asylums twice yearly and expands the Secretary of State's role to inspecting all asylums and madhouses in the country regardless of legal status
1845	Lunatics (Care and Treatment) Act and Regulation of Asylums Act	Set up a board of commissioners to inspect and supervise asylums and all other places where the mentally ill are cared for
1853	Three Lunacy Acts	Further amend the procedure for certification, licensing and regulation of lunatic asylums
1862	Lunacy Acts Amendment Act	Establishes conditions and regulations for the inspection of county asylums
1867	Poor Law Amendment Act and Metropolitan Poor Act	Establish hospitals for the poor, sick and infirm and include separate provision for the poor insane. Set up the Metropolitan Asylums Board
1886	Idiots Act	Provides for the care, education and training of people with a learning disability. It sets up a registration and inspectorate of institutions and hospitals for people with a learning disability, thereby differentiating these from institutions for the insane.

of healthcare. The CHI was set up in response to concern about the variability of clinical practice and standards of care offered by the National Health Service (NHS) across the UK. While some of this variation was explicable in terms of populations and local health culture, much seemed to have no such basis and little reason for its existence. Following a series of high-profile scandals, such as those at the Bristol Royal Infirmary (Bristol Royal Infirmary Inquiry, 1999) and Ashworth Hospital (Fallon *et al*, 1999), the government took action to address what it saw as unacceptable variations in the standard of practice (Department of Health, 1997). This was the beginning of clinical governance and the NHS 'quality agenda' (see Lelliott, 2000).

The government outlined three complementary ways in which standardisation and quality were to be improved within the NHS (Department of Health, 1998*a*, 1999*a*):

- by setting clear national quality standards
- by ensuring local delivery of high-quality clinical services
- by establishing an effective system to monitor the delivery and standards of healthcare

The CHI and later the Commission for Health Audit and Inspection (known as the Healthcare Commission) were created to undertake the monitoring role.

The Commission for Health Improvement (1999–2004) and the Healthcare Commission (2004 onwards)

Function

The CHI was set up by statute under the Health Act 1999. Its functions, powers and structure were stipulated by that Act and subsequently expanded in the NHS Reform and Healthcare Professions Act 2002. It had five statutory roles that underpinned its function of assessing the delivery and standards of healthcare in NHS organisations (Box 5.1). These applied both to purchasers (strategic health authorities and primary care trusts) and providers (NHS trusts).

Box 5.1 The five main functions of the CHI

- Reviews and investigations
- Rating the NHS
- Monitoring of National Service Frameworks
- Clinical audits and surveys
- Patients and public involvement.

Box 5.2 The main functions, roles and duties of the Healthcare Commission

- The primary inspector of public and private healthcare
- Investigations into serious service failures
- Publication of annual performance ratings for all NHS organisations in England
- Production of annual reports to Parliament on the state of health
- The independent review of NHS complaints in England
- To replace the Mental Health Act Commission in providing enhanced scrutiny of the operation of compulsion in the new Mental Health Bill (Department of Health & Home Office, 2000)
- National reviews/audits of particular kinds of healthcare
- Reviews of the quality of data collected by NHS organisations, including patient and staff surveys and national clinical audits
- The independent scrutiny of patients' complaints
- Licensing (in addition to inspection) of private hospitals, medical agencies and clinics)
- Undertaking NHS value-for-money audits on a national (England and Wales) basis.

On 19 April 2002 the Secretary of State for Health announced plans to establish two new independent inspectorates. One of these was the Commission for Social Care Inspection (CSCI). This would exist only in England. It would encompass the functions of the National Care Standards Commission for England, the Social Services Inspectorate in England and the joint review teams of the Social Services Inspectorate and Audit Commission. The second was the Commission for Healthcare Audit and Inspection (CHAI) – in effect a beefed up and broadened CHI. It would function in both England and, probably in a more limited capacity, Wales. In addition to doing the work that the CHI undertook, it is planning also to undertake the inspection work of the Mental Health Act Commission and the NHS efficiency work of the Audit Commission. Furthermore, for the first time it will encompass the assessment of independent healthcare as well as NHS care (thereby replacing the role previously undertaken by the National Care Standards Commission).

The new CHAI was therefore to have similar but expanded roles to the old CHI and to become the primary assessor of healthcare in England (Box 5.2).

The CHAI came into being on 1 April 2004. For general purposes it immediately shortened its name to the Healthcare Commission, although its legal (statute) name remains the Commission for Healthcare Audit and Inspection.

Both the CHI and the Healthcare Commission were set up to be independent of direct government control and to act as a non-departmental public body (NDPB). The broad aim was to assist the NHS and hospitals outside the public sector to improve the quality of patient care, address unacceptable standards, and praise and disseminate good practice.

When it was set up, the CHI had no statutory powers to discipline organisations or individuals, or to order changes. The Health Act 1999 only required the CHI to undertake reviews (and investigations) and to report back with findings and recommendations to the Secretary of State (in England) or National Assembly (for Wales). The NHS Reform and Healthcare Professions Act 2002 gave more teeth to the CHI, by requiring it to publish performance league tables and giving it powers to recommend changes to management, suspension or closure of any service found wanting.

The Healthcare Commission (and its sister organisation, the CSCI) were set up explicitly to be authoritative and independent judges of the quality and efficiency of health and social care in England. The shift from 'Improvement' to 'Audit and Inspection' was not just a name change.

Wales, Scotland and Northern Ireland

The CHI was set up to cover clinical governance of NHS bodies in England and Wales. It never had a remit in Scotland or Northern Ireland.

The Clinical Standards Board for Scotland (CSBS) had a remit similar to that of the CHI, involving both setting standards and quality assessment. On 1 January 2003 the CSBS became part of a new organisation called NHS Quality Improvement Scotland. It was an attempt by the Scottish Executive to rationalise a plethora of healthcare assessors. It brought together the CSBS, the Clinical Resource and Audit Group, the Health Technology Board for Scotland, the Nursing and Midwifery Practice Development Unit and the Scottish Health Advisory Service. NHS Quality Improvement Scotland is therefore an umbrella clinical effectiveness organisation that will help to develop the national strategy on healthcare. However, beneath this umbrella the CSBS remains as a statutory body established as a special health board in April 1999. It boasts commitments to quality, openness and public accountability. Its core aims are:

- to promote public confidence with the services provided by the NHS
- to demonstrate that, with the resources available, the NHS is delivering the highest possible standards of care.

Both England and Scotland have recently taken measures to rationalise healthcare inspection, but in Wales the situation is less clear and is still evolving. In Wales a new healthcare inspectorate, the Healthcare Inspection Unit for Wales, is planned to take over the inspection of NHS facilities and it may also inspect independent hospitals. Meanwhile, efficiency or audit functions may continue to be undertaken by the Audit

Commission in Wales. The approach being taken for social services in the principality is not yet clear. The National Care Standards Inspectorate for Wales will remain (though it will no longer inspect independent healthcare), as will the Social Services Inspectorate for Wales, to inspect social services. Practices of financial efficiency within social services currently remain under the remit of the Audit Commission in Wales.

The situation with regard to Northern Ireland is also not yet clear.

Structure

The CHI had two main bodies: the Commission and a board of directors. The governing body, the Commission, consisted of 14 non-executive commissioners appointed by the Secretary of State for Health in England and the National Assembly for Wales. These 14 comprised a chair and 13 other members, with a built-in lay majority of eight. The Commission appointed the executive directors. These were full-time employees responsible for the day-to-day operations, including the recruitment of assessing staff. The executive directors did not sit on the governing body and were specifically barred from involvement in politics. They included a director of nursing, a medical director and a chief executive.

Like the CHI, the Healthcare Commission is a non-departmental public body and has a chair and commissioners, who are appointed. The power of appointment is delegated by the Secretary of State. The chief executive and other executives are appointed by commissioners in much the same way as for the CHI. One significant difference is that the Healthcare Commission has no medical director. Instead, it has a clinical advisory board, chaired by a commissioner and with eight doctors nominated by the medical Royal Colleges. The Healthcare Commission is a national organisation covering England and Wales. It has no local or regional offices or structure.

Effective and efficient inspection implies the avoidance of unnecessary duplication. There are a wide number of non-NHS bodies that are involved in the regulation of healthcare. In order to formalise the relationship between the CHI and other regulatory bodies, a number of memoranda of understanding were written to provide clarity regarding roles and responsibilities, agreed protocols, confidentiality, data sharing and mutual understanding. These continue under the Healthcare Commission.

The CHI had also maintained 'close working relationships' with organisations that had a similar assessment role within the health or public service.

The primary reason for the creation of the Healthcare Commission and CSCI was to streamline inspection arrangements in view of the plethora of new inspectorates that had been created – essentially rationalisation and consolidation. The lack of duplication will mean a stronger, more streamlined and hence more authoritative organisation. It is also hoped that this streamlining will reduce the burden of work on trusts.

Although the majority of efficiency activities in the NHS in England will be undertaken by the Healthcare Commission, the inspection of purely financial matters will still involve the Audit Commission, particularly at the level of primary care trusts.

Principles

On foundation the CHI had six principles that underpinned its work (Box 5.3). However, as its role developed, it evolved from a body that strongly maintained the view that it was *not* an inspectorate (but rather a facilitator) to one that clearly accepted that it was in the business of inspection and audit. Health workers have therefore questioned whether all of these principles were ever applicable in practice.

The principles that govern the Healthcare Commission are derived from those for the CHI, but are less collaborative and more geared towards inspection. Furthermore, the Healthcare Commission shares its set of principles with the CSCI. These are:

- to put patients' and other service users' experiences of services at the centre of its work
- to consider issues of quality alongside those of efficiency
- to aim to maximise the benefit and reduce the burden of regulation.

The last task will be undertaken by a likely reduction in the number of reviews and a concentration of scrutiny on organisations that are considered to be at risk (i.e. more investigations). The Healthcare Commission will continue the CHI's aims of being evidence based and transparent, of continually seeking improvement, and of being open to independent evaluation of the impact to its work.

Box 5.3 The six principles underpinning the work of the CHI

- The patient's experience will be at the heart of the CHI's work
- The CHI will be independent, rigorous and fair
- The CHI's approach will be developmental rather than confrontational and will aim to support continuous improvement within the NHS
- The CHI's work will be evidence based, not opinion based
- The CHI will be open and accessible
- The CHI will apply the same standards of continuous improvement to itself as it expects of others.

Clinical governance reviews

Of the CHI's five main functions, local clinical governance reviews were arguably the most wide ranging and important. Their aim was to provide independent scrutiny of NHS organisations, including health authorities, primary care trusts, acute hospital trusts, mental health trusts and ambulance trusts. They aimed to be collaborative, to take into consideration local factors, and to comment on good as well as bad practice. Nationally they have been the most visible part of the CHI's work.

The initial plan was for regular reviews to occur on a four-yearly cycle, with the possibility of becoming two-yearly in organisations rated 'red' under the government's system of performance management (Department of Health, 2000b). 'Fast track' reviews could be triggered if concerns were raised about an organisation's performance.

The situation has changed with the advent of the Healthcare Commission: there is a reduction in the frequency and burden of reviews and an explicit concentration on 'failing organisations'. The aim is for the review to be coordinated with other statutory and regulatory reviews, thereby maximising information-sharing, minimising administration and avoiding repetition. With the advent of the Healthcare Commission, many of the roles of the other agencies will be gradually taken over.

The CHI had a review framework for all NHS organisations that was modified according to the type of organisation being assessed. The strict assessment framework was meant to ensure that judgements were reliable, fair, robust, comprehensive and consistent. It also gave a structure for the collation and analysis of data. This is important in principle because it allows for objective comparisons of organisations and the construction of league tables, an increasingly important area.

The design of the review framework used by the CHI was derived from two existing models: the 'excellence model' of the European Foundation for Quality Management (2000) and the Baldrige Healthcare Criteria for Performance Excellence (National Institute of Standards and Technology, 2001). In the area of mental health, the work of the Health Advisory Service (1999a,b) and its classification of standards according to five levels of the care system were influential.

Within the CHI framework, the relationship between clinical governance, capacity for change and health outcomes was seen as the most important measure of the effectiveness of an organisation (Box 5.4). The underlying hypothesis of this model is that good clinical governance leads to better patient outcomes. This could have been put to the test, but with the move from the CHI to the Healthcare Commission it is likely that more emphasis will be put on inspecting key performance indicators and less on the process or quality of management.

> **Box 5.4** The main factors deemed by the Healthcare Commission to determine organisational effectiveness
>
> - Outcomes (patients' experiences and the population's health)
> - An organisation's technical components of clinical governance (audit, risk management, education, staffing, etc.)
> - An organisation's capacity for improvement (leadership, multidisciplinary working etc.).

The CHI review framework recognised the importance of the 'culture' of healthcare organisations and provided criteria by which they could be assessed. For example, Box 5.5 lists the criteria used to assess organisational management. Mental health reviews had adaptations from the generic model; for example, they included a service user who would interview services users during the visit.

The review teams comprised a full-CHI employee (the review manager) and professional healthcare staff seconded to the review. Thus, the process was one of peer review.

A review went through four stages: preparation, visit, report and follow-up. The whole process took about 26 weeks.

The CHI contacted the organisation and established a nominated person, termed the 'trust coordinator', who acted as the primary point of contact. The review team collated information about the organisation and its performance. This required a number of meetings to be organised before the visit. Much of this information would come from external sources. As nationally agreed minimum data-sets (Korner, 1983; Glover 2000), policy objectives (Department of Health, 1999a,b) and key performance indicators were established, they were to play an increasingly key role. Information was also requested from user groups.

Review visits took approximately one week, depending on the size of the organisation. The review team spoke to clinicians, managers and

> **Box 5.5** The Healthcare Commission's criteria for good organisational management
>
> - Strong leadership
> - Consumer focus
> - Results orientated
> - Managed by facts and processes
> - Involve all staff and partners
> - Multidisciplinary working
> - A culture of learning, innovation and improvement.

> **Box 5.6** Summary guide to preparing for a mental health clinical governance review
>
> - Follow a strict assessment framework, based on established models of performance management
> - Assess the structure and function of the organisation, in addition to health outcomes
> - Produce a report that requires an action plan in response.

other staff. The service user representative had the specific task of interviewing service users. All information was treated as non-attributable, unless there was evidence of unsafe practice or risks to patients.

The team then compiled a draft report of its findings. The report was discussed with the organisation, which was allowed to comment on its factual accuracy. The final report was published in full and in summary, and contained the key findings, that is, areas of good practice as well as areas needing improvement. Following the review, the organisation was required by the CHI to produce an action plan.

This review process continues with the Healthcare Commission, but with significant changes. First, reviews can be carried out during random, unannounced visits. Second, it is hoped that the review process will rely more on exisitng standard data, rather than requiring extra data to be collated. Third, the frequency of NHS review visits will be reduced from that seen in the past 4 years. In the independent sector, visits will be carried out annually.

A summary guide for preparing for a mental health clinical governance review under the Healthcare Commission is given in Box 5.6.

Investigations

The conducting, assisting or overseeing of local investigations or inquiries into serious service failures was another major function of the CHI. Although based on the same principles and models as the regular and 'fast track' reviews, there were differences of purpose and process. An investigation is an in-depth examination of a service's alleged failures. It is generally a response to a specific situation and therefore has a narrower focus than a regular review. The purpose of such an investigation is to improve patient care, improve public confidence and avoid repetition of a failure by providing 'learning opportunities' for NHS organisations, a theme echoed in *An Organisation with a Memory* (Department of Health, 2000*b*).

There are three ways in which an investigation could be triggered:

- the Secretary of State for Health (or the National Assembly for Wales) could require an investigation

- the CHI could decide that a NHS body should be investigated
- members of the public, NHS staff or other interested stakeholders could request an investigation.

The Director of Nursing and the Medical Director of the CHI were responsible for investigations. They were the investigation managers and it was their responsibility to organise and support a constituted investigation team, the membership of which was chosen as required for each individual investigation. A layperson was always included. Its brief was to look at management and organisational practices, not at individual staff. It aimed to identify causes of service failure, make findings, come to a conclusion as to why the failures occurred, make recommendations on how the failures can be addressed and give guidance to prevent future similar failures.

The CHI published its report findings and recommendations and made these available to the public. It did not have the powers to dismiss staff or close hospitals, although it could make recommendations. The Healthcare Commission has the power to prosecute, though sadly this applies only to hospitals and providers in the independent sector.

Box 5.7 summarises the key points of investigation under the Healthcare Commission.

Monitoring the implementation of National Service Frameworks

National Service Frameworks were introduced to reduce unacceptable variations in care and treatment standards. They apply only in England, as Wales has its own (albeit similar) frameworks set out in the Mental Health Strategy for Wales (National Assembly for Wales, 2001).

The CHI had a statutory function to undertake reviews of the implementation of National Service Frameworks and the Mental Health Strategy for Wales. This function is now the responsibility of the Healthcare Commission.

The initial aim of the CHI was to audit the implementation of the National Service Frameworks for a defined service or care group and to put in place strategies to support the implementation of these, and then to establish the milestones against which progress could be measured. It

---

Box 5.7 Key points of investigation under the Healthcare Commission

Investigations:

- are undertaken in response to evidence of persistent service failure
- aim to identify the causes of service failure and recommend how they can be addressed
- focus on organisational practice, not individual staff.

was undertaking this in partnership with the Audit Commission on a rolling programme of reviews. The first Framework to be reviewed was that for cancer. Reviews of those for coronary heart disease, older people and mental health were also planned. The Healthcare Commission will continue with this programme, although the time scale and priorities may change.

Rating the NHS (the publication and development of performance indicators)

The CHI originally had no monitoring role and did not see itself as an 'inspectorate'. This role was created and rapidly expanded under the NHS Plan (Department of Health, 2000a) and subsequent changes in the NHS Reform and Health Professions Act. The CHI latterly undertook the annual publication and commentary on performance indicators. Allied with this was the development of new clinical indicators to form part of future performance measurement. This role as the inspector and rater of NHS services had in recent years become headline news. It is likely in future years to become the most high-profile function of the Healthcare Commission. However, this role is controversial because of concerns about the accuracy and utility of league tables and their limited relationship to clinical outcomes. Furthermore, league tables and star ratings have become the basis for trusts being allowed to proceed to foundation hospital status.

Although the Healthcare Commission is responsible for the compil-ation and publication of the performance rating, it is government ministers who retain responsibility for setting both the targets and priorities. It is therefore important to note that politicians will determine the key targets and type of performance indicators that are used for rating and therefore the criteria by which a trust is judged. These will be subject to change and controversy, both clinical and political.

Under the CHI, acute trusts were first to receive performance ratings (of 0 to 3 stars). By 2003, star rating had broadened to include mental health trusts, specialist trusts, ambulance trusts and primary care trusts. There has been considerable controversy about what criteria should be used when giving a star rating to an organisation. Historically, most of the criteria have been not clinical but based on 'patient experience' factors (e.g. waiting times). Furthermore, translating in a meaningful way between large 'general' trusts, small specialist trusts and trusts serving vastly different populations has proved controversial. The CHI attempted to be objective by the use of the 'Finsbury rules'. These reflect the way in which the information obtained from clinical governance reviews is incorporated into an overall star rating (see Box 5.8).

Box 5.8 The Finsbury rules

- A trust will receive a 0 star rating if it fails the Department of Health's criteria on key targets or the CHI's 0 star threshold (the CHI's 0 star threshold is for a trust that scores five or more 1s in a clinical governance review)
- For a trust to be eligible for 3 star status it needs to pass both the Department of Health's criteria on key targets and the balance score card, and in its clinical governance review have scored one or more 3s and no 1s
- If a trust is borderline 2 and 3 stars on key targets and the balance score card, it is promoted to 3 stars if in its clinical governance review it scored three or more 3s and no 1s.

The key performance targets that apply to mental health trusts are likely to evolve. The categories of assessment used by the CHI up to April 2004 are shown in Box 5.9.

The Healthcare Commission will, unlike the CHI, have to publish results of its findings in an annual report directly to Parliament as a statutory requirement.

The utility of healthcare inspection

The UK is in the early stage of the new phase of healthcare inspection. The role of the CHI/CHAI as an 'independent assessor' of health services has not been fully evaluated. There has been little criticism thus far. However, as the national structure of clinical governance has formed, concern has been raised about the conflicting roles of the Commission's work, unnecessary duplication, the validity of the sources of information and the relative unimportance of clinical outcomes.

The Healthcare Commission has four clear roles:

- setting standards (with the Department of Health)
- audit and inspection
- improvement (with the NHS Modernisation Agency)
- enforcement (with strategic health authorities).

Box 5.9 Rating categories for mental health trusts

- Use of information
- Education, training and continuing professional development
- User, carer and public involvement
- Risk management
- Clinical audit
- Clinical effectiveness
- Staffing and staff management.

Some have seen fundamental tensions between these roles. Dewar & Finlayson (2002) argue that, in effect, the Healthcare Commission is acting as lawmaker, prosecutor, judge, jury and probation officer. They point out the irony that this new Commission is undertaking all these roles while other health bodies (such as the General Medical Council and Nursing and the Midwifery Council) are separating and clarifying these boundaries. Is the Department of Health wise in having its routine inspectorate as the same body as its investigator? One can question whether there would objectivity in the investigation of an organisation that had recently been inspected and found not to be wanting and given 3-star status.

There has been a growing raft of governmental regulatory checks on the NHS. Some of these are UK organisations, while others apply to only one of the home countries. Some apply to all healthcare, some only to the NHS. Although they have different functions there is often overlap (e.g. strategic health authorities will be responsible for monitoring the implementation of guidelines from the National Institute for Clinical Excellence, in addition to the Healthcare Commission). Many see this as unnecessary duplication. It is hoped that the creation of the Healthcare Commission (and NHS Quality Improvement Scotland) will reduce and rationalise this, at least in England and Scotland.

We have seen a move from a soft CHI – 'the trust's friend' – to a more examining and inspectorial Healthcare Commission. The Commission has a mission to be rigorous, to motivate staff and to ensure that public funds are efficiently and appropriately spent. This change has been a cause of concern to healthcare professionals for two reasons:

- it is an attempt to centralise planning
- it may have the effect of stifling professional independence and public sector enterprise.

The Healthcare Commission has therefore been seen as a new 'regulatory hybrid' that gives contradictory messages to health professionals (Dewar & Finlayson, 2002). It is adopting apparently different and contradictory approaches that imply competing conceptual ideas of effective regulation. One is the inspectorial and audit process, intended to encourage compliance with government targets. This is largely aimed at pushing through a management-driven process. The second is a qualitative process, a different style that is patient centred and based on care by well-motivated individual staff. This may mean that the Healthcare Commission will face real challenges in establishing a clarity of purpose and a coherence of approach.

Another challenge for the Healthcare Commission will be establishing independence from government. This matter is something that many clinicians and patients are concerned about. Some see the Healthcare Commission as a heavy-handed weapon of central control and see no clear boundary between the inspection of a service and the implementation of government policy. The emphasis is seen to be too much on reviewing a government's agenda and assessing whether a government's key performance indicators (as translated by the independent Healthcare Commission) are met. Are these really the key factors in evaluating what a local service has achieved? The government's agenda of 'improving the patient experience' of the NHS has been accepted by the Healthcare Commission without question. It could, of course, be argued that state-paid healthcare professionals (public servants) have to be realistic and accept that it is impossible to obtain true political neutrality in the allocation of public money.

Although both the inspectorate and the government are keen to talk about Healthcare Commission independence, ultimately the power to appoint commissioners is delegated from the Secretary of State. The nature and purpose of the appointments is therefore set at a political level. Is this top-down 'quango method' the best way of appointing a Commission and overseeing a service? An alternative would be the 'bottom up' approach: the election of commissioners, perhaps representative of the various professional and NHS bodies (including patient groups). Such a body would be similar to the 1774 Commission of Inspectors of Asylums, elected by the Royal College of Physicians.

Increasingly, one of the major concerns of critics, including those who support the principles of centralised inspectorates, is the outcomes that they use. Clinical outcomes do not play a large role in routine inspections or performance ratings. Many of the factors reflect patients' surveys and political targets. Some have criticised this as a tick-box exercise that has little clinical utility. The key performance indicators chosen and rated seem to have little association with the core role of a state-funded health service – public health.

Despite the Healthcare Commission's claims to be objective and to use robust assessment methods, some of these methods remain controversial and have been the subject of criticism (Day & Klein, 2003). Perhaps most controversial is the policy of asking patients to rate services, for example to rate general practitioners according to their medical knowledge, technical ability, trustworthiness and how well they arrange tests. Leaders of that profession have questioned whether such methods are robust and objective or simply populist. The CHI argued that these survey instruments were widely used and validated in primary care settings. The sceptic would question not their validation, but their purpose. Are they directly related to health outcomes and local public health, or only to customer satisfaction?

Ultimately, time may provide the true answers. The interesting outcome for clinicians and those interested in evidence-based practice will be whether the process of regular inspection and the compilation of league tables will have any effect on improving the performance of trusts, the public health or public opinion about the NHS. As yet there is no clear evidence either way.

The implications of healthcare inspection

At such an early stage of its development, the impact of the CHI/ Healthcare Commission on the day-to-day practice of trusts and clinicians is unclear. It is already evident that clinical governance will make individual clinicians and organisations more accountable for their performance and place on them an expectation to embrace best practice, constant improvement and a greater awareness of patient expectation.

Continuing the work begun by the CHI, the Healthcare Commission will influence future health provision in the following ways:

- It will develop a body of opinion with regard to what constitutes organisational good practice and what is bad or unacceptable practice (Palmer, 2000).
- The clinical governance reviews, audits and surveys are being combined to act as the overall measure of organisational performance. Under the government's scheme of performance management they are becoming increasingly influential in deciding the status of organisations, their independence and the funds allocated to those organisations.
- The investigations (and to a lesser extent the reviews) will lead to a clarification of the roles and responsibilities of individual clinicians and managers with regard to ensuring quality. The CHI was quick to address the issue of 'where does medical accountability lie in this situation' (Commission for Health Improvement, 2000a) and pronounced on the need for urgency and uniformity in trust disciplinary procedures (Commission for Health Improvement, 2000b). Its conclusions are likely to build into a significant body of opinion that will influence bodies such as the General Medical Council and the Nursing and Midwifery Council, as well as the civil and possibly the criminal courts.
- The national monitoring of the implementation of National Service Frameworks and guidelines will have effects on the culture and autonomy of trusts and health authorities. They will have to show that they are responding appropriately to centrally led government targets and accept the implications that their performance in these areas will be published in a league table and determine future revenues.
- The monitoring and reviewing role will allow for some evidence-based appraisal of the effectiveness of government policy. It has yet to be established that the implementation of good clinical governance or of a National Service Framework has any impact on

patient outcomes or the health of a given population. (Department of Health, 1998*b*).

- The structure of healthcare inspectorates across the four countries of the UK has never been so disunited. There is now little overlap in the inspectorates of England, Scotland, Wales and Northern Ireland. Although all inspectorates will be producing 'national' league tables and performance information, these are unlikely to be comparable across the four countries. Although arguably not its intention, the presence of devolved health inspection is, more than any other process, likely to ensure that the NHS becomes less national. To some extent this process is already happening (Greer, 2001; Owen, 2001).

- The powers of the Healthcare Commission have implications for patient confidentiality. Legislation allows the Commission to look at individual patients' records if it deems access 'necessary or expedient'. This has provoked understandable protests by both doctors and patients groups. Not only will it allow the Healthcare Commission to see records, but it can do so without asking for the patient's consent and a refusal to cooperate could lead to prosecution (Dyer, 2003). It is not clear whether such draconian powers will be used by the Healthcare Commission. If they are, there would be a clear erosion of the common law right of patient confidentiality, particularly when one considers that this would apply to patients in the independent sector as well as NHS.

Conclusions

- The government will set the broad objectives or standards and these will be interpreted, audited, imposed and enforced by the Healthcare Commission.

- The Healthcare Commission will 'independently' set, assess and measure the standards and then compare organisational performance across the healthcare sector.

- The Healthcare Commission will, over time, clarify the roles, responsibilities and expectations of healthcare staff and healthcare services.

- Over time, the relationship between good clinical governance, patient outcome and public health may become clearer.

- England, Scotland, Wales and Northern Ireland have devolved 'national' health services and devolved health inspection. Comparison across the four countries will become increasingly difficult, particularly as the respective Departments of Health pursue different priorities, different methods of implementation and different methods of audit/measurement.

- The NHS and independent sector will not be treated equally: the latter has a much stricter (annual) programme of review and is liable to prosecution.

Acknowledgements

I thank Dr Jocelyn Cornwell, former Director of Policy and Development at the CHI, for her guidance and support. I also extend my gratitude to Margaret Allen and Karin Wathen for typing and secretarial support.

References

Bristol Royal Infirmary Inquiry (1999) *Final Report*. Available at http://www.bristol-inquiry.org.uk

Commission for Health Improvement (2000a) *Investigation into the North Lakeland NHS Trust: Report to the Secretary of State for Health*. London: CHI

Commission for Health Improvement (2000b) *Investigation into the Carmarthenshire NHS Trust: Report to the Secretary of State for Health*. London: CHI

Day, P. & Klein, R. (2003) *The NHS Improvers: A Study of the Commission for Health Improvement*. London: King's Fund.

Department of Health (1997) *The New NHS: Modern, Dependable*, cm 3807. London: TSO.

Department of Health (1998a) *A First Class Service: Quality in the New NHS*. London: Department of Health.

Department of Health (1998b) *Our Healthier Nation. A Contract for Health*, cm 3852. London: TSO.

Department of Health (1999a) *Clinical Governance: Quality in the New NHS*, HSC 1999/065. London: Department of Health.

Department of Health (1999b) *Effective Care Co-ordination in Mental Health Services. Modernising the Care Programme Approach – Policy Booklet*. London: Department of Health.

Department of Health (2000a) *An Organisation with a Memory: Report of the Expert Group on Learning from Adverse Events in the NHS*. London: TSO.

Department of Health (2000b) *The NHS Plan: A Plan for Investment, a Plan for Reform*, cm 4818-I. London: TSO.

Department of Health & Home Office (2000) *Reforming the Mental Health Act*. London: TSO.

Dewar, S. & Finlayson, B. (2002) The I in the new CHAI. *BMJ*, **325**, 848–850.

Dyer, C. (2003) New powers for CHAI 'threaten patient confidentiality'. *BMJ*, **328**, 580.

European Foundation for Quality Management (2000) *EFQM Excellence Model – Public and Voluntary Sector Version*. Brussels: EFQM.

Fallon, P., Bluglass, R. & Edwards, B. (1999) *The Report into the Committee of Inquiry into the Personality Disorder Unit, Ashworth Special Hospital*. London: TSO.

Glover, G. (2000) The minimum data set. At last information! *Psychiatric Bulletin*, **24**, 163–164.

Greer, S. (2001) *Divergence and Devolution*. London: Nuffield Trust.

Health Advisory Service (1999a) *Standards for Mentally Disordered Offenders*. Brighton: Pavilion Publishing.

Health Advisory Service (1999b) *Standards for Mental Health Services for Older People*. Brighton: Pavilion Publishing.

Korner, S. (1983) *Report of the Working Party in Information Requirements in the National Health Service*. London: HMSO

Leilliott, P. (2000) Clinical standards and the wider quality agenda. *Psychiatric Bulletin*, **24**, 85–89.

National Assembly for Wales (2001) *Adult Mental Health Services for Wales: Equity, Empowerment, Effectiveness, Efficiency. Strategy Document.* Cardiff: National Assembly.

National Institute of Standards and Technology (2001) Baldrige National Quality Program Awards: Healthcare Criteria for Performance Excellence. See www.quality.nist.gov.

Owen, J. W. (2001) *The Machinery of Government for Health Policy: Devolution in Context.* London: Nuffield Trust.

Palmer, C. (2000) Clinical Governance Support Service. *Psychiatric Bulletin*, **24**, 151.

Further information

Healthcare Commission website: www.healthcarecommission.org.uk
NHS Quality Improvement Scotland website: www.nhshealthquality.org
Nuffield Trust website: www.nuffieldtrust.org.uk

The mental health guidance programmes of the National Institute for Clinical Excellence

Peter Littlejohns, Gillian Leng and Carole Longson

- In its first 5 years the National Institute for Clinical Excellence has achieved international prominence for its work of assessing cost-effectiveness as well as clinical effectiveness
- Mental health is the key component of its work programme
- In the future, greater emphasis will be placed on disease prevention.

Introduction

The National Institute for Clinical Excellence (NICE) was established in April 1999 to provide national guidance on the clinical effectiveness and cost-effectiveness of treatments and care for people using the National Health Service (NHS) in England and Wales. The Institute is a special health authority governed by a board consisting of executive and non-executive members, which meets in public (around the country) every 2 months. It is a small organisation (it has around 90 employees) based in London and undertakes its work by commissioning and liaising with a range of professional, specialist and patient organisations. It is supported by a Partner's Council, which includes representatives from all its stakeholders (including the pharmaceutical and medical devices industries). There are formal links with a number of universities and the National Health Service Research and Development Programme. NICE works closely with local trusts and clinical governance professionals to ensure support for those responsible for implementing its guidance. This includes providing audit advice to accompany its guidance.

Mental health is one of the government's priority areas and a range of guidance products have been developed by NICE to support implementation of the National Service Framework for Mental Health in England and its equivalent in Wales. In its first 4 years NICE issued guidance on five technology appraisals and one newly commissioned guideline that were related to the general area of mental health (out of totals of 60 appraisals and three guidelines). Another six mental health guidelines and two mental health technology appraisals were in preparation at the time of writing. The transparent and inclusive approach that NICE has adopted in reaching its decisions has highlighted difficult technical and social issues facing the NHS as it seeks to balance its responsibility for enhancing services for individuals with improving the overall public health.

This chapter describes the processes of appraising technologies and developing guidelines, and future developments in the Confidential Inquiries.

The role of the Institute

The Institute has four main aims:

- to speed the uptake by the NHS of interventions that are both clinically effective and cost-effective
- to encourage more equitable access to healthcare (i.e. to reduce 'postcode' variation in care)
- to provide better and more rational use of available resources by focusing the provision of healthcare on the most cost-effective interventions
- to encourage the creation of new and innovative technologies.

It achieves these aims by providing guidance to the NHS in England and Wales on the effectiveness and cost-effectiveness of clinical interventions. This task is achieved by appraising new and existing technologies, developing disease-specific clinical guidelines and initially by supporting clinical audit – although the responsibility for audit has now been transferred to the Commission for Health Audit and Inspection (known as the Healthcare Commission) (see Chapter 5). In addition, NICE has responsibility for the three national Confidential Inquiries (including the National Confidential Inquiry into Suicide and Homicide by People with Mental Illness) and more recently for assessing the safety and efficacy of new interventional procedures (previously the responsibility of SERNIP – Safety and Efficacy Register of New Interventional Procedures) and advising on the prescription of medical foods.

Quality improvement

The Institute's position in the broader quality improvement picture is illustrated in Fig. 6.1. Its establishment has been part of the government's approach to improving the quality of the NHS outlined in the White Paper *The New NHS: Modern, Dependable* and the consultation document *A First Class Service: Quality in the New NHS* (Department of Health, 1997, 1998). Standards for service configuration are established at a national level through National Service Frameworks and clinical standards are established through the guidance issued by NICE.

Figure 6.1 The quality model for the National Health Service.

The approach was initially presented as a 'quality improvement' model, with education and support being the key driving forces. However, a reduction in public and professional confidence in some of the systems in place to assure professional standards and institutional performance resulted in tough messages from government. Politicians have sought to substitute an 'educational' model with a more directive 'performance management' approach. In this context, NICE considers that one of its main roles is to provide guidance on controversial health issues, where lack of clarity has resulted in regional variation in the care provided by the NHS. The guidance is considered to be a 'national standard' for clinical practice and is expected to be incorporated into local clinical governance mechanisms via the use of local guidelines and protocols. Monitoring of its uptake forms part of the assessment of local trusts undertaken by the Healthcare Commission.

Evidenced-based healthcare policy

The initial step in all technology appraisals and guideline development is systematically to search the literature for research evidence and then to estimate the magnitude of effect of the relevant interventions (for both costs and benefits) by statistical and modelling techniques. In practice the data required for the assessment of clinical effectiveness and cost-effectiveness are usually deficient. This is because the research base necessary to assess the two types of effectiveness is more extensive than that required for the initial licensing of a technology (which is based solely on efficacy and safety). For example, many drugs for the treatment of mental health have been licensed on the basis of short-term trials, which makes assessing their impact on chronic disease difficult.

The Institute recognises the important difference between 'assessment' of the research evidence and 'appraisal', which represents the translation of *all* the available evidence (including patient and professional experience) into practical guidance that is useful to the NHS on a day-to-day basis. Thus, while the guidance produced is firmly based on published evidence, it is also influenced by submissions from a variety of stakeholders, including professional organisations, patient/carer groups and industry. It is apparent that results from the same evidence base can be interpreted differently, depending on the value given to different outcomes by each stakeholder. The final guidance issued by the Institute always draws upon the value judgements inherent to each stakeholder group. This is why it is essential to involve all these groups in the process. NICE, as part of its own research and development strategy, has initiated a number of projects to understand more fully how to integrate information from various sources into its decision-making processes. Examples are a feasibility project on patient impact assessment, undertaken by Birmingham University, and another on the value that the public place on the concept of quality-adjusted life years, undertaken in conjunction with the methodological section of the NHS research and development programme.

Despite the volume and robustness of the evidence base for an intervention, judgement is always necessary when translating clinical research findings into guidance, and can stimulate considerable controversy when the results determine national policy. An American sociologist, David Mechanic (1993), argues that 'research is a form of currency as varying interests negotiate a political solution, but research is never definitive to resolve major issues on which strong political interests differ'. The stakes are now very high, as the acceptance of a new intervention can have enormous financial as well a therapeutic impact. Even clinical research laboratories involved in developing innovative treatments can expect financial reward for contributing to a commercially successful drug.

In summary, although the basis of the Institute's approach to decision-making is evidence based, pure research evidence is necessary but not sufficient. In addition, in order that the decisions made are robust and credible, the process has to be transparent, consultative, inclusive of all key stakeholders and responsive to change. These principles underpin all of the guidance issued by NICE.

Technology appraisals

When a technology appraisal is referred to NICE from the Department of Health and the National Assembly for Wales, all possible stakeholders are identified. They are then consulted on the scope of the appraisal. An independent review of the published literature is commissioned from a university department through the NHS research and development programme. In addition, NICE receives submissions (both written and verbal) from all the stakeholders. The independent multidisciplinary appraisal committee considers all this information and consults on its provisional views (which are set out in an 'appraisal consultation document') via the Institute's website (www.nice.org.uk). The appraisal committee reconsiders its initial decision in the light of the comments and produces a final appraisal determination, which is also placed on the website. Stakeholders can appeal against it if they consider the Institute and the guidance have not fulfilled a number of criteria. NICE then issues the guidance to the NHS. A full description of the process and the principles underlying the appraisal decision-making process is available on the website.

Appraisals relevant to mental health issued so far include:

- newer atypical antipsychotic drugs for schizophrenia
- computerised cognitive–behavioural therapy for anxiety and depression
- donepezil, rivastigmine and galantamine for Alzheimer's disease
- methylphenidate for attention-deficit hyperactivity disorder
- electroconvulsive therapy
- new drugs for bipolar disorders.

Clinical guidelines

The Institute produces clinical guidelines for the NHS in England and Wales in response to a referral from the Department of Health and the Welsh Assembly. Its programme of guideline development is now one of the most extensive in the world – there may be over 30 guidelines in production at any one time. The process – for example, evaluation of the best available evidence and extensive stakeholder consultation (see above) – is based on internationally agreed standards for guideline development (Cluzeau *et al*, 2003). The guideline development process is described in greater detail below.

NICE guidelines in mental health

There are currently many guideline topics relevant to mental health on NICE's programme of work, and it is anticipated that these will eventually span the whole breadth of the mental health field. Current topics that are either published on under development include:

- the management of generalised anxiety disorder and panic disorder (with or without agoraphobia) in adults in primary, secondary and community care

- the management of bipolar affective disorder (manic–depressive illness)
- the management of dementia, including the use of antipsychotic medication in older people
- the management of adult depression in primary and secondary care
- the identification and management of depression in children and young people in primary care and specialist services
- the short-term management of disturbed (violent) behaviour in in-patient psychiatric settings
- the management of anorexia nervosa, bulimia nervosa and binge eating disorders
- the management of obsessive–compulsive disorder in adults in primary, secondary and community care
- the management of post-traumatic stress disorder in adults in primary, secondary and community care
- the short-term physical and psychological management and secondary prevention of self-harm in primary and secondary care
- the core interventions in the treatment and management of schizophrenia in primary and secondary care.

Details of the publication status of these guidelines can be found on the NICE website (www.nice.org.uk).

Links with National Service Frameworks

The focus of a clinical guideline is to provide recommendations for healthcare professionals on the appropriate management of people with a specific disease or condition. This is in contrast to a National Service Framework, where recommendations emphasise service delivery rather than individual patient care. The two programmes should be complementary, with NICE guidelines providing recommendations on best practice in clinical management, supported by recommendations in the National Service Frameworks on how services should be configured to enable healthcare professionals to deliver this best practice. Regular communication between teams developing guidelines and those developing the National Service Frameworks is therefore essential to ensure the boundaries between the work are clear and any overlapping issues are discussed. Detail on the links between NICE guidelines and the National Service Framework for Mental Health are given in Chapter 8.

Integration of appraisals and guidelines

The appraisal programme was established to assess the correct positioning of a single intervention in the management of a disease on the basis of its clinical effectiveness and cost-effectiveness. A guideline in the same clinical area addresses the broader context in which the single intervention fits. This differentiation ensures that a single intervention (usually but not always a drug) does not dominate the guideline developers' time at the expense of other therapeutic interventions. It also ensures that the sponsor of the technology can be assured that NICE has given due consideration to all aspects of assessing its value.

It is apparent that, with two guidance development processes advising NICE on a similar clinical issue, there needs to good integration of the development systems. This is achieved by close liaison between appraisal and guideline technical staff within the Institute, attendance of the chair of the guideline development group at the appraisal meetings and consulter status of the guideline development group for any relevant appraisal. In the end there has to be clarity over the roles of each development process and NICE's policy is that the guideline development group is required to adopt the recommendations of the appraisal process (when appropriate) into the guideline.

The first full guideline issued by NICE was on the management of schizophrenia and this incorporated the appraisal on the use of newer atypical antipsychotics.

National collaborating centres

The Institute commissions seven national collaborating centres (NCCs) to develop guidelines. Each centre is a multidisciplinary collaboration of healthcare professionals, user representatives and technical experts. The NCCs have the capacity, skills and expertise to deliver guidelines that are of a high quality. They:

- are led by professionals and have requisite academic support
- work closely with patient and carer representatives
- complement each other, and share skills and expertise
- have governance arrangements that assure cooperation, wide participation, consultation and clear contractual accountability.

The NCCs are largely based in medical Royal Colleges and cover a range of clinical areas (Table 6.1). Further details on the centre for mental health is given in Chapter 7.

The guideline development process

The development of NICE clinical guidelines is a joint process shared between the NCCs and the Institute, with input at several stages from relevant stakeholders. Stakeholders are those organisations with an interest in the guideline topic, including national patient or professional bodies, companies manufacturing relevant drugs or medical devices, and

Table 6.1 National collaborating centres and their host organisations

National collaborating centre	Host organisation
Acute care	Royal College of Surgeons
Cancer	Velindre NHS Trust, Wales
Chronic conditions	Royal College of Physicians
Nursing and supportive care	Royal College of Nursing
Mental health	British Psychological Society and Royal College of Psychiatrists
Primary care	Royal College of General Practitioners
Women's and children's health	Royal College of Obstetricians and Gynaecologists

NHS organisations. Stakeholder input is vital to ensure all aspects have been appropriately addressed in the guideline, and to support implementation. Guideline development is therefore a complex process – it takes on average 2 years to complete each guideline.

The process of guideline development can be divided into four phases, as described in Table 6.2. More details on each of the phases are given in the guideline manuals available on the NICE website, and specifically in relation to the development of mental health guidelines in Chapter 10.

Guideline review panels

Seven guideline review panels have been established to advise and assist in the guideline programme. Each panel is aligned to one NCC. The panel members provide external validation for the guidelines by overseeing their development, advising on the commissioning of work and monitoring their quality. Members are expected to have an in-depth knowledge of the development of their allocated guidelines and to keep a record of the documents relating to their guidelines.

Publication

Guidelines commissioned by NICE are published in three formats, to make it easier for different groups to access the information most relevant to them: the NICE guideline; information for the public, and the full guideline.

The NICE guideline

This is a short summary publication that contains all the recommendations produced by the guideline development group. A few recommendations (those with the greatest impact on patient care) are prioritised by the group as 'key' recommendations and these are suggested as priorities for implementation. The NICE guideline also contains information on implementation, to advise local NHS bodies on

Table 6.2 Phases in NICE guideline development

Development phase	Key components
1. Initiation	Topic referred to NICE by the Department of Health and the Welsh Assembly NICE commissions appropriate NCC to develop guideline Stakeholders register interest NCC outlines areas to be covered within the guideline for consultation with stakeholders NCC agrees methodology for guideline development with NICE
2. Development	NCC convenes a multidisciplinary guideline development group, which includes patients and carers The group defines the key clinical questions relevant to the topic area, reviews best evidence of clinical and cost-effectiveness and receives stakeholder submissions, produces recommendations and writes the guideline for submission to NICE NICE provides technical input as required
3. Validation and publication	NICE sends guideline to stakeholders for two 4-week periods of consultation NCC revises guideline to take into account stakeholder views NICE approves final guideline in conjunction with the guideline review panel NICE and the NCC publish and disseminate the guideline Implementation of guideline supported by the NCC and NICE
4. Review and update	NCC updates the guideline 2–4 years after publication, depending on whether significant new evidence is available.

how to approach the guideline and to make them aware of any other relevant national initiatives, such as National Service Frameworks.

Information for the public

This publication mirrors the NICE guideline but presents guideline recommendations in lay language, to make them more widely accessible. It also provides some background information about the condition covered by the guideline to help put the recommendations in context.

The full guideline

This contains all the guideline recommendations as well as much more detailed information for interested specialists in the field. It includes detail on the development process, a description of how the evidence was collected, reviewed and assessed, plus full reference details of the relevant literature, detail on how the recommendations were formulated and recommendations for future research.

Implementation

Successful implementation is key to the success of the guideline programme. NICE and the NCCs are involved in dissemination of the guidelines, and help to support implementation through professional organisations and patient groups. Wherever possible, NICE encourages other organisations to republish the recommendations in the most appropriate format to support local use, for example through the development of protocols.

The National Confidential Inquiries

The Institute took over responsibility for the Confidential Inquiries from the Department of Health in 1999, though in April 2005 that resonsibility will transfer to the National Patient Safety Agency (NSPA), a part of the Arm's Length Bodies review. At that time NICE will take on th functions of the Health Development Agency. NICE provides funding to three discrete National Confidential Inquiries:

- Confidential Enquiry into Maternal and Child Health (CEMACH)
- National Confidential Inquiry into Suicide and Homicide by People with Mental Health Illness (NCISH)
- National Confidential Enquiry into Patient Outcome and Death (NCEPOD)

Since 1999, NICE has worked with the Confidential Inquiries to expand their remit and put in place new managerial and budgeting structures. Details of this process, and the structure and function of each Inquiry, can be accessed on the NICE website and on the website of each Inquiry (www.cemach.org.uk, www.national-confidential-inquiry.ac.uk, www.ncepod.org.uk).

In recent years the healthcare and scientific environments in which the Inquiries function have changed dramatically, particularly because a range of other organisations now monitor the delivery and organisation of healthcare. These organisations include:

- the Commission for Healthcare Audit and Inspection (the Healthcare Commission), which has responsibility for monitoring trust performance and establishing national audits.
- the NPSA, which routinely gathers and analyses data on adverse events and disseminates guidance on good practice

- NICE, which issues national guidance on patient care, treatments and interventions.

In addition, the work of the Inquiries is likely to be affected by: recent reviews of procedures surrounding death registration and the use of the coronial system (in particular in the light of the Shipman inquiry); the review of childhood deaths (in the light of the Victoria Climbié inquiry); and the proposals by National Statistics to make birth, death and marriage registrations electronic and to link vital statistics with hospital episode data.

Thus, despite the changes to the Inquiries' remits and structures over the past few years, it is apparent that they will need to develop further. The Institute's proposals in this regard are considered below.

Collaboration

It is essential that the unique role of the Inquiries within the National Framework of data capture and investigation is clearly identified and strengthened, both by collaboration between the Inquiries themselves and their collaboration with agencies that have common objectives or that have common needs for data capture. The establishment of the Confidential Enquiries Advisory Committee (CEAC), with its independent chair, Catherine Peckham (Professor of Paediatric Epidemiology at the Institute of Child Health), has initiated this collaboration. CEAC members include representatives of each Inquiry and a number of relevant national organisations, including NICE, the NPSA and the Healthcare Commission. From April 2005 the NPSA has been managing the contracts for the National Confidential Inquiries, this responsibility having been transferred from NICE.

It is intended that CEAC will advise the NPSA on those functions of the Inquiries that would best be undertaken in collaboration. This may include issues related to informed consent, data protection, ethics approval and the efficient use of resources, such as statistical support. CEAC may also advise on common strategies for the dissemination of the Inquiries' findings and recommendations.

Choosing investigations

The Institute has been working with each Inquiry and CEAC to develop an open and transparent process to identify and prioritise subjects for future investigations. A key factor has been the extent to which study findings have complemented and informed NICE's broader agenda, for example through:

- an evaluation of clinician adherence to existing NICE guidance
- data collection to inform the development of guidance being produced by NICE

- the identification of areas of clinical practice that would benefit from NICE guidance

The Institute has been working with CEAC and the individual Inquiries to develop systems to ensure the scientific rigour and effective analysis of individual studies.

Reporting and dissemination of study findings

With the changing nature and focus of the Inquiries, it is expected that the format and method of dissemination of their findings will need to change. It is unlikely that any one dissemination method will be suitable for the range of investigations that will be undertaken in response to different questions. It is proposed that, as each study is developed, explicit consideration will be given to the dissemination of findings and recommendations, with the aim of reaching as many interested parties as possible.

It is also proposed that output from investigations should include publications in peer-reviewed journals. Publication in peer-reviewed journals gives the Inquiries the potential to reach a wider audience, especially within the international context, than is the case with the current published reports.

Data access and data sharing

As the Inquiries develop and expand their databases, the data held are likely to be useful to other researchers assessing quality of care or the epidemiology of specific diseases. Subject to appropriate safeguards, it is proposed that the Inquiries explore ways of entering into collaborations that maximise the use, for research purposes, of their data.

Education and capacity building

The Inquiries provide a unique opportunity for clinicians and research students to participate in a national research programme. It is proposed that each Inquiry should attract students who wish to undertake a higher degree (for example MSc, MPhil, PhD or MD).

Conclusions

The Institute has been given an ambitious programme of work. It issues guidance to the NHS in various formats, each with its own development process and yet all adhering to core principles. Its activities are likely to increase. The challenge in the future will be to ensure that its programmes are fully integrated. It is imperative that an individual patient, professional or member of the public interested in a particular disease can be assured that there are national evidence-based standards of clinical practice that cover all aspects of care, from prevention through to palliation.

References

Cluzeau, F. A., Burgers, J. S., Brouwers, M., *et al* (2003) Development and validation of an international appraisal instrument for assessing the quality of clinical practice guidelines: the AGREE project. *Quality and Safety in Healthcare*, **12**, 18–23.

Department of Health (1997) *The New NHS: Modern, Dependable*, cm 3807. London: TSO.

Department of Health (1998) *A First Class Service: Quality in the New NHS*. London: Department of Health.

Mechanic, D. (1993) Social research in health and the American sociopolitical context: the changing fortunes of medical sociology. *Social Science and Medicine*, **36**, 95–102.

CHAPTER 7

National support for clinical governance

Adrian Worrall

- This chapter discusses different ways national support for clinical governance is provided and introduces the Clinical Governance Support Service (CGSS)
- National support for clinical governance may be provided using: organisational and clinical audit; external assessment; quality networks; consultancy support; information dissemination; education and training; and policy, guidelines and standards
- CGSS reviews use an organisational audit model. Clinical governance standards are used for self-review and external peer-review. This engages staff in the service development process
- Future support must focus on service development, rather than service evaluation, and clinical teams, rather than trust managers
- Service development work must be sufficiently resourced to avoid the demotivating consequences of extra workload
- Contact details for support organisations are given.

Introduction

Establishing and developing clinical governance in a trust is neither quick nor easy. Although the benefits are obvious to many staff, putting it into practice is quite a different matter. This chapter explains the need for support for clinical governance and discusses the different ways in which this is provided to services. It introduces the Clinical Governance Support Service (CGSS) of the Royal College of Psychiatrists' Research Unit and lists other organisations that offer support.

Why do services need support?

Policy and political context

The Department of Health has embarked on an ambitious programme of change. Ministers and the National Health Service Executive have placed quality at the top of the agenda of the National Health Service (NHS) (Department of Health, 1997, 1998) and the demands on services have never been greater. There are clear responsibilities for trusts to improve the quality of their services but, unfortunately, so far little support has been offered.

There are only a few organisations that are concerned with specifically supporting clinical governance: the Commission for Healthcare Audit and Inspection (known as the Healthcare Commission), which has replaced the Commission for Health Improvement (CHI); the Clinical Governance Support Service (CGSS); and the NHS Clinical Governance Support Team (NCGST). Other organisations do, however, offer support for key areas within clinical governance, such as clinical audit or evidence-based practice.

The Commission for Health Improvement (CHI) reviewed the progress of clinical governance in trusts that provide mental health and learning disability services. The new Healthcare Commission has now taken on this role (see Chapter 5). The NHS Plan announced the establishment of the new Modernisation Agency to support trusts' service development (Department of Health, 2000), within which a Leadership Centre develops leaders to take forward the modernising of services. It is not yet clear how these initiatives will support clinical governance in mental health or learning disability services.

Key stages in implementing clinical governance

The stages that need to be completed to implement clinical governance are outlined in Box 7.1. The key components of clinical governance are listed in Box 1.1 of Chapter 1, and Chapter 3 describes in more detail issues in implementing clinical governance.

The first stage – agreeing aims and objectives – may have been a problem in some trusts. Clinical governance is notoriously difficult to understand or specify and the definition is not always clear. If it is interpreted simply as a 'framework of accountability', then this has more implications for trust managers than clinical teams. However, if it is interpreted as a generic term for a range of quality activities, then clinical team members will be more involved. Objectives and strategies will differ in this way according to the local interpretation.

Progress

Progress to date has been slow. Two years after the government launched its modernisation agenda, a survey of all 47 trusts in the West Midlands found that clinical governance had not advanced beyond the production of strategies, establishing committees and appointing leads (Latham *et al*, 1999). A survey of the minutes of trust boards also found that clinical

---

Box 7.1 Key stages in implementing clinical governance

- Agree and communicate aims and objectives
- Identify resources
- Establish committees and identify responsibilities
- Develop strategy
- Translate strategy into local tasks and responsibilities, and draw up a timetable
- Develop measures of progress and patient outcomes
- Monitor and feedback progress and identify ongoing needs.

---

governance was not appearing as an agenda item in the majority (Palmer, 2000) (see Chapter 4). Good progress may have been made in many trusts since these studies were conducted; however, these early problems may have slowed subsequent progress. A recent study of trusts in the West Midlands region found little further improvement. The trusts lacked time, resources and information to manage clinical governance effectively (Cowpe & Scrivens, 2001).

Trust difficulties

Variation in performance is as much a characteristic of organisations as it is of individuals. It is therefore not surprising that clinical governance has progressed to varying degrees. Some trusts have made good progress in all areas, whereas others have not. Services that are not as advanced are likely to be concerned about their performance in the Healthcare Commission's reviews.

There is a range of reasons why trusts may have difficulties. Often they may have allocated insufficient time and money to planning and delivering the various initiatives. They may also be under stress following a recent, or preceding an imminent, merger. Visible senior-level commitment is needed to help establish the credibility of clinical governance work, and dedicated resources will help staff support it. Some staff may be poorly motivated to take part in it, as this generally means extra workload without necessarily any immediate rewards. Other staff may not be 'engaged' in clinical governance activity; for example, they may be aware of strategies and plans formulated around them but may not be directly involved. It is generally understood that there is still a poor basic understanding of what clinical governance really means on the ground and 'cascading' of information about clinical governance does not always happen. In addition, one-off training events may not be enough and regularly revisiting topics may better sustain interest and momentum.

Box 7.2 Factors helping the implementation of clinical governance

- Committed, enthusiastic leadership by senior managers
- Good working relationships and staff goodwill and enthusiasm
- A supportive culture and a cooperative, 'no-blame' approach
- A pre-existing infrastructure (e.g. for clinical audit)
- Investment in education about clinical governance, particularly at the beginning
- Congruence between existing trust culture and clinical governance
- Regional office framework and visit.

Forty medical and clinical directors from ten mental health and other trusts in the West Midlands region were asked what factors had helped (Box 7.2) or hindered (Box 7.3) their attempts to introduce clinical governance (Cowpe & Scrivens, 2001). Their responses may be a useful reference, together with other information in this section, for managers when they next revise their trust's clinical governance strategy. The researchers concluded that all the trusts in the survey lacked the 'organisational capacity' (i.e. time, resources and information) to manage the clinical governance agenda.

Poorly performing services need support and better performers may need help to sustain momentum. Clinical governance needs dedicated resources and motivated staff. Staff, in turn, need systematic support to improve the consistency and overall quality of the service they provide.

More recent CHI (Commission for Health Improvement, 2003) and National Audit Office (2003) reports show that clinical governance has

---

Box 7.3 Factors hindering the implementation of clinical governance

- Lack of time, both to reflect on practice and risk and to plan and introduce changes
- Lack of resources (both support staff and funding for implementation)
- Lack of a clinically focused information system
- Lack of knowledge, for example of how to do clinical audit
- Negative staff attitudes
- 'Mixed messages' (e.g. a view that the government is, in reality, more interested in quantity than quality)
- Paperwork and bureaucracy
- Turbulence, in terms of mergers, large building projects, major financial pressures.

---

made a difference and is generally well supported. Nearly all trusts have a clinical governance committee and typically, at the time of writing, have about half the key structures and strategies in place.

There are, however, chronic staffing and funding problems, which often undermine managers' good work. There are particular problems with service user and carer consultation, supporting evidence-based practice and managing clinical information. It is also common to see poor internal communications between senior levels of the trust and clinical teams, and also disconnection between various parts of trust. Most importantly, clinical audit, an effective method of introducing change, has been neglected in many trusts, possibly because of the new focus on clinical governance and the Healthcare Commission reviews. It will be interesting to see how clinical governance develops without plans for the Healthcare Commission to conduct another round of clinical governance reviews in the future.

Models of national support

This section outlines what national and external support is available for clinical governance. Chapters 18 and 21 focus more on change from within the service.

Box 7.4 lists a range of support models. There is a good range available, but not a great deal is known about the effectiveness of each. Services are more likely to develop if staff have a sense of ownership of objectives and standards, and if there is good peer support and active involvement in the process itself. Using multiple methods may be more costly but should increase the chance of improvements being made. Combinations of interventions have been shown to be more effective than any one intervention (Grol, 1992).

Box 7.4 Models of national support for clinical governance

- Organisational audit
- Multicentre clinical audit
- External assessment (peer-review, diagnostic review, inspection, accreditation, models from other sectors, such as the European Foundation for Quality Management (EFQM) and the International Organisation for Standardisation's ISO 9000)
- Quality networks
- Consultancy
- Information dissemination
- Education and training
- Policy, guidelines and standards.

Several guides and reviews help explain and evaluate those theories and methods of change management and quality improvement that have implications for managers' implementation of clinical governance (e.g. Audit Commission, 2001; Cameron *et al*, 2001; Iles & Sutherland, 2001; Walshe & Freeman, 2002). They conclude that sustained change is very hard to achieve and that interventions are consistently variable in their effectiveness. The success of interventions appears to be often undermined by contextual factors.

All is not doom and gloom, however, and there are some positive implications. Good project management may compensate for problems caused by contextual factors and so may be critical to the success of a quality-improvement intervention. The recruitment and selection of managers, and their training and support could therefore be a priority for health services in the future. In particular, project management training, such as PRINCE 2 (Central Computer and Telecommunications Agency, 2000), could develop as part of services' training programmes.

Organisational audit

Standards-based service reviews or 'organisational audits' use organisational or service standards to evaluate and further develop services. After standards are agreed, data are collected and the findings are used to identify areas that need further attention. After the necessary action has been taken, the process is repeated to assess whether improvement has been made.

These audits differ from conventional audits in that they are based on comprehensive service standards. The standards used in clinical audit typically focus on a particular area such as prescribing or record-keeping. They also differ from other external assessment methods in that the data collection is just one part of an ongoing learning process. Audit and feedback have been shown to lead to improvements in practice (Jamtvedt *et al*, 2004).

Multicentre clinical audit

Multicentre clinical audit networks can be a very effective way to bring about change in a particular area. These can be national interventions following findings of national research or publication of clinical guidelines. The principles of clinical audit apply, but with the added benefit of sharing innovative ideas and lessons learned at network meetings (see Quality networks, below). Chapter 15 describes the components of clinical audit and gives a diagram of the audit cycle.

External assessment

External assessment is an important way to identify service development needs and hence can facilitate the targeting of resources. Assessment

---

Box 7.5 Characteristics of effective external assessment programmes (Shaw, 2001)

- Give a clear framework of values
- Publish validated standards
- Are patient-focused
- Include processes and results
- Encourage self-assessment
- Have trained assessors
- Measure systematically
- Provide incentives
- Communicate with other programmes
- Quantify improvement over time
- Give public access to standards, methods and results.

---

must, however, be followed by effective intervention to achieve improvements in service delivery. External assessment is now common in the UK. There are about 35 peer-review and accreditation programmes and this number is increasing (Shaw, 2001). There is some concern that unless standards and methods are coordinated there will be duplication of effort, inconsistency and confusion (Shaw, 2001).

The characteristics of effective external assessment programmes are described in Box 7.5 (Shaw, 2001), which may be used as a checklist by any service that is considering taking part in such a programme.

Peer-review

External peer-review typically involves a visiting team of 'peers' from a similar service conducting a standards-based assessment. These are sometimes organised as exchange visits and excellent open and learning relationships between departments or organisations can develop. This should not be confused with the type of peer-review that is used in staff appraisal (see Chapter 13). The combination of feedback and peer-review has been found to be effective (Grimshaw & Russell, 1993; Wensing & Grol, 1994); for example, site visits, peer-review and feedback have proved effective in changing general practice routines (Grol, 1992).

Diagnostic review

Several support organisations and consultancies now offer standards-based diagnostic review, at various levels of the service, using multi-disciplinary or stakeholder teams and interview-based site visits. Review teams will often include a recognised expert, who may advise the team and help write the report. These diagnostic reviews may lead on to a specific piece of service development work.

Inspection

There are several statutory bodies that inspect mental health and learning disability services. There are, for example, fire and environmental health inspections as well as visits from the Mental Health Act Commission and Ofsted in some child and adolescent services. These are generally to ensure that patients' rights and safety are protected. The Healthcare Commission will combine the roles of the CHI, the Audit Commission in its NHS-related work, the Mental Health Act Commission, the independent health sector inspectorate, and the National Care Standards Commission (see Chapter 5). Regulatory scrutiny is an increasingly important focus of new policy initiatives. The Audit Commission (2001) has found that the benefits of external inspection will be limited unless local leaders 'own' the messages and build support for change in consultation with local staff throughout the process.

Accreditation

The accreditation of health services originated in the USA. It uses standards-based external assessment. Services that meet standards are accredited and may have to be re-accredited after a period of time. This may be voluntary or mandatory. The UK Accreditation Forum (UKAF) represents organisations involved in standards-based review and accreditation.

Models from other sectors (EFQM and ISO 9000)

The European Foundation for Quality Management (EFQM) originally used the Baldridge criteria developed in US industry as the basis for its 'business excellence model' (European Foundation for Quality Management, 2000). In the new excellence model this has developed from a process-orientated framework to one now more focused on outcomes for the patient, staff and society. It uses self-assessment and European standards. The assessment of an organisation's impact on society is a particularly interesting component of this model.

The International Organisation for Standardisation has its origins within European manufacturing industry. External assessors use the ISO 9000 series of standards (see www.iso.ch/iso/en/iso9000-14000/iso9000/iso9000index.html) for quality systems in service industries to certify organisations. These assessors are themselves accredited by the national standardisation body. There have been some concerns about how well the standards transfer into health services, and new ISO standards are being developed specifically for this sector.

Quality networks

Services can benefit from sharing information as part of a quality network. This may mean, for example, local or national groups holding regular meetings, participating in an e-mail discussion group and arranging symposia and training events. Multicentre audit may also be organised this way (see above). Members can ask for support from the network and informal meetings may provide solutions to a range of problems. These networks are a means of sharing both innovative practice and experiences of development work. A similar collaborative process has improved the quality of care in 37 mental health services in northern England (Kennedy & Griffiths, 2003).

External peer-review (see above) can be easily developed from this, as the network is likely to provide a good pool of reviewers. Services with common needs can develop as 'learning sets'. The network representatives can act as a collective voice for members, for example when lobbying for resources. With support from enough members a 'critical mass' can be achieved and service development gets more exciting and change happens faster. There is also some reassurance in knowing that you are not battling alone and 'reinventing the wheel'.

Quality networks are also well placed to maintain a register of evaluated service development projects, for example following critical incident reviews, audits or complaints. These can be an important resource to help action planning and strategy development.

Consultancy

Consultancies may be asked to provide diagnostic reviews (the doctor–patient model) (see above) or to provide expert help with a previously identified problem (the expertise model). They may have a register of experts 'on tap' who can help provide solutions. These experts may have, for example, generic skills in change management or specific skills in and experience of specialty areas of the service, such as in risk management in forensic mental health services. Schein (1999) describes two potential problems with these approaches:

- The doctor–patient model can create a dependent client. Information is not always available to a consultant to make a good diagnosis, in which case a joint diagnosis would be more accurate. Also, without joint diagnosis and joint action planning there is less ownership of the problem or solution. Staff will be less likely to be committed to the changes needed.
- The expertise model can also create a dependent client. There may be, in addition, problems with the accuracy of the client's self-diagnosis and in the client communicating this clearly in the consultant's brief.

Schein promotes a 'process consultation model' in which consultants help clients to identify their own problems and solutions and are careful not to seek to solve problems themselves.

Consultancy may be provided internally or externally. Internal consultancy is potentially more cost-effective and ensures continuity and therefore commitment to the longer-term success of projects (Berenbaum, 1997). The work is more likely to be accepted by local staff and the consultants are likely to have a better understanding of the whole system (Holdaway & Saunders, 1996). Internal consultants, however, may be less objective and may therefore have less credibility with senior managers. Also, they may not have the exact skills or expertise required for a specific piece of work, which should therefore be sourced externally. Generally speaking, external involvement helps most when it results in organisations building their own internal capacity and when organisations have a clear sense of direction (Audit Commission, 2001).

Information dissemination

Information about clinical governance is more effectively disseminated using several different methods. These may include publications, conferences and symposia, and the use of e-mail discussion groups and enquiry services.

Most support organisations use a variety of these methods. This is often, however, a one-way flow of information and there may be problems in engaging staff without some kind of dialogue. We do know, for example, that simply distributing guidelines rarely changes clinical behaviour (Freemantle *et al*, 2001). It is also difficult to evaluate the effectiveness of this approach. In its broadest definition 'information dissemination' covers many other models of intervention or support listed here.

Education and training

New training and education curricula are essential to support clinical governance – specifically within continuing professional development (CPD), revalidation and appraisal processes, as well as the National Service Frameworks and the new Mental Health Act. Unfortunately, the NHS has a poor reputation for maintaining or developing the skills of its staff. Budget and time restrictions may not, for example, permit staff to attend any training other than the minimum requirements for safe practice and revalidation. The effects of education are variable but seem to increase when the influence of peers or respected colleagues is included (Grol, 1992; Grimshaw & Russell, 1993; Wensing & Grol, 1994).

Training in project management may be a new priority to support managers' service development work (see above). Education and training for clinical governance, however, need to be targeted at clinical teams as well as senior managers. There are also issues with intensity of training; for example, some topics may need to be regularly revisited to sustain change.

Chapter 14 covers this topic in more detail.

Leadership development

It seems clear with the establishment of the new Leadership Centre (see above) that leaders are expected to play a key role in taking clinical governance forward within trusts. It is widely recognised that, to be successful, they will need to effect a major cultural change.

There are lessons to be learned from the implementation of clinical audit. It is not enough to place mandatory requirements on all clinicians to be involved: a change in culture needs to occur before quality initiatives can be implemented. Unfortunately, it is notoriously difficult to achieve directly a change in culture. It may, indeed, be more realistic to expect cultural change to occur as a result of clinical governance rather than to see it as a precondition for clinical governance.

Trusts have been preparing for clinical governance for several years. Leaders must not only communicate the aims and objectives of clinical governance but now must also help support staff more directly. Managers and practitioners must understand how the effort they invest in clinical governance will improve patient outcomes. They also need practical support. This has several implications for quality leaders:

- Leaders now have to support staff achievement of the strategy objectives more directly.
- In order to change culture and motivate staff, leaders should explain the link between clinical governance and patient outcomes.
- Leaders should use good measures of both clinical governance progress and patient outcomes. This will allow them to feed back any benefits attributable to this extra work.
- Time will need to be set aside both to justify all aspects of the quality strategy to staff and to provide progress reports.

Leadership is also discussed in Chapters 4, 19 and 21.

Policy, guidelines and standards

These provide information to staff and service users and carers about what can be expected of the service, in terms of aims, objectives and current practice. In Chapter 11, Figs 11.1 and 11.2 show how policy, guidelines, procedures and protocols enable clinical governance. The process of development may be local or national and can itself help understanding of the practical problems.

Key points

- There is a range of national and external support available.
- Services are more likely to develop if staff have a sense of ownership of objectives and standards, and if there are good peer support and active involvement in the process itself.
- Good project management may help compensate for those contextual factors that often undermine the success of quality-improvement work.
- Combinations of methods have been shown to be effective, but this approach is likely to be more costly.
- Quality networks and audit networks provide a good way to share information about best practice.

The Clinical Governance Support Service

The CGSS is managed by the Royal College of Psychiatrists' Research Unit. So far it has worked with over half the trusts that provide mental health services in the UK. It produces a range of publications, provides an information service and organises themed events. An important part of this work now includes a national network of clinical governance reviews. These are annual reviews against clinical governance standards. After standards are agreed, data are collected using self-review and external peer review. The results are fed back in local and aggregated reports and action is taken to address any needs identified. The annual cycle is outlined in Fig. 7.1. It is an ongoing process rather than one of two or three iterations.

The CGSS approach promotes several important factors for service development, including active staff involvement, peer support, and ownership of objectives and standards.

Standards

The standards used are statements of best practice relating to clinical governance. These have been agreed by participating trusts and are revised each year by trust members. At present they are aimed at trust managers and are more focused on processes than outcomes. Two sets of standards are listed in Appendices 1 and 2. The range of topics covered by the standards on clinical governance structures and strategies is described in Box 7.6.

The development of the standards involved three main processes: a review of key documents; consultation with CGSS members; and editing. We used the information from members to supplement the standards derived from the literature review. This ensured that the

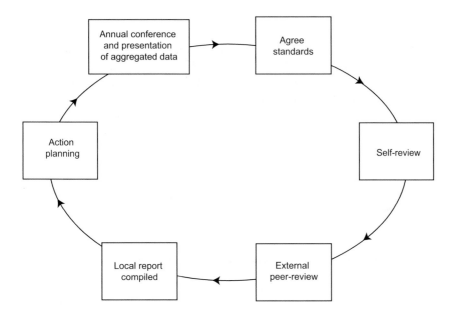

Figure 7.1 The annual review cycle.

standards were up-to-date and that they took account of the views of relevant staff.

A prioritised list of desirable characteristics of review criteria has been produced by a panel of recognised international experts (Hearnshaw *et al*, 2001). The panel recommend that criteria are based on a review of the available research evidence, combined with expert opinion if necessary, and prioritised according to health outcomes and the strength of the evidence. It would, however, be difficult to apply these criteria to clinical governance standards until the effectiveness of

---

Box 7.6 Range of topics covered by the CGSS standards on clinical governance structures and strategies

- The clinical governance committee and strategy
- Service user and carer involvement and experience
- Clinical audit
- Clinical risk management
- Evidence-based practice
- Staffing and staff management
- Education, training and CPD
- Information management.

clinical governance is better understood, particularly in relation to health outcomes.

Standards stimulate a lot of discussion when they are being developed and when they are used in the field. Sometimes they can even create anxiety. They may at first seem very detailed, overwhelming and imposed. Seeing best practice statements relating to all aspects of your work can be quite daunting.

Data collection

Data are collected in a self-review, followed 8 weeks later by an external peer-review by visiting network members. Self-review is an effective way to measure certain parts of a service. It also creates a sense of ownership on the part of the staff team and is an economical way of preparing for an external peer-review. An external peer-review, as well as giving a more objective evaluation, provides a good opportunity for trust managers to meet one another and discuss service standards and identified service deficits in a way that might not be possible in a visit by an inspectorate.

Teams of three people spend one full day in the trust collecting evidence from various sources, including interviews with staff from a range of professions. This provides an important learning experience for the visiting team, as well as the trust being visited.

Feedback on performance and benchmarking

The CGSS prepares local reports and aggregated reports. These give detailed individual feedback about performance:

- against the standards
- in comparison with other members of the network or a specific subgroup (benchmarking)
- in relation to the trust's performance in previous reviews.

They provide an opportunity for trusts to demonstrate their implementation of clinical governance and are a useful reference for trusts' own clinical governance reports. Participating trusts are expected to share their results with key groups locally, including health and local authorities, those making referrals to their trusts and local user and carer groups.

Action planning workshops are held each year and help trusts to develop and implement plans based on the findings in the reports. Given the lack of evidence for the effectiveness of quality improvement interventions, it is particularly important that members meet to discuss the potential of various approaches and share their experiences of service development work.

The impact of the CGSS's work is gauged by monitoring changes in the trusts, as reflected in performance against standards and the benchmarking data.

Benefits

Organisational audit, such as that available through the CGSS, uses standards, self-review and external peer-review in a combination that offers many benefits over a conventional information dissemination approach. Most importantly, the process engages staff in the quality improvement process. Staff become familiar with all aspects of clinical governance through working with the standards, and get to grips with what it means on the ground when collecting evidence of progress. Standards make clinical governance more transparent and explicit. They also allow incremental progress, in that a small number of achievable targets can be set. This is particularly important for services that are under stress. The annual revision of standards ensures they are owned, up to date and relevant.

Learning occurs through discussion and observation in both self-review and external peer-review. The reviews help staff critically examine the service they provide and systematically identify areas of need. This in turn allows training and support to be effectively targeted. The process also exploits people's natural curiosity and competitiveness. Staff like to know about other trusts' ways of working and are keen to do their best within the network.

Although annual improvements would not be expected in all areas, members know that each area will be revisited each year and hence momentum is sustained.

Of course, it is not just clinical governance that can benefit through this system of review. Other standards may be incorporated to monitor progress, for example on the National Service Framework, aspects of the NHS Plan or NICE guidelines.

The College Research Unit has established similar networks for inpatient child and adolescent mental health services (QNIC), therapeutic communities (the Community of Communities) and electroconvulsive therapy clinics (ECTAS). Standards are available at www.rcpsych.ac.uk/cru

Other support organisations

Table 7.1 lists organisations that provide general support for clinical governance and service development. It does not include organisations that support specific components, such as information on clinical effectiveness.

Table 7.1 Organisations that support clinical governance

Organisation	Services	Telephone number	Website
British Association of Medical Managers (BAMM)	Improves and supports the contribution of doctors to management. Provides information on clinical governance, appraisal, events, publications, and the BAMM leadership programme	0161 474 1141	www.bamm.co.uk
Clinical Accountability, Service Planning and Evaluation (CASPE)	Provides a standards-based hospital accreditation programme to review services and assess development needs	020 7307 2879	www.caspe.co.uk
Clinical Governance Resource and Development Unit	Information on courses, projects in progress, audit protocols, publications. Publishes the *Journal of Clinical Governance*	0116 258 4873	www.le.ac.uk/cgrdu
Clinical Governance Support Service (CGSS)	Produces standards, other publications, provides an information service and organises themed events. In addition, it now manages a national network of clinical governance reviews	020 7977 6690	www.rcpsych.ac.uk/cru
Healthcare Commission	Provides clinical governance reviews, (www.healthcarecommission.org.uk) national studies, investigations, clinical governance reports and news releases	020 7448 9200	www.healthcarecommission.org.uk

Organisation	Description	Telephone	Website
European Foundation for Quality Management (EFQM)	Promotion of the use of the EFQM excellence model and excellence concepts in the health sector. Much activity is particularly supported through the health sector community of practice. A package of materials is available	+32 2 775 35 11	www.efqm.org
Health and Social Care Advisory Service (HASCAS)	Provides standards-based reviews and development work, including clinical governance 'health checks', strategy development and action planning; and support and advice relating to investigations of serious incidents and homicides	020 7307 2892	www.healthadvisoryservice.org
Healthcare Quality Quest Ltd	Provides practical help on how to improve the quality of healthcare. Helps to develop clinical effectiveness strategies for clinical teams. Facilitates teamwork across traditional boundaries and provides competency-based education for clinicians and leadership development	023 808 4024	www.hqq.co.uk
Investors in People UK (IiP UK)	Helps services achieve the Investors in People standard. This describes good practice for staff training and development. Organisations are assessed against 12 key standards as part of a cyclical process.	020 7467 1900	www.iipuk.co.uk

Table continues

Table 7.1 *Continued*

Organisation	Services	Telephone number	Website
King's Fund	An independent healthcare charity which gives grants and carries out research. It produces publications and arranges conferences and educational programmes	020 7307 2400	www.kingsfund.org.uk
NHS Clinical Governance Support Team	Part of the NHS Modernisation Agency. It offers development programmes and information about clinical governance	0116 295 2000	www.cgsupport.org/
NHS Quality Improvement Scotland (NHS QIS)	Sets standards, monitors performance and provides advice to NHS Scotland on effective clinical practice and service improvements	0131 623 4300	www.nhshealthquality.org
Health Quality Service	Offers accreditation and develops standards and helps healthcare organisations implement the changes needed to meet them	020 7389 1000	www.hqs.org.uk
Modernisation Agency	Hosts many different initiatives and project teams. It provides expert support to help improve NHS services and implement health policy	0845 600 0700	www.modernnhs.nhs.uk/
National Co-ordinating Centre for	Manages a national research programme	020 7612 7980	www.sdo.lshtm.ac.uk

NHS Service Delivery and Organisation Research and Development (NCCSDO)	to consolidate and develop the evidence base on the organisation, management and delivery of healthcare services		
NHS Confederation	Membership body for all NHS organisations. Produces publications and organises regional and national events to support the improvement of health policy and practice	020 7959 7272	www.nhsconfed.org
Sainsbury Centre for Mental Health	Supports mental health services by influencing national policy and practice through a coordinated programme of research, service development and training	020 7403 8790	www.scmh.org.uk

Statutory organisations

Modernisation Agency

The Agency aims to disseminate information about best practice, provide diagnostics and deliver a range of improvement programmes. How this will affect clinical governance within trusts that provide mental health and learning disability services is, however, not yet clear.

The Agency will also commission research and gain knowledge on the effectiveness of a range of organisational interventions (the National Co-ordinating Centre for NHS Service Delivery and Organisation Research and Development (NCCSDO) will also play a role in this).

The Modernisation Agency will encompass some existing support agencies, e.g. the NHS Clinical Governance Support Team (NCGST). The NCGST development programme uses the RAID (review, agree, implement, demonstrate) model of change to support implementation of clinical governance. This 9-month programme is open to NHS services in England. Five interactive learning days, 8 weeks apart, offer practical help to deliver a 'programme of change'. The Agency is also home to the National Institute for Mental Health in England (NIMHE). This works through eight regional centres to improve mental health and is now part of the Care Services Improvement Partnership (CSIP).

The Leadership Centre

Leadership development is considered a highly effective way of modernising services. The Centre will be part of the new Modernisation Agency and will develop both clinical and non-clinical leaders. Social care leadership will be included and support will be provided for the new

---

Box 7.7 National priorities for clinical governance support

- The focus needs to be more on improving performance rather than simply measuring it
- Dedicated resources for service development need to be identified
- External assessment needs to be nationally coordinated, to prevent duplication of effort and inconsistency
- Standards need to be further promoted, to make clinical governance more explicit and for use in assessment
- Evaluation of the quality improvement interventions and the idenfitication of the determinants of their effectiveness are research priorities
- Clinical teams need to be actively engaged in clinical governance and in critically examining the service they provide. External peer-review is a good way to do this
- Patient outcomes need to be related to clinical governance. The Leadership Centre could promote this in its training curricula
- Clinical governance will need to be developed and integrated within new mental health and social care trusts and within primary care trusts.

---

patient-based groups. The Centre will set the skills and knowledge requirements at all levels, and will assure the quality of providers' programmes. It will commission new work where necessary and will deliver programmes at every level and across the NHS.

Priorities for support

Many services now have the structures and accountabilities in place to take clinical governance forward. Managers and practitioners need support to achieve this (Box 7.7).

Measuring versus improving performance

In NHS trusts today, more attention is being paid to measuring performance than to improving performance. This is the wrong way around. Good measurement is an important starting point but it does not magically reveal easy-fix underlying problems. Even the best report may simply describe what staff already know.

Unless there is sufficient support for improvement, there is a danger that the Healthcare Commission may merely serve to highlight a failure to meet targets. Many targets have been already described as ambitious. Although a range of support does now exist, it is limited and it is not clear to what extent it is being accessed by the services most in need.

We must also understand the differences between measurement for improvement and measurement for judgement or inspection. Measuring for judgement encourages services to bury evidence of errors instead of learning from them and sharing their experience (Berwick, 1998). Services need to deliver sustained improvement in patient care. To do this, staff must not only measure for improvement but must also have access to and use a range of effective organisational interventions.

The effectiveness of quality improvement interventions is a research priority. Increasing amounts of time and money are being spent on supporting clinical governance and service development work. Unless we are more confident of the effectiveness of different interventions and, in particular, know more about the determinants of their effectiveness, we cannot be sure that these resources are being used to maximum effect. The Modernisation Agency and the NCCSDO promise support and will commission research in this area.

A coordinated approach to assessment

External assessment, organisational audit and quality networks are becoming more common. The Academy of Medical Royal Colleges could help NICE and the Healthcare Commission coordinate standards and methods and promote a consistent approach to minimise any duplication of effort, inconsistency and confusion. Quality Improvement Scotland has already established a coordinated standards-based external peer-review programme. It will be very interesting to see how this develops.

Integrated clinical governance

The NHS Plan describes the development of mental health and social care trusts, which will provide integrated care to local communities. In Scotland and Northern Ireland and the Republic of Ireland services are already provided this way. Mental health services will join primary care trusts in some cases. In England and Wales clinical governance needs to develop to incorporate social care. This should not be an impossible task, given the fairly generic quality principles at the core of clinical governance.

The locality will have to establish an expanded clinical governance committee to coordinate a multi-agency quality strategy. More attention will also have to be paid to cross-boundary audit, training and policy development. Chapter 16 discusses these issues in more detail.

Conclusions

Quality is now at the top of the NHS agenda. Some services have made good progress, but there is still a long way to go before clinical governance can be shown to have made sustained improvements to patient outcomes.

New clinical governance support should focus on service development, rather than service evaluation, and on clinical teams, rather than trust managers. The Modernisation Agency has a key role to play in this and also in leading new research.

Leaders can help motivate clinical teams by explaining the links between clinical governance work and improved patient outcomes. Good measures of clinical governance progress and patient outcomes are needed to do this and service development work must be sufficiently resourced to avoid the demotivating consequences of extra workload.

Until we know more about the effectiveness of organisational interventions, the sharing of innovative practice and experience of successful service development is particularly important. Quality networks, based on audit methods or otherwise, are a good way to do this.

Acknowledgements

Thanks to Geoff Shepherd, Barbara Grey, Stephanie Daley and Ceri Diffley for helpful comments.

References

Audit Commission (2001) *Change Here! Managing Change to Improve Local Services.* London: Audit Commission.

Berenbaum, R. (1997) Internal consultancy. In *Developing Organisational Consultancy* (eds J. E. Neuman, K. Kellner & A. Dawson-Shepherd), pp. 71–90. London: Routledge.

Berwick, D. (1998) The NHS: feeling well and thriving at 75. *BMJ*, **317**, 57–61.

Cameron, M., Cranfield, S., Iles, V., *et al* (2001) *Making Informed Decisions on Change: Key Points for Healthcare Managers and Professionals*. London: NCCSDO.

Central Computer and Telecommunications Agency (2000) *Managing Successful Projects with PRINCE 2*. London: TSO.

Commission for Health Improvement (2003) *Emerging Themes from Mental Health Trust Reviews*. London: CHI.

Cowpe, J. & Scrivens, E. (2001) *The Impact of Clinical Governance on Medical and Clinical Directors. Report for the Research and Development Directorate of the NHS Executive, West Midlands*. Keele: Keele University.

Department of Health (1997) *The New NHS: Modern, Dependable*. London: Department of Health.

Department of Health (1998) *A First Class Service: Quality in the New NHS*. London: Department of Health.

Department of Health (2000) *The NHS Plan: A Plan for Investment, a Plan for Reform*, cm 4818-I. London: TSO.

European Foundation for Quality Management (2000) *EFQM Excellence Model – Public and Voluntary Sector Version*. Brussels: EFQM.

Freemantle, N., Harvey, E. L., Wolf, F., *et al* (2001) Printed educational materials: effects on professional practice and healthcare outcomes (Cochrane Review). In *The Cochrane Library 1*. Oxford: Update Software.

Grimshaw, J. & Russell, I. (1993) Effect of clinical guidelines on medical practice: a systematic review of rigorous evaluations. *Lancet*, **342**, 1317–1322.

Grol, R. (1992) Implementing guidelines in general practice care. *Quality in Healthcare*, **1**, 184–191.

Hearnshaw, H. M., Harker, R. M., Cheater, F. M., *et al* (2001) Expert consensus on the desirable characteristics of review criteria for improvement of healthcare quality. *Quality in Healthcare*, **10**, 173–178.

Holdaway, K. & Saunders, M. (1996) *The In-house Trainer as Consultant*. London: Kogan Page.

Iles, V. & Sutherland, K. (2001) *Organisational Change: A Review for Healthcare Managers, Professionals and Researchers*. London: NCCSDO.

Jamtvedt, G., Young, J. M., Kristoffersen, D. T., *et al* (2004) Audit and feedback: effects on professional practice and health care outcomes. In *Cochrane Library*, issue 1. Chichester: John Wiley & Sons.

Kennedy, P. & Griffiths, H. (2003) Mental health 'collaborative' challenges care culture. *Psychiatric Bulletin*, **27**, 164–166.

Latham, L., Freeman, T., Walshe, K., *et al* (1999) *The Early Development of Clinical Governance: A Survey of NHS Trusts in the West Midlands*. Birmingham: Health Services Management Centre, Birmingham University.

National Audit Office (2003) *Achieving Improvements Through Clinical Governance. A Progress Report on Implementation by NHS Trusts*. London: National Audit Office.

Palmer, C. (2000) *Are Boards on Board? Report for the Clinical Governance Support Service*. London: CGSS.

Schein, E. H. (1999) *Process Consultation Revisited: Building the Helping Relationship*. New York: Addison-Wesley.

Shaw, C. (2001) External assessment of healthcare. *BMJ*, **322**, 851–854.

Walshe, K. & Freeman, T. (2002) Effectiveness of quality improvement: learning from evaluations. *Quality and Safety in Healthcare*, **11**, 85–87.

Wensing, M. & Grol, R. (1994) Single and combined strategies for implementing changes in primary care: a literature review. *International Journal of Quality in Healthcare*, **6**, 115–132.

CHAPTER 8

Clinical governance and the National Service Framework for Mental Health

Melba Wilson

- Background to development of the National Service Frameworks
- Links and impact of clinical governance
- Key areas for successful implementation: (a) leadership, ownership and accountability within NHS organisations; (b) involvement of users and carers; (c) monitoring and evaluation
- Pointers to implementation
- Involvement of Black and minority ethnic communities

Development of the National Service Frameworks

The National Service Frameworks are part of the government's modernisation agenda for the National Health Service (NHS) and their aims – to drive up quality and cut wide variations in health services – were set out in the White Paper *The New NHS: Modern, Dependable* (Department of Health, 1997). The NHS Confederation (1997) characterised the White Paper as setting the tone for a 10-year vision based firmly on co-operation, not competition.

There is little doubt that it was a marked departure from the previous government's focus on free market competition – exemplified by the internal market and general practitioner fundholding of the 1990s; and under which regime NHS trusts actively competed with each other. The new NHS – of which the National Service Frameworks are a major and integral part – heralded a 'third way' based on partnership and driven by performance. Six key principles underlined the changes:

- renewing the NHS as a genuinely national service, with consistently high quality across the country
- making the delivery of healthcare against national standards a matter of local responsibility
- getting the NHS to work in partnership by breaking down organisational barriers and forging stronger links with local authorities

- driving efficiency through a more rigorous approach to perform-ance by cutting bureaucracy
- shifting the focus on to quality, so that excellence is guaranteed to all patients
- rebuilding public confidence in the NHS as a public service.

Criteria

All the National Service Frameworks are aimed at reducing unacceptable variations in health and social care. In order for a clinical area to become the focus of a National Service Framework, certain criteria have to be met:

- it has to have demonstrable relevance to the government's agenda for health improvement and tackling health inequalities
- it has to be an important health issue in terms of mortality, morbidity, disability or use of resources
- it has to be an area of public concern
- there must be evidence of a shortfall between actual and acceptable practice
- it has to be an area where local services need to be reorganised to ensure service improvements
- it must be a problem which requires new, innovative approaches.

The National Service Frameworks for Mental Health, Older People and Children

The National Service Framework for Mental Health (NSF-MH) was the first (Department of Health, 1999), and this is described in more detail below. It was followed by the publication of the National Service Framework for Older People (Department of Health, 2001). Both are concerned with setting targets for improvements in service delivery. That for older people focuses on:

- rooting out age discrimination
- providing person-centred care
- promoting older people's health and independence
- fitting services around people's needs.

Its implementation is generally the joint responsibility of health and social care providers. For example, with regard to older people with mental health problems, standard 7 calls for 'older people who have mental problems [to] have access to integrated mental health services, provided by the NHS and councils to ensure effective diagnosis, treatment and support, for them and their carers' (p. 19).

Implementation is monitored by multi-agency local implementation teams. In April 2004, the National Service Framework for Older People came into force. Among other things, it emphasises the importance of taking account of the needs of older people from Black and minority ethnic communities, and the need for 'culturally biased' assessments of needs (p. 19).

The National Service Framework for Children continues to progress. The first part of it (*Getting the Right Start*; Department of Health, 2003) focuses on services for children and young people (up to 19 years of age) in hospitals. This hospital services standard has three parts:

- child-centred services
- quality and safety of care
- quality and setting of environment.

Getting the Right Start emphasises that 'strong links need to be drawn with the NSFs for Mental Health [and others]' (p. 7). The safety part of the standard discusses children's mental health. It notes that 'attention to the mental health of the child, young person and their family should be an integral part of any children's service, and not an afterthought'. The standard goes on to note that:

'It is ... essential for a hospital with a children's service to ensure that staff have an understanding of how to assess and address the emotional wellbeing of children, and are able to identify significant mental health problems.' (p. 26)

It calls for 'robust arrangements' to secure child and adolescent mental health services, including psychiatry, psychology, individual and family psychotherapy, social work and specialist nursing.

The standard calls for all hospitals that assess and treat children and young people to have policies and arrangements in place that can deal with:

- management of overdoses and deliberate self-harm
- acute psychiatric crisis
- direct clinical work
- complex cases
- child protection cases
- long-term and life-threatening diseases
- the death of a child.

The development of the NSF-MH

The rolling programme of National Service Frameworks utilises expert reference groups as the vehicle for development. The expert reference group for the NSF-MH included health professionals, users, carers, managers, partner agencies and other advocates, in order that a range of views would be represented in the formulation of the Framework.

Graham Thornicroft, who chaired the group, has described the NSF-MH as follows:

'a strategic blueprint for services for adults of working age for the next ten years. It is both *mandatory*, in being a clear statement of what services must seek to achieve in relation to the given standards and performance indicators, and *permissive*, in that it allows considerable local flexibility to customise the services which need to be provided to fit the framework.' (Thornicroft, 2000)

The significance of the method and manner of development of the NSF-MH is that it underscored the government's firm intention that service delivery had to be informed *not only* by service providers but also, importantly, by those for whom services are intended. This includes their involvement in planning and monitoring the delivery of services at a sustainable level and on an equal basis. This has been welcomed by Mind and other organisations concerned that the diverse voices of users of mental health services should, *as a matter of right*, be given status equal to that of mental health professionals. Chapter 9 looks at the involvement of service users and their relatives in more detail.

The NSF-MH also recognises issues such as race and gender, and calls for specific arrangements to be in place to ensure:

- service user and carer involvement
- advocacy arrangements
- integration of care management and the care programme approach (CPA)
- effective partnerships with a range of partners.

The NSF-MH is intended to promote and provide seamless healthcare. As such, the aims of the NSF-MH are not stand-alone concepts, but depend, for their workability, on related initiatives and an emerging framework of agencies, structures and processes. These include the National Institute for Clinical Excellence (NICE) (for appraisal and review of treatments and guidance on their use); the clinical governance framework (for accountability for quality of service delivery), which is itself underpinned by professional self-regulation and lifelong learning; and the Commission for Healthcare Audit and Inspection (known as the Healthcare Commission) (for monitoring and inspection). Further monitoring is carried out through the National Performance Assessment Framework and the National Survey of Patients.

Scope

The NSF-MH focuses on the mental health needs of working-age adults (i.e those up to 65 years of age). It has been developed on the premise that one in four adults suffers at any one time from a mental health problem. It covers health promotion, assessment and diagnosis,

Table 8.1 The seven standards of the NSF-MH and lead organisations

Standard	Area covered	Lead organisation
1	Mental health promotion	Health authority
2 & 3	Primary care and access to services	Primary care trust
4 & 5	Effective services for people with severe mental illness	NHS trust
6	Carers for people with mental health problems	Local authority
7	Preventing suicide	Health authority

access, treatment, rehabilitation and care. It encompasses primary and specialist care agencies and their roles – individually and as partner agencies.

The standards

In all, there are seven standards that together cover five areas (see Table 8.1), each with a stipulated lead organisation. Each standards is aligned to an evidence and knowledge base and is supported by service models and examples of good practice.

Strengthening the evidence base

One of the greatest challenges for the NSF-MH concerns whether it can enable the user perspective to achieve equal weight and validity to that of the service provider. In a discussion on the evidence base for mental health services, Thornicroft & Tansella (1999) note the importance of acknowledging the wider evidence base:

'it is misleading to discuss mental health needs without consideration of wider family and other social networks. Further, the specialist mental health services do not operate alone, but rather function at a whole series of interfaces with other social and healthcare agencies, all of which are under the influence of the wider social, political and cultural climate.'

Mind's view, and that of many mental health service users, is that without a fundamental shift in professional attitudes, one that acknowledges the extent to which service users can contribute to the wider evidence base to bring about informed and effective service delivery, the brave new world of the National Service Frameworks will not be realised.

Partnerships

Those with lead responsibility for implementation of the NSF-MH are expected to work in partnership with other service providers and commissioners to ensure that needs are met appropriately. It can thus be characterised as approaching mental health service delivery from a *corporate* or *holistic* perspective, one which looks at the spectrum of care and need, and attempts to meet that need across a range of sectors. From the perspective of the voluntary sector, this is welcome.

The development of *integrated services* through proactive partnership working is a key strand of the NSF-MH. Integrated care requires partnerships: between those who use services and those who provide services; between clinicians, practitioners and professional groups; across different parts of the NHS; and between the NHS and local government. It also demands a reaching out to the community, to individual groups and organisations, including the voluntary, in-dependent and business sectors. According to the Department of Health (1999):

'All mental health services must be planned and implemented in partnership with local communities, and involve service users and carers. Partnership will be vital if, for example, services are to meet the needs of black and minority ethnic communities and reduce present inequities.'

The NSF-MH calls for a unified commissioning process that involves partnership arrangements between health and social care providers. The ultimate aim is for a single budget to enable more comprehensive and 'joined up' healthcare. The intent is that accountability rests within the commissioning framework (i.e. all partners within the framework will be accountable).

Implementation

Effective implementation of the framework requires mental health trusts to demonstrate:

- senior leadership of and commitment to mental health services
- clinical governance, including continuing professional develop-ment and lifelong learning
- evidence of a commitment to the underpinning programmes, including education and training, recruitment and retention, information services, and research and development
- clear lines of accountability for mental health services.

Successful and sustainable implementation will depend on achieving systemic and systematic change. The executive summary of the NSF-MH states that the standards 'will be challenging for all mental health services' (Department of Health, 1999). This is not least because the Framework proposes: local milestones for each standard; time scales that require agreement with NHS Executive's regional offices and social care regions; and the monitoring of progress.

Clinical governance and the NSF-MH

The NSF-MH is an ambitious and welcome programme of action. It is worth noting, however, that much of what is contained within it reinforces what is already widely regarded as good practice in mental health. Many within the voluntary sector, including Mind, have long argued for more involvement of users and carers, greater linkage between professions and across sectors, including local authorities, and more involvement of voluntary sector service providers in the planning as well as the provision of services.

Effective and *sustainable* implementation of the NSF-MH, however, will depend on:

- an understanding of the different needs of users and carers and enabling effective input from each
- views of users and carers being actively sought and incorporated
- users of mental health services being *supported* to participate equally
- clear lines of responsibility and accountability within and between trusts, primary care and local authorities
- a focus on creating clarity in the detail of implementation (e.g. how will a common purpose be achieved between health and social care professionals in relation to the integration of the CPA and care management?)
- the provision of staff training that is relevant to diversity and need
- assessment of the resource implications for implementation and steps to back up good ideas with the necessary financial and human resources.

Clinical governance – the tie that binds

The requirement to incorporate a clinical governance framework in the implementation of the National Service Frameworks is, it can be argued, the crucial element. It can mean the difference between the NSF-MH being just another good idea and it being an effective programme of comprehensive, relevant and accountable NHS service delivery.

One survey of health authorities and trusts (Mental Health Strategies, 1999) found that while there was a unanimous welcome for the NSF-MH, only 53% of respondents felt that their current services complied with the standards it set out. While an overall majority of health authorities and trusts (76%) felt they could partially meet the demands of NSF-MH implementation through available skills and resources, only a quarter (24%) felt wholly able to meet the NSF-MH agenda for implementation. Issues raised by respondents included:

- the degree to which working partnership arrangements with other mental health organisations could be a reality
- the need for training for all staff on new ways of working and new mindsets
- the need for strategic change skills, and an acknowledgement that mental health is not always seen as a management area with these attributes.

A survey of mental health service managers in London, carried out by the Centre for Mental Health Services Development (Peck & Wigg, 2001) found that while a large majority rated the NSF-MH as the 'top national policy intervention' and largely welcomed it, there was 'concern about the prescriptivity of the NSF implementation process'.

The challenge for clinical governance is to progress implementation of the National Service Frameworks in the context of these tensions. The success of clinical governance will be judged by the extent to which it enables understanding and ownership among a diverse range of constituencies – users, carers and staff (both clinical and non-clinical). This will require:

- leadership that helps to generate cultural and organisational change
- effective integration of the voices of users and carers (which are, it must be emphasised, two distinct voices)
- a clear framework for accountability – with monitoring and evaluation of progress.

The successful implemenation of clinical governance

Williams (2000) has identified a number of key factors for the successful implementation of clinical governance. These include the need for:

- having in place a framework for it
- understanding the context in relation to organisational culture
- having appropriate leadership and communication skills
- professional development, education and training
- multidisciplinary team working
- monitoring and evaluation programmes.

In a discussion on leadership and organisational change, trusts recognised that organisational culture was of prime importance and had to be transparent to all working within an organisation. The influence of the trust board, and particularly of non-executive members, was thought to be paramount in changing attitudes, 'winning hearts and minds' and addressing leadership issues.

Implementation of clinical governance at local level: case study

The experience of the development of clinical governance at South West London and St George's Mental Health NHS Trust provides a good learning point (see the trust's annual report for 1999/2000). The trust approached clinical governance in 'shadow' form in the year before the statutory requirement for implementation. Work began in November 1998, when a clinical governance steering group was charged with setting out the parameters and making recommendations to the board about the direction and priorities that should be pursued. The board established a clinical governance committee from April 1999 (the statutory deadline). The trust began work in earnest to establish what its priorities would be in the first year and how to implement them.

The author was involved as a non-executive director and as joint chair of the committee (with the medical director). This afforded first-hand experience of the development and implementation of the clinical governance process at local level.

Staffing

The trust board embraced the concept of clinical governance, as its requirements for accountability and monitoring of the quality of service delivery were key aims of the trust.

A first staffing appointment was that of clinical governance manager. The fact that the trust was able to make an excellent appointment meant that the work of the committee and the board was made very much easier. The qualities required of the post-holder included:

- clear vision
- an ability to think conceptually and practically
- an ability to bring people along with the ideal as well as the reality, in order that they could understand their roles within clinical governance.

The trust was fortunate in being able to appoint such a person as clinical governance manager. The clinical governance team has since been strengthened by the appointment of a clinical risk manager, a CPA coordinator, a clinical audit coordinator and a part-time evidence-based practice coordinator. This is augmented with a secretarial function.

Finance

It is clear from the staffing that implementing clinical governance does come at a price. It is not possible to do the work without having in place an enabling infrastructure. The clinical governance committee sought and gained, during the early stages of its development, a budgetary commitment from the trust board to carry out its statutory duties on behalf of the trust. This enabled the recruitment of staff and expenditure on training, as well as some provision for information technology.

Priorities and aims

The multidisciplinary clinical governance steering group undertook its work within the context of the short- and medium-term priorities set by the trust for effective service delivery. Steps were also taken to involve staff, users and carers as an integral part of the process. This met with mixed results, as discussed below.

Early and key priorities were:

- to promote understanding of roles and responsibilities in clinical governance
- to identify achievable targets and development plans
- to develop workable and transparent frameworks for implementation
- to involve users and carers
- to identify practical and useful monitoring mechanisms.

Subsequently, the clinical governance committee agreed on a number of aims:

- to ensure that there were robust corporate structures to support active implementation of clinical governance at all levels of trust business
- to continue to seek and support user and carer involvement in this process
- to provide leadership in developing a culture that is user and carer centred, and that continually aims to improve services
- to evaluate existing trust structures and processes to ensure that they follow and support the principles of clinical governance
- to act as an information point for the trust and external agencies regarding its clinical governance implementation programme.

In addition, the clinical governance steering group identified four areas through which it recommended that the trust begin to undertake its responsibilities for implementation of the clinical governance framework. These were intended to reflect the NSF-MH standards:

- *Clinical and non-clinical audit.* This focused on a baseline assessment of services and measuring progress in implementing the trust's clinical improvement targets. A number of directorates also carried out audits at team or service level, supported by the audit department. This work was reported on at board and directorate levels.

- *Evidence-based practice.* The clinical governance committee took the view that implementation required a change in the way of working, access to sources of evidence and the development of skills. Work in this area concentrated on developing the capacity of staff to access, critically appraise and use evidence (including the evidence of users and carers) in the course of routine practice. A digest of trust key practice guidelines and policies, was produced as part of the work of the evidence-based practice advisory committee.
- *Performance and appraisal.* The performance and appraisal advisory committee developed a trust-wide system of appraisal. Implementation involved a series of briefings and cascade training.
- *Risk management.* Development work concentrated on clinical risk issues. Areas of common concern (e.g. controls assurance and health and safety) were addressed via quarterly meetings of the chairs of each of the trust's committees with a risk brief. The key achievement for 2000–01 was the development and implementation of core, unified CPA/risk assessment documentation across the trust and social services.

It is also important to note that agreeing these priorities was also early recognition by the board that, while clinical governance was a welcome development, it needed to be contextualised and broken down into a *manageable* framework if it was to be effective.

Baseline assessment

The baseline assessment (required as part of the implementation) enabled the trust to determine the degree of ownership and understanding of the clinical governance process. The self-assessment exercise, which was completed in January 2000, aimed to establish the extent to which teams had systems consistent with the principles of clinical governance. Consistently positive answers were explicitly *not* expected – the aim was to enable teams to make an honest appraisal of their position, so as to inform directorates what the key areas for the development of clinical governance were, and to allow the clinical governance committee to identify where supporting resources were most needed.

The assessment addressed:

- operational policies
- continuing professional development (including training, appraisal and supporting practice change)
- risk assessment and management
- service delivery (including assessment, record-keeping, care protocols and discharge arrangements)
- user and carer involvement

- access (including ethnic monitoring and meeting the needs of a diverse population)
- outcome measures (use of monitoring, audit and peer review)
- efficiency (bed usage, readmission, 'did not attend' (DNA) rates and use of agency staff).

The results showed that:

- many teams did not have an up-to-date operational policy
- staff appraisal was not taking place consistently
- access to sources of clinical evidence to support practice was patchy
- some elements of good practice in service delivery were inconsistent
- involvement of service users and their carers at the individual, team and directorate levels needed to be developed
- clinical risk assessment was not being carried out systematically
- teams had limited access to performance management information to drive change.

The assessment also revealed, however, a willingness by significant numbers of staff to engage with the clinical governance process. This led, among other things, to a proactive programme to engage with staff, users and carers. A series of seminars was held in order: to outline what clinical governance was (and was not; for example, it was not about blame but was about working together to bring about genuine service improvements); to develop the user perspective; and to demonstrate the links between clinical governance and a strong evidence base, allied to audit. These seminars met with a high degree of engagement among staff, users and carers.

The view was that a multifaceted approach could result in a greater understanding and acceptance of clinical governance as a process for improvement. One measure of the success of this has been in the business planning process. One year on, all the directorates have identified clinical governance leads and all directorate business plans contain reference to programmes of implementing the clinical govern- ance framework.

Clinical improvement targets

The trust took the view that it was important for staff, users and carers to see pragmatic improvements, particularly those recommended by inquiries into serious incidents, complaints and national strategies. The clinical improvement targets set by the trust in the first year had their basis in one or more of these. Although largely generic, not all targets applied to all directorates (for 2001–02, each directorate had set two clinical improvement targets as part of its own development plan). The targets have not only been important in their own right, but have helped to identify problems in the logistics of communication, implementation and data collection across the trust. Each directorate was asked to self-report progress against the targets on a monthly basis, via a 'traffic light' system.

The targets were:

- all users discharged from in-patient care to be seen by their keyworker within 1 week of discharge
- review of all potential fixed ligature points (e.g. curtain rails) on in-patient units
- all users to have a formal regular monitoring of side-effects of medication
- every user to have a structured risk assessment completed at referral and review (the plan resulting from the assessment should include a strategy agreed with users and carers to minimise risk of relapse)
- shared prescribing arrangements for all users receiving medication from their general practitioner to be in place at discharge, to include concordance monitoring
- all users to have a current care plan (or clear reason for delay)
- complete adherence to trust standards for discharge planning
- all users on the enhanced care programme approach to have included in their care plan written arrangements for out-of-hours care
- adherence to trust standards for record-keeping
- adherence to the trust's revised antipsychotic prescribing protocol.

In a review of its first year, the clinical governance committee made a number of recommendations – not least being the development of more useful structures for involving users and carers.

Involvement of users and carers

As noted earlier, a key feature of the NSF-MH is its emphasis on ensuring that the evidence base for improved mental health service delivery is strengthened by the input of users and carers.

The NSF-MH identifies local implementation teams as a multi-agency vehicle for the involvement of a wide range of partners. This has the potential to provide a good avenue for user and carer involvement through, for example, greater alignment with the voluntary sector. The evidence is, however, that there is a high degree of reluctance on the part of the statutory sector to view the voluntary sector as a natural partner in planning and developing services, with the result that opportunities are lost for the kind of seamless service provision envisaged by the NSF-MH. Local implementation of the NSF-MH can be made more effective by enabling agencies like, for example, the local Mind associations (of which there are more than 200) to take an active role as partners.

It is important that statutory sector providers recognise and make real attempts to bridge the gap between sectors because:

- the voluntary sector represents a real resource and can offer a ready-made infrastructure for the involvement of users and carers
- it obviates the need to 'reinvent the wheel'
- it promotes capacity-building and can lead to more effective use of resources – financial and human.

An Office for Public Management (2000) study on the involvement of patients in the implementation of clinical governance in an acute trust noted:

'Meshing the health concerns of users and the public with internal strategic work is not easy. It means finding practical and effective methods to identify and distil lay experiences, needs, concerns, values, expectations and ideas about services .... To integrate these lay voices with other partnership working arrangements and internal development work means creating a safe environment for all stakeholders to talk together and support action plans. Finding ways of supporting both patients and professionals in the process, so that the former can contribute properly and the latter can be receptive enough to respond properly, is the key to success in patient and public involvement initiatives.'

One of the early successes of the trust's engagement with clinical governance was a seminar organised to promote understanding of user involvement, entitled 'Getting Started – How to promote user and carer involvement in clinical audit, research and clinical governance'. Its importance lay in the facts that: first, it signaled the priority the trust placed on developing and incorporating user involvement; and second, it was multi-contributory in nature – it was organised as a joint effort between the clinical audit, research and clinical governance departments, as well as service users.

The seminar resulted in a number of important learning points. They included:

- the need to appoint a trust development worker to coordinate user involvement and guide directorates
- the importance of understanding the tensions between partnership and power
- the importance of finding ways to give a voice to the very ill and very frail
- the need for staff training on how to involve users and carers
- the need for training for users and carers to enable them to become involved effectively
- the need for support and supervision for users and for carers

- the importance of including and incorporating the views of users and carers from Black and minority ethnic communities.

The trust is making progress in these areas. It has: recruited of a user and carer coordinator; supported user and carer training; supported users and carers *to train* staff; and sought ways, through examining the clinical governance structure itself, to enhance input from users and carers at a strategic as well as an operational level.

Race, culture, diversity

As noted earlier, the NSF-MH specifically recognises the mental health needs of people from Black and minority ethnic communities. It states:

'Combined evidence suggests that services are not adequately meeting mental health needs, and that black and minority ethnic communities lack confidence in mental health services. All mental health services must be planned and implemented in partnership with local communities and involve service users and carers. If services are to match the needs of black and minority ethnic communities and reduce the present inequities, this principle is especially important.'

Working effectively with Black and minority ethnic communities is reinforced throughout the NSF-MH. In its submission of evidence to the expert reference group, Mind identified a number of performance indicators that focused on meeting the needs of diverse communities. The NSF-MH integrates work in relation to Black and minority ethnic communities throughout. For example, standard 1 notes that some Black and minority ethnic communities have higher diagnosed rates of mental health problems than the general population, and calls for specific programmes of service development for these communities. Standards 2–6 discuss the need for performance assessment to include the 'experience of service users and carers, including those from BME [Black and minority ethnic] communities'.

With respect to performance indicators, the NSF-MH notes that measures of experience should include: evidence of the appropriate care of African-Caribbean service users; and evidence of adequate access to ensure better assessment of mental health problems in the Asian community. In particular, it acknowledges that concerns about cultural competence need to be addressed and that this should be an early priority for the National Survey of Patients and local surveys of need.

Monitoring and evaluation

Monitoring and evaluation are the linchpins for clinical governance *and* the NSF-MH. As noted earlier, the NSF-MH is an ambitious programme for improving mental health service delivery. Its successful implementation over 10 years will require trusts, health and local authorities, and primary care trusts to have in place milestones by which to demonstrate genuine improvements. These improvements, it should be added, ought to be recognisable as such by users and carers.

Before it became the Commission for Healthcare Audit and Inspection (the Healthcare Commission), the Commission for Health Improvement (CHI) indicated the areas in which it would assess implementation of the National Service Frameworks. In summary, these relate to:

- management style – that is, two-way communication, supportive, clear leadership and 'succession planning' for roles
- high-quality implementation and communication
- information support for managers and clinicians – for example with regard to risk, evidence-based practice, audit, deployment and basic performance data
- a comprehensive approach to risk management, backed up by audit and organisational learning, including the need to incorporate 'near-miss' policies
- good working relationships across departments – clinical and non-clinical
- cleanliness and hospitality
- emphasis on innovations that recognise the importance of the patient journey
- progress on human resource issues, including supervision and appraisal, staff sickness and turnover, and integrated, effective training, tied to organisational needs
- evidence that trusts link effectiveness with consequences
- involvement of users and carers.

Conclusions

It has been said that clinical governance is 'a state of mind'. The inference was that the strategies concerned with implementation of the National Service Frameworks and the quality agenda – information gathering and dissemination; staff development; involvement of users and carers; education and training – should actually result in organisational change. The aim of that change should be to support staff to do the job that is needed, and to make a difference to the quality of life of service users.

The key points in the implementation of the NSF-MH are:

- effective leadership
- clarity of vision about what needs to be accomplished
- an ability to prioritise clear aims, objectives and outcomes
- measurable progress in involving users and carers
- educating staff and developing ownership

- involving others, including primary care trusts and voluntary agencies
- using information and information technology effectively.

A 10-year time scale in which to accomplish this may just be enough.

References

Department of Health (1997) *The New NHS: Modern, Dependable*, cm 3807. London: TSO.

Department of Health (1999) *National Service Framework for Mental Health*. London: Department of Health.

Department of Health (2001) *National Service Framework for Older People*. London: Department of Health.

Department of Health (2003) *Getting the Right Start: National Service Framework for Children*. London: Department of Health.

Mental Health Strategies (1999) *The Mental Health NSF – An Ambition Too Far?* Manchester: Mental Health Strategies.

NHS Confederation (1997) *Briefing – The White Paper, Issue No. 6*. London: NHS Confederation.

Office for Public Management (2000) *Patients as Teachers – Linking Patient Knowledge with Clinical Governance at the Princess Alexandra Hospitals NHS Trust*. London: OPM.

Peck, E. & Wigg, S. (2001) Managing mental health services in London: the annual London managers' survey 2000. *Institute News* (Institute for Applied and Social Policy), January/February, p. 1.

Thornicroft, G. (2000) National Service Framework for Mental Health. *Psychiatric Bulletin*, **24**, 203–206.

Thornicroft, G. & Tansella, M. (1999) The evidence base for mental health services. In *The Mental Health Matrix*, p. 109. Cambridge: Cambridge University Press.

Williams, A. (2000) Clinical governance: key success factors. *Clinician in Management*, **9**, 107–114.

Part II

Building blocks/key elements

CHAPTER 9

Involving service users and their relatives

Rachel E. Perkins and Kim L. Goddard

- The unique expertise of those who use services and their relatives should be recognised
- They need to be involved at all levels of service: individual, operational (including monitoring and evaluation) and strategic
- This must be a core component and not an 'add on' to existing ways of working
- The views both of those who use services and of their relatives are important but they may differ from each other
- Comprehensive information should be easily accessible, to enable involvement
- A range of different modes of involvement should be used creatively, rather than reliance on a single method (e.g. the questionnaire)
- The mechanisms for involving users and their relatives must be as 'user-friendly' as possible
- Information, training and support for staff are essential for good working partnerships with users and their relatives.

Introduction

'Patients provide a uniquely valuable perspective on services, and it is impossible to get the best from a change process without actively involving them.' (Department of Health, 1999b)

The experience of service users and their relatives lies at the heart of clinical governance: the framework through which NHS organisations and their staff are accountable for the quality of patient care. The involvement of service users and their relatives is required by all recent legislation relating to mental health, such as the National Service Framework for Mental Health (Department of Health, 1999a) and the

Throughout this chapter the term 'relatives' has been used. This is intended to refer to relatives, friends and 'significant others' in the individual user's life, whether or not these people are considered, or consider themselves, to be 'carers'.

NHS Plan (Department of Health, 2000). Yet service users often feel that a great deal of ambivalence remains towards their involvement.

'On the one hand professional organisations publicly encourage greater involvement of service users (and carers) and acknowledge the legitimacy of direct experience, however, on the other there is a resistance to non-expert views ... many mental health workers are wary of those service users now involving themselves in mental health service development.' (Campbell, 2001)

In relation to clinical governance, the involvement of users and their relatives needs to be addressed at a number of levels:

- *individual* – involvement in making decisions about the treatment and support that they need and the ways in which this will be provided
- *operational* – involvement in decisions about the way in which different services – community teams, wards, day facilities, residential units – are run
- *strategic* – involvement in the development, planning and organisation of services – including clinical governance structures
- *service monitoring and evaluation* – involvement in providing feedback about treatment and support received as part of audit or evaluation exercises to inform service improvements and developments.

A number of research studies have shown that users' involvement can contribute to changes in service provision (Crawford *et al*, 2002). However, making a reality of the involvement of users and their relatives involves a great deal more than the simple inclusion of token representatives on committees or a signature on a care plan. If the involvement of service users and their relatives is to be meaningful, it requires a major cultural change for service providers: a move away from a perspective in which the professional is the sole expert who determines what patients need, to one in which the expertise of experience is acknowledged, respected and heeded. Many services have already achieved large strides in this direction, but users, carers and staff would all acknowledge that there is still some way to go. In order to examine how further progress might be achieved, this chapter first addresses some of the barriers to involvement and then offers practical suggestions for how these might be overcome (Simpson & House, 2003).

Barriers to the involvement of users and their relatives

Users and relatives

While service users and their relatives may have some common interests and concerns, the priorities and preferences of the two groups are often different (Shepherd *et al*, 1994). This is hardly surprising. Irrespective of the quality of family relationships, few of us would wholly share the aspirations of our kinfolk (parents, partners, children, etc.) or would wish for them to speak on our behalf. Adults with mental health problems, no matter how serious or disabling these may be, are no different. Therefore, the lumping together of 'users and carers' into a single interest group is problematic (Perkins & Repper, 1998).

The primary concerns of service users tend to focus on information, choice, control, dignity and respect (Read & Reynolds, 1996). The most common unmet needs they describe include an adequate income, intimacy and privacy, a satisfying sex life, meaningful work, a satisfying social life and happiness (Bond, 1994; Dunn, 1999). Service users typically say that it is practical help that is important: help with income, benefits, housing, child care and finding employment, as well as advocacy and assistance to access specialist services (Sainsbury Centre for Mental Health, 1997).

Relatives' interests tend to revolve around: receiving acknowledgement from professionals of their role as primary carers; a recognition of their value as partners in care; access to the professional support and services they need to sustain their role as carers; information about the illness and regular updates from professionals; effective service co-ordination; good communication with professionals; and opportunities to learn coping strategies (Shepherd *et al*, 1994; Sainsbury Centre for Mental Health, 1997).

The perspectives of both users and their relatives are important but it cannot be assumed that they are the same.

The 'token' user or carer

Sometimes user involvement can be somewhat tokenistic (Bowl, 1998). Such tokenism is reflected at all levels, as the following examples of procedure show:

- Service users are given a copy of a care plan that has already been decided by professionals and are asked to sign it – involvement becomes little more than 'You do agree, don't you?'
- 'Community meetings' are held within residential or day facilities which decide only where the next 'outing' should go, or at the most what colour the walls should be painted. Alternatively, such forums are sometimes used to explain why staff are unable to respond to service users' requests (safety, lack of time, lack of resources, etc.) or why these were misguided in the first place. 'Relatives' groups' sometimes serve a similar function.
- Staff-designed 'satisfaction questionnaires' (which often bear little relationship to users' concerns and allow no scope for detailed

feedback concerning personal experience) are handed out to users but the results are used for nothing more than to produce a report to show that consultation has occurred (rather than to inform service developments).

- One or two 'user' or 'carer' representatives (who often have little idea of the parameters of the discussion) are included alongside many more professionals on planning or clinical governance committees whose priorities and agendas are set by service providers. Mere presence is not enough.

'There are times when, as someone who has been and still is a recipient of mental health services, I feel as though I am shaking hands with the devil. The feeling tends to be strongest when I find myself sitting on a high powered committee which is intent on sending out signals that the mere presence of people using services is evidence of its good will and obvious commitment to delivering user centred services.' (Conlan, 1996)

'You don't know what you are talking about'

Involving service users and their relatives is a straightforward matter when their views accord with those of service providers. It is when opinions diverge that problems arise. The involvement of users and relatives is meaningless if their views are disregarded as soon as they disagree with professionals.

Service users have commented that, when they express their views, staff seem to be 'humouring' them – listening but not responding to their concerns. Alternatively, their views may be vigorously refuted by staff. Lucksted & Coursey (1995) found that 58% of service users felt they had been pressured or forced into taking some form of treatment/ therapy, and the most common type of force reported was 'verbal persuasion'.

It is clearly important to brief service users and their relatives fully, and there are likely to be both legal limitations and resource constraints on what is possible. However, the purpose of involving service users and relatives is precisely to add the 'expertise of experience' to decision-making at all levels. It is important that such expertise is not automatically overridden when it diverges from that of professionals.

On the other hand, there remains considerable concern among service users that their views, concerns and complaints are dismissed as manifestations of their psychopathology (Spaniol & Koehler, 1994; Read & Reynolds, 1996; Rose, 2001).

'I can speak but I may not be heard. I can make suggestions, but they may not be taken seriously. I can voice my thoughts, but they may be seen as delusions. I can recite experiences, but they may be interpreted as fantasies. To be an ex-patient or even an ex-client is to be discounted.' (Leete, 1988)

'You're not representative' or
'That's not the remit of this committee'

There are two further barriers to involvement that particularly affect those users and their relatives who sit on committees and planning groups at an operational or service development level. Their views and opinions may be disregarded either as 'unrepresentative' of 'service users as a whole' (Crepaz-Keay, 1996) or outside the remit of the particular group of which they are a part.

It is unlikely that professional members of a committee are strictly representative of their profession. Indeed, it is typically the case that professional members of planning groups have been specifically selected for their 'unrepresentativeness': because they have a special interest, expertise or role in the area under consideration. However, when the charge of 'unrepresentativeness' is levelled, it is generally reserved for user and carer members in order to dismiss or marginalise their input.

Similarly, the views of users and their relatives can be dismissed with the assertion that 'You can't agree with each other'. A rich diversity of politics, perspectives, interests and experiences exists among those who experience mental health problems and their relatives, just as exists among service providers and the population as a whole. Diversity among different professions, although sometimes a cause of conflict within teams, is also seen as an asset of multidisciplinary working: a way in which decisions can be informed by a range of different perspectives and points of view. However, when such diversity is evident among users and their relatives it may more often be construed as a problem – 'We don't know who to believe'.

The challenge of effective user involvement is to ensure that service user members of committees have opportunities to consult with their constituencies (via user forums etc.) and to ensure that decisions are informed by the range of perspectives that exist. It is especially important to include the perspectives of those who find it less easy to get their voice heard, like people from minority ethnic groups, older people, young people, women, lesbians and gay men.

In addition, users and their relatives have complained to us that concerns and issues that they raise in clinical governance meetings are 'outside the scope' of that particular committee. This probably occurs when representation of users and their relatives is somewhat piecemeal, not coordinated throughout the organisation (see, for example, Commission for Health Improvement, 2000). If this is the case, then they lack the opportunity to raise concerns in the appropriate forum. Clearly, a single planning group or clinical governance committee cannot deal with everything. The challenge is to ensure that service users and their relatives are fully involved in all planning and decision-making forums within an organisation, and have access to opportunities for communication with their colleagues in these different arenas to ensure that their voices are heard in the appropriate place.

Meaningful involvement of users and their relatives

Individual care planning

If service users and their relatives are to be involved at the level of individual care planning, then the first requirement is information. However, a chorus of complaints continues from relatives (Shepherd *et al*, 1994) and service users about the lack of information available (Read & Reynolds, 1996; Campbell *et al*, 1997; Faulkener & Layzell, 2000; Rose, 2001).

'Most basically, if it is not known that something is available, it cannot be used, it cannot be chosen. Good information makes effective choice possible ... We consistently find information provision falling short of what at least half of users would like and this has to be the benchmark – if users do not feel well informed then they will be unable to exercise choice and they will be unable to become involved in their care.' (Rose, 2001)

On the basis of extensive user-focused monitoring of a number of services throughout the UK, Rose (2001) makes the following key recommendations with respect to the provision of information:

- All prescriptions for psychotropic medication, including prescriptions from hospital pharmacies, should be accompanied by full information on the benefits and side-effects of the drugs.
- In-patient units should hold this information in accessible leaflet form for all the medications used on the ward.
- Non-medical staff who take on the role of care coordinator, such as social workers and occupational therapists, should be trained in the main side-effects of common psychiatric drugs.
- Community mental health teams should develop central, indexed stores of information concerning community resources, housing, benefits, work projects and advocacy. All staff should have basic knowledge of what these stores contain.
- In-patient units should have freely available leaflets on the main resources in their locality.
- All information should be provided in all the locally spoken languages and in forms accessible to those with sensory impairments.

If people are to be involved in their care planning, then information must be provided in such a way that a person has time to think about it and to discuss the implications of different options. People need time and 'space' to talk through the options available and make decisions about what they want. It is critical that information is provided in a form that people can understand, and there are numerous leaflets available from organisations such as Mind (www.mind.org.uk), the Manic Depression Fellowship (www.mdf.org.uk), the Mental Health Foundation (www.mentalhealth.org.uk), the Depression Alliance (www.depressionalliance.org) and Rethink (formerly the National Schizophrenia Fellowship) (www.rethink.org), as well as from professional organisations such as the Royal College of Psychiatrists (www.rcpsych.ac.uk).

It may not be possible to discuss fully with users all the available options when they are in acute crisis (e.g. at the point of admission). However, such information and discussion can occur when the crisis has abated and users are able to consider the options available to them.

There are now a number of publications available to assist service users and professionals in the process of assessment and care planning from the perspective of users and their relatives. These include:

- *Direct Power* (Leader, 1995), which was developed by service users as a resource pack for people to develop their own care plans and support networks
- *The Avon Mental Health Measure* (Avon Measure Working Group, 1996), which was developed to help service users to assess their own strengths, wants and needs, to express their views to mental health workers and to have more control over the help they receive
- *The Carers' and Users' Expectation of Services* questionnaires (CUES) (Lelliott *et al*, 1999, 2001; National Schizophrenia Fellowship, 2000*b*) – two instruments – one for service users, the other for carers – developed as part of the Department of Health's OSCA (Outcomes of Social Care for Adults) initiative to enable users and their relatives to contribute to care plans (as well as inform health and social care workers of social function and outcomes from their perspective), to participate in audit of outcomes of care, to provide service monitoring and evaluation information and to help educate mental health and social care workers about user- and carer-focused outcomes
- *Carers' Assessment Pack* (National Schizophrenia Fellowship, 2000*a*), which was developed according to carers' self-reported information and specifically designed for mental health carers' assessments (this pack includes the carer's version of CUES).

Having ascertained the views of service users, it is essential that these are actually used in designing care plans. While this may seem obvious, there is worrying research evidence that care plans are not always based on assessments performed (Conning & Rowland, 1992), and that even when the views and preferences of users are sought, they are not always included in care plans (Perkins & Fisher, 1996). It is easy to include users' wishes and preferences in care plans when these are in accord with those of the professionals involved: it is when the user wants something that is at odds with what the professional thinks is best that the real challenge of involving service users arises. While legal constraints exist, professionals are sometimes tempted to go beyond these in a desire to protect service users from treatment failure (which they believe may further erode their already fragile self-confidence). But in order to have the possibility of achieving things, a person has to risk failure: which of us would have the relationships and occupations that we enjoy had we not taken such risks? It is also the case that many service users have more experience of dealing with failure than the staff who wish to protect them. Helping a person to try to get a job, or do a college course, is often more likely to enhance engagement and enable the person to move towards what is wanted than assuming that the person will fail and refusing this assistance. Helping the person to do things, even when the professional may not consider these things ideal, makes a reality of user involvement. For example, if someone is adamant that she wishes to take less medication, or a different medication, it may be preferable to help her to try this in a planned and supported way rather than refusing to entertain her wishes and risking complete disengagement.

The whole process of deciding on the contents of the care plan and actually writing it should be a collaborative exercise – and the language used should be that of the user rather than the professional. The language that is familiar to professionals can be vague, obscure and sometimes distressing to others. For example, a young man became very upset at an item on his care plan which said 'prevent sexual exploitation'. Unfamiliar with the term 'sexual exploitation' he believed he was being accused of unusual sexual practices. When this was rephrased as 'help to have sex when he wants to and not to have sex when he doesn't', his anxieties were alleviated. All service users should be given a copy of their care plan in a form that they can understand – and given a new copy each time it is changed or updated.

While the framework of the care programme approach offers an opportunity to involve service users in the planning and delivery of their own treatment and support, it is important to ensure that the structures and processes adopted are 'user-friendly'. The large ward round or case conference, for example, can be an extremely daunting event: it would be difficult for anyone to express his views and talk about personal issues in a room of, say, six people, many of whom are strangers. However, even when reviews and care planning meetings involve only those who are directly involved in a person's care, it remains all too easy for the user to feel overawed by mental health workers.

'Professionals might not feel very intimidating but there's something about the relationship that we have with you. It's not easy for us to say ... what we want ...

especially when we fear that what we want to say is not what mental health workers want to hear.' (Read, 1996)

The presence of a friend or advocate can help people to express their concerns. The National Service Framework for Mental Health (Department of Health, 1999a) says that services must ensure that users have access to advocacy. When people have difficulty in speaking for themselves, others who have experienced similar difficulties and situations are probably in the best position to assist them: other service users in the form of peer advocacy (Conlan et al, 1994). If it is to be effective, advocacy must be independent of the services to which the individual must represent his/her interests and concerns: mental health workers cannot act as advocates within mental health services because they are a part of those services. Initially, many mental health workers feel wary of advocates, but, as Leader & Crosby (1998) argue in their resource pack for the development of peer advocacy programmes, advocacy has a central role to play in improving genuine partnership working between service users and mental health workers.

From the operation of teams/services to clinical governance and planning structures

There is often no clear distinction between the forums in which operational and strategic decisions are made: the two often shade into another as one moves from community meetings in individual units through team business meetings to directorate and trust-wide planning and clinical governance structures. However, if services users and their relatives are to be able to express their views, inform staff of their experiences and influence the nature and range of services from which they can choose, then involvement at every level is critical.

The clinical team is the organisational structure with which service users and their relatives have most contact, and the operation of services – how to get hold of help in an emergency, how long they are kept waiting, how they are treated by professionals – is the area about which they have the greatest concerns. Paradoxically, this is the arena where meaningful service user involvement has been least developed (Onyett et al, 1994). There are a number of reasons for this. Team working is a fairly new concept in mental health care and to date, although its central importance over and above the contribution of individual staff members in delivering good services is well established (Thornicroft & Tansella, 1999), team development has not been well resourced. Teams largely remain a group of individuals with dynamics that reflect established power structures: doctors tell nurses what to do and psychologists dissociate themselves from their medical models! In addition, problems with recruiting and retaining experienced clinical staff, major national and local organisational changes, and a perception that public expectations of services cannot be met mean that conditions are often not conducive to team learning and partnership working. Confident, valued teams are typically less threatened by partnership working with service users and their relatives than are less-confident, less-valued teams.

Particular barriers to real involvement at this level include:

- a belief that any time spent away from actual service delivery ('seeing patients') is time wasted
- the assumption that it may result in expectations on the team that they are unable to meet
- the mistaken assumption that involvement requires something complicated or that services do not have the resources to effect
- the belief that visits by community health councils and other bodies, or consultations with single user/carer 'development workers', are sufficient to constitute 'involvement'
- the delegation of attendance at meetings with service users to junior members of staff who have no or little power to effect change.

Meeting service users and their carers outside the immediate clinical setting is a novel experience for most clinicians. Equally, operational managers' contact with them is often limited to the investigation of complaints. In other words, clinicians and managers at this level may lack the skills required for partnership working and, as a result, become defensive or seek to impose a structure that is familiar to them (such as a committee) but not necessarily effective. Service users then feel unwelcome and overawed. There is a danger that the experience as a whole is unpleasant for both staff and service users, and this in turn becomes an excuse not to persist with developing involvement.

Good preparation is therefore essential. Senior staff must be committed to the principle of involvement, understand how it will result in quality improvements and be prepared to act as role models for the service: a sceptical or half-hearted response will be quickly picked up by service users and more junior members of staff. Discussing potential pitfalls (real and imagined barriers to involvement) and staff hopes and fears with someone who has experience of involvement at this level will help. Some professional organisations have begun to produce material and training programmes to support this (e.g. British Medical Association, 2000). It cannot be assumed that, simply because individuals have good clinical skills, they necessarily have the skills to facilitate partnership working. The trust must 'legitimise' time spent on involving service users and carers by building this into its expectations of professionals and services (e.g. as part of job, business and clinical governance development plans).

There is room for creativity at this level: different modes of involvement can be used, but it makes sense to begin by looking at those already in existence. 'Community meetings' and patient business meetings have a long history in day and in-patient services. These are often poorly attended or attended because continued use of the facility is dependent on attendance. The purpose of these meetings is often vague or not couched in terms meaningful to service users (or staff). Service users will attend if there is clarity of purpose, their agenda is listened to and their input is acted on. This requires that those with the power to effect change also attend and hear this agenda first hand.

Community-based services increasingly run support groups for service users with particular illnesses and their carers, or based on gender, sexual orientation or ethnicity. Feedback sessions with senior clinicians/ managers in attendance can be attached to these groups at intervals, with the advantage that those involved are already comfortable and supportive of each other. Patient satisfaction questionnaires have their place, with certain caveats (see below), particularly for non-clinical aspects of the service (Young, 1996). However, a simpler format has been suggested by the College of Health – a stamped addressed postcard to fill in after the statement 'If you could change two things about the service, they would be ...'. This approach is more likely to reach those who would not otherwise attend a meeting or complete a traditional questionnaire.

In many trusts, user forums or councils have existed for some time (Barker & Peck, 1996). But at this level 'representativeness' is an appropriate consideration. The structure of these forums should reflect trust service-delivery and decision-making structures. It is all too easy for views expressed by a general patients' council to be dismissed by a specialist service as being unrepresentative of 'their' clients and therefore for key people responsible for managing different services not to attend. Regular forums for each broad service area or directorate, with the senior management team in attendance, allows the directorate to benefit from feedback, and allows users and their relatives to engage with an agenda that has an immediate impact on their experience of care. Setting this up at directorate level ensures that appropriate arrangements to facilitate attendance can be made that meet the needs of the people who use the directorate's services and that the agendas are appropriate to the population served.

All these efforts will come to nothing if the organisation is not proactive in regularly publicising these events, and also makes clear what they are for and why they are important. Clear information, as always, is essential if involvement is to be genuine (Rose, 2001).

There is an explicit expectation that 'Patients and the public should be actively involved in work to develop and monitor clinical governance arrangements locally' (Department of Health, 1999*b*).

The key work group in any organisation at this level is the traditional committee, often inhabited by senior managers in grey suits! These barriers are compounded by the somewhat abstract nature of 'clinical governance' and a complex and rapidly changing agenda. Most staff sitting on these committees will be senior, with many years' experience of this form of working. It is easy for service users and relatives to feel marginalised and dispirited in such an atmosphere.

Campbell & Lindow (1997) offer a comprehensive 'meetings checklist' of things that practitioners should do if they are inviting service users to meetings that mainly involve service providers. This is presented in Box 9.1.

Service users on committees need to have access to a constituency of the people they are supposed to represent, and should be considered appropriate representatives by these constituencies. It is therefore important to support – both financially and administratively – existing user forums/groups (or new ones if none exists locally) from which representatives can be drawn. It is also worth remembering that senior staff can be invited to attend service user forums, rather than always expecting service users to come to meetings organised by provider organisations. It is also important specifically to encourage representation of groups who may have specific issues to raise or have difficulty getting their voice heard (such as older people, younger people, people from ethnic minorities, women, lesbians and gay men).

The involvement of users and their relatives in service planning is important because it will ensure that strategic initiatives are properly focused on the ultimate aim of making improvements in services that are visibly responsive to the wishes of those who use them. This is the acid test of strategy. If service user representatives cannot see that a strategy will achieve anything of benefit to them, then the strategy is probably not worth pursuing.

Service monitoring and evaluation

Historically, the involvement of users and their relatives in service monitoring and evaluation has essentially been as subjects in a process designed and controlled by mental health workers. Involvement has meant little more than completion of questionnaires or interviews, whose content is determined by mental health workers; the latter also analyse the results and draw their own conclusions. Even the large number of patient and relative satisfaction scales available have been devised by clinicians and therefore reflect their concerns rather than those of service users (Ruggeri, 1994). However, in recent years this has been changing. An increasing number of methods and instruments have been developed by service users for service users in monitoring and evaluating services.

Box 9.1 Meetings checklist: things that practitioners should do if they are inviting service users to meetings that mainly involve service providers (Campbell & Lindow, 1997)

Membership
- Service user representatives should be service users or ex-users, rather than carers or voluntary sector organisations speaking on their behalf (although these groups may be represented separately, if appropriate, to speak about their own needs).

Support
- Meeting attendance payments should be made to users attending meetings: staff are paid to be there – service users should be similarly recompensed for contributing their time and expertise
- Travel costs should be paid on the day of the meeting – many service users live on small incomes and can ill afford to wait for the payment of expenses they incur
- Find out what service users need to consult other service users and to report to them issues raised at the meeting
- Produce papers, including the next agenda, soon after the meeting (rather than immediately before the next meeting) so that representatives can consult other people
- Avoid unnecessary paperwork.

Power and decision-making
- Make the committee's purpose and limits clear
- Make it clear where the power to make decisions lies
- Do not assume that there are areas where service users are not competent to take part
- Do not pass the buck of difficult or controversial decisions to service users
- Invite service users to put items of concern to them on the agenda – and do not place them at the end, as there may be little time left in the meeting to address them properly.

At the meeting
- Avoid jargon: practitioners and managers who are present should take responsibility for challenging use of jargon as well as being open to challenges from the service users present
- Make statements about the equality of everyone's contribution at the meeting
- Be clear about issues of confidentiality
- Be clear to practitioners, managers and service users that no one will be victimised for taking part in consultation and representation (fear of possible consequences can sometimes prevent service users saying what they wish to say)
- Provide drinks: many psychotropic medications dry the mouth
- Be prepared for meetings sometimes to take longer
- Be prepared for strong emotional expression – even anger – and do not regard such expressions as symptoms of the person's mental health problems
- Provide regular breaks for people to have a cigarette and so on
- Let individuals and groups know that you appreciate their input.

Access
- Hold meetings in user-friendly places that are accessible via public transport (or provide transport) and at times that are convenient to those involved – ask people about these things
- Remember that mental health service users may also have physical impairments and make meetings accessible in this sense as well.

As many services express the intention of 'empowering' their users, Rogers *et al* (1997) have developed a consumer-constructed scale to measure empowerment among service users. A user researcher began by bringing together a diverse group of service users, who developed a definition of the attributes of empowerment from a user perspective, on the basis of which a scale was constructed and tested. Good psychometric properties were demonstrated (internal consistency, construct validity, known groups validity) and a factor analysis revealed five factors:

- self-esteem and self-efficacy
- power and powerlessness
- community activism and autonomy
- optimism and control over the future
- righteous anger.

The resulting instrument therefore offers a way of evaluating the extent to which services are successful in achieving the user-defined goal of empowerment.

Similarly, the development of the Carer and User Expectation of Services Questionnaires (Lelliott *et al*, 2001) involved service users and their relatives. However, it is not simply in the design of outcome measures that important methodological questions arise. The person asking the questions can significantly influence the responses obtained: service users often express understandable concerns that the treatment and services they receive may be influenced by the answers they give. Srebnick *et al* (1990) described how, given the power differentials that prevail, in assessments of user preference and satisfaction an acquiescent response set can be induced if professionals ask the questions: people endeavour to please the questioner by saying what they think the questionner wishes to hear. There is no reason to assume that the same would not apply to relatives. This can be avoided by involving service users as researchers. Service users trained to perform assessments and interviews are more likely to be able to offer proper reassurance to user interviewees and obtain richer, more accurate information about their concerns.

Such an approach has been developed and used to good effect by a number of user researchers (East Yorkshire Monitoring Team, 1997; Rose *et al*, 1998; Faulkener & Layzell, 2000; Rose, 2001). These approaches are user-led at all stages: service users have defined the issues and methods of investigation, user researchers collect the information, and service users analyse and report on the results.

Rose (2001) and her colleagues have developed 'user focused monitoring'. This is an approach to the systematic investigation of what service users think about hospital and community services that provides both quantitative and descriptive information and is 'user focused' in at least five ways:

- The research and evaluation are centrally coordinated by users and ex-users of psychiatric services who also have professional qualifications.
- The instruments are constructed by groups of local service users who are in touch with grass-roots services.
- Local service users are trained to carry out the practical research work: one-to-one interviews, site visits and focus groups.
- Informants are people who make heavy use of psychiatric services: those people with severe and enduring mental health problems who are often denied a voice.
- The results are interpreted and reports written from a service user's perspective: that of the qualified user coordinators of the programme.

Real user involvement in service monitoring and evaluation does not simply involve professionals giving out their questionnaires. Neither is it a way of performing audits 'on the cheap' by getting unpaid, or poorly paid, service users to collect information.

Conclusions

A number of practical ways forward have been presented here, but there is no 'right' model for developing real involvement. While key lessons and principles can be shared, importing standard formulas developed elsewhere is unlikely to result in a system that is genuinely responsive to local populations and services. Each trust needs to develop a coordinated strategy for the involvement of service users and their relatives at all levels. This strategy should relate to its own structures and decision-making processes. Piecemeal efforts in particular services or committees are inadequate.

Agendas within mental health services remain contradictory, with simultaneous demands that we are responsive to the wishes of those who use them, while at the same time protecting the public and offering only 'evidence-based' interventions. No service restricts care and treatment to those for whom their effectiveness has been proven in randomised controlled trials. Research is required into the effectiveness of interventions in terms of those outcomes that users consider important, since most research to date has focused on those outcomes deemed important by professionals (Perkins, 2001). In addition, if effective ways of involving service users and their relatives are to be developed, then these too must be the subject of systematic investigation (Simpson & House, 2003).

The development of services that are genuinely responsive to the needs and wishes of those whom they serve demands a major change in assumptions, attitudes and practices. While information, training and

145

support are important for service users and their relatives, they are equally important for staff. The goal posts have shifted.

'Changes in power relationships do not mean that professionals have no skills, rather that these skills might be used in a different way .... There is a need to move away from the idea of professionals as experts who know best, controlling services and telling patients what to do. An alternative model where professionals place their expertise and services at the disposal of those who need them is both possible and desirable. This is the model within which many professionals (like lawyers) work.' (Perkins, 1996)

References

Avon Measure Working Group (1996) *The Avon Mental Health Measure. A User-Centred Approach to Assessing Need*. Avon: Mind.

Barker, I. & Peck, E. (1996) User empowerment – a decade of experience. *Mental Health Review*, 1(4), 5–13.

Bond, G. R. (1994) Psychiatric rehabilitation outcome. In *An Introduction to Psychiatric Rehabilitation* (ed. Publication Committee of the International Association of Psychosocial Rehabilitation Services). Columbia, MD: IAPSRS.

Bowl, R. (1998) Involving service users in mental health services: social services departments and the NHS and Community Care Act 1990. *Journal of Mental Health*, **5**, 287–303.

British Medical Association (2000) *Involving Patients in Quality Improvement Activities: An Introduction for Clinicians*. London: BMA.

Campbell, P. (2001) The role of users of psychiatric services in service development – influence not power. *Psychiatric Bulletin*, **25**, 87–88.

Campbell, P. & Lindow, V. (1997) *Changing Practice. Mental Health Nursing and User Empowerment*. London: Mind Publications/Royal College of Nursing.

Commission for Health Improvement (2000) *North Lakeland Healthcare NHS Trust*. London: CHI.

Conlan, E. (1996) Shaking hands with the devil. In *Speaking Our Minds* (eds J. Read & J. Reynolds), pp. 207–208. Milton Keynes: Open University Press.

Conlan, E., Gell, C. & Graley, R. (1994) *User Group Advocacy: A Code of Practice*. London: Department of Health Mental Health Task Force.

Conning, A. & Rowland, L. A. (1992) Staff attitudes and the provision of individualised care: what determines what people do for people with long-term psychiatric disabilities? *Journal of Mental Health*, **1**, 78–80.

Crawford, M. J., Rutter, D., Manley, C., *et al* (2002) Systematic review of involving patients in the planning and development of health care. *BMJ*, **325**, 1263–1268.

Crepaz-Keay, D. (1996) Who do *you* represent? In *Speaking Our Minds* (eds J. Read & J. Reynolds), pp. 180–183. Milton Keynes: Open University Press.

Department of Health (1997) *The New NHS: Modern, Dependable*, cm 3807. London: TSO.

Department of Health (1998) *A First Class Service: Quality in the New NHS*. London: Department of Health.

Department of Health (1999a) *National Service Framework for Mental Health*. London: Department of Health.

Department of Health (1999b) *Clinical Governance: Quality in the New NHS*, HSC 1999/065. London: Department of Health.

Dunn, S. (1999) *Creating Accepting Communities. Report of the Mind Inquiry into Social Exclusion and Mental Health Problems*. London: Mind Publications.

East Yorkshire Monitoring Team (1997) *Monitoring Our Services Ourselves. User-Led Monitoring of Mental Health Services*. Hull: East Yorkshire Community Healthcare.

Faulkener, A. & Layzell, S. (2000) *Strategies for Living: A Report of User-Led Research into People's Strategies for Living with Mental Distress*. London: Mental Health Foundation.

Laugharne, R. (1999) Evidence-based medicine, user involvement and the post-modern paradigm. *Psychiatric Bulletin*, **23**, 641–643.

Leader, A. (1995) *Direct Power: A Resource Pack for People Who Want to Develop Their Own Care Plans and Support Networks*. Brighton: Pavilion Publishing.

Leader, A. & Crosby, K. (1998) *Power Tools. A Resource Pack for Those Committed to the Development of Mental Health Advocacy into the Millennium*. Brighton: Pavilion Publishing.

Leete, E. (1988) The role of the consumer movement and persons with mental illness. In *Rehabilitation of Persons with Long-Term Mental Illness in the 1990's*. Report of the 12th Mary E. Switzer Memorial Seminar. Alexandria, VA: National Rehabilitation Association.

Lelliott, P., Beevor, A., Hogman, G., *et al* (1999) *The CUES Project. Carer and User Expectations of Services. A Part of the Department of Health's SCA Initiative (Outcomes of Social Care for Adults). Final Report*. London: Royal College of Psychiatrists' Research Unit/National Schizophrenia Fellowship.

Lelliott, P., Beevor, A., Hogman, G., *et al* (2001) Carers' and Users' Expectations of Services – User version (CUES–U): a new instrument to measure the experience of users of mental health services. *British Journal of Psychiatry*, **179**, 67–72.

Lucksted, A. & Coursey, R. D. (1995) Consumer perceptions of pressure and force in psychiatric treatments. *Psychiatric Services*, **46**, 146–152.

National Schizophrenia Fellowship (2000*a*) *Carers Assessment Pack*. London: National Schizophrenia Fellowship.

National Schizophrenia Fellowship (in conjunction with the Royal College of Psychiatrists' Research Unit, Royal College of Nursing Research Institute and University of East Anglia Department of Social Work) (2000*b*) *CUES – Service User Version*. London: National Schizophrenia Fellowship.

Onyett, S., Heppleston, T. & Bushnell, D. (1994) A national survey of community mental health teams. *Journal of Mental Health*, **3**, 175–194.

Perkins, R. E. (1996) Seen but not heard: can 'user involvement' become more than empty rhetoric? *Mental Health Review*, **1**, 16–19.

Perkins, R. E. (2001) What constitutes success? The relative priority of service users' and professionals' views of the effectiveness of interventions and services. *British Journal of Psychiatry*, **179**, 9–10.

Perkins, R. E. & Fisher, N. (1996) Beyond mere existence: the auditing of care plans. *Journal of Mental Health*, **5**, 275–286.

Perkins, R. E. & Repper, J. M. (1998) *Clinical Dilemmas in Community Mental Health Practice. Choice or Control*. Oxford: Radcliffe Medical Press.

Read, J. (1996) What we want from mental health services. In *Speaking Our Minds* (eds J. Read & J. Reynolds), pp. 175–179. Milton Keynes: Open University Press.

Read, J. & Reynolds, J. (eds) (1996) *Speaking Our Minds*. Milton Keynes: Open University Press.

Rogers, E. S., Chamberlin, J., Ellison, M. L., *et al* (1997) A consumer-constructed scale to measure empowerment among users of mental health services. *Psychiatric Services*, **48**, 1042–1047.

Rose, D. (2001) *Users' Voices: The Perspectives of Mental Health Service Users on Community and Hospital Care*. London: Sainsbury Centre for Mental Health.

Rose, D., Ford, R., Lindley, P., *et al* (1998) *In Our Experience. User-Focused Monitoring of Mental Health Services*. London: Sainsbury Centre for Mental Health.

Ruggeri, M. (1994) Patients' and relatives' satisfaction with psychiatric services: the state of the art and its measurement. *Social Psychiatry and Psychiatric Epidemiology*, **29**, 212–217.

Sainsbury Centre for Mental Health (1997) *Pulling Together: The Future Roles and Training of Mental Health Staff*. London: Sainsbury Centre for Mental Health.

Shepherd, G., Murray, A. & Muijen, M. (1994) *Relative Values: The Differing Views of Users, Family Carers and Professionals on Services for People with Schizophrenia in the Community*. London: Sainsbury Centre for Mental Health.

Simpson, E. L. & House, A. O. (2003) User and carer involvement in mental health services: from rhetoric to science. *British Journal of Psychiatry*, **183**, 89–91.

Spaniol, L. & Koehler, M. (1994) *The Experience of Recovery*. Boston, MA: Center for Psychiatric Rehabilitation.

Srebnick, D., Robinson, M. & Tanzman, B. H. (1990) *Participation of Mental Health Consumers in Research: Empowerment in Practice* (CI-10). Burlington, VT: Center for Community Change through Housing and Support. http://www.cccinternational.com/consumer.htm.

Thornicroft, G. & Tansella, M. (1999) *The Mental Health Matrix: A Manual to Improve Services*. Cambridge: Cambridge University Press.

Torrey, E. F. (1986) Finally, a cure for homelessness: but it takes some strong medicine. *Washington Monthly*, **10**, 95–97.

Young, C. F. (1996) *The Usefulness and Quality Implications of Service Level Agreements Within a Large Scale Facilities Management Contract*. Report in part submission for Postgraduate Diploma in Business Research, University of Brighton.

CHAPTER 10

Evidence-based practice

John Geddes

- Clinicians have considerable difficulty keeping up-to-date with the scientific literature
- Evidence-based practice (EBP) is a problem-based approach to help clinicians keep up to date
- EBP is based on advances in clinical epidemiology and knowledge management
- The successful introduction of EBP requires the acquisition of critical appraisal skills and the easy availability of high-quality sources of evidence
- EBP helps to identify areas of high priority for primary research.

Keeping up-to-date with the literature

All clinicians need to keep up with the increasingly rapid pace of research advances in mental healthcare, including new treatments (pharmacological, psychotherapeutic and models of service organisation and delivery) as well as advances in diagnosis, prognosis (including assessment of risk) and aetiology. Increasingly, with the introduction of clinical governance, health service managers also need to be aware of the emerging evidence. This chapter provides an overview of evidence-based practice (EBP), a methodology that has been developed to facilitate this process.

The problem is how to help decision-makers get rapid access to research evidence, filter out the quality research from the poor, and implement the research findings in clinical practice, using their clinical judgement and in line with patients' preferences. There are two associated problems: first, time in clinical practice is very limited; and second, many clinicians do not have the skills needed critically to appraise and interpret the findings of research studies efficiently. The number of primary research papers published every year – estimated even in the mid-1990s at two million papers published in 20 000 biomedical journals (Mulrow, 1994) – means that it is clearly unfeasible for busy clinicians themselves to access the primary literature routinely. A strategy is required to identify research that is both methodologically sound and clinically relevant.

Traditionally, clinicians have used a number of methods of keeping up to date with research, including consulting colleagues and reading textbooks and journals. The problem with these resources is that there tends to be an inverse correlation between validity and usefulness and availability (Smith, 1996). In other words, it is very easy to ask a colleague, but the answer is of uncertain reliability, while it requires more effort to find and use a high-quality review article. Traditional methods of obtaining information (such as conventional textbooks and lecture-based continuing medical education) are more widely available, but of limited validity.

The difficulty of accessing reliable information means that the clinician is often more uncertain about decisions than necessary. Furthermore, the clinician is often unable to meet the increasing demands for accurate information about treatment options and prognosis from patients and users of mental health services. The ensuing gap between research and practice is often filled by an unsystematic combination of experience and information rapidly gathered from sources of unknown reliability. This rather chaotic approach sometimes leads to unnecessary variations in clinical practice. Variations may simply imply the lack of good evidence (Gilbody & House, 1999), but they sometimes imply the failure to implement research findings effectively. In mental health practice, variations have been observed in the use of electroconvulsive therapy, the use of antipsychotics and the treatment of depression (Geddes & Harrison, 1997). These variations probably mean that some patients are not receiving the optimum treatment.

Evidence-based practice as a method of ensuring access to the best available evidence

Evidence-based medicine (EBM), which is called evidence-based practice (EBP) in a multidisciplinary setting, refers to a set of strategies designed to assist clinicians in their attempts to base their practice on the best available evidence (Sackett *et al*, 1996). EBP is a problem-based approach and splits the process into five stages (Box 10.1). To make EBP useful and feasible in clinical practice, each of the stages requires the development of a range of skills and resources.

Asking a structured, answerable clinical question

First of all, the clinician needs to be able to recognise uncertainty, or a need for information, and to be able to translate that uncertainty into a structured, answerable, question (Geddes, 1999). Framing a well-structured

---

Box 10.1 The five stages of evidence-based practice

- Asking a structured, answerable clinical question
- Finding the evidence
- Critically appraising the evidence
- Applying the evidence to the clinical problem
- Assessing and improving the process.

---

question is fundamental to the process of EBP because it allows the question to be classified according to its type. Most common clinical questions are to do with treatment – both the benefits and the risks – but common questions also include prognosis (including risk assessment), diagnosis, aetiology and cost-effectiveness. Classifying the question allows the identification of the study design that is most likely to provide a reliable result and indicates the best and most efficient place to look for the evidence. Table 10.1 shows the common types of question with the study designs that are most likely to be helpful.

Having classified the question, it is then helpful to break the question down into four parts – the patient's problem, the intervention, the comparison (either an alternative treatment or no treatment) and the outcome.

Example

You have been discussing maintenance treatment with a 26-year-old male patient who has recently recovered from a second severe episode of mania. You are aware that valproate (or, more specifically, valproate semisodium) is increasingly used as first-line therapy in the United States – in preference to lithium. You therefore formulate a *therapy* question:

- In a 26-year-old patient with bipolar disorder (*the problem*)
- how effective is long-term valproate treatment (*the intervention*)
- compared with lithium or placebo (*the comparison intervention*)
- in preventing future relapses? (*the outcome*).

Finding the evidence

The formulation and classification of the clinical question allows the clinician to perform a rapid and efficient literature search. One of the main advances in EBP has been the development of methods of *research synthesis,* or the process of identifying, appraising and summarising primary research studies into clinically usable knowledge. Two methods of research synthesis have become increasingly available: systematic reviews and evidence-based clinical practice guidelines (CPGs). The recognition of the need for systematic reviews of randomised controlled

Table 10.1 Types of clinical question and most reliable study architecture

Type of question	Form of the question	Most reliable study architecture
Diagnosis/problem	How likely is a patient who has a particular symptom, sign or diagnostic test result to have a specific disorder?	A cross-sectional study of patients suspected of having the disorder that compares the proportion of the patients who have the disorder *and* a positive test with the proportion of patients who do *not* have the disorder *and* a positive test result
Treatment/intervention	Is the treatment of interest more effective in producing a desired outcome than an alternative treatment (including no treatment)?	A study in which patients are randomly allocated to receive either the treatment of interest or the alternative. This is usually a systematic review of randomised controlled trials (RCT) or a single high-quality RCT
Prognosis/outcome	What is the probability of a specific outcome for this patient?	A study in which an inception cohort (patients at a common stage in the development of the illness – especially first onset) are followed up for an adequate length of time
Aetiology	What has caused the disorder?	A study that compares the frequency of an exposure in a group of persons with the disease of interest ('cases') with a group of persons without the disease (controls). This may be an RCT, a case-control study or a cohort study

Table 10.2 Hierarchy of evidence for studies of treatments

Category	Criterion
Ia	Evidence from a systematic review of randomised controlled trials
Ib	Evidence from at least one randomised controlled trial
IIa	Evidence from at least one controlled study without randomisation
IIb	Evidence from at least one other type of quasi-experimental study
III	Evidence from non-experimental descriptive studies, such as comparative studies, correlation studies and case-control studies
IV	Evidence from expert committee reports or opinions and/or clinical experience of respected authorities

trials and the development of the scientific methodology of reviews have been two of the most striking developments in health services research over the past decade. The founding of the Cochrane Collaboration, an international organisation with the objective of producing regularly updated systematic reviews of the effectiveness of all healthcare interventions, has been one of the main driving forces behind these advances.

Both systematic reviews and CPGs are based on an explicit methodology that uses a *hierarchy of evidence* in which certain forms of research architecture are recognised as usually being more reliable than others. The hierarchy of evidence used for therapy is shown in Table 10.2. The production of a CPG should always (but often do not) include a systematic review, but go one stage further because they include recommendations for clinical practice – again, according to explicit criteria (see Table 10.3). CPGs are usually developed at a national level and need tailoring to suit local circumstances. Professional bodies have often initiated the development of CPGs, but the quality of such guidelines has been variable (Grilli *et al*, 2000). In the UK, the National Institute for Clinical Excellence is now in charge of national guideline development (www.nice.org.uk/) and has developed a thorough methodology for ensuring both methodological quality and that all stakeholders have been consulted (National Institute for Clinical Excellence, 2004).

Table 10.3 Grading of recommendations in clinical practice guidelines

Grade	Criterion (see Table 5.2 for category criteria)
A	Directly based on category I evidence
B	Directly based on category II evidence or extrapolated recommendation from category I evidence
C	Directly based on category III evidence or extrapolated recommendation from category I or II evidence
D	Directly based on category IV evidence or extrapolated recommendation from category I, II or III evidence

Concurrent developments have also taken place to improve *access* to high-quality evidence. These include the Cochrane Library, the journal *Evidence-Based Mental Health, Clinical Evidence* and the National electronic Libaries for Health and for Mental Health.

The Cochrane Library

The Cochrane Library includes the Cochrane Database of Systematic Reviews, which contains hundreds of systematic reviews of the effect of interventions in all areas of healthcare – a large number concerning the treatment of schizophrenia, and mood and anxiety disorders. The Cochrane Library also includes the Database of Abstract of Reviews of Effectiveness and the Cochrane Controlled Trials Register, which is the best source of randomised controlled trials. The Cochrane Library is published quarterly on CD-ROM and on the internet. The online Cochrane Library is available to NHS service users and staff free of charge via the National electronic Library for Health (www.nelh.nhs.uk).

Evidence-Based Mental Health (EBMH)

The journal owned jointly by the Royal College of Psychiatrists, the British Psychological Society and the British Medical Journal Publishing Group. The aim of *EBMH* is to provide rapid access to structured summaries of emerging high-quality evidence in the field of mental health. This evidence can cover treatment (including specific inter-ventions and systems of care), diagnosis, aetiology, prognosis/outcome research, quality improvement, continuing education and economic evaluation. One of the most important features of the journal is that explicit methodological criteria are used to select articles, which are included only if they are both methodologically sound and clinically useful (see Box 10.2). The articles are then summarised in value-added abstracts and a commentary by a clinical expert is added.

The full text of *EBMH* is available online (ebmh.bmjjournals.com/), which allows searching across all the previously published issues.

Clinical Evidence

Clinical Evidence is a regularly updated compendium of the best available answers to common clinical questions published twice a year by the British Medical Journal Publishing Group. The sections are organised by specialty and there is a mental health section with chapters on most disorders. It is published in both paper and electronic forms (www.clinicalevidence.com) and is available to NHS users via the National electronic Library for Health.

National electronic Libraries for Health and for Mental Health

Although each of the above resources meets a specific need, their very proliferation causes a new problem, in that the clinician may need to

Box 10.2 Examples of the criteria for selection and review of articles for abstracting in the journal *Evidence-Based Mental Health*

Basic criteria:
- Original or review articles
- In English
- About humans
- About topics that are important to the practice of clinicians in the broad field of mental health.

Studies of prevention or treatment must meet these additional criteria:
- Random allocation of participants to comparison groups
- Follow-up (end-point assessment) of at least 80% of those entering the investigation
- Outcome measure of known or probable clinical importance
- Analysis consistent with study design.

Studies of diagnosis must meet these additional criteria:
- Clearly identified comparison groups, at least one of which is free of the disorder or derangement of interest
- Interpretation of diagnostic standard without knowledge of test result
- Interpretation of test without knowledge of diagnostic standard result
- Diagnostic (gold) standard (e.g. diagnosis according to DSM–IV or ICD–10 criteria after assessment by clinically qualified interviewer) preferably with documentation, or at least with reproducible criteria for subjectively interpreted diagnostic standard (e.g. report of statistically significant measure of agreement among observers)
- Analysis consistent with study design.

Studies of prognosis must meet these additional criteria:
- Inception cohort (first onset or assembled at a uniform point in the development of the disease) of individuals, all initially free of the outcome of interest
- Follow-up of at least 80% of patients until the occurrence of a major study end-point or to the end of the study
- Analysis consistent with study design.

Studies of causation must meet these additional criteria:
- Clearly identified comparison group for those at risk of, or having, the outcome of interest (i.e. randomised controlled trial, quasi-randomised controlled trial, non-randomised controlled trial, cohort analytic study with case-by-case matching or statistical adjustment to create comparable groups, or case-control study)
- Masking of observers of outcomes to exposures (this criterion is assumed to be met if the outcome is objective); observers of exposures masked to outcomes for case-control studies; masking of subjects to exposure for all other study designs
- Analysis consistent with study design.

search each separately. In recognition of the need for an internet-based portal that allows rapid access across all these resources, the National Health Service is developing a National electronic Library for Health (www.nelh.nhs.uk/). Extra content tailored to the needs of a range of users (patients, primary and secondary care clinicians and policy-makers) is being provided online by a number of 'virtual branch libraries', including the National electronic Library for Mental Health (www.nelmh.org).

There have also been developments in Medline – including the introduction of filters into PubMed (www.ncbi.nlm.nih.gov/PubMed/clinical.html) and the creation of PubMed Central (www.pubmedcentral.nih.gov/) which may herald the end of paper-based journals, at least as the principal medium for published research (Delamothe & Smith, 2001). All these continuing developments in the organisation of clinical knowledge mean that, increasingly, it is possible for a clinician to search rapidly and efficiently for current best evidence. Obviously, this situation will continue to evolve as new methods of organising knowledge are developed.

Critically appraising the evidence

Once the evidence has been found, it needs to be critically appraised for its reliability and usefulness. Clinicians need to be able to assess the scientific value and clinical importance of a study. This requires a range of epidemiological and biostatistical skills that have not traditionally been considered to be key skills for psychiatrists. In the UK, the Royal College of Psychiatrists introduced in 1999 a new part of the main professional examination that is designed to test these skills, in recognition of their fundamental importance for clinical psychiatrists (Critical Review Paper Working Party, 1997).

The structured critical appraisal of articles is an *active* process that involves a systematic assessment of the key methodological aspects of the paper. In particular, critical appraisal focuses systematically on those aspects of the study methodology that are most likely to lead to unreliability of results. A number of checklists, designed to make the appraisal quicker and more systematic, have been produced for different research study designs and these are widely available in several books (e.g. Geddes & Harrison, 1997; Sackett *et al*, 2000; Lawrie *et al*, 2001).

Applying the evidence to the clinical problem

After critically appraising the study for its validity, the clinician needs to determine what the results are, and how important they are for a particular patient. Patients in research studies are *always* different from those in clinical practice, in ways that may be difficult to assess. The use of results from research studies in clinical practice therefore should be cautious and *always* requires a degree of extrapolation. However, it is probably better than extrapolation from unsystematic and probably idiosyncratic clinical observation. One of the key contributions of clinical epidemiology has been to develop simple methods of applying research results to individual patients that are biologically and statistically robust and are explicit about any assumptions made.

Perhaps the most useful question to ask when applying the results of a research study is 'Is my patient *so different* from those in the study that the results *cannot* be used at all?' The next step is to try to interpret the study results for a particular patient, in terms of that patient's clinical characteristics and treatment preferences. One example of a simple measure that seems to be clinically helpful is the *number needed to treat* (NNT). The NNT is an estimate of the number of patients who would need to be treated with the intervention of interest, compared with the alternative (which may be no intervention or an alternative treatment), in order to achieve one good outcome, or to avoid one harmful outcome. The NNT is calculated by taking the reciprocal of the difference between the rates of the outcome of interest in the experimental and control groups. The NNT is a measure of *how* effective the treatment is and the interpretation depends on: how serious the outcome is; and the nature (and cost) of the intervention.

Assessing and imporving the process

Improving and updating one's own skills is the final stage of EBP. Practice leads to improvement in formulation of questions; search skills – and access to recent developments – must be kept up to date; and critical appraisal and clinical application of the evidence need to be practised and developed.

Training in EBP

The skills in information technology and clinical epidemiology that are required for effective EBP have only recently been included in under-graduate and postgraduate curricula. Most practising clinicians therefore need some new training to obtain the skills. Probably the most effective way of learning the skills is to attend a workshop. A number of workshops in EBP are available, ranging from half-day introductions through to 3- or 5-day residential workshops (see www.cebmh.com for details). In addition, a number of distance-learning packages are becoming available through the National Health Service Critical Appraisal Skills Programme (www.phru.nhs.uk/casp/casp.htm).

Developing the evidence base

Finally, if clinical practice is to be based on evidence, then research needs to be relevant to it (Knottnerus & Dinant, 1997). The process of EBP inevitably leads to the identification of important areas of clinical uncertainty. In turn, this can lead to primary research being focused on these important unanswered questions. One such area is the increasing recognition of the need for trials of drug treatments that are conducted independently of the pharmaceutical industry. Clinicians and patients often have different questions from the pharmaceutical industry and this means that it is often difficult to obtain clinically useful results from published trials. However, there are major challenges to overcome in setting up such trials, because of the narrow window of opportunity between the introduction of a drug and its widespread adoption into clinical practice. One example of an attempt to evaluate a newly available drug is the BALANCE trial, which is currently being conducted in the UK (www.psychiatry.ox.ac.uk/balance/). BALANCE aims to compare lithium and valproate (Depakote) monotherapy with the combination of the two drugs and the maintenance treatment of bipolar disorder. Depakote has only recently been licensed within the UK and is now being marketed; it is therefore an ideal, although again narrow, window of opportunity in which to assess its effectiveness.

References

Critical Review Paper Working Party (1997) MRCPsych Part II examination: proposed critical review paper. *Psychiatric Bulletin*, **21**, 381–382.

Delamothe, T. & Smith, R. (2001) PubMed Central: creating an Aladdin's cave of ideas. *BMJ*, **322**, 1–2.

Geddes, J. (1999) Asking structured and focused clinical questions: essential first step of evidence-based practice. *Evidence-Based Mental Health*, **2**(2), 35–36.

Geddes, J. & Harrison, P. J. (1997) Evidence-based psychiatry: closing the gap between research and practice. *British Journal of Psychiatry*, **171**, 220–225.

Gilbody, S. & House, A. (1999) Variations in psychiatric practice. Neither unacceptable nor unavoidable, only under-researched. *British Journal of Psychiatry*, **175**, 303–305.

Grilli, R., Magrini, N., Penna, A., *et al* (2000) Practice guidelines developed by specialty societies: the need for a critical appraisal. *Lancet*, **355**, 103–106.

Knottnerus, J. A. & Dinant, G. J. (1997) Medicine based evidence, a prerequisite for evidence based medicine. *BMJ*, **315**, 1109–1110.

Lawrie, S. M., McIntosh, A. M. & Rao, S. (2001) *Critical Appraisal for Psychiatry*. Edinburgh: Churchill Livingstone.

Mulrow, C. D. (1994). Rationale for systematic reviews. *BMJ*, **309**, 597–599.

National Institute for Clinical Excellence (2004) *The Guideline Development Process – An Overview for Stakeholders, the Public and the NHS*. London: NICE. www.nice.org.uk/page.aspx?oa=114268.

Sackett, D. L., Rosenberg, W. M., Gray, J. A., *et al* (1996) Evidence based medicine: what it is and what it isn't. *British Medical Journal*, **312**, 71–72.

Sackett, D. L., Straus S. E., Richardson, S., *et al* (2000) *Evidence-Based Medicine: How to Practise and Teach EBM* (2nd edn). London: Churchill Livingstone.

Smith, R. (1996) What clinical information do doctors need? *BMJ*, **313**, 1062–1068.

CHAPTER 11

Evidence-based policies, guidelines, procedures and protocols

Mary Lindsey

Policies, guidelines, procedures and protocols should:

- be compatible with the culture and purpose of both the trust and the wider National Health Service
- be congruent with the strategic framework and business plan of the trust
- be proactive and include strategic, operational and clinical levels of organisational function
- be person-centred and developed through consultation with all stakeholders
- be evidence-based and flexible enough to evolve through continuous learning
- be mapped to avoid duplication and to ensure comprehensiveness
- be understandable and related to behaviours and outcomes
- address issues of implementation
- reflect good organisational practice
- exist for a good reason
- be developed, ratified, disseminated and reviewed in a systematic way
- be linked to an implementation plan
- be adopted by staff in their day-to-day practice through staff induction and other training
- be monitored and audited for effectiveness.

Introduction

This chapter examines the organisational culture required for the development of policies, guidelines, procedures and protocols that will contribute effectively to clinical governance. The key principles that underpin policies and procedures are identified and good and bad practice outlined. The reasons for their development and the procedure to be followed are then described. For the purposes of this chapter, the following definitions apply:

- a *policy* is a statement of intent that describes the principles of actions that are adopted or proposed by a government, party, business or individual
- a *guideline* is a principle or set of rules or criteria that guides or directs actions and behaviour
- a *procedure* is the mode in which a task is performed, that is, a series of actions conducted in a certain order or manner
- a *protocol* is the set of rules, or formalities, of any procedure or group behaviour, and is a formal statement of a transaction (it is generally applied in a local context)
- a *standard* is an object, quality or measure that serves as a basis, example or principle to which others conform or should conform, or by which the accuracy or quality of others is judged; it is the required level of performance determined by agreed criteria.

The organisational culture and strategic framework

The National Health Service (NHS) is an extremely large and complex organisation that has to interface with other complex organisations such as local authorities. Each NHS trust has to develop its services within this context. Strategies for mental health and learning disability services should be jointly produced by health and social care authorities and should be based on national policies and guidance. Clinical governance requires an approach that looks at the organisation as a whole and identifies the key values and beliefs that need to be embedded in the culture to deliver such strategies (Figs 11.1 and 11.2).

Recent management theories emphasise the importance of vision and mission within the organisation. This shared sense of purpose and values has to be developed in such a way that there is widespread acceptance of them within the workforce. The process of translating aspirations into practice requires not only leadership and communication but also empowerment of the workforce, users and carers. This style of engagement with stakeholders is very different from the more traditional, patriarchal cultures of command and control akin to the more military model used in the past. The 'softer' management styles have to be carefully and skilfully orchestrated to prevent anarchy and to ensure that clear standards of practice are developed and adhered to. Certain standards of attitudes and behaviour are essential. If staff are to understand these changes, it is essential that the underpinning values of the organisation are made explicit and prominently displayed. It is then possible to test all other policies against these values and standards to ensure that they are clearly related to the aspirations of the organisation.

Trust policies and procedures should be embedded in, and mapped against, the strategic framework that is designed to underpin the

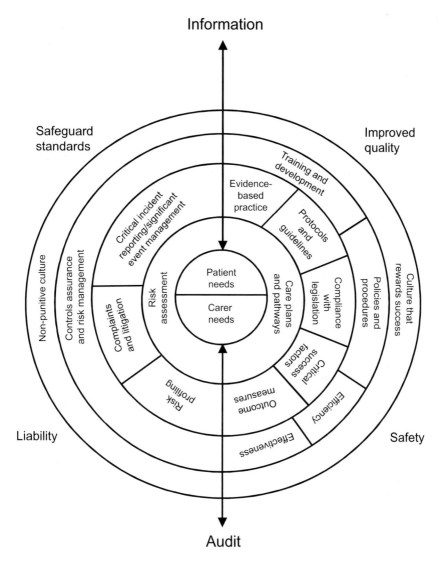

Figure 11.1 Patient-related systems and processes that enable clinical governance.

cultural changes necessary for clinical governance (Figs 11.1 and 11.2). This strategic framework also has to encompass a wide diversity of services. In the UK a considerable proportion of mental health and learning disability services were part of large community NHS trusts and are now part of primary care trusts or specialist mental health and/or learning disability trusts. It is inevitable that the configuration of the trust will influence its organisational structure and purpose, and thus

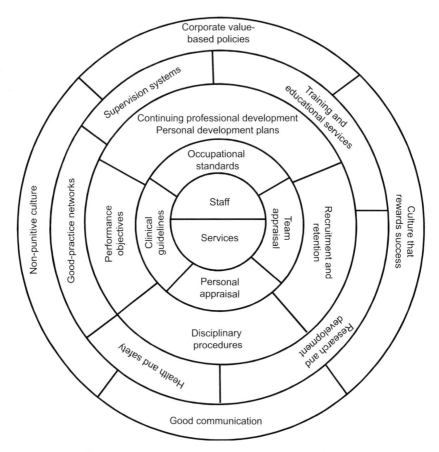

Figure 11.2 Staff-related systems and processes that enable clinical governance.

its culture. Other factors that influence cultures include the local history of service development, geographical factors, demography, the personalities of key individuals, the resources available and the interfaces with related services and organisations. The degree of diversity is such that managerial approaches that are effective in one setting can rarely be transferred directly to another. Therefore it is more appropriate to think in terms of the principles, the systems that underpin these and the policy framework in which they sit.

In the same way that at a national policy level, the clinical governance system has evolved with identification of the key players, organisations, roles and responsibilities, so too this has to be translated at a local level. At present the framework is fairly fluid, allowing for evolution through a process of experimentation and learning. It has yet to be seen to what extent it will become more prescriptive and centrally determined, as it is also clear that the present government is concerned about the great variation in access, standards and practice in healthcare and the consequent lack of equity for service users. This particularly applies to mental health and learning disability services (Department of Health, 1999a,b, 2001). The current approach to this in England and Wales is based on centrally determined standards (including those set by the National Institute for Clinical Excellence) and monitoring (through the Commission for Healthcare Audit and Inspection), while responsibility for planning and securing provision is transferred to primary care trusts (Department of Health, 2002).

Key principles

Proactivity

In the past, policies and procedures within the NHS have tended to evolve in reaction to local circumstances, with occasional prompts from government initiatives and legislation. This reactive response has been encouraged by recent high-profile cases of professional and system failure. However, the reactions to such cases are often excessive and the intense focus on one area of practice can often lead to other areas being neglected. Nowadays there is greater emphasis on the 'prevention is better than cure' approach and there is a strong drive to be more proactive at each level of an organisation, from the overall cultural and strategic framework to the detailed procedures and competencies required for a clinical intervention. Therefore corporate policies have been and are being developed that are more strategic and provide direction, and that set the scene for more detailed policies, guidelines, protocols and procedures. Examples include corporate strategies for service user involvement, communications, clinical governance, risk management, research and development, and training and education.

Person-centred services

Two of the most important cultural changes that appear to be taking place in the NHS as a whole, driven by both government policy and social pressures, are the development of a strong user and carer orientation and a culture that supports the staff. These two are interlinked and require the development of 'can do' attitudes, willingness to learn, openness in communication and a strong ethos of mutual respect between staff and with patients and carers. Staff should be expected to 'sign up' to them through staff and patient charters, which provide clear expectations and standards.

The 'no blame' culture that supports staff is, of course, in conflict both with the adversarial legal system when it comes to litigation and with the media pressures to scapegoat individuals as much as possible. In order to counteract these pressures, some trusts have developed explicit 'no blame' policies through which the board pledges to support those staff who are prepared to learn from their mistakes.

Using the evidence base

Another major change is the strong drive towards evidence-based and reflective practice. The importance of this to the organisation is signalled within the research and development, and training and education strategies.

Systemic approach

There is also a tendency to reduce the compartmentalisation of services and to think in terms of the whole system of care that surrounds the patient. This approach is seen in the development of 'care pathways', which are based on the actual patient experience and which cross professional and departmental boundaries in the exchange of information and in the way that interventions are orchestrated. However, the effective implementation of care pathways will depend on the wider systems that underpin the delivery of services. There has been a shift from the control of people to the control of the systems within which they work. Here, the development of policies and procedures plays a key role. There are also tensions and conflicts that have to be recognised and addressed. The system must remain fluid enough to allow for continuous improvement but rigid enough to give clear direction, stability and accountability to the workforce. Excessive bureaucracy should be avoided while measuring and monitoring become more important. Staff should have a 'mindset' of particular attitudes and behaviours but should also be prepared to question and challenge the status quo. The equilibrium between these opposing forces will be continuously changing and the aim should be to develop the systems in such a way that a degree of homoeostasis will be achieved. For example, there should be a policy of regular review of policies and procedures so that these can be challenged, updated and changed. There should also be audits of their effectiveness.

While there will be policies and procedures that clearly relate to clinical governance, these cannot be divorced from those that relate to other aspects of organisational health and well-being. There is a great deal of mutual interdependence. For example, an organisation with poor financial and resource management is likely to struggle with the delivery of the clinical governance development plan. An organisation that does not have a business plan is much more likely to be 'muddling its way through'.

Good organisational practice

In light of the above, the starting point for the development and coordination of policies and procedures must be the organisation as a whole. It is important to consider whether the organisation has, or needs to have:

- a statement of mission, purpose or values
- a business plan
- a staff charter and a strategy for involving and empowering staff (such as Investors in People)
- a service user and carer charter, and a strategy for user and carer involvement
- a communication charter and strategy
- a clinical governance strategy
- a risk management strategy
- a training and education strategy
- an information strategy
- a research and development strategy
- a health and safety policy
- a 'no blame' policy
- a whistle-blowing policy
- a strategy for the development and review of policies and procedures.

This list is not comprehensive and each organisation needs to decide what it requires through a combined process of scanning external factors and self-examination. It is necessary to identify the areas in which policies and procedures are needed. This is important because many NHS trusts have policies that evolve in a piecemeal way, are never reviewed and become irrelevant or out of date, while other important areas are ignored. It is also important to be able to map the interfaces between the many areas of policy development. Some of these, such as those relating to staff involvement and empowerment, will underpin many other policies, such those for 'no blame', anti-harassment, zero tolerance of violence to staff, appraisal, supervision, reflective practice, mentoring, disciplinary procedures, public interest disclosure, recruitment and retention and so on. Professional development – through appraisal, personal development planning, peer review and continuing education – is essential if the organisation is to establish policies and procedures that are relevant, up to date and incorporated into practice. Professional organisations produce standards for behaviour, such as *Good Psychiatric Practice* published by the Royal College of Psychiatrists (2001) and the *Code of Professional Conduct* published by the Nursing and Midwifery Council (2002).

The strategy for service users should relate to other policies, such as those for confidentiality, consent and information sharing. The clinical governance strategy should be clear about the links with risk management, complaints, health and safety, critical incidents, communication, users and carers, and so on.

Table 11.1 summarises what is good practice and what is bad practice for organisations in relation to policies and procedures.

Strategic corporate policies

The corporate policies that have a more strategic role should be written in such a way that they reflect and are congruent with the underlying principles, values and purpose of the NHS as a whole, and with those of the organisations responsible for service delivery at a local level. Local strategies for mental health and learning disability services should have been based on clear criteria and be linked with plans for implementation, quality assurance and service agreements.

These policies should provide direction and standards for individuals and teams within the workforce. The emphasis should be on what is to be achieved and why this is necessary. The details of 'how' and 'when' should form the subsequent implementation plan, protocols or procedures, and at the strategic level it will be necessary to identify the organisational systems needed or responsible for the implementation.

Consultation with stakeholders is needed in the development of strategic policies. Even those policies that are 'givens' (because they are governmental or legislative imperatives) can be developed through consultation with stakeholders, at least in the process of determining the way in which they are to be implemented. For example, the National Service Framework for Mental Health (Department of Health, 1999a) provides clear standards and expectations of services but is not prescriptive about the approach to local implementation. The processes for consultation with users, carers, referrers, commissioners and front-line staff should be well planned and coordinated in a manner appropriate to the task in hand. Often short-life groups with specific purposes are more focused and therefore more effective than standing committees. These may be referred to as working groups, project teams, taskforces or whatever is the latest fashion in terminology. Such groups may employ techniques such as surveys or focus groups to obtain as broad a view as possible and the process of such policy development should be iterative, that is, with ongoing opportunities for further development.

In the development of strategic policy it is important to draw on information from outside the organisation, including that available from research, from other NHS trusts and from specialist sources of advice, such as the Royal College of Psychiatrists, the King's Fund, the Sainsbury Centre for Mental Health and the Institute for Applied Health

Table 11.1 Good and bad organisational practice in relation to policies and procedures

Good practice	Bad practice
Checking that the necessary policies and strategies are available and appropriate in style and content	The existence of many policies that are never referred to because they are irrelevant and/or the absence of those that are needed
Ensuring that policies relate to the organisational culture and purpose	Developing policies in isolation, without reference to the context in which they apply
Clarity about why they are necessary and what it is important to achieve	A lot of woolly rhetoric
Being clear about the relationships between policies that apply to similar areas of work	Policies in existence that contradict each other
Identifying and involving the stakeholders at the outset, including users, carers and clinicians	People in powerful positions unilaterally dictating the way that clinical staff operate
Ensuring that the person leading the process has the necessary leadership and facilitative skills	Asking people to take the lead just because they are clinical experts
Being open and encouraging information sharing within the organisation and with other organisations	Reinventing the wheel or being secretive and competitive about a project
Encouraging testing and challenging in order to learn from others and from experience	Assuming that you know best
Ensuring that there is someone in the team who can write up the work coherently and succinctly	Producing a policy that is verbose and confusing
Recognising that policies and procedures will never be perfect but always ready for adjustment and improvement	Being defensive or introducing delay while in search of the perfect policy
Providing skills, support and supervision for project teams	Expecting staff to be able to generate good policies and procedures without any training or experience
Introducing and maintain systems for reviewing and updating policies and procedures	Accumulating policies and procedures that are redundant or out of date

and Social Policy. Priority should be given to monitoring and auditing services and systems in order to evaluate and learn from current practice.

Any policy should be able to be readily translated into understandable and practicable behaviours and outcomes.

Finally, it is important to recognise the management skills required for the implementation of the strategy. These may include project management, training, facilitation, negotiation, communication and report writing. Appropriate support and supervision are required from senior management.

Reasons for developing policies and procedures

Policies and procedures are important because they provide information about what can be expected of the organisation and its staff. Staff function best when they are clear about their role and the way in which they are expected to perform. Standards need to be clearly understood.

The need for a policy may be triggered in many ways. These include:

- a change in the law – British or European
- directives or guidance from the NHS Executive
- guidelines issued by the National Institute for Clinical Excellence
- recommendations of professional or academic organisations
- decisions made by the board of the NHS trust
- partnership working arrangements with other organisations
- new areas of service development
- changes to buildings or equipment
- needs for systems management (e.g. inconsistencies discovered)
- adverse or critical incidents
- complaints, disciplinary action or litigation
- areas identified through the risk management process (risk audit)
- new areas of clinical practice
- new research evidence
- need for service user information
- feedback and suggestions from service users or carers.

More general strategic policies will inevitably lead to the development of more specific policies, protocols and procedures. These will include operational policies and clinical policies. Each service will need an operational policy and in addition there may be specific protocols for dealing with referrals, admissions, discharges and so on. For example, the assertive outreach teams, established as a result of the National Service Framework for Mental Health, each need operational policies that either include the referral policy or relate to a separate referral policy or procedure. Clinical policies are often in the form of good practice guidelines, such as those for physical restraint, person-centred planning, the care programme approach (CPA), administration of medication or health records; there are many others that involve the adoption of professional standards or national guidance.

On occasion it will be the imposition of external guidelines that leads to the development of procedures. For example, recent guidelines from the National Institute for Clinical Excellence should lead to the development of local shared care and prescribing policies and protocols for methylphenidate and for the anti-dementia drugs.

Competent and well-motivated staff working within clinical governance initiatives will also identify areas of their work that can be improved by the development of protocols and procedures. The development of care pathways and individual care plans are examples. The priorities will depend on feedback from staff and from service users. Such feedback may come from critical incidents, complaints, suggestions, patient diaries, clinical audit and performance management. Professional bodies such as the General Medical Council, the Royal College of Psychiatrists, the Royal College of Nursing and the British Psychological Society also set standards for professional behaviour and competence that can lead to the development or adoption of protocols and procedures in particular areas of work. These will provide many of the standards against which services can be delivered and monitored.

As the clinical evidence base develops from the information derived from research and clinical trials, tighter and more specific protocols and procedures for assessment, investigation, treatment and care will be developed. In many areas of psychiatry there is already sufficient evidence on the use and the potential side-effects and benefits of medication to enable clear guidelines and protocols to be developed. For example, the National Institute for Clinical Excellence has provided guidance on the use of methylphenidate for attention-deficit hyperactivity disorder in childhood (National Institute for Clinical Excellence, 2000) and, more recently, on core interventions in the treatment and management of anorexia nervosa, bulimia nervosa and related eating disorders (National Institute for Clinical Excellence, 2004). Where there is not an evidence base for good practice, then accepted best practice has to be identified.

Development, ratification, dissemination and reviewing

A major challenge facing the management of organisations is the establishment of systems that ensure that staff are aware of, and familiar with, those policies and procedures that apply to their practice. Unless this is achieved there is no point in having them. Therefore it is essential to ensure that all policies and procedures are:

- up to date
- sent to and received by all who need them
- read and understood by all who need them
- linked to an implementation plan, which may include training needs
- acted upon
- reviewed and revised periodically.

It is advisable for each NHS trust to have a specific procedure and guidelines for staff on good practice in creating, writing, implementing and monitoring policies and procedures. The board should approve this procedure. Such a procedure should include the following eight steps.

Step 1. Is a policy needed?

First, it is necessary to involve the key stakeholders to establish that there is a need for a policy in this area. A process of consultation should take place. If the policy has implications for terms and conditions of service, it is important to consult with the human resources department. It is important to consider this in the context of the wider trust culture and strategies (see above).

Step 2. Does one already exist?

There should be a central register of policies through which it is possible to check those that are currently available in order to find out whether there is a similar or related policy and to be aware of potential areas of overlap. If so, ensure that existing policies comply with the latest legislation, national guidelines, clinical evidence or best practice by carrying out a literature search. If there is an existing policy, it may be possible to adapt and update it to cover a wider area. This needs to be done through cross-service or cross-specialty consultation.

Step 3. Register an intention to develop a policy

Each trust should have a policy coordinator who administers the central register of policies. The policy coordinator should enter the basic information (name of policy) on to a database so that others can be made aware that such a policy is being developed. At this stage it is usual to give the policy a unique reference code, which should appear on all drafts that are developed. The time scale for completion should also be agreed.

Step 4. Draft policy produced in consultation with key stakeholders

The trust should have a standard format for policies. The headings should include:

- title (policy name)
- developed by (originator – post title or group)
- document status (corporate, clinical, local, etc.)
- document stage (draft or consultation – this heading ceases to exist once the policy has been ratified)
- ratified (date, title of executive director ratifying it)
- date to be reviewed

- purpose
- responsibility (who it applies to and who needs to act on it)
- definition (whether it is a policy, guideline, protocol, standard or procedure – see Introduction).

This should be followed on the next page by the text of the document. The content will depend on the purpose, but there should be headings and numbered paragraphs for ease of reference. When planning a more complex policy, a 'spider diagram' can be used on a flip chart, with each of the main areas to be covered written within separate circles around the page. The main points to be made in relation to each are attached to lines coming out from each circle (hence the page will be covered by several 'spiders'). The person drafting the policy will then organise these into headings and subheadings or numbered paragraphs. However, the design of procedures and protocols may require a different approach, with the use of a flow diagram to track the sequence of events that need to be covered.

When working on a draft it is important to date it, to include the unique document reference number given by the policy coordinator, and to include the word 'draft' as a watermark. Once it has reached the formal consultation stage it should be watermarked with the words 'Consultation draft'. Marking it in this way prevents the implementation of unratified policies.

Because of the expectation that all NHS practice is underpinned by evidence-based policies, the document should be referenced to show supporting evidence. Personnel policies should refer to relevant legislation, whereas clinical policies may refer to research evidence or literature reviews. It should also be cross-referenced to other relevant policies.

It is essential that policies are written in plain language, without jargon or abbreviations.

Step 5. The consultation process

The policy should then be distributed for wider formal consultation and a record of all consultations should be kept. The consultation route and rationale for all amendments must be recorded to ensure that the policy is both robust and credible. A document trailing process can be used. It may be necessary to include an appropriate specialist group and the consultation process should be agreed with the policy coordinator.

Step 6. Ratification

An executive director should ratify the policy once he or she is satisfied that full consultation has taken place and that the policy is necessary and appropriate. Policies that have far-reaching implications, that challenge existing values or that could be controversial may need to be approved by the board.

Step 7. Distribution

The policy coordinator will distribute the policies, enter them on the central database and make them available through the intranet (in read-only format). The master is held in a central policy library and managers will keep their local policy libraries up to date and hold a list of places in which manual copies are required.

Step 8. The review process

Policy reviews should take place annually unless there is a need for them to be more frequent. The policy author will be responsible for this but will be prompted by the policy coordinator.

Policy and procedure awareness

In addition to this administrative process there need to be rigorous systems for staff induction and training to ensure that all the necessary information relating to policies and procedures is available and fully understood. If this information is to be remembered and used, it may well be necessary also to have regular training and checks of staff awareness through supervision sessions or refresher courses. Questionnaires or supervised practice can be used to show that staff have the level of knowledge and competence required. Even at consultant level, practices such as peer review, peer supervision and 360-degree appraisal have recently been introduced. Whenever there is concern that policies and procedures are not being followed, it is essential to investigate this. Audit is usually the least threatening and most effective way of doing so.

Conclusions

Policies and procedures are an integral part of a systemic approach to management and should be firmly embedded in the culture and mission of an NHS trust. They underpin clinical governance and require a rigorous and corporate approach to for their development and dissemination into day-to-day practice.

Acknowledgement

Many of the ideas and much of the information in this chapter are derived from the experience and opportunities provided by working as

Medical Director of Cornwall Healthcare NHS Trust (now Cornwall Partnership Trust) and Trecare NHS Trust. The Cornwall Healthcare Trust Clinical Governance Strategy and Policies and Procedures Guidance were particularly useful.

References

Department of Health (1999a) *National Service Framework for Mental Health*. London: Department of Health.

Department of Health (1999b) *Facing the Facts: Services for People with Learning Disabilities*. London: Department of Health.

Department of Health (2001) *Valuing People: A New Strategy for Learning Disability for the 21st Century*, cm 5086. London: TSO.

Department of Health (2002) *Shifting the Balance of Power: Next Steps*. London: Department of Health.

National Institute for Clinical Excellence (2000) *Guidance on the Use of Methylphenidate for Attention-Deficit Hyperactivity Disorder (ADHD) in Childhood*. Technology Apprasial Guidance no. 13. London: NICE.

National Institute for Clinical Excellence (2004) *Eating Disorders: Quick Reference Guide*. Clinical Guideline 9. London: NICE.

Nursing and Midwifery Council (2002) *Code of Professional Conduct*. London: NMC. Available at www.nmc-uk.org/nmc/main/publications/CodeOfProfessionalConduct.pdf

Royal College of Psychiatrists (2001) *Good Psychiatric Practice*, CR90. London: Royal College of Psychiatrists. Available at www.rcpsych.ac.uk/publications/cr/cr90.htm

CHAPTER 12

Risk management

Tim Amos and Peter Snowden

- Risk management is a key component of clinical governance
- The aim of risk management is to reduce the risk of adverse incidents
- Risk recognition, risk assessment and risk reduction or containment are the main stages
- Many government initiatives contribute to national risk management
- Trusts should have a written and agreed risk management strategy
- A systems approach is the most effective way of learning the lessons from adverse incidents. This recognises that such events occur as a result of a series of failings rather than a single one
- For individual patients, full risk assessment and management are crucial. There are several risk assessment instruments that can aid, but not replace, clinical judgement
- Training of staff in the many areas of risk management is fundamental.

Introduction

Risk is part of everyday clinical practice. Risk management plays a major role in the current emphasis on quality in the National Health Service (NHS) and is one of the cornerstones of clinical governance. Within mental health, risk assessment and management have always been essential aspects of psychiatric care, particularly with reference to harm to self or others.

Risk

Risk has been defined as 'the possibility of beneficial and harmful outcomes and the likelihood of their occurrence in a stated timescale' (University of Manchester, 1996). The harmful outcomes may be for:

- patients (e.g. increased morbidity from drug errors, increased mortality from suicide)
- carers (e.g. increased need for care, disruption to their lives, occasionally more serious outcome such as homicide)
- staff (e.g. concern about errors, by themselves or others)
- the public (e.g. hospital errors resulting in longer in-patient stays, longer waiting times for all patients)
- the hospital/health provider (e.g. extra resources required to provide corrective treatment, damage to hospital reputation)
- professions (e.g. the reputation of the health professions as a whole suffers when unwanted outcomes receive widespread publicity)
- the NHS (e.g. concern about the ability of health services to provide ongoing good-quality or even adequate care).

In order to avoid these and many other unwanted outcomes, risk needs to be minimised. However, risk is also an integral part of everyday healthcare.

'By its very nature healthcare is a risky activity. Indeed, doctors and healthcare professionals should not be discouraged from taking some risks in developing more effective methods of treatment and care for patients and clients. But it is important that such risks are taken as a result of a positive decision to do so, on the basis of good information and a sound understanding of the possible consequences and the likely outcome of treatment.' (NHS Executive, 1993)

If a service or individual clinical team does not take risks, then this in itself is a gamble, as risk cannot be assessed fully or managed if no risk is taken. For example, if an in-patient is not given leave, then, while this reduces the risk of untoward incidents outside the ward to zero during the in-patient stay, there is no experience on which to assess the risk of such incidents in the community, when the patient is discharged.

So risk needs to be contained, rather than reduced to zero. Services need to be able to tolerate risk. However, risk should be managed, usually in whatever setting it occurs and risk tolerance may be 'the level of risk which is not significant enough to be considered unreasonable' (Davies, 1999). It is important to note that risk goes beyond the individual professional and is part of the responsibilities of both local and national services.

Definitions and models

Risk management is a means of reducing the risks of adverse events occurring in organisations. It involves systematically identifying, assessing and reviewing the risk of adverse events, and then seeking ways to prevent their occurrence (NHS Executive, 1999).

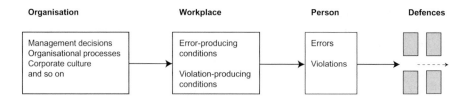

Figure 12.1 Modelling organisational accidents (after Reason, 1995).

All parts of an organisation have a role to play in risk management because adverse events occur as a result of a series of failings rather than a single one. Failings may occur as a direct result of one individual's action (*active human failures*); in addition, the culture or environment of the organisation may make active failures more likely (*latent conditions*). Organisations recognise that individuals are prone to error and to break rules or protocols, and so put into place control systems (or *defences*) that reduce the likelihood of human fallibility leading to an accident. Such defences may either be engineered (e.g. alarms) or rely on people or on procedures and administrative controls. Reason (1995) has put these components together in a single model (Fig. 12.1) which emphasises the need for risk management to be part of the ethos of an organisation at all levels.

More recently, Reason (2000) has used the 'Swiss cheese model' (slices of Swiss cheese have many holes) to explain how hazards may come into damaging contact with victims if the holes on all the defensive layers 'momentarily line up to permit a trajectory of accident opportunity'.

Risk management may therefore be seen as a framework designed to help identify the varied causes of latent conditions, inadequate or inappropriate defences and active human failure. This framework needs to permeate throughout the whole workforce, as 'the management of risk is a key responsibility of every line manager and the concern of every employee' (NHS Executive, 1993). The recent emphasis on safety in healthcare has been as much on latent conditions, which can be longlived and therefore identified and removed, as on active human failures, which are usually shortlived and less predictable (Department of Health, 2000). Thus there is an emphasis on the 'system approach', which concentrates on the conditions under which people work and tries to build defences to avert errors or mitigate their effects (Reason, 2000).

Risk management in the health service

Risk management in the health service covers various spheres. Primarily there is clinical risk management, which takes place in a clinical setting. However, there are other areas that impinge on patient care, for example financial risk management, estate management, health and safety, and infection control. Risk management is seen as the common thread linking clinical governance and wider controls assurance. Controls assurance is a holistic concept based on best governance practice and is a process designed to provide evidence that NHS organisations are doing their 'reasonable best' to manage themselves so as to meet their objectives and protect patients, staff, the public and other stakeholders against risks of all kinds (NHS Executive, 1999). It is seen as complementary to, and proceeds in tandem with, developments in clinical governance.

Clinical risk management should benefit patients, individuals caring for a patient in a personal or professional relationship, and health services in general. However, until recently, risk management was not an integral part of health services in the same way that it is in, for example, the aviation and nuclear industries.

There are two main reasons why there has been a major shift in thinking on risk management in the NHS: litigation and a new emphasis on quality. The costs of litigation have increased dramatically: in 1975 the total costs for settling all claims within the NHS was around £1 million, but at the start of the 1990s the cost of litigation was around £50 million a year. By 2000, the estimated value of outstanding claims was £2.6 billion, with an additional estimated potential liability of a further £1.3 billion for episodes that were likely to have occurred but for which claims had not yet been received (National Audit Office, 2001).

Since the early 1990s there has been an increasing emphasis on quality within the NHS. Medical, and then clinical, audit were introduced. Then concerns of variations across the NHS led to a series of government actions intended to ensure equitable access to good-quality health services throughout the UK.

'The new NHS will have quality at its heart. Without it there is unfairness. Every patient who is treated in the NHS wants to know that they can rely on receiving high quality care when they need it. Every part of the NHS, and everyone who works in it, should take responsibility for working to improve quality.' (Department of Health, 1997)

Risk management was seen as a crucial aspect of quality, with one key observer stating that 'safety should be recognised as the first dimension of quality' (Vincent, 1997).

In view of these two drivers, risk management has been defined in terms of quality and costs:

'The aim of clinical risk management is to improve the quality of care by preventing occurrences which harm, or may harm, patients, with the twin intent of both reducing the risk of such adverse events for patients and of reducing the costs of such events to healthcare providers.' (Walshe & Dineen, 1998)

Key stages of risk management

Risk management in whatever setting can be viewed in a standard manner. This is well described by a model in which risk management is a three-stage dynamic process (Fig. 12.2):

- risk identification (or recognition)
- risk assessment/analysis
- risk management/reduction.

The three stages may be common to all risk processes but they differ markedly in nature. This may be seen at two main different levels – national and local. These are examined in the next two sections.

National risk management

Reducing risk and enhancing patient safety are seen as an integral part of the NHS quality programme (Department of Health, 2001a). Elements of this programme include the setting of both national standards, such as the National Service Frameworks, and clinical standards, such as suicide prevention. The National Institute for Clinical Excellence is involved in setting these standards. The programme also includes the

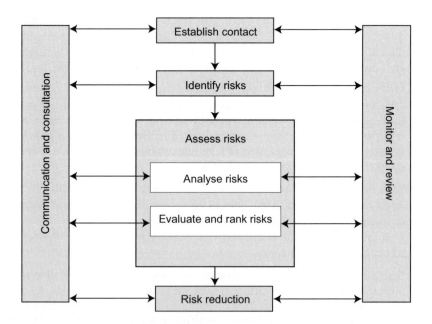

Figure 12.2 Model of risk management (from NHS Executive, 1993).

implementation and monitoring of the standards, and here the National Patient Safety Agency, the Commission for Healthcare Audit and Inspection, the Clinical Negligence Scheme for Trusts and the NHS Performance Assessment Framework have a role.

National Service Frameworks

The National Service Framework for Mental Health (Department of Health, 1999a) sets out seven national standards, one of which is the prevention of suicide by a number of means, including training staff in risk assessment. One of the themes of the Framework is an emphasis on risk reduction and the importance of risk assessment and management.

National Institute for Clinical Excellence (NICE)

The National Institute for Clinical Excellence acts as a nationwide appraisal body for new and existing treatments, and disseminates consistent advice on what works and what does not (see Chapter 6). One specific role of NICE is the overseeing the National Confidential Inquiries, which cover maternal deaths, infant deaths, perioperative deaths and deaths linked to mental illness.

National Confidential Inquiry into Suicide and Homicide by People with Mental Illness

The National Confidential Inquiry into Suicide and Homicide by People with Mental Illness was established in Manchester in 1996, having been previously based in London. Its main aims are to collect detailed clinical data on people who die by suicide or commit homicide and who have been in contact with mental health services, and to make recommendations on clinical practice and policy that will reduce the risk of suicide and homicide by people under mental healthcare.

In *Safety First*, the report based on the first 5 years of the Inquiry, there is a series of recommendations that address policy and practice in mental health (Appleby *et al*, 2001). The list below includes the most important clinical recommendations:

- staff training in the management of risk of both suicide and violence (with updating every 3 years)
- all patients with severe mental illness and a history of self-harm or violence to receive the most intensive level of care
- individual care plans to specify the action to be taken if the patient is non-compliant or fails to attend
- prompt access to services for people in crisis and for their families
- assertive outreach teams to prevent loss of contact with vulnerable and high-risk patients

- atypical antipsychotic medication to be available for all patients with severe mental illness who are non-compliant with 'typical' drugs because of their side-effects
- strategy for dual diagnosis, covering training in the management of substance misuse, joint working with substance misuse services, and staff with specific responsibility to develop the local service
- in-patient wards to remove or cover all likely ligature points, including all non-collapsible curtain rails
- follow-up within 7 days of discharge from hospital for everyone with severe mental illness or a history of self-harm in the previous 3 months
- patients with a history of self-harm in the past 3 months to receive supplies of medication covering no more than 2 weeks
- local arrangements for information-sharing with criminal justice agencies
- policy of post-incident multidisciplinary case review and information to be given to families of involved patients.

Individual homicide inquiries

The National Confidential Inquiry into Suicide and Homicide by People with Mental Illness was initially set up in 1992, partly as a response to public concern about a few well-publicised cases of homicides by individuals with mental health problems. At the same time there was also a requirement on health authorities to hold an independent inquiry whenever there was a homicide by an individual who had been in contact with mental health services. Most of these inquiries produced substantial reports, with many recommendations, which were often similar in nature and covered various areas of practice, including risk.

In her review of the lessons for risk management, Reith (1998) identified four key themes:

- *thoroughness* – this emphasised the importance of comprehensive history-taking, with attention to detail and accurate recording; and that staff should not minimise incidents, should link incidents when appropriate and 'ask the unaskable' when necessary
- *multidisciplinary teams* – teams should involve, and listen to, all members, including junior members; discrepancies between team members should be examined; 'effective teamwork is the only means whereby the range of necessary skills to address the problems can be brought together'
- *inter-agency working* – there should be proper inter-agency co-operation, with appropriately shared sources of information; all local agencies should be involved, including primary and secondary healthcare, social services, housing departments, police, probation

and voluntary sector organisations; for effective liaison, there should be regular meetings at which key individuals can get to know each other

- *listening to carers and relatives* – relatives should be given the opportunity to talk (away from the patient if necessary); a working alliance between staff and relatives needs to be encouraged; the feelings and the views of the family should be an important part of risk management; professionals need to be trained to trust the experienced judgement of close family.

Another overview of homicide inquiries emphasised the importance of good risk management:

'Inquiries into homicides by psychiatric patients suggest that, when things do go wrong, it is usually because of basic failures in procedure. If services are based on good clinical practice, most risk can be safely managed.' (Maden, 1996)

The inquiries into individual homicides have been criticised for being inefficient, financially costly, potentially unjust and of limited value (Eastman, 1996), as well as for having harmful consequences of themselves (Szmukler, 2000). This has been recognised by the Department of Health (2001a), which describes the system as 'adversarial, not lending itself to a learning environment and not meeting the needs of victims' families for support and information'.

The mandatory nature of homicide inquiries is therefore changing. The strategic health authorities now have discretion about the setting up of such inquiries, in conjunction with the primary care trusts. Lessons may not be learnt if blame is felt to be a priority by clinical staff. It is hoped that the new process and methodology will encourage a shift away from the culture of blame.

Suicide prevention

Suicide prevention is currently a major national, and international, health priority. Risk management is seen a vital part of suicide prevention.

Saving Lives: Our Healthier Nation

The White Paper *Saving Lives: Our Healthier Nation* (Department of Health, 1999b) developed out of an earlier White Paper, *The Health of the Nation* (Department of Health, 1992). Both set national targets for improvement in the nation's health in the areas of heart disease, cancer, accidents and mental health. Within mental health, targets were set relating to a reduced suicide rate. Ways of achieving this included emphasising the importance of risk recognition, assessment and management in clinical practice.

National Suicide Prevention Strategy for England

The National Suicide Prevention Strategy (Department of Health, 2002) identified six intermediate goals to support the target of reducing the death rate from suicide:

- to reduce risk in key high-risk groups
- to promote mental well-being in the wider population
- to reduce the availability and lethality of suicide methods
- to improve the reporting of suicidal behaviour in the media
- to promote research on suicide and suicide prevention
- to monitor progress towards the target for reducing suicide.

Most of the goals had related actions referring to the pivotal role of risk assessment and risk management.

National Patient Safety Agency

The National Patient Safety Agency (NPSA) was one of the main measures introduced by the government in response to *An Organisation with a Memory*, the report of an expert group on learning from adverse events in the NHS, chaired by the Chief Medical Officer (Department of Health, 2000). *Building a Safer NHS for Patients* states that the NPSA has a single core purpose of improving patient safety by reducing the risk of harm through error (Department of Health, 2001a). The NPSA is designed to achieve this by implementing and operating the 'new national system for learning from adverse events and near misses'.

The national reporting system is founded on five principles:

- the system is mandatory for individuals and organisations
- it is confidential but open and accessible
- generally a blame-free and independent approach is taken
- the system is simple to use but comprehensive in coverage and data collection
- systems learning and change at local and national levels are emphasised.

The system comprises five linked key components:

- identifying and recording reportable adverse events
- reporting by individuals to local sites and to the national system, and by institutions to the national system
- analysing incidents, including root cause analysis, and trends
- learning lessons, from analysis, research and other sources of information, and disseminating them
- implementing change at local level and national level.

Four specific areas for action were determined in order to assess what might be achieved. In mental health, the target was set as reducing to zero the number of in-patient suicides as a result of hanging from non-collapsible curtain rails (shower or bedroom rails).

Commission for Health Audit and Inspection (Healthcare Commission)

The Commission for Health Audit and Inspection (more commonly known as the Healthcare Commission) was established in April 2004, replacing the Commission for Health Improvement (CHI) (see Chapter 5). A report from the CHI summarised the key themes from its clinical governance reviews of 20 mental health trusts (Commission for Health Improvement, 2003). The main conclusions relating to risk management were that trusts, in general, had good systems for incident reporting and reviewing serious untoward incidents but that there was little evidence of feedback to staff or dissemination of learning or sharing of results or trend analysis.

Clinical negligence

The marked increase in litigation in the 1980s resulted in clinical negligence becoming the responsibility of health authorities in 1990 and then NHS trusts when they were created. As claims became larger, the Clinical Negligence Scheme for Trusts (CNST) was established in 1994 as a mutual fund that would provide cover against negligence claims, to which trusts paid premiums. The NHS Litigation Authority (NHSLA; www.nhsla.com/home.htm) was then set up as a special health authority to run the CNST. The objectives of the CNST are:

- to protect NHS trusts in England from the financial consequences of clinical negligence
- to promote good risk and claims management
- to improve the quality of patient care.

The CNST attempts to achieve these objectives by setting risk management standards (www.nhsla.com/RiskManagement/CnstStandards). The standards apply to all trusts providing hospital services and are revised annually. There are currently eight standards, which are listed in Box 12.1. Within each standard there are a number of criteria (not listed here) relating to specific policy and procedures. For example, the criteria for standard 1 include 'Patient adverse incidents and near misses are reported in 50% of all specialities' and 'The Trust applies the advice of the National Confidential Inquiries'.

For mental health and learning disability trusts, the NHSLA is currently developing and piloting new standards. These will be based on the current general standards shown in Box 12.1, with an emphasis on

---

Box 12.1 The eight CNST general clinical risk management standards (after NHS Litigation Authority, 2004)

1	Learning from experience	*The trust proactively uses internal and external information to improve clinical care*
2	Response to major clinical incidents	*There is a policy for rapid follow-up of major clinical incidents*
3	Advice and consent	*Appropriate information is provided to patients on the risks and benefits of the proposed treatment or investigation, and the alternatives available, before a signature on consent form is sought*
4	Health records	*A comprehensive system for the completion, use, storage and retrieval of health records is in place. Record-keeping standards are monitored through the clinical audit process*
5	Induction, training and competence	*There are management systems in place to ensure the competence and appropriate training of all clinical staff*
6	Implementation of clinical risk management	*A clinical risk management system is in place*
7	Clinical care	*There are clear procedures for the management of general clinical care*
8	The management of care in trusts providing mental health services	*There are clear systems for the protection of the public and service users*

---

standard 8, which is specific to mental health trusts. The current criteria for this standard are shown in Box 12.2

Trusts are judged against the criteria of the standards and achieve one of three levels for each standard. The higher the level, the greater the discount on the trust's CNST membership contributions, on the grounds that good risk management should lead to fewer claims.

Performance Assessment Framework and performance indicators

The NHS Performance Assessment Framework (Department of Health, 1999*c*) is a means of monitoring the delivery of health services against the plans for improvement. It identifies six areas, such as fair access and effective delivery, in which service quality and performance can be measured. For mental health services a seventh area of risk management

---

Box 12.2 Standard 8 of the CNST clinical risk management standards

Standard 8: The Management of Care in Trusts providing Mental Health Services
There are clear systems for the protection of the public and service users.

8.1.1 All service users are assessed for the possibility of self harm or harm to others.

8.1.2 All staff undertaking assessments of service users have received appropriate training.

8.1.3 Appropriate control measures are in place to reduce the risk of self harm or harm to others by service users.

8.1.4 There is a multidisciplinary care programme approach.

8.2.1 The Trust has a mechanism for ensuring that there is detailed provision of care and supervision of service users following their discharge from hospital.

(NHS Litigation Authority, 2004: p. 53)

---

has been identified and key performance indicators include: the assessment of risk; training to deal with risk; the availability of risk assessment tools; and the number of occupied bed-days per untoward incident.

Royal College of Psychiatrists' External Clinical Advisory Service

The Royal College of Psychiatrists provides a service for NHS trusts where there are concerns about a clinical service, a multidisciplinary team, or occasionally individual practitioners. The service provides a team appropriate to the psychiatric specialty with, if necessary, a nurse or psychologist, once the External Clinical Advisory Service has been contacted by a medical director or chief executive. There must be agreement with all those involved before a visit takes place. The objective of the visits is to analyse the situation concerning professional staff and services, and to issue a considered report with recommendations.

Risk management for local services

Risk management at the level of local services is crucial for patients. The implementation of national policies and how local services review their own serious incidents in order to 'learn the lessons' are the two major aspects that underpin a local risk management strategy and that are important for trust boards and risk management (or equivalent) committees. There are a number of other process, for example clinical audit, that play a role in a comprehensive risk management strategy.

Finally, practical risk assessment and management are vital for front-line staff.

Local implementation of national policies

Many policies and priorities have been determined by the NHS centrally and by the government, as detailed above. For individual patients, risk is likely to be reduced if there is local scrutiny of national policies, with consideration of the implications for local services and how relevant procedures might be implemented locally. On a local level, one of the main ways of achieving this is through the local implementation plan (LIP), which is the local translation of the National Service Framework and other national priorities. The local implementation team (LIT) provides leadership and is made up of primary care trusts, hospital trusts and public health representatives. The LIP is monitored by the relevant strategic health authority.

Systems also need to be put into place for local mental health services to implement national guidelines (e.g. from NICE) and lessons from both local and national inquiries and other bodies, such as the CHAI. These systems usually fall under the 'service' or 'clinical governance' umbrella. For example, some trusts' clinical governance committees use the standards from the CNST (Box 12.1) either as a reference for their own monitoring purposes or as a framework for risk management reports. Similarly, many trusts use the most recent clinical recommendations from the National Confidential Inquiry into Suicide and Homicide by People with Mental Illness (see above) as guidance for services (Appleby *et al*, 2001). Another example of a useful instrument for a specific purpose is the checklist that relates to compliance with the Code of Practice for the 1983 Mental Health Act (Roberts, 1999). Using the tool, those individuals responsible for monitoring the use of the Mental Health Act and the Code of Practice can 'examine present practice within their service and identify areas where improvements may need to be made'.

Learning the lessons: the systems approach

'Learning the lessons' is a crucial part of risk management. There are adverse events occurring all the time within medicine. One recent study found that around 11% of all patients admitted to two London acute hospitals experienced an adverse event (Vincent *et al*, 2001), mirroring similar results from other countries (Berwick & Leape, 1999). One of the main ways to improve risk assessment and management is to learn from such events.

Reason (2000) suggests that the 'basic premise in the systems approach is that humans are fallible and errors are expected, even in the best organisations' and that 'errors are seen as consequences rather than causes'. He argues that 'countermeasures are based on the assumption that we cannot change the human condition, we can change the conditions under which humans work'. *Building a Safer NHS for Patients* concurred with this view and emphasised that 'modern healthcare is a complex, at times high risk, activity where adverse events are inevitable' and that 'systems thinking is the only route to definitive risk-reduction solutions' (Department of Health, 2001*a*).

The main ways to reduce adverse events are to design safe systems and to investigate errors when they arise.

System design

Systems can be designed to help prevent errors, to make them detectable so that they can be intercepted, and to provide means of mitigation if they are not intercepted (Nolan, 2000). Nolan has suggested a number of strategies in system design to help reduce adverse events. These include the following:

- *Reducing complexity*, as complexity causes error. Simplifying a complex task can be achieved by considering: the steps in the task, the number of choices, the duration of the task, the information content and the patterns of intervening and distracting tasks.
- *Optimising information processing*, by increasing understanding, reducing reliance on memory and preserving short-term memory for the essential tasks for which it is needed.
- *Automating wisely*, by keeping the aim focused on system improvement rather than automating what is technologically feasible, by using technology, to support, not supplant the human operator, and by being aware of the implications of new technology, particularly during the initial stages of implementation.
- *Using constraints* to restrict actions that result in error, whether constraints are physical, procedural or cultural.
- *Mitigating the unwanted side-effects of change*, by using a formal process to predict possible opportunities for error, by testing changes on a small scale, and by monitoring outcomes and errors during the time of change.

Ways of investigating an incident

The emphasis on taking a system approach is central to investigating an adverse event and to putting that event in context. In considering a single incident, it is necessary to examine all the factors that influence clinical practice and not just to focus on those factors that appear to have an immediate effect. Vincent *et al* (1998) have developed a framework for all the relevant factors, so that a full analysis of the background to any individual event can be investigated (Box 12.3).

Box 12.3 Framework for analysing risk and safety in clinical medicine (Vincent *et al*, 1998)

Institutional context
- Economic and regulatory context
- National Health Service Executive
- Clinical Negligence Scheme for Trusts.

Organisational and management factors
- Organisational structure
- Financial resources and constraints
- Policy standards and goals
- Safety culture and priorities.

Work environment
- Staffing levels and skills mix
- Workload and shift patterns
- Design, availability and maintenance of equipment
- Administration and managerial support.

Team factors
- Verbal communication
- Written communication
- Supervision and seeking help
- Team structure.

Individual (staff) factors
- Knowledge and skills
- Motivation
- Physical and mental health.

Task factors
- Task design and clarity of structure
- Availability and use of protocols
- Availability and accuracy of test results.

Patient characteristics
- Condition (complexity and seriousness)
- Language and communication
- Personality and social factors.

Root cause analysis is a similar approach, which aims to provide answers to the question of why something happened by determining the underlying (root) causes of events and near misses and thus avoiding the counterproductive process of blaming an individual. The key features of a thorough root cause analysis include:

- determination of the human and other factors most directly associated with the event, *and* the processes and systems related to its occurrence
- analysis of the underlying systems and processes through a series of 'why' questions to determine where redesign might reduce risk
- identification of risk points and their potential contributions to the event
- determination of potential improvements in processes or systems that would tend to decrease the likelihood of such events in the future, or a determination, after analysis, that no such opportunities exist.

Identification of incidents

The identification of appropriate incidents to be investigated is fundamental to the whole process. Events with high-profile outcomes, such as death, will be recognised, but it is important also to examine incidents that appear to be minor but may be an indication of problems within the system. It can also be useful to investigate 'near misses', not least to prevent actual adverse incidents of a similar nature taking place in the future.

Organisations need to have policies and procedures that optimise the reporting of adverse events and near misses. McCracken (2000) has given details of the development of a local working procedure for incident reporting, which includes the following principles and practice:

- anyone can report anything, anonymously if they so wish
- report cards are designed to gather the details of any untoward incident
- the cards are posted in locked boxes and collected weekly
- the cards are confidential and are seen by only a small group of impartial people
- staff are not censored or criticised for reporting any matter
- the identity of the sender is protected when a follow-up or action is instigated
- cards are shredded after use
- cards are not used as evidence in disciplinary proceedings
- there is feedback to the staff involved.

Despite some initial concerns among the professional staff, this scheme received 30–40 reports a week, with the vast majority (80%) signed, which suggests a recognition of the value of the system and the development of a more open culture.

The process of investigation

The actual inquiry process needs to examine not only the chain of events that led to the incident and the actions of those involved but also the

---

Box 12.4 Summary of investigation of an incident (Vincent *et al*, 2000)

- Ascertain that a serious clinical incident has occurred and ensure that it is reported formally.

- Trigger the investigation procedure. Notify senior members of staff who have been trained to carry out investigations.

- Establish the circumstances as they initially appear and complete an initial summary; decide which part of the process of care requires investigation; prepare an outline chronology of events; and identify any obvious management problems.

- Structured interview of staff: establish chronology of events; revisit sequence of events and ask questions about care management problems identified at the initial stage; use framework (fig. 3) to ask supplementary questions about reasons for each care management problem*

- If new care management problems have emerged during interviews, add them to the initial list. Interview again if necessary.

- Collate interviews and assemble composite analysis under each care management problem identified.

- Compile report of events, listing causes of care management problems and recommendations to prevent recurrence.

- Submit report to senior clinicians and management according to local arrangements.

- Implement actions arising from report and monitor progress.

*Care management problems are actions or omissions by staff in the process of care.

---

conditions under which the staff were working and the organisational context in which the incident occurred. A summary of the steps of an investigation is given in Box 12.4 (Vincent *et al*, 2000).

Reports by different members of the multiscipliplinary team can give differing viewpoints and these are likely to enhance an understanding of the circumstances. However, this process must not be devisive and set one professional or professional group against another. The local service should encourage incident reporting as a means of wanting to learn rather than wanting to blame.

Incidents will vary as to their severity and frequency, and will therefore require different types of investigation. There will need to be local agreement on the categories of incidents and at what level local and external reviews take place. For example, a single case of suicide may give rise to a review of the involved team's management, while a series of suicides in a hospital may require a more in-depth and probably external review. So, in some cases the investigation will be undertaken by internal staff, and in others it may be necessary for an external review to take place. This may, for example, be by a panel of external professionals, chaired by a non-executive member of the trust board. The Royal College of Psychiatrists' External Clinical Advisory Service (see above) is another example of an external review.

Changing practice

One of the most vital aspects of learning from adverse incidents is the attempt to change practice to prevent similar adverse incidents form occurring in the future. It is therefore important that there is widespread dissemination of the recommendations of the investigation to the appropriate front-line staff, followed by discussion and then agreement on changes that should be implemented. Finally, there needs to be monitoring of the changes and their effect on practice and patients.

It is therefore important that the outcome of any investigation is considered by the apposite local authorities, for example the trust board, risk management and/or adverse incident subcommittees, as well as local health services management. There also needs to be a key individual – probably a senior clinician or risk manager – within a hospital or service to whom all reports go. The identification of such a person will ensure that incident reports are collated, as this will facilitate the identification and understanding of common organisational problems.

The trust board, usually by means of clinical governance arrangements, should have procedures to ensure that an action plan is developed so that the necessary changes to the organisation and clinical practice are made.

Feedback to all relevant staff is a crucial part of the process. Staff are more likely to report adverse clinical incidents if it is seen that doing so improves patient care and the operation of the system.

It is important that the 'local lessons are of use locally' (Amos & Shaw, 2000). One large mental health trust in Oxford has reported the experience and the benefits, particularly in terms of the changes to local services, of 6 years of a rolling programme of serious incident reviews (Rose, 2000). The Oxford clinicians found the use of external facilitators (who were senior mental health professionals from outside the local trust) of particular value. Others have described the advantages of having ethnographers, trained in qualitative observational research, to assist health professionals' own discussions about adverse events and near misses, which then provided good information for proactive error prevention (Andrews et al, 1997). More simple procedures, such as the use of feedback notes on medical devices, have also revealed the multi-factorial causes of adverse incidents and the procedures to minimise repetitions (Amoore & Ingram, 2002).

Other local processes contributing to risk management

Clinical audit

Clinical audit may be considered to be the systematic critical analysis of the quality of clinical care, including the procedures used for diagnosis and treatment, and associated use of resources, and the resultant outcome and quality of life for the patient (see Chapter 15). There is a clear and close link between risk management, clinical audit and quality systems. Clinical audit and risk management are both seen as essential stages towards improving the quality and safety of health services.

Clinical audit has a clear role in the monitoring and assessment of the changes implemented after a serious incident review. A range of possible audit topics are relevant to risk management and different services will have different priorities. Audit can scrutinise primarily clinical matters, for example suicide risk assessments on individual patients. The audit process can ensure that these have been undertaken in an appropriate way and, equally vitally, that the results of the assessments have been recorded and are available to those who may need them. Audit can also examine service issues. Examples of such audits include assessing the general hospital management of individuals presenting with self-harm against recognised standards (Royal College of Psychiatrists, 1994) and establishing how many of those individuals, who are then admitted to psychiatric in-patient care, are followed up within 1 week of discharge.

Praise, suggestions and complaints systems

These ensure that the views of users and carers are communicated to suitable individuals within the trust. They can identify areas where possible untoward events may happen before a serious incident occurs.

Whistle-blowing

Guidelines on whistle-blowing in the NHS have clarified the suitable course of action for individual clinicians should they be concerned about aspects of care within their service (Department of Health, 1999d). The appointment of a dedicated non-executive director in every trust to hear such concerns is an example of the measures undertaken in this field.

Good clinical standards

Another important factor in local risk management is to ensure that good clinical standards are maintained. 'The starting point for promoting high standards of practice is helping doctors to keep their skills up to date so that problems are prevented' (Department of Health, 2001b). Recent initiatives in this area include:

- continuing professional development (CPD) – the means by which doctors, like other healthcare professionals, ensure that their practice is up to date

- appraisal – a regular, usually annual, process that involves meeting with a senior colleague to review aspects of work performance, linking to job plans and professional development plans
- revalidation – a cornerstone of the General Medical Council's strategy in its overseeing of doctors and which will be mandatory.

Reporting poor performance

All trusts should have procedures in place for the proper reporting of poor performance where there is a concern. The National Clinical Assessment Authority (NCAA) has been established to act as a performance and assessment service to help when an individual doctor's performance falls short of what is required (Department of Health, 2001b). A doctor can be rapidly referred to the NCAA, where concern about practice will be promptly assessed and an appropriate solution devised.

Involving patients

Involving patients in risk management is important because this is the group most likely to suffer and very likely to observe adverse incidents and near misses. In the United States, the Agency for Healthcare Research and Quality has produced patient fact sheets (see www.ahcpr.gov/consumer) which emphasise the importance of patients being 'active members of their health teams' and asking questions if they have any concerns; they also give practical advice, for example taking a list of all medications to an appointment. The sheets' titles (e.g. 'Five steps to safer healthcare' and '20 tips to help prevent medical errors') indicate the role of patients in helping to manage the risks inherent in healthcare.

Practical clinical risk assessment

Within hospitals and trusts, local risk assessment strategies are often outlined for the benefit of all clinicians. Some trusts prescribe detailed risk assessment schedules, while others give brief guidelines only (North Bristol NHS Trust, 2000; South London and Maudsley NHS Trust, 2001). For front-line staff, these strategies tend to concentrate on the risk of harm to self or others.

A plethora of risk assessment scales can be used, but any tool is only an aid to the assessment process and is not sufficient in itself. Risk assessment is primarily a clinical skill and 'the decision on risk is made when all these strands [of information] come together in what is known as clinical judgement' (West Midlands Regional Health Authority, 1991). Snowden (1997) suggested that 'the assessment and management of risk is an approach' that is 'best taught in a clinical apprenticeship situation', thus emphasising the importance of training for staff who are required to make risk decisions as part of their professional work.

Many suicide prediction scales have been published in the professional literature (Rothberg & Geer-Williams, 1992). Few appear to be used widely in clinical practice, which perhaps suggests that they lack practicality. Some clinical services use the variables identified by research as a checklist for junior staff to aid with the management of individual patients. Some of the scales were actually designed to be used in this way. For example, SAD PERSONS (Patterson et al, 1983) is a 10-item checklist of demographic and clinical variables found in the literature to be associated with suicide. The scale is meant for adult psychiatric patients and is partly based on the subjective judgement of the evaluator. The authors' guidelines for proposed clinical actions based on the scores are as follows: 'send home with follow-up' (0–2); 'close follow-up: consider hospitalization' (3–4); 'strongly consider hospitalization, depending on confidence in follow-up arrangement' (5–6); and 'hospitalize or commit' (7–10).

Other scales are designed to be used to differentiate between two groups to help with prediction. Examples include: the Suicide Risk Measure (Plutchik et al, 1989), which has been found to discriminate suicide attempters from controls; the Reasons for Living Inventory (Linehan et al, 1983), which distinguished, in trials, between suicide ideators and suicide attempters; and the Suicide Intent Scale (Beck et al, 1974), which was shown to differentiate suicide completers from attempters.

There has been less interest until recently in the development by health professionals of risk assessment scales for violence. This reflects the less-clear link between violence and mental illness and the recent emphasis on the management of violence by clinicians. The main clinical instruments used in this area have been reviewed by Blumenthal & Lavender (1999) and Dolan & Doyle (2000). They include the following.

The HCR-20

The HCR-20 is a structured clinical guide designed to assess the risk of future violence (Webster et al, 1995). It is a checklist of 20 items that are considered risk factors for violent behaviour (Table 12.1). An important aspect of the HCR-20 approach is the inclusion of past, present and future considerations: static historical factors are weighted equally with present clinical and future risk management variables. Preliminary findings suggest that the HCR-20 has good inter-rater reliability and is reasonably predictive of violence.

Violence Risk Appraisal Guide (VRAG)

Following a series of studies investigating the link between a variety of factors and violent recidivism, Harris and colleagues combined samples and common factors in the construction of a statistical prediction instrument, originally named the Risk Assessment Guide (RAG) and

Table 12.1 HCR-20 (Webster *et al*, 1995)

Historical (past)	Clinical (present)	Risk management (future)
Previous violence	Lack of insight	Plans lack feasibility
Young age at first violent incident	Negative attitudes	Exposure to destabilisers
Relationship instability	Active symptoms of major mental illness	Lack of personal support
Employment problems	Impulsivity	Non-compliance with remediation attempts
Substance use problems	Unresponsive to treatment	Stress
Major mental illness		
Psychopathy		
Early maladjustment		
Personality disorder		
Prior supervision failure		

Items are scored 0 (no), 1 (maybe) and 2 (yes)

later the VRAG (Rice & Harris, 1995). The VRAG is a list of 12 predictor variables, nine of which are reported to be positive and statistically significant predictors of violent recidivism. These are: separation from parents before age 16; lack of adjustment at primary school; never married; relatively young at index offence; history of property offences; failure on prior conditional release; history of alcohol misuse; diagnosis of personality disorder; and high score on the Psychopathy Checklist (PCL) (see below). The other three variables are reported to be negatively predictive: female sex; victim injury in index offence; and diagnosis of schizophrenia.

The advantage of the VRAG is that variables are weighted according to their importance in predicting violence. An individual score is placed in one of nine categories of risk, each of which is associated with a percentage chance of violent offending within 7 and 10 years. Rice & Harris (1995) recommended anchoring clinical judgement with the use of actuarial data and combining this with dynamic (i.e. changeable) variables, such as treatment progress, change in cognitive distortions associated with offending and level of supervision included in the release plans, in order to adjust the actuarial prediction. The VRAG was developed using a sample of offenders released from Canadian high-security hospitals; both this fact and its reliance on historical data are limitations to its use. Change and reduction of risk, for whatever reason, will not be reflected by the VRAG.

Psychopathy Checklist (PCL)

The PCL and the revised version (PCL-R) (Hare, 1991) serve to operationalise the construct of psychopathy. The items on the PCL-R are glibness and superficial charm, grandiose sense of self-worth, need for stimulation and proneness to boredom, pathological lying, conning and manipulative, lack of remorse or guilt, shallow affect, callous and lacking empathy, parasitic lifestyle, poor behavioural controls, promiscuous sexual behaviour, early behaviour problems, lack of realistic long-term goals, impulsivity, irresponsibility, failure to accept responsibility for own actions, many short-term marital relationships, juvenile delinquency, revocation of conditional release, and criminal versatility. The assessment is based on a semi-structured interview, with the items rated between 0 and 2 according to specific criteria. In North America, those who score over 30 are deemed to have met the criteria for psychopathy, while in the UK a score of over 25 is used.

Psychopathy is used to define an extreme personality disorder that involves ego-centred impulsive self-gratification and a callous disregard for others. There is significant overlap between psychopathy and dissocial personality disorder. It is important to note that psychopathy is not used according to the Mental Health Act 1983 definition of the term.

In some studies psychopathy has been found to be a better predictor of violence than either psychiatric diagnosis or substance misuse (unfortunately, explanation of this is beyond the scope of this chapter).

MacArthur Risk Assessment Study

The MacArthur Risk Assessment Study assessed a large sample of psychiatric patients on a wide range of variables that had previously been reported to be predictors of violence. These risk factors fall into four generic 'domains': dispositional, historical, contextual and clinical (Steadman et al, 1994) (see Table 12.2).

The study investigated the relationship between the variables in each of the domains and the criterion variable of violence in the community. The advantage of this scheme is that it incorporates both the risk assessment and management goals of the research, all domains being concerned with risk assessment. However, only contextual and clinical domains are the concern of risk management, since dispositional and historical factors are given and cannot be managed. The major findings of the study have highlighted the role of clinical factors such as substance misuse and psychopathy in the prediction of violence (Steadman et al, 1998). The investigators, from their results, have developed a risk assessment tool called the Iterative Classification Tree, which aims to catagorise individuals as high or low risk (Monahan et al, 2000).

Other scales

The Royal College of Psychiatrists (1998) has reviewed all the evidence and has produced a list of risk factors which are associated with violence (Box 12.5).

Table 12.2 MacArthur Risk Assessment Study domains and factors

Factors	Example items
Dispositional factors	
Demographic	Age, gender, race, social class
Personality	Personality style, anger, impulsiveness, psychopathy
Cognitive	IQ, neurological impairment
Historical factors	
Social factors	Family history (child-rearing, child abuse, family deviance), work history (employment, job perceptions)
Educational history	
Hospitalisation	Prior hospitalisations, treatment compliance (mental)
Crime and violence	Arrests, incarcerations, self-reported violence, violence towards self
Contextual factors	
Perceived stress	
Social support	Living arrangements, activities of daily living, perceived support, social networks
Means for violence	Guns
Clinical factors	
Axis I diagnosis	
Symptoms	Delusions, hallucinations, symptom severity, violent fantasies
Axis II diagnosis	
Functioning	
Substance abuse	Alcohol, other drugs

There are a number of other scales that may be of use in considering violence: some assess historical factors (e.g. OGRS, Static99); some assess clinical factors (e.g. Maudsley Assessment Delusional Scale); some assess personality factors (e.g. Barratt's Impulsivity Scale, Novaco Anger Scale); and some assess general aggression (e.g. Overt Aggression Scale, Buss Durkee Hostility Inventory). There are also general guidelines that aim to aid the process of assessment and management (e.g. Royal College of Psychiatrists 1996; O'Rourke *et al*, 1997).

The plethora of scales and instruments indicates the difficulty of producing a tool that is relevant and useful to the many individual professionals working in this field. A survey of forensic units in the UK showed that while every unit used some form of risk assessment tool, there was a startling lack of consensus on the most appropriate tools to employ (McGregor-Kettles *et al*, 2000). This lack of agreement

---

Box 12.5 Royal College of Psychiatrists' list of risk factors associated with violence

Demographic or personal history
- A history of violence
- Youth, male gender
- Stated threat of violence
- Association with a subculture prone to violence.

Clinical variables
- Alcohol or other substance misuse, irrespective of diagnosis
- Active symptoms of schizophrenia or mania, in particular if: delusions or hallucinations are focused on a particular person; there is a specific preoccupation with violence; there are delusions of control, particularly with a violent theme; there is agitation, excitement, overt hostility or suspiciousness
- Lack of collaboration with suggested treatments
- Antisocial, explosive or impulsive personality traits.

Situational factors
- Extent of social support
- Immediate availability of a weapon
- Relationship to potential victim.

---

indicates the importance of remembering 'that none of these measures are a substitute for a comprehensive history and clinical examination of the patient' (Pereira & Lipsedge, 2001).

Summary and conclusions

Risk management is a key component of clinical governance and, in essence, is a means of reducing the risk of adverse events. It is important to note that risk can rarely be reduced to zero and, indeed, some risk-taking in certain clinical situations will be appropriate. Risk management within the health service occurs particularly in the clinical field, but also in non-clinical areas such as finance, and health and safety. Risk management can be seen as a three-stage process: risk recognition, risk assessment and risk reduction or containment.

Risk management, at a national level, has a number of aspects. A number of national bodies (e.g. NICE and the CHAI) whose main aims are to improve the quality of the NHS bear directly on to risk management. Risk management is important in the National Service Frameworks and in the Performance Assessment Framework. Patient safety, dependent on the reduction of risk, is a major government priority, as is seen by the development of the NPSA. Risk management is also the key component of the CNST. National projects also inform risk management, for example the National Confidential Inquiries.

Implementation of risk management at a local level depends on the risk to be managed. For an individual patient, clinical decisions depend on risk management, particularly in relation to risk to the patient or risk to others. It is crucial that there is recognition of the risk in the first place and that a full assessment is carried out, which may be informed by the use of various risk tools. Once risk has been assessed, it is, of course, important for that risk to be managed for that individual patient.

For a team it is important that risk is managed within that team. For example, many mental health teams are multidisciplinary and it is necessary for each individual to provide information and skills to aid the risk assessment. The team also needs to contain anxieties about risk.

For a hospital or a trust, there need to be a number of processes linked to risk. Most trusts have a risk management strategy, which will cover a number of aspects. One of the most important of these is a process of risk assessment for the guidance of clinicians where necessary. There will also need to be policies around the reporting and collation of adverse events, so that the organisation can learn from these. Local procedures for serious incident reviews must have a system approach, to ensure that the correct lessons are learnt and that the reviews are widely disseminated, to allow changes to be implemented and monitored. Other processes, such as audit, will also be a way of assessing risk management and ensuring that appropriate changes are made when possible weaknesses are identified.

Risk management, used appropriately, will benefit the patient, the professional, the multidisciplinary team and local mental health services, as well as improving quality throughout the whole NHS.

References

Amoore, J. & Ingram, P. (2002) Learning from adverse incidents involving medical devices. *BMJ*, **325**, 272–275.

Amos, T. & Shaw J. E. (2000) Reviewing serious incidents. *Psychiatric Bulletin*, **24**, 241–242.

Andrews, L. B., Stocking C., Krizek, T., *et al* (1997) An alternative strategy for studying adverse events in medical care. *Lancet*, **349**, 309–313.

Appleby, L., Shaw, J., Sheratt, J., *et al* (2001) *Safety First. Five-Year Report of the National Confidential Inquiry into Suicide and Homicide by People with Mental Illness.* London: Department of Health.

Beck, A. T., Schuyler, D. & Herman, I. (1974) Development of suicidal intent scales. In *The Prediction of Suicide* (eds A. T. Beck, H. L. P. Resnick & D. J. Lettieri), pp. 45–56. Bowie, MD: Charles Press.

Berwick, D. M. & Leape, L. L. (1999) Reducing errors in medicine. *BMJ*, **319**, 136–137.

Blumenthal, S. & Lavender, T. (1999) *Violence and Risk*. London: Greenwich Publications.

Commission for Health Improvement (2003) *Emerging Themes from Mental Health Trust Reviews*. London: CHI. Available at www.chi.nhs.uk/eng/cgr/mental_health/index.shtml.

Davies, M. (1999) A simple approach to the management of service risk in a local mental health service. *Psychiatric Bulletin*, **23**, 649–651.

Department of Health (1992) *The Health of the Nation*. London: HMSO.

Department of Health (1997) *The New NHS: Modern, Dependable*, cm 3807. London: TSO.

Department of Health (1999*a*) *National Service Framework for Mental Health*. London: Department of Health.

Department of Health (1999*b*) *Saving Lives: Our Healthier Nation*, cm 4386. London: TSO.

Department of Health (1999*c*) *The NHS Performance Assessment Framework*. London: Department of Health.

Department of Health (1999*d*) *The Public Interest Disclosure Act 1998: Whistleblowing in the NHS*, HSC 1999/198. London: Department of Health.

Department of Health (2000) *An Organisation with a Memory. Report of an Expert Group on Learning from Adverse Events in the NHS*. London: TSO.

Department of Health (2001*a*) *Building a Safer NHS for Patients. Implementing an Organisation with a Memory*. London: Department of Health.

Department of Health (2001*b*) *Assuring the Quality of Medical Practice. Implementing Supporting Doctors, Protecting Patients*. London: Department of Health.

Department of Health (2002) *National Suicide Prevention Strategy for England*. London: Department of Health.

Dolan, M. & Doyle, M. (2000) Violence risk prediction. Clinical and actuarial measures and the role of the Psychopathy Checklist. *British Journal of Psychiatry*, **177**, 303–311.

Eastman, N. (1996) Inquiry into homicides by psychiatric patients: systematic audit should replace mandatory inquiries. *BMJ*, **313**, 1069–1071.

Hare, R. D. (1991) *Manual for the Hare Psychopathy Checklist – Revised*. Toronto: Multihealth Systems.

Linehan, M. M., Goodstein, J. L., Neilsen, S. L., *et al* (1983) Reasons for staying alive when you are thinking of killing yourself: the Reasons for Living Inventory. *Journal of Consulting and Clinical Psychology*, **51**, 276–286.

Maden, A. (1996) Risk assessment in psychiatry. *British Journal of Hospital Medicine*, **56**, 78–82.

McCracken, M. (2000) Developing risk reporting in a hospital trust. *Clinical Governance Bulletin (Risk Management)*, **1**(2), 7–8.

McGregor-Kettles, A., Robinson, D. & Moody, E. (2000) *A Review of Clinical Risk and Related Assessments Within Forensic Psychiatric Units*. Nottingham: Rampton Hospital.

Monahan, J., Steadman, H. J., Appelbaum, P. S., *et al* (2000) Developing a clinically useful actuarial tool for assessing violence risk. *British Journal of Psychiatry*, **176**, 312–320.

National Audit Office (2001) *Handling Clinical Negligence Claims in England. Report by the Comptroller and Auditor General*, HC403. London: TSO.

NHS Executive (1993) *Risk Management in the NHS*, EL(93)111. London: Department of Health.

NHS Executive (1999) *Governance in the New NHS: Controls Assurance Statements 1999/2000: Risk Management and Organisational Controls*, HSC 1999/213. London: Department of Health.

NHS Litigation Authority (2004) *CNST General Clinical Risk Management Standards*. London: NHS Litigation Authority. www.nhsla.com/NR/rdonlyres/4F4EC0A8-FE84-40CA-8966-24ACCB327C7A/0/CNSTGeneralStandardsApril2004.pdf

Nolan, T. W. (2000) System changes to improve patient safety. *British Medical Journal*, **320**, 771–773.

North Bristol NHS Trust (2000) *North Bristol NHS Trust Risk Management Strategy. Clinical Governance Policy*. Bristol: North Bristol NHS Trust.

O'Rourke, M., Hammond, S. & Davies, E. (1997) Risk assessment and risk management: the way forward. *Psychiatric Care*, **4**(3), 104–106.

Patterson, W. M., Department of Health, H. H., Bird, J., *et al* (1983) Evaluation of suicide patients: the SAD PERSONS scale. *Psychomatics*, **24**, 343–352.

Pereira, S. M. & Lipsedge, M. (2001) Risk assessment and management. In *Psychiatric Intensive Care* (eds M. D. Beer, S. M. Pereira & C. Paton), pp. 215–238. London: Greenwich Medical Media Ltd.

Plutchik, R., van Praag, H. M., Conte, H. R., *et al* (1989) Correlates of suicide and violence risk: 1. The Suicide Risk Measure. *Comprehensive Psychiatry*, **30**, 296–302.

Reason, J. (1995) Understanding adverse events: human factors. In *Clinical Risk Management* (ed. C. Vincent), pp. 31–54. London: BMJ Publishing Group.

Reason, J. (2000) Human error: models and management. *British Medical Journal*, **320**, 768–770.

Reith, M. (1998) Risk assessment and management: lessons from mental health inquiry reports. *Medicine, Science and the Law*, **38**, 89–93.

Rice, M. E. & Harris, G. T. (1995) Violent recidivism: assessing predictive validity. *Journal of Consulting and Clinical Psychology*, **63**, 737–748.

Roberts, G. (1999) *Risk Management in Practice. Complying with the Code of Practice Mental Health Act 1983. A Checklist for Action*. Glossop: GRA Ltd.

Rose, N. (2000) Six years' experience in Oxford. Review of serious incidents. *Psychiatric Bulletin*, **24**, 243–246.

Rothberg, J. M. & Geer-Wiliams, C. (1992) A comparison and review of suicide prediction scales. In *Assessment and Prediction of Suicide* (eds R. W. Maris, A. L. Berman, J. T. Maltsberger & R. I. Yufit), pp. 202–217. New York: Guilford Press.

Royal College of Psychiatrists (1994) *The General Hospital Management of Adult Deliberate Self-harm*. London: Royal College of Psychiatrists.

Royal College of Psychiatrists (1996) *Assessment and Clinical Management of Risk of Harm to Other People*. London: Royal College of Psychiatrists.

Royal College of Psychiatrists (1998) *Management of Imminent Violence: Clinical Practice Guidelines to Support Mental Health Services*. London: Royal College of Psychiatrists.

Snowden, P. (1997) Practical aspects of clinical risk assessment and management. *British Journal of Psychiatry*, **170** (suppl. 32), 32–34.

South London and Maudsley NHS Trust (2001) *Framework for Clinical Risk Assessment and Management of Harm*. London: South London and Maudsley NHS Trust.

Steadman, H. J., Monahan, J., Appelbaum, P. S., *et al* (1994) Designing a new generation of risk assessment research. In *Violence and Mental Disorder: Developments in Risk Assessment* (eds J. Monahan & H. J. Steadman), pp. 101–136. Chicago, IL: Chicago University Press.

Steadman, H. J., Mulvey, E. P., Monahan, J., *et al* (1998) Violence by people discharged from acute psychiatric inpatient facilities and by others in the same neighborhoods. *Archives of General Psychiatry*, **55**, 393–401.

Szmukler, G. (2000) Homicide inquiries. What sense do they make? *Psychiatric Bulletin*, **24**, 6–10.

University of Manchester (1996) *Learning Materials on Mental Health Risk Assessment*. Manchester: School of Psychiatry and Behavioural Sciences.

Vincent, C. (1997) Risk, safety and the dark side of quality. Improving quality in healthcare should remove the causes of harm. *BMJ*, **314**, 1775.

Vincent, C., Taylor-Adams, S. & Stanhope, N. (1998) Framework for analysing risk and safety in clinical medicine. *BMJ*, **316**, 1154–1157.

Vincent, C., Taylor-Adams, S., Chapman, E. J., *et al* (2000) How to investigate and analyse clinical incidents: Clinical Risk Unit and Association of Litigation and Risk Management Protocol. *BMJ*, **320**, 777–781.

Vincent, C., Neale, G. & Woloshynowych, M. (2001) Adverse events in British hospitals: preliminary retrospective record review. *BMJ*, **322**, 517–519.

Walshe, K. & Dineen, M. (1998) *Clinical Risk Management: Making a Difference?* London: NHS Confederation.

Webster, C. D., Eaves, D., Douglas, K., *et al* (1995) *The HCR-20: Assessing Risk of Violence to Others (Version 2)*. Burnaby, BC: Mental Health Law and Policy Unit, Simon Fraser University.

West Midlands Regional Health Authority (1991) *Report of the Panel of Inquiry Appointed to Investigate the Case of Kim Kirkham*. Birmingham: West Midlands Regional Health Authority.

CHAPTER 13

Appraisal

Sheila Mann and Cornelius Katona

- Appraisal within the National Health Service is a mixture of an assessment of the educational needs of the individual, and performance review, which assesses individual performance in relation to the needs of the organisation
- A personal development plan (PDP) reviews the job plan, sets objectives, measures performance against previous objectives, identifies areas where change is needed and includes an action plan to achieve change
- Appraisal should include clinical performance in all areas, research and teaching, as well as personal and organisational matters
- Opinions from peers and from service users and carers are important and can help in the assessment of a clinician's availability, team-working skills and communication
- Every appraiser needs training in how to appraise
- An integral part of the PDP is a programme of continuing professional development (CPD)
- The CPD process of peer-review closely parallels that of appraisal but solely focuses on the individual's needs
- Revalidation aims to identify and remedy poor performance. This will be dependent on the evidence of appraisals, participation in CPD, participation in audit, peer feedback and user/carer feedback.

Introduction

Regular appraisal is commonplace for employees in most businesses, and for university academics. For hospital doctors, as for other hospital-based employees of the National Health Service (NHS), appraisal is now a key component of clinical governance. The prime purpose of clinical governance is to improve the clinical service being delivered. The implications of appraisal for hospital doctors (including psychiatrists) are, as yet, poorly understood. Some still see appraisal as a threat to existing practice rather than as an opportunity and a support for improvement.

This chapter covers the appraisal of doctors, although similar principles underlie appraisals of other health professionals. Practical issues are covered in publications by their professional bodies and other guidance. The Chartered Society of Physiotherapy (1998) has produced a good briefing paper on performance appraisal. Others tend to recommend generic advice offered by other organisations (e.g. at www.appraisaluk. info/; www.gmc-uk.org; or www.dh.gov.uk/).

Definition and benefits of appraisal

In the wake of 'scandals' seen to result from the poor performance of a small number of individual doctors (e.g. at Bristol and Alder Hey), it is clear that the early identification and, where possible, remediation of poor performance will be perceived as a major function of appraisal.

There are two main approaches to appraisal. One concentrates on the needs of the individual, while the other concentrates on the needs of the organisation and assesses an individual's performance in the light of these. The former is adopted by theorists and the latter by the English Department of Health.

Educational theorists view appraisal as a formative, positive exchange between an informed and trained appraiser and a suitably prepared appraisee with the intention of identifying educational and developmental needs which, if met, would result in an improvement in the performance of the appraisee in terms both of knowledge base and of performance. As such, it should encourage the appraisee to aim for higher standards. In this educational context, appraisal should be appraisee-focused and confidential. The process should encourage the appraisee to discuss present or potential deficiencies in knowledge, skills or attitudes, some of which may not be readily apparent. It also provides a platform for the appraisee to identify, negotiate and plan for personal work-related aspirations.

The English Department of Health defines appraisal as: 'a positive process to give someone feedback on their performance, to chart their continuing progress and to identify development needs' (Department of Health, 1999). In this context appraisal is seen as broadly synonymous with 'performance review' – a means of measuring progress against explicit corporate (clinical governance) objectives, rather than emphasising personal objectives.

Possible trust approach to appraisal

A trust's appraisal process may well include elements of both the above approaches. Enhancing personal aspiration is likely to improve the contribution of the individual. An individual psychiatrist's personal aspirations may, however, be relatively low on a trust's clinical governance priority list. The NHS view of appraisal is likely to be a (sometimes uncomfortable) mixture of educational appraisal and performance review. In addition, there may be a tension (although possibly a creative one) between using performance reviews to identify poor performance and the efforts of the appraisee to put pressure on employers to provide better resources and meet development needs.

Personal development plans

The appraisal process needs to have an 'output'. This is the appraisee's personal development plan (PDP), which will help to direct the individual's professional development. Such a PDP has five main components:

- reviewing the appraisee's job plan
- setting objectives – these may include service objectives, multidisciplinary team priorities, those identified from user/carer feedback, and personal aspirations
- measuring performance against previous objectives
- identifying areas where objectives are not being met or where change is needed
- devising and implementing an action plan to achieve change (such changes may involve the individual, the organisation or both).

Who needs appraisal?

The short answer is, of course, 'everyone'. Lifelong learning and keeping up to date with recent developments and practice are essential not only for doctors but for everyone in the professions and, indeed, in most other occupations. Appraisal should have a major positive developmental function, as discussed above. The 'seal of approval' function of appraisal is, however, also an important one, although many find this uncomfortable. Although some people believe they can 'appraise themselves' and may really have considerable insight into their practice, a process that provides some objective validation of performance is clearly more robust.

The appraisal process is likely to be particularly valuable for staff grades and associate specialists (those in the former 'non-consultant career-grades' (NCCGs)), for whom there have been difficulties in finding a means of easily identifying problems and ensuring continuing professional development (CPD) in the past. It should be emphasised that the Royal College of Psychiatrists' CPD scheme is open to staff grades and associate specialists as well as to consultants. Medical staff in training grades now are appraised on a regular basis. For specialist registrars this is led by regional deaneries and generates a 'record of in-training assessment' (the RITA). For senior house officers (SHOs) the appraisals are currently more informal and carried out within rotational training schemes, though it is likely that SHO RITAs will soon be introduced.

What aspects of work may be covered within the appraisal process?

The starting points for an appraisal are the appraisee's job plan and its context in terms of the organisation's contracted work programme. The British Medical Association and the government have agreed that consultant appraisal should be based on the core headings in *Good Medical Practice* (General Medical Council, 2001) and should also consider the contribution made to management and delivery of local services. It is important that appraisers are trained and that both appraiser and appraisee are adequately prepared. The content proposed is to include:

- clinical performance in all areas, not just for NHS employers, to include concerns as a result of clinical complaints, adherence to and preparation of clinical guidelines, risk management and adherence to clinical governance policies, professional relation-ships and CPD
- research
- teaching
- personal and organisational matters
- other matters, for example the appraisee's general health and well-being.

A document has now been produced which may be used in a consultant's appraisal. Appraisal 'toolkits' are available for consultants in England (www.appraisals.nhs.uk) and in Scotland (www. cybermedicalcollege.com) and a useful framework for appraisal information and documentation has been described (Brown *et al*, 2003).

Professional standards

The appraisal process includes assessment of professional probity. As specified in *Good Medical Practice*, individuals will need to confirm that they have both adhered to the organisational rules on hospitality, gifts and so on, and have also not fallen foul of any disciplinary procedures, either local (which is likely to be known) or national, such as the General Medical Council's.

Adherence to protocol

Adherence to locally agreed protocols or clinical guidelines, for example the management of first-episode schizophrenia, early-onset dementia or severe behavioural disturbance in an adolescent, or specific treatments such as rapid tranquillisation, clozapine or cholinesterase inhibitors, may be a useful outcome measure. In this context it is important to remember that slavish adherence to guidelines without sufficient flexibility to allow for individual need may be a problem rather than a virtue! More generally, the appraisal process should examine whether the appraisee's clinical work is appropriately evidence-based. Other clinical aspects that form a legitimate part of the appraisal process include note-keeping and confidentiality.

Keeping up to date

The good standing of the appraisee in a recognised CPD programme (like that of the Royal College of Psychiatrists) will form the main evidence that the individual is keeping up to date. This is discussed in more detail below.

Management

All psychiatrists with managerial responsibility need to identify the nature of that component of their work within their job plan. Examination of performance measures will be an important part of the appraisal process for psychiatric as indeed for other NHS managers. Senior medical managers may indeed be 'performance managed' in terms of specified management outcomes. The effectiveness of the psychiatric managers' appraisal of other staff will in turn be a part of this appraisal.

Research

All medical staff, and indeed all professional staff in the NHS, are expected to be able to appreciate the significance or otherwise of research findings and to assess the likely validity of these. The appraisal may identify the need to update critical research skills. Where individuals actually carry out research, such research activity needs to be reviewed within the appraisal. This may involve mechanisms for obtaining ethical approval, publication and other forms of dissemination, and, if appropriate, peer-review.

Teaching

Most consultants (and many NCCGs) are involved in teaching and training. The quality of teaching offered within a trust needs to be 'quality assured' to the same extent as more directly clinical functions, and a review of the quality of an appraisee's teaching forms part of the normal appraisal process. It is worth mentioning in this context that the British Medical Association recommends that individual doctors should only be involved in *one* appraisal cycle. Thus, academics with a major teaching (and/or research) commitment may more appropriately go through a university rather than a trust appraisal process. However, for those engaged in significant clinical as well as teaching work, joint appraisal by both organisations is effective.

An appraisee's teaching commitments should be clearly indicated in the job plan, which forms the starting point of the appraisal process. The appraisal of teaching quality extends beyond identifying the number of hours of supervision, the number of lectures given and participation in local teaching activities such as case conferences and journal clubs. Feedback from recipients of the teaching may be helpful; such feedback is now routine in, for example, most MRCPsych courses. Review of the trainee's agreement with the regular appraisals carried out on SHOs and specialist registrars is also helpful. Encouraging an appraisee to update his/her teaching or supervision skill may be a useful objective within the appraisal. The Department of Health has launched an appraisal scheme with supporting documents for academic clinical consultants (www.dh.gov.uk/PolicyAndGuidance/HumanResourcesAndTraining/LearningAndPersonalDevelopment/Appraisals/fs/en).

Personal and organisational matters

These will include the appraisee's contribution to the development of services, relationships with colleagues and patients, time-keeping (both personal and in relation to service standards, such as responses to referrals and communication with others involved in patient care) and the management and supervision of staff.

Health and well-being

Although it is likely that local knowledge will be available concerning ill-health, there needs to be some method within the appraisal of recording that a doctor's fitness to practise is not impaired by health problems.

Appraisal measures and comparisons

Benchmarking and comparisons

Any appraisal measure needs to take into account the context in which the practitioner is carrying out his or her work. Both appraiser and appraised need accurate and relevant data, including the context of local resources and needs. It is impossible to judge the performance of a consultant working in a catchment area of 30 000 in a socially upward suburb against that of a consultant of similar experience and age working in a catchment area with high deprivation indices and a population of 60 000. Relevant local data may, for example, be needed on:

- bed numbers
- day patient places
- supporting medical staff
- staffing levels of nurses and other professions allied to medicine and their configuration (e.g. in community mental health teams)
- social service staffing and resources
- number of in-patient admissions
- number of day patients
- readmission rates.

In addition to the actual workload and the means of carrying out clinical practice, information will be required on critical incidents, complaints and compliments. Homicide and suicide figures, although likely to be small for any individual, are also relevant. It is useful to have comparative prescribing data for the appraised doctor and colleagues. Unfortunately, many information technology systems do not provide such data easily or indeed at all.

Reviews

Most discussions on appraisal indicate the importance of peer-review, in the form of systematic obtaining of opinions from psychiatric, other medical and multidisciplinary team colleagues and from service users and carers. Aspects of working that can best be appraised from such sources include availability (during office hours and when on call), team-working skills and communication. The interpretation of this information (particularly that from users and carers) may be problematic for psychiatrists, and appropriate methods are currently being devised and validated.

How does appraisal fit with CPD?

An integral part of the PDP is a programme of CPD aimed at continuing the individual psychiatrist's lifelong learning. Active participation in CPD is essential to enable the practitioner to keep up to date and to maintain and improve the knowledge base, skills and attitudes necessary for good (or even adequate) performance.

The Royal College of Psychiatrists has recently revised its CPD programme to make it more complementary to appraisal. Within the

College's new programme, CPD is no longer primarily a matter of 'credit counting'. Instead, it is now pre-planned in terms of the individual's CPD needs as identified in the job plan. Participants form small peer groups (usually three to six psychiatrists) who review and validate each other's CPD plans by reviewing job plans, agreeing on what CPD objectives are appropriate and realistic for each participant, and reviewing progress in meeting these objectives. This process closely parallels that of appraisal but has the crucial difference of solely focusing on the individual's needs and allowing a more objective identification of CPD needs, undistorted by potentially conflicting corporate priorities. Evidence of participation in a CPD peer group and of progress in identifying and fulfilling CPD objectives will not only allow the College to accredit an individual's good CPD standing but also inform the appraisal process. Discussion of the accredited CPD record will be an important element in the appraisal process, particularly in terms of negotiating the resources (study leave, locum fees, meeting expenses) necessary to meet the identified and agreed CPD objectives.

Appraisal and revalidation

The main purpose of revalidation is reaffirmation that the individual doctor has maintained appropriate minimum standards. The revalidation 'agenda' is, to a greater extent than that for appraisal, driven by the need to identify and remedy or root out poor performance.

The definitive framework for revalidation is still in preparation by the General Medical Council. However, it is expected that:

- it will be compulsory for all doctors who wish to continue in practice
- it will be cyclical – almost certainly every 5 years
- doctors to be revalidated will be expected to keep a 'revalidation folder' comprising evidence of appraisals, participation in CPD and in audit, peer feedback and user/carer feedback
- in order to be able to fulfil the functions of a registered medical practitioner (e.g. to prescribe prescription-only medication, to sign death certificates) doctors will require a 'licence to practise' and this will be obtained when the doctor is revalidated
- the licence to practise will be measured in terms of standards relevant to all doctors, as defined in *Good Medical Practice*, and those relevant more specifically to psychiatrists, as delineated in the Royal College of Psychiatrists' (2001) *Good Psychiatric Practice*.

It seems likely that the great majority of doctors will succeed in being revalidated and that the main evidence for such will be the information collected during annual appraisals.

Who should be involved in the appraisal process?

Appraisal consists of a meeting between two individuals, in private and in confidence. This is particularly valuable when the appraiser is a peer acquainted with the appraisee's performance. Within NHS trusts, however, appraisal has a hierarchical element. The clinical director will appraise most consultants, the medical director will appraise clinical directors, and a senior consultant nominated by the chief executive will appraise medical directors. In the past, chief executives, who are most likely not registered medical practitioners, let alone psychiatrists, have appraised some medical directors. However, the General Medical Council specifies that appraisal must be carried out by a registered medical practitioner to comply with revalidation, and this now has to be the case.

The chief executive is responsible for ensuring that appraisers are trained and able to undertake this role. This emphasises the 'performance review' rather than the 'educational appraisal' aspect of the clinical governance appraisal process – and justifies the Royal College of Psychiatrists' parallel structure of peer-review of at least the CPD element of PDPs.

Training and preparation for appraisal

Training

Appraisal is becoming an integral part of the work of the increasing number of psychiatrists taking on managerial or senior academic positions. Every appraiser needs training in how to appraise. More fundamentally, since all psychiatrists are going to be involved in the appraisal process as appraisees, there is also a need for some training in 'being appraised'. Such training may be seen as a legitimate individual CPD objective.

Positive appraisal requires considerable (bilateral) trust and the ability to agree on realistic objectives. It is necessary not only to be able to assess an appraisee's working practice, but also to do so in an encouraging and non-judgemental way. There may be long-held or entrenched beliefs and opinions that would be detrimental to the process but that can, with training, be identified and remedied. It is particularly important that the appraisal process is not contaminated by bias related to religion, ethnicity, gender or sexual orientation.

A solution-focused appraisal technique may be more constructive and may allow difficulties to be discussed with less defensiveness (Cole, 2002). Positive goals should help, such as 'take more support from peers' rather than 'try less to struggle through problems alone'. Problems should be described as unwanted behaviours rather than personality characteristics, because it is easier to envisage doing something different than being something different.

Training in the appraisal process is widely available in universities and more specifically in medical schools. Some trusts and some NHS regions have also organised training courses on appraisal.

Preparation

In addition to training, advance planning is required by the organisation, the appraiser and the appraisee.

The organisation needs to ensure that:

- protected time is available to appraiser and appraisee to plan and conduct the appraisal
- appraisees have up-to-date job plans and timetables
- the necessary information is available relating to the service as a whole and for the individual appraisee's component of it, including service objectives, guidelines and protocols, demographic data, statistical information (e.g. number of referrals, staff profiles, referral rates, etc.), population indices, and complaints, critical incidents and compliments and outcome, where applicable.

Preparation undertaken by the appraiser should include:

- arranging the date and time for appraisal well in advance
- ensuring that the appraisee has the necessary information and is aware of what the appraisal itself involves
- giving some thought to the performance of the appraisee, both within the organisation and as an individual
- considering how both aspects of performance may be improved and what resources will be necessary for this.

The appraisee similarly should ensure that all information, particularly on individual matters, is available and has been considered. In addition, the appraisee should undertake a critical self-examination to consider the following questions:

- How effective am I in my expected role?
- How do I work within a team?
- How up to date am I?
- In what areas could I improve my knowledge and performance?
- What resources do I need to achieve this?
- Where are such resources available?

Outcome of appraisal

Appraisal should improve the effectiveness and performance of the appraisee.

During the discussion, notes should be made of key points and these should be considered by both participants at the end. It is likely that there will be agreement and therefore that both will be willing to sign the appropriate documentation. If, however, there is disagreement, then a detailed record of the points of disagreement should be made and arrangements made for a meeting with the medicald director as soon as possible to consider the specific points of disagreement.

When agreement has been reached either initially or after further discussion, a clear record of what further action has been suggested should be made. This will then be considered as part of the next appraisal, to assess whether objectives have been achieved.

Conclusions

Appraisal is playing an increasingly important part in the working life of psychiatrists. The challenge is to use such appraisal (from the viewpoints of both appraiser and appraisee) as a positive instrument for developing individual skills and confidence, and for improving the standards of care within a managerial unit. There also needs to be bilateral commitment. The appraisee has to be prepared to accept constructive criticism and use it as an opportunity to change and progress. The appraiser has to recognise the appraisee's individual needs as well as those of the organisation, and to support (with resources as necessary) the CPD and other activities necessary for the appraisee to achieve agreed and realistic objectives.

References

Brown, N., Parry, E. & Oyebode, F. (2003) Appraisal for consultant medical staff. *Advances in Psychiatric Treatment*, **9**, 152–158.

Chartered Society of Physiotherapy (1998) *Performance Appraisal*. London: CSP. Available at www.csp.org.uk/workplace/publications.cfm?id=90.

Cole, M. (2002) Appraising your colleagues. *BMJ*, **324**, S156.

Department of Health (1999) *Supporting Doctors, Protecting Patients. A Consultation Paper on Preventing, Recognising and Dealing with Poor Clinical Performance of Doctors in the NHS in England*. London: Department of Health.

General Medical Council (2001) *Good Medical Practice* (3rd edn). London: GMC. Available at www.gmc-uk.org/standards/good.htm.

Royal College of Psychiatrists (2001) *Good Psychiatric Practice*, CR90. London: Royal College of Psychiatrists. Available at www.rcpsych.ac.uk/publications/cr/cr90.htm.

CHAPTER 14

Education and training

Lesley Stevens and Pearl Hettiaratchy

- Education and training are central to clinical governance
- The development needs of individual staff, clinical teams and the service as a whole must be considered
- Quality standards for the delivery and monitoring of education and training should be set and regularly reviewed
- Continuing professional development is regulated by professional bodies, and relies on a learning cycle of review, objective setting, action planning and monitoring.

Introduction

Education and training are central to clinical governance. This was emphasised in *A First Class Service: Quality in the New NHS,* which stated 'clinical governance needs to be underpinned by a culture that values lifelong learning and recognises the key part it plays in improving quality' (Department of Health, 1998). The quality standards set by the National Institute for Clinical Excellence (NICE) and the National Service Frameworks rely upon a combination of lifelong learning by health professionals (i.e. continuing professional development, CPD), professional self-regulation (i.e. revalidation) and clinical governance to ensure dependable local delivery. The standards are monitored within organisations through clinical governance procedures, and at a national level by the Commission for Healthcare Audit and Inspection, the National Performance Framework, and the National Patient and User Survey.

A cultural change in attitudes to education and training is clearly required. The National Health Service (NHS) has invested heavily in training new staff, but until recently it took little interest in maintaining or further developing their skills. As the pace of change in medicine accelerates, this neglect of trained staff has become increasingly untenable. Although a relatively 'low-tech' branch of medicine, the changes in mental health services have been rapid and dramatic. The closure of the large asylums, establishment of community mental health teams, massive reduction in bed numbers, and advances in pharmacological and psychotherapeutic treatments have presented enormous challenges to all mental health professionals. And, of course, the changes continue with the implementation of the National Service Framework for Mental Health; there is also the prospect of a new Mental Health Act.

The necessary changes in education and training are being driven by clinical governance, CPD, revalidation, and appraisal processes (on the last, see Chapter 13).

Clinical governance

Developing a strategy for training and education

Change is needed across the whole organisation in order to improve the quality of education and training. The development needs of individual staff, clinical teams and of the service as a whole must be considered. These can be identified through systems of appraisal, clinical audit, risk management processes, national guidance and other sources. A training and education strategy is required that focuses both on the needs of the local population and on the requirements of the wider modernisation agenda. The strategy should be based on a systematic 'training needs analysis', which will describe the difference between job requirements and the individual's or team's skills and knowledge.

A training needs analysis should incorporate assessment of the following:

- Organisational needs – considering present and future needs, and the skills and knowledge available in the organisation. Any training plan must take account of the trust's mental health strategy.
- Individual skill and knowledge levels – in order to provide training that is best suited to the individual and that person's own goals and ambitions.
- The requirements of the task – the local population's health and social care and appropriate clinical guidelines should be considered. A health and social care needs assessment should have been conducted by the trust or health authority, and the key guidelines so produced could include the management of depression or schizophrenia. A 'job analysis' is essential, in which direct observation, surveys and interviews should be used to identify the key elements of the job.
- Organisational factors – such as the opportunity to practise, develop and adapt new skills and knowledge on the job. Training should be linked to targets. Management support can affect the outcome of

training and the extent to which it successfully transfers to the workplace.

- Contextual considerations. These could include economic climate, imminent mergers, joint working and joint training arrangements.

Alternatively, a competencies approach could be taken to identify training needs. This is a hierarchical approach in which the trust's overall objectives are broken down into component tasks, and those tasks into their component activities. The skills, skill levels and knowledge required of staff are then identified. The specified competencies can then become training objectives.

Two current projects should provide an important resource for those developing training strategies or specific programmes. First, the Royal College of Psychiatrists' Research Unit is designing and piloting a training needs analysis method, aimed at both mental health and social care services (Royal College of Psychiatrists' Research Unit, 2003). It describes the mental health needs of the local adult population and the evidence-based interventions available to meet these needs. It also considers the number of staff needed to deliver interventions and identifies the competencies needed to implement the National Service Framework for Mental Health, the NHS Plan and clinical governance. It assesses the local mental health workforce and calculates the 'skills deficit' (which is the training need).

Second, the Sainsbury Centre for Mental Health has produced a 'framework of capabilities' required of mental health practitioners to implement the National Service Framework for Mental Health (Sainsbury Centre for Mental Health, 2001). Many of these apply well to clinical governance. The term 'capability' extends the concept of 'competence', to include the ability to apply necessary knowledge, skills and attitudes to a range of complex and changing settings. The report describes specific statements of capabilities in five areas: ethical practice, knowledge, process of care, interventions, and application.

The quality of the education and training provided needs to be considered. Links are therefore required with the key organisations and individuals commissioning and providing the education and training in order to exert some influence over the content and quality. These include:

- education and training consortia, which plan and commission education and training for non-medical professional staff
- postgraduate deaneries, which commission postgraduate medical education
- universities, which are providers of education
- professional bodies, including the Royal College of Psychiatrists and the Nursing and Midwifery Council (NMC), which set standards for postgraduate education and training, and grant training approval to trusts.

Box 14.1 Considerations in setting standards for education and training

Levels and scope of knowledge required in:
- technical/professional areas, which should be contemporary and evidence-based
- information management
- particular topic areas.

Standards of skills expected in:
- evidence retrieval and synthesis
- team working and clinical leadership
- data handling and analysis.

Attitudes expected in relation to:
- using the evidence base and guidelines
- team working and organisational support.

Behaviour expected in:
- using evidence-based practice
- communication and managing relationships with patients and colleagues.

The development of evidence-based practice (see Chapter 10) must be actively supported by the organisation. This will involve the development of an integrated library and information technology strategy. Clinical governance processes should monitor professional staff to ensure they are gaining access to the knowledge and evidence they need to improve the quality of their work.

Setting standards for education and training

Clinical governance and education and training committees should set quality standards for the delivery and monitoring of education and training, and ensure that these are regularly reviewed. Standards should consider knowledge, skills, attitudes and behaviour (see Box 14.1). Examples of education standards implemented in a mental health service are shown in Box 14.2.

Education and training to support the implementation of clinical governance

Clinical governance is unlikely to have a significant impact on improving the quality of mental health services if it is applied as a top-down process, with an elite and aloof committee of senior clinicians issuing documents that outline the standards to be implemented. In order to succeed, it has to be incorporated into the day-to-day life of the service, with all individuals, teams and professional groups working to improve quality. A bottom-up approach allows all staff to feel a sense of ownership

---

Box 14.2 Standards in education and training

- The trust has a written training and education strategy, which has been locally agreed
- A training needs assessment will be conducted to systematically identify needs across the trust
- All professional groups to satisfy regulatory bodies' requirements for continuing professional development
- All staff have training objectives that relate both to identified priorities for the service/professional group and to service development/identified issues
- Attendance at the trust induction event for all new staff within their first 6 weeks of service
- Attendance at trust-approved recruitment and selection events for all staff with staff supervisory or managerial responsibilities, both within 6 months of recruitment and on refresher courses every 2 years
- All newly appointed staff are trained in avoidance and break-away techniques within 3 months of starting employment.

---

of the process, as they address issues pertinent to their own working environment by setting standards, monitoring their performance against these standards and looking for ways of driving up quality. The role of senior managers and senior clinicians in this scenario is to provide an environment that supports and facilitates this process, and to provide an overview. All staff therefore require access to the following:

- library services
- information technology (including bibliographic databases and the internet)
- local and national training programmes to support the practice of evidence-based practice
- appraisal, which results in the development of personal development programmes (see Chapter 13)
- specific training for individuals and teams to meet local priorities for service development
- training and supervision in clinical audit
- information about clinical governance and quality improvement priorities, such as the National Service Framework
- dedicated resources
- multidisciplinary training
- protected time for education and training (e.g. study leave).

The following items are examples of skills required for the implementation of clinical governance:

- clinical skills, including clinical risk management and the ability to involve patients and carers

- the ability to appraise evidence critically
- clinical audit skills
- computer skills, including the use of a word processor, spread-sheets and accessing the internet
- staff management skills, including effective supervision and appraisal.

Continuing professional development

Continuing professional development includes a very wide range of educational experiences – didactic teaching in conferences and lectures, specific courses, workshops and seminars, and less formal events, such as case conferences, clinical audit meetings, journal clubs, research and personal study. A major challenge for clinical governance is to facilitate the move from uni-professional education to multi-professional development. Successful CPD requires support, including protected time, incentives to participate and rewards for success.

The CPD requirements of the various professions involved in mental health services vary, and so are separately described below.

Psychiatrists

Continuing professional development for psychiatrists is regulated by the Royal College of Psychiatrists. A new CPD policy was implemented in 2001. This policy aims to ensure that CPD is a proactive process that can meet the needs of individuals. CPD is guided by personal development plans, which are reviewed and monitored by peer groups, usually of three to six individuals. The intention is to ensure a learning cycle of review, objective setting, action planning to achieve objectives, and monitoring that implementation is completed (see Fig. 14.1). In this

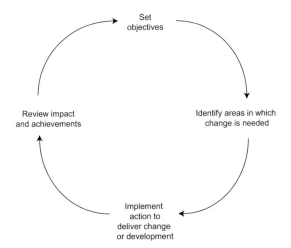

Figure 14.1 The learning cycle in continuing professional development.

process, CPD activities become an essential component of the actions required to achieve targets in a personal development plan. This results in CPD becoming forward-looking and focused on the needs, roles and activities of participants. The Royal College of Psychiatrists set minimum annual requirements for the time that should be spent on CPD activities. These are 20 hours of external CPD time, which includes didactic teaching, courses, workshops and seminars, and 30 hours of internal CPD time, which includes local educational events such as case conferences and journal clubs, supplemented by 100 hours of reading or other self-directed learning.

Nurses

Continuing professional development for nurses is regulated by the Nursing and Midwifery Council (NMC). The NMC requirements are known as post-registration education and practice (PREP), and must be fulfilled for maintenance of registration with the NMC. PREP is designed to maintain and improve standards of knowledge and competence achieved at the point of registration, in order to promote higher standards of practice. There are four key elements to PREP:

- completing a notification-of-practice form at the point of re-registration every 3 years
- a minimum of 5 days or equivalent study activity every 3 years
- maintaining a personal professional profile, which contains details of professional development
- a return-to-practice programme if practice has been less than a minimum of 750 hours or 100 working days in the 5-year period leading up to the renewal of registration.

The study activity may be a conference, seminar, distance learning, visits to other areas of practice to observe care delivery, personal research or a course. The learning cycle of review, action planning, implementation and monitoring is recommended, as for psychiatrists.

Social workers

The General Social Care Council (GSCC) offers post-qualification awards for social workers. They are the Post-Qualifying Award in Social Work (PQSW), which is assessed as the academic equivalent of the final year of an undergraduate degree, and the Advanced Award in Social Work (AASW), which is assessed at the equivalent of a master's degree. Credits towards the awards are obtained in three ways:

- development of a portfolio that provides evidence of learning from work-based activities, personal study, and in-service training
- completion of an accredited programme
- accreditation of prior learning and experience (APEL).

Occupational therapists

The College of Occupational Therapists (COT) requires all occupational therapists to take individual responsibility for maintaining professional competence, to ensure that they undertake continued learning, and to maintain a portfolio of additional education and training. The appraisal process is used to develop annual objectives for personal and professional development.

Psychologists

The qualifications of clinical psychologists are regulated by the British Psychological Society (BPS). Registration is voluntary. The guidelines offered on CPD include the following.

- Every clinical psychologist should have a minimum entitlement of 10 days per annum for CPD. This should be recorded and reviewed regularly.
- All clinical psychologists should ensure the continual supervision of their own work throughout their career.
- Clinical psychologists should pursue CPD experience appropriate to their present duties and level expertise.
- Clinical psychologists should ensure that they keep up to date with current developments and the applied scientific knowledge base of their profession.
- CPD should extend beyond purely clinical applications to include the development of skills and knowledge such as research and development, audit and evaluation, management and organisational issues.

Revalidation of doctors

The regulation of individual doctors through registration with the General Medical Council (GMC) and the regulation of the quality of care through clinical governance share the same aim – the well-being of patients. Arrangements for clinical governance and professional registration should therefore be complementary, and avoid duplication wherever possible.

The GMC has worked with the Royal Colleges and other professional bodies to develop proposals to make the Medical Register an up-to-date statement of each doctor's fitness to practise, rather than simply a record of qualifications obtained in the past. Every 5 years doctors would be required to demonstrate that they are fit to practise in their chosen field(s), in line with the seven headings of the generic guidance on *Good Medical Practice* (General Medical Council, 2001). This guidance has been elaborated in specialty-specific terms by the Royal College of Psychiatrists (2001) (see Box 14.3). This requirement must be met as economically as possible, consistent with effectiveness.

221

Box 14.3 Key topics covered by *Good Psychiatric Practice* (Royal College of Psychiatrists, 2001)

- *Core attributes –*
  - clinical competence
  - being a good communicator
  - having a basic understanding of group dynamics
  - operational management
  - effective teamwork
  - ability to be decisive
  - ability to appraise staff
  - understanding of the role and status of the vulnerable patient
  - bringing empathy, encouragement and hope to patients and carers
  - having a critical self-awareness of emotional responses to clinical situations

- *Trusting relationships* – with patients, carers and colleagues in all disciplines

- *Good clinical care* – providing the best level of clinical care commensurate with training and experience
  - Consent to treatment
  - Note-keeping and inter-agency/inter-professional communication
  - Confidentiality
  - Availability and emergency care
  - Working as a member of a team

- *Referring patients* – between services, across agencies and between disciplines

- *Clinical governance*

- *Teaching and training*

- *Research*

- *Being a good employee and employer* – awareness of the probity required of a doctor and as an employee of an organisation.

The link between annual appraisal, a central element of clinical governance, and 5-yearly revalidation is crucial. The government has emphasised that appraisal must apply to all doctors working in the NHS and that doctors should be appraised against the headings of *Good Medical Practice*. The information that doctors and the NHS will bring to appraisal will also be used for revalidation. The appraisal will allow the NHS appraiser and the doctor being appraised to consider whether the information is sufficient to allow revalidation and whether there are aspects of the doctor's practice that need attention. The 5-yearly decision by people appointed by the GMC to conduct the revalidation should, the Council has emphasised, involve no surprises for the doctor.

Clinical governance systems will make it much easier for the GMC to be confident that the information presented by doctors every 5 years is a true reflection of their practice. Information systems in the NHS, which bring together data about doctors' practice from sources such as routine indicators, logs of critical incidents, clinical audit and complaints handling, will be an essential part of this. To ensure that there are no surprises, that information must be reviewed regularly and appraisal is ideal for this. The information and appraisal systems must also be subject to the robust quality assurance that will be provided by the Commission for Healthcare Audit and Inspection, the Clinical Standards Board for Scotland and other NHS agencies. The revalidation decisions will also be a form of quality assurance, as they will draw attention to any difficulties in information gathering and appraisal, allowing revalidation arrangements to feed back into clinical governance systems, just as clinical governance provides a core support to revalidation.

Conclusions

It is clear that the provision, form and content of education and training will have to change in order to achieve full implementation of clinical governance. The training needs of individuals, professional groups, teams and the service as a whole will need to be identified in a systematic and reliable way. This will require much closer integration of management processes and systems such as clinical audit, appraisal and CPD. The education and training programmes delivered to staff must be relevant, evidence based and of high quality, and must address their identified needs. To ensure this, quality standards for education and training must be agreed locally, and implemented. Ultimately, the benefits of the improvements in education and training should be realised in terms of higher-quality patient care.

References

Department of Health (1998) *A First Class Service: Quality in the New NHS*. London: Department of Health.

General Medical Council (2001) *Good Medical Practice* (3rd edn). London: GMC. Available at www.gmc-uk.org/standards/good.htm

Royal College of Psychiatrists (2001) *Good Psychiatric Practice*, CR90. London: Royal College of Psychiatrists. Available at www.rcpsych.ac.uk/publications/cr/cr90.htm.

Royal College of Psychiatrists' Research Unit (2003) *Training Needs Analysis Pilot Project*. London: Royal College of Psychiatrists' Research Unit. Available at www.rcpsych.ac.uk/cru/complete/tna.htm

Sainsbury Centre for Mental Health (2001) *The Capable Practitioner*. London: Sainsbury Centre for Mental Health.

CHAPTER 15

Clinical audit

Robert F. Kehoe

- Doctors are still required to perform clinical audit
- Clinical audit is different from research
- Clinical audit increasingly focuses on outcomes
- The choice of key people can increase the success of audit
- Change in clinical practice is part of the audit cycle
- More involvement of service users is expected
- There is a vast amount of clinical audit experience to draw upon in the National Health Service

History of clinical audit

For many centuries clinicians have (at least on occasions!) been reflective of their practice and considered the outcome of the individual being treated. Audit meetings were an established part of clinical practice within certain medical specialties before the promotion of the more widespread practice of medical audit throughout the National Health Service (NHS) (Department of Health, 1989). At that time medical audit was defined as 'a systematic, critical analysis of the quality of medical care, including the procedures used for the diagnosis and treatment, resources and the resulting outcome and quality of life for the patient'. Over subsequent years it became recognised that audit needed to encompass the wider aspects of care and outcome, and hence clinical audit was promulgated. This was defined as a process of 'systematically looking at the procedures needed for diagnosis, care and treatment, examining how associated resources are used and investigating the effect care has on the outcome and quality of life for the patient' (Department of Health, 1997).

The development of 'clinical effectiveness' brought an emphasis on wider quality issues, aided by critical appraisal and systematic reviews of evidence (NHS Executive, 1996). More recently there has again been a widening of the quality agenda and an increase in accountability under the theme of clinical governance. Paradoxically, however, much of the drive for clinical governance arose through incidents that were seen as mainly medical in origin (for example, the Bristol inquiry) and this has brought about an increased focus on the competence and performance of medical staff. Whereas clinical audit highlighted the role of the multidisciplinary team within the delivery of health services, clinical governance has focused on the role of doctors. Clinical audit remains at the centre and is an integral part of clinical governance, as a tool to monitor and improve the effectiveness not only of direct patient care but also of processes such as risk management, clinical performance, complaints and continuing professional development. Under the umbrella of clinical governance, clinical audit has, if anything, acquired greater importance.

Psychiatrists should not need to be reminded that it is a requirement of all doctors to 'work with colleagues to monitor and maintain their awareness of the quality of care they provide'. In particular, they 'must take part in regular and systematic clinical audit' (General Medical Council, 1998). In these times of regular appraisal and revalidation, there is thus more pressure on all doctors to partake in clinical audit. The issue then becomes one of how to perform clinical audit.

What is clinical audit?

Audit is:
- a tool to assist implementation of clinical governance
- a means of checking that things are being done correctly
- an activity that involves clinicians and users of the service
- a means of ensuring that the treatments used have been shown by research to be effective.

Conversely, audit is not:
- a means of demonstrating that a type of treatment works
- an excuse to collect endless data
- an activity exclusively for the audit department
- an activity that always works.

The audit cycle

Several cycles have been suggested over the past 10–15 years, from the very simple to much more complex and involved. The audit/effectiveness cycle outlined by the National Health Service Executive (1996) is extremely simple: 'inform–change–monitor–inform'. Clinical audit would by some be considered to be the 'monitor' part of that cycle, although in practice successful audit projects tend to involve all three

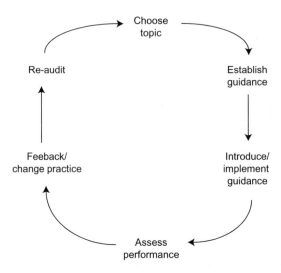

Figure 15.1 A full cyle of audit.

parts of the cycle. Figure 15.1 shows a home-grown hybrid, which hopefully emphasises that re-audit is an integral part of the cycle, which aims to ensure good practice or to improve practice and then maintain such practice.

It should be recognised that clinical audit is not simply doing a survey of practice. Clinical audit involves the whole cycle. It is often difficult to introduce better practice, but it is even more difficult to maintain it. To do this, it is often necessary to pass through the cycle several times, over a number of years.

There is an increasing focus on auditing the outcome of procedures, this sometimes being close to research. Unless clinical audit establishes that practice accords with guidelines, or that practice has improved, then it is difficult to justify the use of the practitioners' time spent on clinical audits.

Successful audits

Choice of topic to audit

The degree of simplicity or complexity of audit topics chosen will depend much on local circumstances. Some departments and organisations may be more advanced in terms of clinical audit procedures and implementation of change than others. If there is little tradition of change through clinical audit, then it would be best to choose simple topics that do not involve too many people and that are likely to achieve some

---

Box 15.1 Planning an audit

- Choose topic
- Determine objectives
- Establish team of practitioners to be involved
- Review current practice and search the literature to identify examples of good practice
- Set criteria and standards
- Assign roles and responsibilities
- Decide the methodology of the audit – for example, define the study population, and decide whether a retrospective or prospective study would be the more appropriate
- Produce a written plan, with time scales
- Collect data
- Analyse data
- Present results to team, directorate or service
- Make recommendations or produce an action plan
- Get management/managers to assist in the implementation of changes
- Re-audit
- Further refinement
- Re-audit.

---

success. Organisations that are further along the audit/governance trail may pursue more ambitious topics that may cross organisations and be more difficult in terms of judging success.

When choosing an audit topic, one should consider the following questions:

- Is it possible to envisage any change in clinical practice in that area?
- Would any changes in practice have significant resource implications?
- If there are resource implications, are such resources available?
- Is the topic of sufficient local interest and importance?
- Is the topic consistent with other local or national priorities, such as the National Service Framework for Mental Health?

Topics that are suitable for clinical audit are likely to have some of the following characteristics:

- they are measurable
- they are locally important
- they are of national interest
- there are clear, evidence-based guidelines in place
- the associated procedures or treatments are expensive
- they involve common conditions or situations

- they relate to rare but significant procedures or conditions
- there are high risks involved
- they are in areas where omissions or mistakes can lead to litigation.

Who should be involved?

Before a clinical audit project is embarked upon, thought should be given as to whose practice may have to change as a result of the findings of the audit. This may not be entirely clear at the outset, but it is often possible to identify those individuals or groups of healthcare staff who may have make changes in their practice. It is often wise to involve a 'diagonal slice' of such staff in the project. An example of this would be the involvement of a specialist registrar in psychiatry, a ward manager, a staff nurse and a nursing auxiliary or healthcare assistant from an in-patient ward in a clinical area in which violent incidents are being audited. In such an audit it would also be valuable to have some input from mental health service users or a patient advocate. By employing such a spread of staff it would then be easier to make any necessary changes in an effort, in this example, to reduce the number of violent incidents.

Some projects may be performed by a single member of staff; indeed, there is a tradition within medical circles of such audits being carried out by junior doctors. The difficulty here is that their recommendations are often forgotten as they move to another department or specialty, as their recommendations are not 'owned' by those working in the clinical area that they audited. There are few processes that involve only one clinician within mental health.

Audit methodology

Setting and agreeing standards

Ideally, standards of care should be based upon evidence that, by delivering that aspect of healthcare in that particular manner, patient outcomes are improved. Although psychiatry has its fair share of evidence-based treatment (Geddes *et al*, 1996; Summers & Kehoe, 1996*a*), there are few evidence-based guidelines. Other guidance may be nationally accepted, although only partly evidence-based. Examples would be guidance from the National Institute for Clinical Excellence (NICE) on attention-deficit hyperactivity disorder, and that from the Royal College of Psychiatrists on the management of imminent violence. It is entirely legitimate to adopt and implement such guidance locally. In other clinical areas, local services have developed their own guidelines. Examples include collaborative guidelines between primary and secondary care for the treatment of anxiety and depressive disorders. It does appear that many such guidelines have been drawn up in different localities, with little learning from the other localities, partly through a lack of national coordination of clinical audit findings and guideline development. There has therefore been much replication with respect to audit and guideline development.

There may also be areas where no clinical guidelines exist and no standards have been produced. In such circumstances, standards can be set by local agreement. Such standards should specify the parameters of the procedure structure or outcome, and should be measurable and be realistic.

Gathering data

Useful sources of data include:
- routine practice data (e.g. number of admissions, diagnoses, cases)
- external data (e.g. coroners' information on suicides)
- case records (e.g. clinical decisions)
- activity analysis (e.g. out-patient attendance over several years)
- prospective recording of specific data (e.g. instances of rapid tranquillisation on in-patient wards, compliance with Mental Health Act Code of Practice guidance)
- surveys (e.g. patient satisfaction questionnaires).

Some types of data can be collected more easily than others. Audit projects often reveal the poor quality of data, or indeed a lack of data. It is often necessary to improve data input before meaningful conclusions can be drawn.

At the outset of an audit project it will be necessary to identify who is going to collect the data, from where, and how. Somebody will need to analyse the data and this may require statistical expertise. Data collection and analysis are made easier by the use of score sheets with boxes that can be read by an optimal mark reader – the local audit department will most likely be familiar with this method. Then there is the important question of how the findings are to be reported. This could take many forms, including an oral presentation at an audit meeting, a brief written report, or individualised feedback on performance.

Confidentiality

Confidentiality of clinical audit data is a complex issue. The findings of audit projects should usually be made widely available. Individual practitioners should be anonymised, but individuals should be informed of their identity in terms of the findings. The General Medical Council (2000) suggests the patient's consent to disclosure of information for audit must be obtained unless the data have been effectively anonymised. Most authorities would suggest that approval by the local research or ethics committee should be sought for clinical audits where there is any direct patient contact. The Data Protection Act 1998 may be relevant in clinical audit projects. Further information and advice on confidentiality issues in relation to audit should be available within NHS organisations from their 'Caldicott guardian', a local clinician appointed to oversee issues relating to information on patients (Department of Health, 1999).

Types of audit

Different types of audit include:

- self-review (e.g. how often do I provide supervision for my senior house officer, what can I do about it, how can I improve it?)
- external review (e.g. Royal College of Psychiatrists' inspecting team for a training scheme, Mental Health Act Commission reviews of hospitals with regard to standards of care for detained patients)
- sentinel event audit (e.g. reviewing procedures for dealing with the aftermath of in-patient suicide)
- peer-review, in which one group of professionals audits another within the same organisation or across different organisations (e.g. staff from one ward use explicit criteria to review quality and activity in a different psychiatric ward).

Changing practice

What is done with the audit report?

It is essential that audit reports are not produced and then put into the back drawer (or worse!). Mental health organisations need to have an established mechanism by which audit findings can be fed into clinical practice. This may be via a management group or equivalent. Changes in practice may require a number of people within a clinical area to make changes and the management group (or equivalent) should enable this to occur, or at least assist.

Specific interventions to implement audit findings

Specific interventions could include:
- dissemination of educational materials
- educational outreach
- local opinion leaders
- feedback
- reminders
- computer prompts for patient education and treatment.

It is recognised that change is at the core of clinical audit (Malby, 1995). Different methods of facilitating changes in clinical practice have been reviewed (NHS Centre for Reviews and Dissemination, 1999) and the main conclusion is that a variety of interventions can lead to change. Experience suggests that often more than one intervention is necessary to change any single aspect of clinical practice, usually because different professions are involved and different people respond to different types of encouragement. This is particularly the case in the field of mental health.

Culture

Some clinical services or organisations have a culture of learning and change, whereas others do not. Culture cannot be changed overnight but cultural change is a likely (and perhaps necessary) by-product of clinical governance. Clinical audit, where successful, can assist in such cultural change. This is helped by an emphasis on training, open views on audit findings and positive service development closely related to clinical audit projects.

An example of a successful clinical audit: post-suicide review

Following various national and local concerns, a protocol was introduced at Airedale NHS Trust Mental Health Unit to guide practitioners in steps to be taken in the aftermath of suicide, either on an in-patient or out-patient basis. Standards were set following a literature review in 1996. The guidance was discussed with consultant medical staff, community mental health leaders, in-patient ward nursing staff and mental health managers. It was drawn up by a topic group that consisted of a consultant psychiatrist, a community mental health team leader and a ward manager. It was presented at various forums, such as the clinical audit group, consultant meetings and team meetings. The guidance was widely distributed and a copy of it placed in appropriate clinical areas, with protocol books and protocol folders that contained policies or other guidance literature.

An audit of compliance with the guidelines was completed 2 years later. It showed that correct procedures had largely been adhered to and that each suicide had been followed by a meeting within the next couple of months of the appropriate staff involved with that patient. This assisted in reducing the blame culture and ensured that the general practitioners and relatives received timely contact and support in the aftermath of suicides. A re-audit was then undertaken.

This 'sentinel event' audit and the associated guidance were relatively simple to implement but did require much discussion about the procedures to be followed, and junior doctors and consultants needed to be reminded of the existence of the guidance. Such guidance is helpful to turn to in the aftermath of suicide, when at times it is difficult to think calmly.

Involving users in clinical audit

There is an increasing emphasis on involving users in service planning and clinical effectiveness procedures. Various models have been described about how user or lay participation in audit and guideline development can be achieved (Summers & Kehoe, 1996b; van Wersch & Eccles, 2001). Much will depend on local organisation, but most services should be able to encourage some users or their representatives to participate in an audit programme. This could be at the review stage for a particular topic, although confidentiality issues can often be problematic. Participation may also be at a committee level, or attendance at regular monthly audit meetings. Services will have to ensure that those representing users are offered training in clinical audit and consideration should be given to their payment. Representatives may come from advocacy groups, representatives of local voluntary groups, MIND, the Manic Depressive Fellowship, Rethink, community health councils and so on. Active service users may be engaged in this manner or through local patient councils. My own experience over 6 years at Airedale is that user involvement in clinical audit has brought only advantages and positive challenges, and has in no way impeded progress.

Structures, committees and audit reports

No single model of organisational grouping has been shown to be more effective in clinical audit. With the advent of clinical governance, the chief executive of each trust is charged with ensuring clinical quality as well as financial effectiveness, and thus, through various routes, clinical audit activity should feed through to the trust board. Many organisations now have a clinical governance committee that oversees the development of clinical governance and monitors activity by other groups or activities such as risk management, clinical effectiveness, audit, continuing professional development, research and development, and complaints.

Whether performing national or local clinical audit projects, it is often valuable to have an identified lead for that topic together with a small team of appropriately qualified staff and perhaps users. This team would follow the outlined plan and would feed back to a larger clinical audit group, which could criticise and support that ongoing project in terms of its methodology and findings. Recommendations could be made through the larger clinical audit group and most likely a local management group.

Implementation of recommendations or guidelines is in many cases the most difficult step. It may well be necessary to have a 'product champion' involved in encouraging others to make appropriate changes in clinical practice to enable improvements to be made. Improvements in the service or patient outcomes, together with evidence of good practice, is the information that should be presented to the trust-wide clinical audit group or directly to the trust's clinical governance group.

There is a temptation for the whole exercise of clinical governance to involve many monitoring exercises and to produce reports full of numbers, from which it is difficult to identify any real service development or improvements in patient outcome. A briefer report can more easily demonstrate the benefits of clinical audit activity.

Whichever approach is taken, it is helpful for the audit or governance group to have a written annual plan listing, in priority order, audit topics with target dates and the personnel involved. These plans should have a space in which to record 'improvements made' or 'standard reached' so as to emphasise the required end-results and in turn make it easy to summarise them.

Clinical audit – a good or a bad thing?

Problems with audit

It may be questioned whether clinical audit is not good value for money at a national level. It is important to consider the factors that tend to block successful clinical audit projects. These include lack of priority given by the trust board and the audit being a 'tick box' exercise undertaken only because trusts need to be seen to be doing something. It has to be stated that most audits do not complete the audit cycle. Even those that are published are often single surveys with a list of recommendations that do not get followed, or at least there is no 'closure of the loop' to demonstrate that any change has occurred.

Common reasons for failure of clinical audit topics include:

- the topic chosen was too wide or otherwise too ambitious
- there was a lack of data
- the data used or sought were of poor quality
- the topic was not a local priority
- there was a lack of consultation about the choice of topic
- there was a lack of resources (human or financial) with which to complete the audit or to make the changes
- recommendations were made but were not presented to or endorsed by an appropriate group

- the recommendations were not widely discussed
- the recommendations were not implemented
- the implementation of recommendations was resisted by local staff
- the audit did not involve the staff who needed to change their practice
- there was a lack of time
- key staff moved to a different area.

Benefits of audit

In addition to the successful demonstration of good practice or the improvement of clinical practice, there are other benefits of audit activity. These include:

- training in audit techniques for junior (and senior) staff
- involvement of users leads to services being viewed more positively
- professional development of healthcare workers, including those directly employed in clinical audit roles
- changes in strategic thinking for the organisation
- changes in local policies
- better collaboration with health and social 'partners'.

Although the evidence is not entirely clear, there are at least some reviews and studies that have outlined that audit works in terms of ensuring good practice or improving practice, and some of those have identified the characteristics of successful audit projects (Hearnshaw *et al*, 1998; Johnston *et al*, 2000).

Topics for audits

There is no nationally recognised requirement to carry out particular audits. The following, however, could be considered as 'essential' by any mental health unit:

- rates of emergency readmission to a psychiatric unit (required nationally as a high-level performance indicator – see NHS Executive, 1996)
- implementation of the Mental Health Act (e.g. duration of section 5(2) orders, as required by the Mental Health Act Commission)
- aspects of care plan written on CPA care plan (as specified in the national audit tool)
- adherence to NICE guidelines (e.g. on attention-deficit hyper-activity disorder)
- ensuring that the delivery of electroconvulsive therapy meets the standards set by the Royal College of Psychiatrists (see www.rcpsych.ac.uk/cru/qual.htm).

Suggested topics for mental health audit are almost endless but may include:

- improving the quality of information given to users
- audit of consultant case-loads (in-patients and out-patients)
- audit of record-keeping
- audit of reporting to, and using the recommendations of, the National Confidential Inquiry into Suicide and Homicide by People with Mental Illness
- seeing severely ill and suicidal patients within 7 days of hospital discharge (one recommendation of the National Confidential Inquiry – see Appleby *et al*, 2001)
- standards of delivery of high-dose antipsychotic medication (Royal College of Psychiatrists' guidance)
- critical incident reviews (post-suicide reviews)
- adherence to schizophrenia and depression guidelines produced by NICE.

At a national level, various bodies have been established to set standards, produce guidelines and encourage good practice. They have been established, at least in part, to prevent failures of clinical practice. The responsibility for managing the national programme of clinical audits (in England and Wales) transferred to the Commission for Health Improvement (CHI) in 2002 and is now the remit of the Commission for Healthcare Audit and Inspection (CHAI). Its involvement in clinical audit is controversial and some argue that this is incompatible with the role of an inspectorate or regulator.

Where to get further help

- Royal College of Psychiatrists' Research Unit (www/rcpsych.ac.uk/cru)
- NICE, which is developing audit advice to assist in the introduction of NICE guidelines (www.nice.org.uk)
- Scottish Inter-collegiate Guideline Network (SIGN) (www.sign.ac.uk)
- Commission for Health Improvement (www.chi.nhs.uk/eng/audit)
- NHS Information Authority (www.nhsia.nhs.uk/def/home.asp).

References

Appleby, L., Shaw, J., Sheratt, J., et al (2001) *Safety First. Five-Year Report of the National Confidential Inquiry into Suicide and Homicide by People with Mental Illness.* London: Department of Health.

Department of Health (1989) *Working for Patients.* London. HMSO.

Department of Health (1997) *The New NHS: Modern, Dependable,* cm 3807. London: TSO.

Department of Health (1999) *Clinical Governance: Quality in the New NHS*, HSC 1999/ 065. London: Department of Health.

Geddes, J. R., Gaye, D., Jenkins, N. E., *et al* (1996) What proportion of primary psychiatric interventions are based on evidence from randomised controlled trials? *Quality in Healthcare*, **5**, 215–217.

General Medical Council (1998) *Duties and Responsibilities of Doctors*. London: GMC.

General Medical Council (2000) Confidentiality: Protecting and Providing Information. London: GMC.

Hearnshaw, H., Baker, R. & Cooper, A. (1998) A survey of audit activity in general practice. *British Journal of General Practice*, **48**, 979–981.

Johnston, G., Crombie, I. K., Davies, H. T., *et al* (2000) Reviewing audit: barriers and facilitating factors for effective clinical audit. *Quality in Healthcare*, **9**, 23–26.

Malby, B. (1995) Getting started on audit. In *Clinical Audit for Nurses and Therapists*. London: Scutari Press

NHS Centre for Reviews and Dissemination (1999) Getting evidence into practice. *Effective Healthcare*, **5**(1). London: Royal Society of Medicine Press.

NHS Executive (1996) *Promoting Clinical Effectiveness: A Framework for Action In and Through the NHS*. London: Department of Health.

Summers, A. & Kehoe, R. (1996a) Is psychiatric treatment evidence-based? *Lancet*, **347**, 409.

Summers, A. & Kehoe, R. (1996b) Involving lay participants in clinical audit. *Psychiatric Bulletin*, **20**, 719–721.

van Wersch, A. & Eccles, M. (2001) Involvement of consumers in the development of evidence based guidelines: practical experiences of the North of England evidence-based guideline development programme. *Quality in Healthcare*, **10**, 10–16.

Further reading

Firth-Cozens, J. (1993) *Audit in Mental Health Services*. Hove: Lawrence Erlbaum Associates.

Irvine, D. & Irvine, S. (1995) *Making Sense of Audit*. Oxford: Radcliffe Medical Press.

National Institute for Clinical Excellence (2002) *Principles for Best Practice in Clinical Audit*. London: NHS.

CHAPTER 16

Multi-agency working

Paddy Cooney and Barry Wilson

- Multi-agency working is a key element in the government's plans for all mental health service providers
- Closer integration of service planning and delivery between agencies is a national priority
- Effective and long-lasting multi-agency working does not just happen: it requires positive thinking, and appropriate structures and investment
- Modern standards promote multi-agency working as the foundation for effective service delivery
- The clinical governance and 'best value' approaches have elements in common and are key tools for the delivery of effective multi-agency working.

'Every organized human activity – from the making of pots to placing man on the moon – gives rise to two fundamental and opposing requirements: the division of labour into various tasks to be performed, and the co-ordination of these tasks to accomplish the activity. The structure of an organisation can be defined simply as the sum total of the ways in which it divides labour into distinct tasks and then achieves co-ordination among them.'

(Mintzberg, 1978)

This introductory section explores the reasons why multi-agency working is important and where the drive and direction for recent developments has come from.

Multi-agency working and partnership have been a key tenet of practically every national mental health programme and initiative announced in the past 10 years (Table 16.1). Indeed, there is rarely a paper or directive issued by any government department that does not stress the importance of breaking down 'Berlin Walls'. Mental health services in particular have been subject to two decades of homicide and other inquiries, every one of which has referred in some degree to the failure of communication – between individuals, professionals, teams

Table 16.1 Recent national guidance that has highlighted multi-agency working

Guidance	Reference	Nature of guidance
Building Bridges	Department of Health (1995)	A guide to arrangements for inter-agency working for the care and protection of people with a mental illness
Still Building Bridges	Social Services Inspectorate (1999)	Report of a National Inspection of Arrangements for the Integration of Care Programme Approach with care management
Health Act 1999		Established primary care trusts and outlined the cooperation required between health and other organisations
Finding a Place	Audit Commission (1994)	A review of mental health services for adults
Saving Lives: Our Healthier Nation	Department of Health (1999a)	Set four targets for reducing death rates in priority groups, including reducing the death rate from suicide and undetermined injury by at least one-fifth by 2010
National Service Framework for Mental Health	Department of Health (1999b)	Framework addressing the mental health needs of working-age adults up to 65
Shared Care of Patients with Mental Health Problems	Royal College of General Practitioners (1993)	Strengthening the relationship between primary and secondary care through shared care between GPs and CMHTs of people with mental health problems
The Spectrum of Care	Department of Health (1996)	A summary of comprehensive local services for people with mental health problems; 24-hour nursed beds for people with severe and enduring mental illness; an audit pack for the care programme approach
Working in Partnership	Department of Health (1994)	Describes a collaborative approach to care
Modernising Mental Health Services	Department of Health (1998a)	Set out the government's planning and investment strategy for mental health services
A Guide to Clinical Governance Reviews in NHS Acute Trusts	Commission for Health Improvement (2001)	Introduction to the clinical governance review process
Together We Stand	Hancock *et al* (1997)	Describes effective partnerships in mental health
Taking Your Partners	Sainsbury Centre for Mental Health (2000)	Reviews opportunities for partnership working in mental health following implementation of the Health Act 1999

and agencies. Indeed, working in partnership refers to improving communication and collaboration at every level of the service. This is essentially about subsuming a local, departmental or professional interest in order to achieve more efficient or higher-quality outcomes. It therefore applies equally to individual professions working together and to organisational and structural partnership. At its simplest, it is about a shared assessment process that determines a care plan that all sign up to. At its most complex, it is about bringing the strategies of various organisations to bear on agreed, shared priorities, such as the dovetailing of a local authority's community plan with the health community's health improvement plan, to ensure effective health promotion for people with mental health problems.

Partnership between health and social care providers is a key aspect of the reforms to the National Health Service (NHS). It is critical to the delivery of patient-centred care and the improved quality and effectiveness of services. In May 2001 the Health and Social Care Act permitted the creation of new 'care trusts', first announced in the NHS Plan (Department of Health, 2000), and promoted flexibilities that will enable the NHS to work with local authorities to respond to local needs rather than organisational boundaries.

In addition, the effective delivery of mental health services is dependent on a range of partnerships between statutory services and the other organisations providing services, for example housing, leisure, voluntary sector and independent sector. There is also the crucial partnership with those using the services and their carers. This chapter by necessity looks at multi-agency working in general and the relationship between health and social services in particular. However, this is the beginning of partnerships and effective multidisciplinary working is only a stepping stone to a wider range of relationships.

Models of partnership

Multi-agency working may take many forms. In this section we explore why this is the case and give examples of different arrangements.

Models of partnership need to develop from the current services and – because of differences in the local history, relationships, needs and nature of services – what works in one area will not necessarily work in another. There is no universal model that can be applied nationally and across different organisations. Partnerships in mental health are formed around a discrete client group, but in organisations like primary care trusts the partnerships will need to accommodate a number of client groups. Equally, geographical boundaries both help and hinder the process. Co-terminous borders can facilitate the establishment of multi-agency working. However, in the case of a mental health trust that

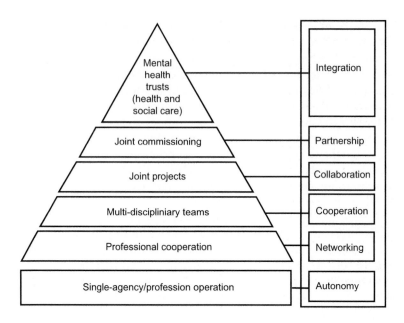

Figure 16.1 The continuum of levels of partnership working.

covers three or more local authorities the structures will need to be established on a different basis, which can result in as many forms of partnership as there are authorities.

That said, the opportunities for agencies to work in partnership lie on a continuum, as shown in Fig. 16.1. Box 16.1 gives details of a particular example of partnership working at the partnership/integration end of the continuum.

Standards

Many national guidelines promote standards for multi-agency working. Here we examine what this involves.

Standards can help services in several ways. They can systematically identify a range of issues in detail and make common goals explicit. They usually stimulate discussion on their development and, when used in service evaluation or in organisational audit, they can be used as a lever for practitioners and managers to argue for better resourcing if a particular aspect of the service is deficient. They can also provide a useful structure for analysis and report-writing (e.g. strategy documents and interface evaluations). It is important that standards are agreed by all relevant parties, so that the issues are 'owned', and so that they are regularly reviewed to incorporate new policy and practice.

Box 16.1 Commissioning and service integration in Somerset

From 1 April 1999 a Joint Commissioning Board for Mental Health was established in Somerset with devolved responsibility for all spending by health and social services on mental health. At the same time, the Somerset Partnership NHS & Social Care Trust was established as the first integrated trust in Britain.

The Joint Commissioning Board
The Joint Commissioning Board was established under a legal framework that did not allow pooled budgets. To work around this, the health authority established a mental health subcommittee and appointed four people with devolved responsibility for mental health commissioning, and the social services committee of the county council mirrored this arrangement by establishing a mental health subcommittee, which again had all spending devolved to it. These two subcommittees then met at the same time in the same room with the same agenda and agreed one chair, which in the first year was held by a representative of the county council but rotated thereafter. This overcame the restriction on pooled budgets. Each of the four primary care groups has an associate representative and as each became a primary care trust, so their members replaced the health authority members as the voting members of the Joint Commissioning Board. The Board also has two users and two carers as associate members. The Board agrees strategic direction and issues contracts to the integrated trust and performance manages the trust. The success of the Board so far has meant that there are no immediate plans to use the new freedoms allowed under the Health Services Act introduced from 1 April 2000, though no doubt use will be made of them in time.

The integrated provider
The initial intention had been to transfer all staff within the social services department and with a mental health brief into a reformed mental health trust. However, it soon became clear that it would not be possible to transfer the employment of social workers, who were approved social workers under the 1983 Mental Health Act, to a trust. Therefore, their contracts remained with the county council, but their management was devolved to the trust. All other staff transferred on to NHS contracts. The director of social care on the trust management board was appointed as an executive member. The structure within the trust also followed the boundaries of the four primary care groups, with each locality having a locality manager and an assistant locality manager responsible for all services within their area. The amalgamation of management posts continued within the community mental health teams, as team leader posts were balanced among designated social worker or health team leaders, and this also applied where day services were amalgamated.

Box continues on next page

Standards and guidance contained in policy documents centre around common themes. These range from the macro to the micro in terms of who and what may be involved (Table 16.2).

Box 16.1 *Continued*

Recent developments
Later developments in integrated mental health trusts have addressed commissioning and integration in different ways, subject to local priorities and circumstances. Integration was taken forward in the NHS Plan, published in July 2000, by proposing the creation of mental health and social care trusts 'to ensure that mental health and social care provision can be properly integrated locally'. The Health and Social Care Act 2001 provides the legal framework for the establishment of care trusts, including mental health and social care trusts. The mental health and social care trust will provide integrated services covering health and social services. Designation as a mental health and social care trust will lead to a change in governance arrangements, so that local authorities will play a full role in the governance of the care trust. The Secretary of State for Health will need to be persuaded that care trust status is likely to promote the effective exercise by the care trust of any delegated health-related functions of the local authority alongside the mental health trust's existing NHS functions. Four such trusts have been established, in Bradford, Manchester, Sandwell and Camden & Islington.

'Best value' and clinical governance

Two key standards-based systems for mental health services are the 'best value' system used for local authority services and the clinical governance arrangements operating within the NHS. In this section these two approaches are compared.

Getting the best out of mental health services, both professionally and organisationally, has been a major area of activity in recent years. For health organisations this has been driven by clinical governance, for local authorities by 'best value'. But these two approaches share many features and a common aim and, as such, bringing them together offers a key opportunity to develop multi-agency working.

Clinical governance and 'best value' are approaches that often draw upon common sources. Both operate alongside professional self-regulation, employer monitoring and personal learning responsibilities to promote the highest level of professional and organisational performance. Both may incorporate 'in-house' and external monitoring and are based on the development of common standards for the whole country and action to improve standards.

Clinical governance is defined on the NHS Modernisation Agency website (www.cgsupport.nhs.uk/About_CGST/Clinical_Governance_defined.asp) as:

'A framework through which NHS organisations are accountable for continuously improving the quality of their services and safeguarding high

Table 16.2 Key themes from policy documents

Theme	Source(s)[a]
The integration of care management and the care programme approach	*The New NHS*; *Modernising Social Services* (Department of Health, 1998*b*)
Effective partnerships between agencies (primary healthcare, social services, housing, the independent sector and other agencies)	National Service Framework for Mental Health
Unified local commissioning process involving pooled budgets and joint or agreed lead commissioning	*Modernising Mental Health Services*
Integrated services	National Service Framework for Mental Health
Disciplines and agencies not working alone	National Service Framework for Mental Health
Effective care coordination (a whole-systems approach that incorporates joint assessment, shared care planning, audit, etc.)	*Building Bridges*; *Still Building Bridges*
Involvement of partner organisations in clinical risk management	*A Guide to Clinical Governance Reviews in NHS Acute Trusts*
Involvement of partner organisations in clinical audit, research and effectiveness work, and staffing and staff management reviews	*A Guide to Clinical Governance Reviews in NHS Acute Trusts*
Partnership approach to service delivery	*Together We Stand* (NHS Health Advisory Service, 1995)

[a]See Table 16.1 for details of sources.

standards of care by creating an environment in which excellence in clinical care will flourish.' (Scally & Donaldson, 1998)

Similarly the core goals for 'best value' are described (Department of Transport, Environment and the Regions, 1999) as:

- ensuring that public services are responsive to the needs of citizens, not the convenience of service providers
- ensuring that public services are efficient and of high quality
- ensuring that policy-making is more 'joined up' and strategic, forward-looking and not reactive to short-term pressures.

Health service organisations do not have the same duty of 'best value' as local authorities, but they are encouraged work in concert with local authority colleagues. The Department of Health recommends that the lessons of 'best value' operating within a partnership arrangement should be absorbed by the NHS to influence future patterns of service delivery. In addition, NHS bodies already work to a similar rigorous set of standards to ensure that the services they provide are of the required quality and value for money. There is already a strong performance management framework for the NHS, which mirrors many elements of the local government model. Likewise, local authority social services departments have systems largely based on the care management model and service specification approaches, which link specifically with individual client needs.

As such, clinical governance and 'best value', with their accompanying performance management and care management arms, may be seen as different but largely overlapping approaches to the delivery of large-scale, individualised services to users. Table 16.3 provides a brief comparison of the two.

The comparison reveals great similarity between clinical governance and 'best value', although different language may obscure this at times. However, clinical governance may be viewed as starting more at the level of the individual patient and best value at the level of the whole service, although both approaches attempt to encompass the individual–service spectrum in their own ways.

The overlap between the two approaches is encouraging efforts to build bridges and to use the best of each. More multi-agency working in the mental health field will both facilitate and drive this trend. Many of the new integrated trusts have termed their quality assurance structure 'service governance' to encompass the local authority 'best value' and health service clinical governance arrangements.

A useful bridge between clinical governance and best value and the benefits of partnership is provided by the Health Development Agency in its Working Partnership (see Box 16.2). It is an approach predicated on the value of the widest possible multi-agency working as the only way to properly address the socio-economic factors that underpin ill-health.

Multi-agency working in practice

In this section we look at the benefits and challenges of multi-agency working and what is involved in delivering it.

The benefits of multi-agency working

'Integrated Care is a concept bringing together inputs, delivery, management and organisation of services related to diagnosis, treatment, care rehabilitation and health promotion. Integration is a means to improve the services in relation to access, quality, user satisfaction and efficiency.'

(Gröne & Garcia-Barbero, 2001)

Table 16.3 Clinical governance and 'best value' compared

	Clinical governance	Best value
Brief description	A framework in which NHS organisations are accountable for continuously improving the quality of their services and safe-guarding high standards of care by creating an environment in which excellence in clinical care will flourish.	Requires local authorities to subject all the activities and services for which they are responsible to a review every 5 years. Best value is about securing the best service.
Main components	Quality improvement processes (e.g. clinical audit). Leadership skill development at clinical team level. Evidence-based practice with the infrastructure to support it. Good practice, ideas and innovations systematically disseminated. Clinical risk reduction programmes. Adverse events detected and openly investigated, and the and the lessons learned promptly applied. Lessons for clinical practice systematically learned from complaints made by patients. Problems of poor clinical performance recognised at an early stage and dealt with. All professional development programmes reflect principles of clinical governance. High-quality data for the monitoring of clinical care.	A local focus. Accountability and inclusiveness. Breaking departmental and organisational boundaries and engendering cooperation between local agencies and partners. Partnerships with the private sector, with communities and other agencies, and between authorities. The delivery of cost-effective services based on competitiveness and keeping up with the best. Performance measurement and management linked to a frame-work of national performance indicators (including some minimum performance standards as well as a national formula for improvement targets). Comparability: local authorities are expected to be working to match the best performers – in the private or public sector. Continuous improvement based on a cyclical review process, with regular monitoring, measurement, review and change. Learning will be an important part of the process.
Key methodologies	Clinical audit Quality monitoring and improvement Education and professional development initiatives External scrutiny	Cyclical review process by service areas Consultation with communities and interested parties Information collection and research National comparisons External scrutiny
Useful sources of information	Department of Health, www.dh.gov.uk/ Wisdom Centre for Networked Learning, www.wisdomnet.co.uk Clinical Governance Research and Development University of Leicester, www.le.ac.uk/cgrdu/ Clinical Governance Support Service, www.rcpsych.ac.uk/cru/cgss.htm	Department for Transport, Local Government and the Regions, www.local.dtlr.gov.uk/research/bvsummar/bvres1.htm Local Government Association, www.lga.gov.uk Improvement and Development Agency, bestvalue/

Box 16.2 'The Working Partnership' (Health Development Agency, 2003)

The six elements of effective working partnerships

Leadership and vision: the management and development of a shared, realistic vision for the partnership's work through the creation of common goals. Effective leadership is demonstrated by influencing, communicating with and motivating others, so that responsibility for decision-making is shared between partners.

Organisation and involvement: the participation of all key local players, and particularly the involvement of communities as equal partners. Not everyone can make the same contribution. Most voluntary organisations are small and locally based, with few staff. They may need resources and time to enable them to become fully engaged.

Strategy development and coordination: the development of a clear, community-focused strategy covering the full range of issues supported by the relevant policies, plans, objectives, targets, delivery mechanisms and processes. Development of local priorities for action will rely on the assessment of local needs, sharing of data and a continuing dialogue between partners.

Learning and development: effective partnerships will not only invest in shared objectives and joint outcomes, but will also add value through secondments and other opportunities to share learning and contribute to professional and organisational development in partner organisations. Willingness to listen and to learn from each other builds trust.

Resources: the contribution and shared utilisation of information, financial, human and technical resources. The new freedoms to pool budgets and to provide integrated services, for example between NHS primary care and local authority services, can help remove some of the traditional barriers to joint working. Cooperation can start by resourcing what everyone wants, for example IT skills and training.

Evaluation and review: assessing the quality of the partnership process and measuring progress towards meeting objectives. Partnerships need to demonstrate that they are more than talking shops. They must also be able to show that they are making real improvements to services.

The benefits of multi-agency working are often presented as a self-evident truth, but staff are more likely to proceed willingly and effectively down the road of change if they are clear about the advantages of integrating systems. There is often a limit, however, to how clear one can be, as the production of research evidence lags behind practice innovation. Often, the initial start is an act of faith, based on good relationships between individuals in specific teams. However, we can begin to make some reasonable claims for the added value that inter-disciplinary working and integration can bring about, and these are discussed under separate headings below.

Combining community leadership with health improvement

As indicated above, local authorities have a responsibility for offering leadership to the local community for such issues as the environment, transport, the local economy and education. Health authorities have a responsibility for the health improvement of the local population. It is therefore imperative to bring these two responsibilities within all communities together, to be sure that the respective plans enhance each other's objectives.

Enhanced capacity from simplified management structures

Often partner organisations have individuals doing broadly similar tasks. Management structures can be rationalised if responsibility is transferred to one person. Inter-disciplinary working and integrated teams allow single management of those teams, cross-discipline supervision and freeing up of clinical time.

Deliver complex packages of care in a tailored way

One of the greatest challenges is to deliver packages of care to people with severe disability or high needs. This generally involves more than one agency. A failure to tailor the response of each agency to individuals can mean critical care is not provided. Integration allows greater coordination of that package of care and a clarity both about who is managing the care and about the role of those involved.

New outcomes not achievable as individual organisations

Bringing professionals and organisations together can often result in creative solutions to old problems.

Financial flexibility and efficiency

In bringing budgets together, there is often a fear of one organisation subsidising the other. However, it can allow greater flexibility in the way that monies are used, so that the best value possible is achieved.

Encourage shared learning and training

Despite a long history of inter-disciplinary working within mental health, there is still a paucity of shared learning and training, particularly at pre-qualification stage. A greater understanding of other professions at pre-qualified level would mitigate the worst excesses of inter-disciplinary stereotyping, which can hinder inter-disciplinary working.

Delivering multi-agency working

The history of joint working and partnership between local authorities and health services has provided examples of real innovation and imagination. However, such innovation is all too often hampered by mutual suspicion and failed opportunities. In more recent years, political imperatives, financial constraints and creative practice have slowly created a momentum towards multi-agency working at the level of the organisations as well as at team level.

In moving into partnership arrangements (whether temporary or permanent) it is necessary to be aware of this history, and the suspicion that both sides can bring into planning. This is not so that old grievances can be brought out and polished, but so that they can be recognised and worked through rather than avoided. The strength of a good partnership either in multidisciplinary teams or between agencies is measured by how they deal with differences.

Partnership is dependent upon relationships

Strong relationships with partner agencies are a prerequisite to close working. Such relationships are built on individual staff within both organisations understanding each other's roles and responsibilities.

Clear aims and benefits of collaboration

Some partnerships seem to take place as an alternative to clear strategy and vision. Integration is seen as an end in itself rather than the means by which services can develop. There is still a need for a strategy or a goal that partners can agree and sign up to and which will be facilitated by partnership working.

Recognition of differences

Cultural differences can be overplayed but still need to be addressed. These should be viewed as difficulties to be overcome, not insurmountable barriers.

Wider ownership

While the imperative for partnerships may be between health and local authority services, their success is dependent on the partnerships being widely 'owned', both within the organisations and, equally important, within the wider community and by other local stakeholders, including in the voluntary sector and user groups. The providers of services may see integration and 'single-door access' as progressive and desirable. It may, however, appear to the user as a monopoly, which has restricted the right to choose between health and social services.

Local champions

Strong champions are needed at the most senior levels of the organisations. Partnership also needs to be modelled throughout the organisations, otherwise it is dependent on individuals, who may leave, rather than being an embedded part of the culture.

Political support

Some staff working in the health service see the local authority elected member as an obstacle to decision-making rather than as a representative whose cooperation may be a critical factor in the success of a project. There needs to be a greater willingness on the part of the health sector to understand and respect the role of the elected member. The health policy outlined in the NHS Plan (Department of Health, 2000) has reinforced this issue in establishing the right of local authority scrutiny committees to summon representatives of local NHS trusts and to question them on their activities.

The challenges of multi-agency working

Models of partnership and multi-agency working are still at an early stage of development. There is therefore a need to give time to gaining ownership and to sign up to an exploration of different models. The aim must be to address local circumstances in a way that will gain commitment from the stakeholders in that area.

In the early stage of partnerships there is a tendency for all to check that they are getting a 'fair share of the cake'. This tendency to patrol the boundaries, whether professional or organisational, is understandable but can be self-defeating. It is not a question of identifying parts of the old organisation in the new, but rather of determining whether the previous organisations' values have been transferred to the new organisation.

What does this mean for managers?

It is not always possible to have clear management structures when working in partnership. In establishing clarity of responsibilities, the authority to act and make immediate decisions needs to be devolved to the appropriate level, so that there is an efficiently managed service. Managers will therefore need to refine their thinking and practice. They will need to develop new ways of viewing the world, new communication channels and a wider understanding of the environment in which mental health services are to be delivered.

Need to negotiate, not direct

Partnerships cannot be dictated and frustration is often experienced by managers who have been used to a hierarchical line-management system. Working in inter-disciplinary teams requires us to have skills of negotiation and persuasion to achieve a shared vision about the direction of the service.

Understand the culture, needs and roles of other professions

It is important that we understand the requirements and pressures on the other disciplines with which we work.

Greater communication skills

The communication problem may be summed up as 'What you think you heard is not what I said'. The language that we get used to hearing within our own profession does not always translate as well as we think it will.

Leadership rather than authority

While we need to negotiate and manage within a service, leadership is often much more influential in inter-disciplinary working than the influence bestowed by a management title. Leadership skills are important and they do not always reside in the manager, which can often be a point of tension.

Understand the local political concerns and the role of the scrutiny committee

In partnerships between health and local authorities, there is often a failure on the part of the health authority to appreciate the role of the elected councillor in local authorities.

References

Audit Commission (1994) *Still Building Bridges*. London: Audit Commission.
Commission for Health Improvement (2001) *A Guide to Clinical Governance Reviews in NHS Acute Tusts*. London: CHI.
Department of Health (1994) *Working in Partnership: A Collaborative Approach to Care. Report of the Mental Health Nurses Review*. London: Department of Health.
Department of Health (1995) *Building Bridges*. London: Department of Health.
Department of Health (1996) *The Spectrum of Care: A Summary of Comprehensive Local Services for People with Mental Health Problems; 24-hour Nursed Beds for People with Severe and Enduring Mental Illness; An Audit Pack for the Care Programme Approach*. LASSL (96)16. London: Department of Health.
Department of Health (1998a) *Modernising Mental Health Services*. London: Department of Health.
Department of Health (1998b) *Modernising Social Services*. London: Department of Health.

Department of Health (1999*a*) *Saving Lives: Our Healthier Nation*, cm 4386. London: TSO.

Department of Health (1999*b*) *National Service Framework for Mental Health*. London: Department of Health.

Department of Health (2000) *The NHS Plan: A Plan for Investment, a Plan for Reform*, cm 4818-I. London: TSO.

Department of Transport, Environment and the Regions (1999) *Implementing Best Value – Consultation Paper on Draft Guidance*. London: DTER.

Gröne, O. & Garcia-Barbero, M. (2001) Integrated Care: A position paper of the WHO European office for integrated health care services. *International Journal of Integrated Care*, 1 (June). www.ijic.org.

Hancock, M., Villeneau, L. & Hill, R. (1997) *Together We Stand: Effective Partnerships in Mental Health*. London: Sainsbury Centre for Mental Health.

Health Development Agency (2003) *The Working Partnership*. London: NICE.

Mintzberg, H. (1978) *The Structuring of Organizations*. London: Pearson Education.

NHS Health Advisory Service (1995) *Together We Stand*. London: HMSO.

Onyett, S. (1997) Collaboration and the community mental health team. *Journal of Interprofessional Care*, 11, 257–267.

Richards, H. & Heginbotham, C. (1989) *The Enquire System: A Workbook on Quality Assurance in Health and Social Care*. London: King's Fund.

Royal College of General Practitioners (1993) *Shared Care of Patients with Mental Health Problems*, Report of a Joint Royal College Working Group, Occasional Paper 60. London: Royal College of General Practitioners.

Sainsbury Centre for Mental Health (2000) *Taking Your Partners: Using Opportunities for Inter-Agency Partnership in Mental Health*. London: Sainsbury Centre for Mental Health.

Scally, G. & Donaldson, L. J. (1998) Clinical governance and the drive for quality imporvemnt in the new NHS in England. *BMJ*, 317, 61–65.

Social Services Inspectorate (1999) *Still Building Bridges*. London: SSI.

Part IV

Translating clinical governance into the clinical context

CHAPTER 17

Clinical information systems

Martin Briscoe

- It is important that clinicians are involved in developing the information technology strategy
- Trusts should ensure good access to computers and the internet for staff
- Trusts should encourage the use of e-mail as a means of communication
- Clinicians should insist that information systems produce reports that are useful to them
- Simple information systems work best.

Introduction

Information should be a key ingredient of an effective mental health service. This chapter describes the types of data and the systems that a mental health service should be able to access. It uses the Department of Health's (1998) information strategy as its framework and attempts to describe how the strategy can be developed by trusts in order to deliver the following:

- information about illnesses and local resources for patients and carers
- up-to-date information for clinicians about treatments and best practice guidelines
- a system for monitoring effectiveness
- a system for measuring local provision against local and national standards
- an electronic health record (from 'cradle to grave') for every person in the area
- an efficient and rapid means of communication between professionals.

A link to the strategy and all other online documents and websites mentioned in this chapter can be found at www.rcpsych.ac.uk/college/sig/comp/docs.htm.

The national strategy

In 1998 the government introduced a 7-year plan entitled *Information for Health* (Department of Health, 1998). The document accepted that information technology in the National Health Service (NHS) fell a long way behind that available to most other organisations. It said:

'Holidays can be chosen, availability checked, and the package booked at the touch of a button in even the smallest travel agent. We can check our bank balance, order statements and new cheque books, and even pay bills electronically. But the NHS still relies on pen, paper and post – and often several staff – to book a simple outpatient appointment. This leads to unnecessary delays, frustration for patients and staff alike, and the potential for mistakes. There is no reason why the NHS should be second best. Information for Health is the Government's strategy for putting this right. The NHS is to invest £1 billion over the next few years modernising how we collect, store and use information.'

The strategy went on to detail the information resources that each of the 98 identified 'health communities' would be expected to have in place by the year 2005. In order to implement the strategy, each community was to take the vision described in the strategy and develop its own local implementation strategy (LIS) by April 2000. The LIS is important because it will be used to determine what developments take place in trusts and how much of the extra funding comes to each 'health community'.

Mental health clinicians should have been involved in the development of all LISs. Their development was not an easy task for mental health services, as the strategy had to be submitted before the national mental health information strategy was even written – it was not published in final form until April 2001 (Department of Health, 2001). There are no new issues in this strategy, but it does give clear guidance on how the original strategy's aims can be tailored to mental health. In many ways it is more achievable than the original strategy and it has put back the deadline for implementation of some areas until 2007. It will be developed locally by 'implementation teams'.

Key points

- Ensure that mental health is clinically represented in the development of information systems.
- Be aware of the goals and targets set out in the LIS.

The main elements of *Information for Health*

Health information and details of local resources for patients

Many organisations have developed information leaflets for the general public. However, these are of variable quality. The quality issue has become even more important with the rise in popularity of the internet and the ease with which information can be made available to large numbers of people. The strategy seeks to ensure that the public has access to 'consistent, comprehensive, comprehensible and up-to-date advice from accredited sources on a wide range of health related issues'.

The evaluation and cataloguing of public health information is to be carried out by NHS Direct. To this end a section of its website (www.nhsdirect.nhs.uk) has been developed to provide a searchable index of evaluated information. Evaluation is carried out using DISCERN (Charnock *et al*, 1999), an instrument jointly developed by the British Library and the NHS Research and Development Programme. DISCERN assesses quality by scoring the leaflets on 16 items such as clarity, authorship, treatment choices and referencing. The leaflets are then given a final score of between 0 and 5.

The aim of providing evaluated health information to the public is an excellent and achievable aspect of the strategy. A single point of entry to gain access to such leaflets, via NHSdirect, will also be very valuable. The scoring system should also encourage people to improve the quality of leaflets. This exercised the Public Education Committee of the Royal College of Psychiatrists, as its very popular 'Help is at hand' leaflets scored only 3 out of 5. A significant amount of rewriting was required to improve their ratings.

The author would advise trusts not to write new self-help material, as there already is a wealth of good information and there is little point in reinventing the wheel. However, trusts are expected to develop information about local resources, for example to let people know how to get help and what facilities are available locally, as well as to give them pointers to nationally available information and perhaps an indication of success rates for local services, rather like the league tables produced by schools. Trusts should also consider how best to make this information available to the public – whether as paper leaflets or through facilities to fax leaflets to enquirers, websites, collaboration with NHS Direct, walk-in centres or telephone help-lines.

Key points

- Patients should have ready access to nationally developed information leaflets.
- Trusts should prepare and keep information about local resources.

257

- Consideration needs to be given to how this information is to be published (e.g. booklets, website, help-lines).

Information and guidelines for clinicians

In recent years there has been an explosion of information about treatments, aimed at clinicians. However, it has been hard to access and evaluate this information. Fortunately, a number of national resources are being developed that simplify the task. The Cochrane Collaboration is an international organisation that formed in 1993 in response to Archie Cochrane's call for systematic, up-to-date reviews in healthcare. Cochrane was an epidemiologist who observed that:

- healthcare practice is not always based on good evidence
- there is too much information for any individual to access and use
- resources are always limited, so it is all the more important to know which interventions work.

The Cochrane Library has an online database of evidence-based practice (www.update-software.com/cochrane). It focuses on meta-analysis studies and provides excellent, freely available summaries of its findings and access to the complete studies to those who have a password. These materials are also published on CD-ROM for libraries and personal use. Provided an institution has a subscription to the database, then the librarian should be able to provide users with a password with which to access the service via the internet, from home or work.

The National electronic Library for Mental Health (www.nelmh.org) was set up as a direct result of the strategy. It aims to be an online library that enables clinicians to access clinical information rapidly. Dr Muir Gray, the Library's director, has said that, for such a service to be useful, clinicians must be able to get hold of the information they need, at the bedside, within 30 seconds. There is no doubt that the internet has made it much quicker to access information, but there are still many problems to be overcome before we can reach Dr Muir Gray's target. All too often scenarios not unlike the following take place:

See patient – need to find information about the disease – walk to nearest computer terminal – switch it on – wait 5 minutes for it to boot up – telephone help-line as your password has lapsed – log onto the computer – try to remember the address of the website – perform a search that returns 100 000 hits – find the site – search for the relevant file – wait for the file to download – switch to another computer which has a printer that works – wait 5 minutes for the file to print out – return to patient who has got bored and left the hospital.

The challenge for trusts is to overcome some of the problems highlighted above. The following points should help.

- The trust should ensure that there is a high computer:staff ratio. Ideally there should be one computer to each clinician; many trusts currently aim for one between three clinicians.
- The trust should develop an intranet (Hicks *et al*, 2000). This is a local private network that can link to key material, such as policies and treatment guidelines. Developing an intranet is also an easy way of giving staff internet access.
- The trust should ensure that staff have good training in information technology.
- The trust should develop a philosophy that encourages the use of computers to access and convey information.
- The trust should consider developing a help-line and appointing an information manager who can research or answer clinical questions from clinicians. It is often quicker to speak to an expert than to spend hours searching for information on the internet. This is particularly important for those clinicians who do not feel comfortable sitting in front of a computer.

Key points
- Staff should have good access to computers and the internet.
- Staff need adequate training in information technology.
- The trust should encourage the use of computers for information storage and exchange.

Medical records

The strategy expects that by 2005 everyone will have an electronic health record (EHR), which will be a summarised clinical history from 'cradle to grave'. The EHR will be maintained in the primary care setting. Mental health services, and other secondary providers, will also develop electronic patient records (EPRs). These EPRs will need to be able to communicate with each other and to update the EHR.

There are numerous potential advantages of electronic records over paper records: for example, they would enable rapid access to information when someone is admitted to hospital or seen in an out-patient department, and a specialist's comment in the hospital record could be instantly seen in the general practitioner's record and vice versa. This would greatly aid communication between hospital and primary care. Increasingly, general practitioners are working towards this and a number of practices are already paperless, but developing an electronic record in mental health will be much harder, partly because so much information is collected.

The strategy also emphasises the coding systems that need to be developed in order to make such a system work. The UK is developing a coding system of its own, called READ. This has been around for some years and it currently has over 250 000 codes. It is still not finished.

Informatics experts generally seem to think this is a vital step in developing electronic records. The author, however, has some concerns about READ as a potential white elephant, for the following reasons:

- Computers and databases are developing very quickly and computer memory is now very cheap. Because of this it is no longer necessary to reduce information to codes in order to save space.
- There seems to be something inherently wrong with a system that produces over 250 000 codes to do what could be achieved with just 60 000 words of English.
- Language is a constantly changing and living thing, whereas a coding system is essentially dead. So every time a new word is developed to describe a medical procedure someone is going to have to create a new code.
- Proponents of coding say that they overcome the problems of different national languages. This may be so, but what happens if other countries do not buy READ? (The author doubts that many will.) This coding system, which has taken years to develop and has cost millions, could well become another Esperanto, a language invented in 1887 in an attempt to overcome the problems of communication between countries and which went nowhere.

Fortunately, the Department of Health has devised a minimum dataset for mental health, which defines the minimum amount of data that trusts should collect on patients. This is being piloted in a number of trusts and will go a long way to satisfying the requirements of the EPR for mental health.

For an excellent debate about the pros and cons of coding systems and other aspects of health informatics, readers are recommended to consult Coiera (1997).

Key points
- Trusts will need to develop a system for capturing electronic patient records.
- Electronic delivery of the minimum dataset is achievable, but caution is needed in attempting to develop a more substantial EPR.

Communication between health professionals

In mental health it is common for several professionals to be involved in a case. In an ideal world it would be good if all involved knew what everyone else was doing. The government has attempted to address this in the concept of the care programme approach (CPA). However, the process of getting all staff together for reviews is almost impossible and highly inefficient, especially in trusts that cover wide geographical areas. A good information system should aid the process of CPA and communication between professionals. This could be achieved by storing care plans and reviews on computer and through the effective use of e-mail. A number of issues need to be resolved before this can happen, however.

Low levels of computer use in trusts

It has been mentioned above that many trusts work on the assumption that a community team can function well with one computer between three workers. This is a serious error. Unless the computer is seen as an essential personal tool, staff will not use it unless they have to and they will never become adept at the technology. It therefore is important to explore ways in which more computers can be made available to staff. One way might be to use smaller, even pocket-sized computers, which cost less than desktop machines. Other savings may be possible by more use of networked printers or encouraging the use of competitive office software packages rather than the very expensive and complex packages purchased by most trusts.

Inability to send health information by e-mail

Currently most trusts do not allow confidential information to be transferred by e-mail. It was originally understood from the information strategy that the government would set up a secure network called the NHSNet. This would link all NHS facilities and enable them to transfer patient information between each other in a secure electronic environment. Unfortunately this is probably an oversimplification of what will happen. The author understands that the NHSNet is more of a 'virtual network', in that it does not exist as a distinct physical entity. Individual hospitals have their own secure networks, as do most primary care centres, but these are to be linked together using existing and public lines of communication.

Understandably this design creates some risk of data being obtained by outside elements. The two weakest points are: the junction between the trust network and the internet; and while the information is passed between trusts on public lines of communication. The first weak point is protected by a 'secure gateway' or 'firewall'. Here electronic 'bouncers' check the identity of people and data trying to go through the gateway and reject any unauthorised visitors. In general this system is quite effective. Sending electronic information over public lines is more problematic. The way to protect such data is to encrypt or scramble the information before it is posted, and to supply the authorised receiver with the code to unscramble the data at the other end. Exactly the same system has been used for years to protect high-security telephone conversations. Although secure encryption techniques exist and are routinely used in the United States to transmit clinical data, approval has not been given for its use in the UK. Until this problem has been solved, the strategy will not succeed.

Key points

- Trusts need to ensure that there are enough PCs for those who need them.
- The embargo on e-mailing patient information, because of confidentiality concerns, needs to be overcome.

Monitoring effectiveness and measuring services against local and national standards

All too many information systems in the NHS are best described as 'data graveyards' – places where information is entered into a computer never to be seen or used again. This leads to a number of problems. Staff become cynical about computers and view them as a waste of time and resources. People who input information realise that it will probably never be seen again, or at least not be of any further use to them, and therefore do not care about the quality of information that they input. However, the ability to evaluate performance depends on having access to high-quality data.

Deciding on what information people should expect from an information system is quite hard. Some suggestions are offered in Box 17.1. Delivery in this area is probably the only effective way of evaluating the success of an information system. A system has really succeeded if employees in all professions within the trust can indicate how the system has helped them do a better job. It will of course also improve efficiency within the trust and enable performance targets to be more easily set and monitored.

Key points

- What reports the system should produce needs to be determined.
- All levels of staff should be included – the system should provide something for everyone.

What can go wrong?

The five main aims of the strategy set some important challenges for trusts and health communities. Some of them are going to be much easier to achieve than others. It is worth looking at some of the problems that could limit success. Millions of pounds have already been spent on informatics and health in the UK over many years and yet there are few examples of the benefits of this investment. It is important to try to understand why this is so before any more money is squandered.

Why do so many systems fail to deliver?

First, information technology departments in the NHS are poorly resourced. In industry, companies usually spend a much higher percentage

---

Box 17.1 The information required at different levels of the organisation

Senior management level
- Number of patients seen in last year by diagnosis, CPA level, sector or specialty
- Activity data (number of referrals or contacts) for wards, community mental health teams or day services
- Waiting lists and times
- Adverse events databases – suicides, assaults on staff, complaints
- Time taken for reports and letters to be written and complaints dealt with.

Clinical level
- Numbers of patients on case-load, by CPA level or severity score on a rating scale
- EHR from clinic to enable checking of prescribed medications
- Lengths of stay and readmission rates by wards and sector
- Mental Health Act information – rates of use, tribunal results, automated tasks such as reminders for second opinions, renewal and after-care procedures
- Changes in rating scale severity scores over a course of treatment, by team and disorder
- Prescribing differences and costs by teams.

Practical level
- Automated clinic appointment system
- Semi-automated preparation of discharge and clinic letters
- Reports on CPA reviews due and contacts overdue for those on high CPA levels
- Automated CPA forms
- Online expense claim forms, study leave requests, and claims and accident forms
- One-off customised reports using an online wizard that enables the user to set up the report without needing to call in a programmer.

---

of their revenue on information technology than does the NHS. This means that resources are stretched, back-up and training are often inadequate and equipment is out of date. Linked to this is the fact that health informatics is complex and in such areas as security and reliability a higher standard is required than in many areas of industry.

Second, information technology staff never say 'It can't be done'. It is generally true to say that computers can be programmed to do anything that a clinician wants, but what we fail to grasp is that it might take tens of thousands of working hours to achieve the desired outcome. Software developers and informatics consultants constantly overestimate their efficiency, and this has led to a number of high-profile failures.

Some parts of the NHS information strategy may similarly fail, especially the coding areas and the EHR. Such projects would be hard enough to achieve in the private sector, but within the cash-constrained NHS they may be impossible. The strategy does come with £1 billion in funding, but the aims of the strategy are by no means easy to realise. In fact, they are probably the most ambitious health informatics goals any country has ever aimed for, and some of the areas, like the EHR and the coding system, have never been achieved on a national scale anywhere before.

Third, people tend to rush in to develop a system, without first determining what they want out of it and whether it is going to be cost-effective to take an electronic approach.

How can these problems be overcome?

The following are suggestions to help ensure that the strategy's aims can be achieved. Trusts should:

- ensure that clinicians are involved in every stage of the development, and avoid using only those clinicians with a passion for computers – sceptics are needed to keep the ideas practical
- insist on sufficient funding to ensure a 1:1 ratio for computers to clinicians
- encourage the universal use within the trust of an intranet, so that staff become used to getting all their information off the network
- encourage the use of e-mail as one of the main methods of communication
- before new data input or project development is agreed, demand to know what the benefits and the new outputs will be
- insist on seeing the output at work and the advantages it will bring before approving the project
- insist that staff who will use the system are involved in its development (e.g. secretaries for discharge and clinic letters, or members of the community mental health team for CPA material)
- aim small – it is better to have a system that does one or two things really well than one that does hundreds of things badly.

Conclusions

It is good news that money is being released for informatics and that health providers are being brought together within health communities to share expertise and coordinate developments. Many parts of the information strategy are easily achievable and should reap measurable rewards, particularly in terms of access to information for patients and clinicians, and encouraging electronic communication between pro-fessionals, provided the concerns about confidentiality can be overcome.

It will be possible to introduce electronic health and patient records into general practice, but developing these in mental health, if we wish to deliver more than the minimum dataset, will be a major challenge and almost certainly unobtainable within the time scale, given the financial constraints and all the other major changes taking place in mental health at the moment. As for coding, I hope my fears are proved wrong.

References

Charnock, D., Shepperd, S., Needham, G., *et al* (1999) DISCERN: an instrument for judging the quality of written consumer health information on treatment choices. *Journal of Epidemiology and Community Health*, **53**, 105–111.

Coiera, E. (1997) *Guide to Medical Informatics, the Internet and Telemedicine*. London: Chapman & Hall.

Department of Health (1998) *Information for Health: An Information Strategy for the Modern NHS*, HSC 1998/168. London: Department of Health.

Department of Health (2001) *Mental Health Information Strategy*. London: Department of Health.

Hicks, T., Stubbs, B. & Briscoe, M. (2000) Intranets – 'safe surf'. *Psychiatric Bulletin*, **24**, 312–313.

CHAPTER 18

Monitoring and improving performance

David Roy

This chapter will:

- focus on the means by which individuals and clinical teams continuously improve clinical performance
- show that performance can be accounted for, monitored and improved only if it is measured against agreed standards or expected outcomes
- suggest some ways of measuring performance.

The continuous cycle of standard setting, monitoring and improving clinical performance is a central tenet of clinical governance. While mental health services are mostly delivered by multiprofessional teams, and organisations develop the means of measuring whole-service and team performance against targets and standards, the development of measures is not the role of healthcare providers alone, but also a key responsibility of individual healthcare praticitioners. Professional bodies also have a major role to play in elaborating clear codes of professional conduct and clinical standards, and healthcare providers and regulatory bodies in dealing with poor performance.

Performance and accountability

'Performance' is defined by the *Oxford English Dictionary* as 'the fulfilment of a process undertaken or ordered'. Healthcare professionals have undertaken to perform and are held accountable for that performance.

'Accountability' is the bedrock of clinical governance, and lies at the core of clinical practice and the provision of high-quality services. It incorporates responsibility for the quality of care, assessing and managing risk, identifying and monitoring poor performance and improving that performance. For their own performance, healthcare practitioners are accountable to professional bodies, to the National Health Service (NHS) and its governing structures, to the organisation in which they work or with which they are associated, to the local service, to the clinical team, to local stakeholders and other professionals involved in the care of the patient and, foremost, to the patient and carer(s).

The relationships mental healthcare professionals have with their professional bodies depend on their discipline. The General Medical Council (GMC) and the Nursing and Midwifery Council are statutory bodies with which all practising doctors and nurses are required to register, and to which they are accountable for their personal, professional and ethical practice and conduct. The Royal Colleges (for doctors and nurses) provide the professional and training framework for practice. They are specialty-specific for doctors, while the Royal College of Nursing has an added negotiating role on terms and conditions of service, similar to that of the British Medical Association for doctors. The Health Professions Council provides registration for occupational therapists, radiographers, physiotherapists, speech and language therapists, art, music and drama therapists, and other professions allied to medicine. The British Psychological Society provides a voluntary register.

Clinical psychologists can currently call themselves healthcare professionals and practise independently without being registered, as can psychotherapists from a wide variety of backgrounds and 'schools'. Statutory regulation now extends to healthcare providers using 'protected titles' (for example, occupational therapist or drama therapist), although it is difficult to see how effectively all psychotherapists and counselling practitioners can or will be regulated.

'Applied psychologists' are likely to come under the auspices of the Health Professions Council, covering clinical psychologists, clinical neuropsychologists, counselling psychologists, and health educational, forensic and occupational psychologists.

Standards

Healthcare practitioners have a responsibility and obligation to deliver care to professional and ethical standards for each professional group or individual practitioner. There are standards in the practice of healthcare that are value driven, qualitative and often difficult to pin down or define with sufficient clarity to allow measurement. These standards can be described as *implicit*. Most healthcare professionals strive to provide the highest standard of care possible, albeit they do not always fully achieve it. Implicit standards are difficult to measure and often rely on consensus and the prevailing social, moral and political climate in healthcare. An example of an implicit standard relates to a patient's consent to a standard treatment, where patients are increasingly viewed as partners in the delivery of healthcare and make choices of treatment based on professional advice and options.

Explicit standards place on individual practitioners the responsibility and obligation to deliver healthcare to absolute contractual, organisational and professional standards that are either legally or professionally binding. Referring again to the example of consent, standards required for consent within a research project will be explicit and measurable. Another example of explicit standards will be those that relate to consent to treatment enshrined in the current Mental Health Act. These standards have little room for flexibility, and the outcomes are more easily measured and clearly defined.

Performance standards and accountability

In their capacity as individual clinicians and team members, and as professionals with ethical and professional obligations, healthcare professionals are actively involved, to a greater or lesser degree, in:

- the setting and adopting of professional/clinical standards, both explicit and implicit
- the measurement of performance against those standards by a variety of means
- the improvement of performance to meet those standards in an ongoing and reflective way.

All services and professional groups have developed, or have adopted, standards of clinical and professional practice, either implicit or explicit (or sometimes a complex mixture of the two). In addition, new sets of standards are continuously being developed and translated into policy and protocol. This setting/adoption of standards should then enable clinicians to have a range of methods of assessing performance against these standards.

How organisations and clinicians can monitor and improve performance using standards

Organisational structures for clinical governance that reflect a process of standard setting/policy development, and monitoring of performance against those standards, can go some way to bringing clarity within the organisation to the process of clinical governance and the improvement of performance. Figure 18.1 describes an example of one organisational model that links standards, policy and structures for the monitoring of performance and support of clinical services, clinical teams and individual clinicians. Clearly, the complex nature of organisations and their differing histories suggest almost infinite variations.

Clinicians, either individually or as part of a clinical team, should engage in a continuous cycle of assessing performance against a range of standards, and should continuously strive to improve that performance.

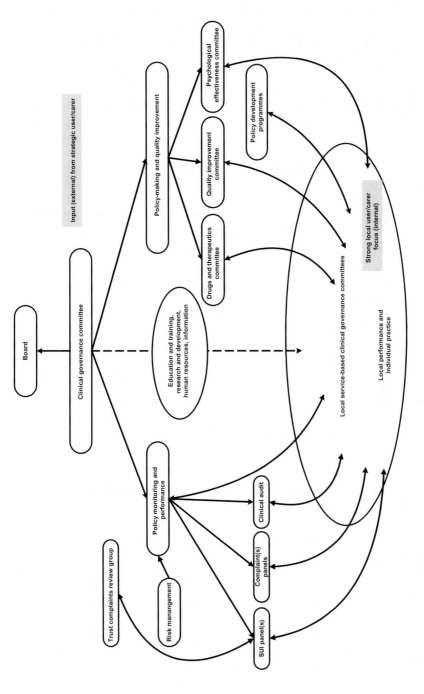

Figure 18.1 An organisational structure that will support performance improvement. SUI, serious untoward incident.

The *active* engagement of all clinical teams and clinicians at individual and team level in a 'bottom-up' process poses a major challenge to mental health services. Clinical audit is an essential part of this process, although, in the main, the results, until now, have often been disappointing when evidence is sought for change in practice occurring directly as a result of individual audits. Clinical audit is the process whereby the cycle of standard setting and monitoring and improving performance is operationalised at service level. However, it is easily marginalised and needs to be integrated into the whole clinical governance process within trusts. Individual clinicians in different professional groups will increasingly be expected to demonstrate their active participation in the clinical governance programme in general and the clinical audit programme in particular, as part of their accountability for quality and their own personal development plans. Figure 18.2 provides a limited pictorial overview of the often complex relationships between monitoring, standards and individual performance.

Setting and adopting standards

Introduction of sensible policy and guidelines

Policies should be clear and simple. Clinical staff need ongoing education and guidance about the implementation of key policies, and should have a clear understanding of the expectations of the organisation with regard to these policies. Adherence to policies and guidelines has become a means by which individual staff are assessed with regard to the clinical care they deliver. There will be many instances where clinical care is of a high standard despite policy or guidelines not being adhered to. Although good clinical care is not dependent on the adherence to sensible policy and procedure, it is likely that when errors do occur, or less than satisfactory standards of care are delivered, these policies and guidelines were ignored.

New policies should be implemented only after assessments have been undertaken of the education and training needs to implement the policy, and of the impact on clinical services generally in terms of change in practice. It is essential that local policies are in line with national initiatives, and that in large mental health trusts local policies are coordinated between services.

Clinical effectiveness programmes

Clinical effectiveness programmes are the means by which clinicians can assess 'What should I do?' as the yardstick against which to judge 'How well do I do it?'

There is a burgeoning of clinical effectiveness literature. However, knowledge does not flow smoothly round an organisation and individual

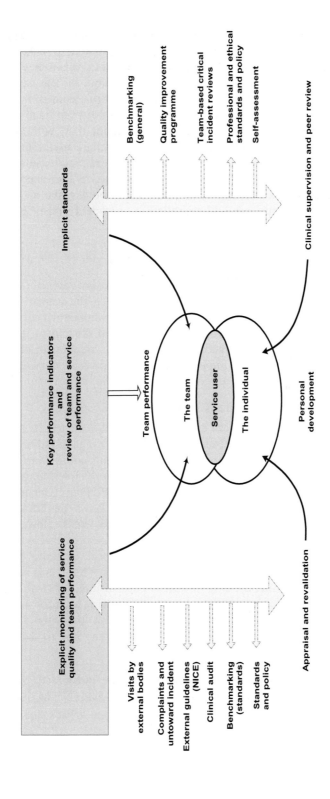

Figure 18.2 The relationshiop between monitoring, standards and invidivual performance.

clinicians find it difficult to assimilate the vast array of often highly technical effectiveness material available. It is possible to make a limited impact on this through clinical supervision, but this relies on more experienced individual clinicians having the time or the expertise to make use of the material available, and much of the material is often not easily accessible or digestible. Sackett *et al* (2000) encourage a positive approach to evidence-based medicine, and claim that, with new technologies and skills available, clinicians can, with relatively little effort, access high-quality evidence-based summaries and practice guidelines or protocols and introduce these into everyday practice. Increased access to information-based intra- and internet sites could make a significant impact on clinicians' use and assimilation of evidence (see Chapters 10 and 17).

Measuring performance against standards

It is not the responsibility of the organisation alone to provide performance measures, to undertake large-scale audit against guidelines or to commission or respond to external assessment/review of services or performance: it is also the responsibility and domain of the clinical team and the individual practitioner, and regular assessment of performance against explicit and implicit standards is possible through simple, good clinical supervision and peer review, and, of course, clinical audit.

Personal performance measures provided by the service

Many mental health services currently find it difficult to provide robust measures of individual or team performance on a regular basis. There are few routinely collected measures that reveal subtle variations in performance. The National Service Framework for Mental Health (Department of Health, 1999*a*) and the NHS Plan (Department of Health, 2000*a*) contain clear indications of how the NHS will try objectively to measure the performance of NHS trusts. However, there are at present few examples of performance measures that will directly benefit the individual clinician and allow for local, objective discussion about performance at team or clinician level. There is a significant challenge in reaching the stage where the Department of Health asks for sensible and useful information capable of allowing accurate assessment of trust performance, and these measures allow the trust to provide teams and clinicians with the kind of data appropriate to daily clinical practice.

Personal performance measures provided by the individual

Increasingly, staff will be asked to prepare documents in support of their annual appraisal (see Chapter 13) to demonstrate 'What I do' and 'How well do I do it'. These data might include:

- individual case-loads, dependency levels and case mix, detailed job plans and timetables, and service-related statistics
- outcomes for patients, complaints and untoward incident management, feedback from referrers, patients and carers, and other members of the team.

Particularly (although not exclusively) for mental health professionals, these data will reflect a mix of team performance and individual performance.

Team and service performance measures

Trust- or service-wide key performance indicators (KPIs) have been developed for mental health. In addition, as outlined above, measures of performance will increasingly be published and expose trusts to a benchmarking process that is likely to be based on data that are very blunt, often out of date, or frankly incorrect. The data at present have little relevance to the clinical team, and trusts should be encouraged to develop KPIs that reflect how well the organisation is doing in delivering quality healthcare to service users right down to individual practitioner level. Examples of KPIs include the number of patients on the standard or enhanced Care Management Approach (CPA), by team or practitioner, the number of patients discharged from acute admission wards who are seen face-to-face by a mental health professional within 7 days, and waiting times for psychological therapies.

Clinical teams should be encouraged to participate in this process and to develop or adopt a small number of indicators that they feel reflect how the team functions. They should consider how they want their own team's performance to be measured more centrally. Useful team-based data could include the number of (relevant) untoward clinical incidents appropriate to the work of the team, well-run user satisfaction surveys, the number of patients who receive a particular treatment/therapy that is germane to the service being provided (cognitive–behavioural therapy, family interventions, compliance therapy, etc.). The aim must be for teams and services to match performance to clinical outcomes, and services and interventions to need and measure these accurately (the 'Holy Grail' for clinical information systems).

Complaints

An efficient complaints system can provide teams and individuals with useful feedback material on 'how others think we are doing'. The commonest complaint in mental health services is about staff attitude, though environment and food follow closely. Many services still do not receive regular feedback on trust- or service-wide complaints. This is a missed opportunity.

Benchmarking

One means by which clinical teams can assess their service is on a range of measures against a number of other similar services. This can be particularly useful for clinical teams that work in a more specialised area and where clinical information that is routinely reported within the organisation can be difficult to interpret. These data might include staffing profiles, case-loads, referral processes, therapeutic interventions and outcomes, in a variety of modalities.

A recent structured example of a national benchmarking programme has been reported by the Department of Health (2001d) which, although essentially nursing based, has interesting lessons for all members of clinical teams and clinical governance programmes generally, and which should be extended to the full multidisciplinary team in mental health services. Other examples of benchmarking could involve the use of reports such as *Safety First*, the report of the National Confidential Inquiry into Suicide and Homicide by People with Mental Illness (Appleby *et al*, 2001), to measure local services against newly recommended standards. The CPA and the *Audit Pack for the Monitoring of the Care Programme Approach* (Department of Health, 2001a) provides a similar opportunity.

External assessments

Mental health services are regularly visited by outside organisations, either by statute or by invitation. Examples include the Mental Health Act Commission, the Commission for Healthcare Audit and Inspection (known as the Healthcare Commission and which has replaced the Commission for Health Improvement), the Health and Social Care Advisory Service (HASCAS), and commissioned user assessments (examples include the Sainsbury Centre for Mental Health and Breakthrough). These can provide a valuable sounding board for evaluating service performance as well as for identifying areas of good or weak performance (see below).

Improving performance to meet implicit and explicit standards

Peer-review

Peer-review can be done either through team-based 'benchmarking' or by individual clinicians ensuring that their performance is open to critical review in an ongoing way. Clinical teams benefit from meeting with similar teams and comparing ways of working and staffing levels, therapeutic interventions and clinical outcomes. In the same way clinicians benefit from the opportunity to meet with colleagues to discuss these issues, perhaps in a more confidential way (see 'The personal development plan', below).

Feedback from clinical colleagues and referrers

Clinical teams should canvas views about their service without individual team members feeling personally criticised. It is more problematic to ask clinicians, and particularly senior clinicians, to invite the same level of critical evaluation, as it will often involve interpersonal issues that are difficult to deal with.

Styles of open feedback and honest, supportive in-team appraisal need development and piloting.

Feedback from service users and carers

Simple user and carer questionnaires can be a quick and regular way of receiving feedback. Other means include direct interviewing of users and carers (preferably by people with appropriate training), the employment of user consultants, the involvment of users in feedback sessions, and the use of facilitated focus groups. The newly created patient advocacy and liaison services (PALS) may help move this agenda forward in trusts.

Service improvement initiatives

There are various developing or established means by which services can be assessed and improvement programmes put in place. These include facilitated 'care pathway' projects, whereby the service examines the progress of an individual patient or group of patients through the healthcare system, and develops ways of improving the experience of the patient, the efficiency of the delivery of service, and eventually the clinical outcome.

This process can be assisted by trying to analyse the whole system by breaking it down into constituent parts, examining the relationship between those parts, and putting them back together, perhaps in a more appropriate way. This can ensure that key clinicians within the system are actually in agreement with the models of care that are being delivered, and working together to provide care. It can give an opportunity for all teams within the system to combine their efforts and to engage with the NHS modernisation agenda.

External, commissioned assessment of local services against agreed standards can help a service to develop an improvement action plan, although both the assessment process and the development of actions require considerable commitment and effort to see the process through.

Team-based initiatives

The role of individual teams and team members in quality improvement is a key question posed within the review process of mental health services by the Healthcare Commission.

There are a number of ways in which clinical teams can engage in the process of improving performance once the information about their performance has been gathered and outlined. These include the original 'quality circle', which has been used within the NHS for many years, and which involves all members of the team looking at how services and the performance of the team can be improved by simple changes or modifications to how they work. While the quality circle does not seem to have much currency at present, clinical teams still find the concept useful and, often under different names (team development meetings, clinical governance meetings, clinical improvement meetings), it can enshrine the principle of all members of the team, whatever their grades, contributing to the process of regular improvement to the service. The process of clinical governance now provides a structure within which these highly valued team-based improvement programmes should thrive. Clinical governance is everybody's business!

Clinical audit will also provide a critical means by which teams and services can pull together standards and monitoring, to create a local action plan and change in practice that will 'make improvement happen'. It is important to include service users and other stakeholders in this process. A range of service and team redesign tools are being encouraged for use within the NHS through the Modernisation Agency.

Key points

- Improving performance is everyone's business
- It can be undertaken by the individual, the clinical team, the service, and organisations as a whole
- Crucial elements include the setting of clear, measurable standards and the monitoring of those standards to provide outcomes and feedback relevant to teams and services.

The role of organisations and the professions in improving performance

Participating at team level in critical incident reviews

The critical incident review (CIR) is the means by which a clinical team openly explores all the issues surrounding a serious unexpected or negative outcome. The culture of the organisation is crucial. When staff believe that the trust genuinely operates a 'no blame' policy – the organisation 'learning' rather than the organisation 'blaming' – CIRs become a valued activity within all clinical teams.

Clinical teams should participate actively in CIRs following serious untoward incidents (including near misses). Ideally, they should be externally facilitated, and a summary of the review (and its recommendations for the practice of the team) be made available for external review of the incident. CIRs are not a managerial tool to investigate an incident, nor a replacement for a more formal inquiry when required, but they do give the clinical team(s) an opportunity to reflect on practice where the outcome was significantly less than optimal. The focus of these CIRs should be developmental, learning exercises, and the outcome a team-based discussion about actions that could be taken by the team, or individuals within the team, to improve performance. The recently formed National Patient Safety Agency is promoting the use of the root cause analysis in the investigation of untoward incidents. This is a laudable attempt to move away from a (generally) less-successful patient-centred approach to a more rigorous systems-based approach, using the notion of 'the organisation with a memory' (Department of Health, 2000b) to draw out themes common to services across trusts. As the name implies, the methodology, although requiring training and investment, can help services to move to an understanding of the real cause of problems, and enable problem-solving strategies to be put in place at an organisational level. This will enable team involvement in untoward incidents to make a difference.

Key point

- Ideally teams should actively participate in a post-incident learning process that is conducted in a 'no blame' environment.

Participating in and responding to service review (including single case reviews) and panel inquiries

Service reviews can be difficult for managers and clinical staff. The key elements of a good service review are clear terms of reference, shared with all staff, clear standards against which the review will be conducted, and clear standards by which the outcome of the review will be measured (both the report and the actions taken).

Review reports that are well designed (Box 18.1) can provide the necessary impetus for service improvement and can support those who wish to promote change.

Unfortunately staff often find reviews and inquiries threatening. It is helpful for clinical staff to have a clear idea about what they should or should not expect from the process. For example, staff should ensure that they have access to the terms of reference, and if they are concerned, they should receive appropriate advice, either from the organisation or independently. Most reviews should be developmental and intended to improve services (some inquiries are, however, by their nature fault-finding). Reviewers are generally hoping to find staff who are both reflective in their practice and receptive to different models of working. Once the reports are prepared, staff should respond speedily and constructively to draft reports and actions plans, either as a team or individually.

Box 18.1 Guidance on preparing review/inquiry reports

- The report should be properly referenced against standards and accepted practice
- Reviewers should work to a clear code of conduct in dealing with professionals, service users and carers and other stakeholders in the review setting
- Recommendations should be clearly referenced and should not rely on individual reviewers' clinical preferences (or prejudices)
- Recommendations should, where possible, be negotiated with the service in order to promote ownership
- Recommendations should be clear and achievable and relate, where possible, to performance issues that are within the domain of the service being reviewed
- Local action plans should be sensible and achievable, and, where possible, these action plans should be rigorously shared across the local service
- Reviewers should have a view as to whether the organisation has the capacity to take the recommendations on board, and if not to make recommendations or comment as to how change could be achieved.

It is worth bearing in mind that not all change is beneficial, however, and managers should take care to observe the rules of implementing service change, and actively involve all staff and key stakeholders.

Clinical supervision

The use of good clinical supervision can be instrumental in establishing high-quality practice and change on the ground. There are several structural models for clinical supervision. Many teams follow a profession-specific model, nurses supervising nurses, occupational therapists occupational therapists, and so on. Many healthcare organisations need to make a significant culture shift to embed structured clinical supervision into everyday practice for all staff. There are frequent and often heated discussions within organisations about the difference between clinical and managerial supervision and a belief that these two processes should be rigorously kept apart. Given the large number of staff who currently receive neither, it is perhaps best to combine the two and aim for every member of clinical staff to receive at least one face-to-face meeting on a regular basis (between weekly and monthly, depending on experience and security), even if it does not satisfy the purists.

Key point

- Clinical supervision is possibly the most effective direct means of improving individual performance.

Appraisal

Appraisal should be firmly linked to ongoing personal development, clinical supervision and, for doctors, revalidation. All staff should have some form of appraisal at least annually. For doctors, the appraisal process is a requirement stipulated in the consultant contract and a generic appraisal pro forma has been agreed between the profession and the Department of Health (2001*b*). For other staff the appraisal process is by local agreement. It is important to note that appraisal is essentially an employer-led process, while revalidation is 'profession led' through the General Medical Council.

The cycle of appraisal is designed to help all clinicians reflect on and improve elements of their personal clinical performance. It should be supportive, bring about changes in the way healthcare professionals work and help shape their job plans. However, it is unlikely that this process will lessen the difficulty of dealing with the small number of staff whose performance gives significant cause for concern.

Key points

- Appraisal is often a mix of personal development and performance review.
- Appraisal should be supportive and developmental.

The personal development plan

All clinical staff should have a personal development plan that provides a framework for professional activities. Doctors in training currently have fairly structured training plans, and nurses and professions allied to medicine are well advanced in providing structures within healthcare organisations to ensure that these plans are in place. Consultant medical staff are increasingly engaging in a more formal process of personal development based on peer review (e.g. Royal College of Psychiatrists, 2004).

Personal development plans should:

- provide a framework for professional activities
- identify professional needs
- identify service needs
- be held and owned by the individual practitioner
- be a collection of statements
- be a record of plans
- be a record of activity
- establish a learning cycle
- contribute to continuing professional development
- provide an audit of activity that contributes to appraisal (and, for doctors, revalidation).

Education and training (continuing professional development and lifelong learning)

Clinical teams should be actively contributing to the trust's education and training plan each year. This should become clearer with the development of workforce developement confederations, which should provide a strategic overview of all education and training across larger geographical areas. The individual personal development plan gives practitioners an opportunity, together with their clinical supervisor or peer group, to plan their own response to the education and training available within the organisation and to ensure that this training also meets the needs of the team and service as a whole. All clinicians will have to account for attendance at some mandatory training (without which they may not be able to practise), some core training (which is highly desirable) and more individualised or team-based training.

The more explicit training requirements become, the greater will be the challenge to the organisation (and the NHS as a whole) to provide sufficient resources to ensure there is fair access to continuing professional development across all disciplines.

Key point

- Continuing professional development should link directly to a plan for personal development rather than a disparate set of unconnected educational opportunities.

The development of professional standards of performance

It is essential that individual clinicians have clear guidance from their professional bodies, developed through a rigorous peer process, of expected standards of professional conduct. The General Medical Council (2001) has published *Good Medical Practice*, which provides the yardstick against which doctors should measure their own conduct and general performance. The Nursing and Midwifery Council (2002) has similar guidance for nurses. The Royal College of Psychiatrists (2004) has published *Good Psychiatric Practice*, which outlines the core attributes of a psychiatrist (Box 18.2) and elaborates on the duties of a doctor registered with the General Medical Council contained within *Good Medical Practice*.

Alongside the development of core competencies, professional bodies are developing clear guidance on what constitutes unacceptable practice. Core competencies will provide a useful tool for self-assessment and external assessment of performance, and a benchmark against which individuals can prepare their personal development plans.

> **Box 18.2** The core attributes of a psychiatrist (Royal College of Psychiatrists, 2000)
>
> - Clinical competence
> - Being a good communicator and listener
> - Having a basic understanding of group dynamics
> - Being able to create an atmosphere within a team where individual opinions are valued, and team members have a sense of ownership of decisions
> - Ability to be decisive
> - Ability to appraise staff
> - Basic understanding of the principles of operational management
> - Understanding and acknowledgement of the role and status of the vulnerable patient
> - Bringing empathy, encouragement and hope to patients and their carers
> - A critical self-awareness of emotional responses to clinical situations.

Dealing with poor performance

Healthcare professionals and organisations often find it difficult to deal with performance that consistently falls below a minimum acceptable standard. For individual practitioners who are performing poorly, this poor performance is often common knowledge among the team, other fellow professionals and managers. Unfortunately, often the professional has not been given a clear indication of the cause for concern until a disciplinary process is formally begun, which is often late in the process. Some clinicians who perform poorly find themselves quite isolated and do not actively pursue, or welcome, critical feedback, and respond in a very negative way to feedback when it is given. This can set up a cycle from which it is difficult to escape. Managers and clinicians in managerial positions should not be deflected by the difficulty that some health professionals have in accepting a critical view of their practice, but clear evidence in the form of written complaints or performance measures can be helpful. It can be particularly problematic for senior healthcare professionals who are used to working autonomously, or as part of a clinical team in a leadership position.

Managing professional performance and conduct creates significant challenges for the healthcare organisation. Managers are often not given sufficient training in performance management, and as a result dealing with poor clinical performance even by a junior member of staff is often extremely time-consuming and unproductive. Unfortunately, even the most well-established organisations find themselves moving staff from one part of the service to another rather than dealing openly with the issue, and providing the (often relatively inexperienced) manager with the support to manage the poor performance appropriately. In large healthcare organisations, an individual clinical manager may only rather infrequently have to deal with a significant performance problem, and therefore require high-quality support from a human resources department, but this is often beyond the capacity of the organisation to provide. A well-resourced and expert human resources department is an integral part of the clinical governance structure of a trust.

Key principles of good individual performance management include:

- early identification of clinical standards not being achieved
- bringing the cause of concern to the notice of the practitioner as early as possible, and discussing remedial actions (through peer review, the personal development plan, clinical supervision, training opportunities)
- keeping clear records of all meetings, and following up any face-to-face discussion with a written agreement of the actions
- follow-up of agreed actions rather than accepting that the problem is resolved merely because 'things have gone quiet'.

Where there is a significant difference of opinion between a more senior and experienced clinician and the clinical manager, a commissioned external view can be helpful in achieving resolution.

Although it should only be used as a last resort, the disciplinary procedure of the trust gives the manager the tools to deal with poor performance that is not improving through training and other means, or where the poor performance is not acknowledged, actively resisted or, of course, where patient care is being placed at risk.

The situation for doctors is somewhat different, and Department of Health guidance issued in 1990 provides a cumbersome, legalistic and expensive framework within which trusts have to work (Department of Health, 1990). This is out of line with the situation of all other healthcare professionals, but is the only current means by which trusts can formally deal with issues of professional conduct or competence where the alternative means of improving performance have failed, or the safety of patients is considered at risk. There have been a number of recent initiatives to improve the accountability of doctors and enable employers to intervene and deal with poor performance. Unless a doctor's performance is so bad as to place patients significantly at risk and the trust is able to provide clear evidence that this is the case, poor performance often goes unchecked.

Performance management of doctors is extremely time-consuming and is seen by many medical managers as enervating and unfulfilling. Many medical managers do whatever they can to avoid proceedings, and while on occasion this can in fact be helpful, and allows organisation to take a more supportive and developmental approach to the poorly performing doctor, it does mean that there are a few doctors whose practice is giving cause for some concern but for whom the problem cannot be resolved.

Categories of problems concerning poorly performing doctors are outlined as follows by the Department of Health (1999b):

- clinical performance or professional conduct
- personal misconduct
- failure to fulfil contractual requirements
- clinical performance serious enough to warrant referral to the General Medical Council.

A new special health authority has been created, the National Clinical Assessment Authority (NCAA), which provides an assessment of a doctor's clinical practice and gives advice on any action that should be taken. A workable policy for trusts dealing with intractable poor medical performance is long overdue, and new disciplinary procedures for doctors are currently under development.

Conclusions

Senior professional staff in all disciplines will need to develop further easy-to-use measures of team and individual performance and new skills to satisfy the public need for accountability for outcomes of service delivery and the scrutiny of that performance.

- Monitoring performance that leads to tangible improvements in clinical practice and outcomes for service users is complex and multi-faceted.
- Within healthcare organisations, individual performance is often best assessed through the performance of the team.
- Senior and experienced healthcare professionals have a key leadership role to play in clinical teams in assuring quality and continuously improving performance.
- All clinicians are increasingly subject to performance scrutiny, and the introduction of appraisal, personal development plans, and formal revalidation procedures for doctors will lead to changes in job planning, the expectations placed on the individual, and roles within the clinical team.

References

Appleby, L., Shaw, J., Sheratt, J., et al (2001) Safety First. Five-Year Report of the National Confidential Inquiry into Suicide and Homicide by People with Mental Illness. London: Department of Health.

Department of Health (1990) Disciplinary Procedures for Hospital and Community Medical and Dental Staff. HC(90)9. London: Department of Health.

Department of Health (1999a) *National Service Framework for Mental Health*. London: Department of Health.

Department of Health (1999b) *Supporting Doctors, Protecting Patients*. London: Department of Health.

Department of Health (2000a) *The NHS Plan: A Plan for Investment, a Plan for Reform*, cm 4818-I. London: TSO.

Department of Health (2000b) *An Organisation with a Memory. Report of an Expert Group on Learning from Adverse Events in the NHS*. London: TSO.

Department of Health (2001a) *An Audit Pack for the Monitoring of the Care Programme Approach*. London: Department of Health.

Department of Health (2001b) *Assuring the Quality of Medical Practice*. London: Department of Health.

Department of Health (2001c) *Appraisal for Consultants Working in the NHS*. London: Department of Health.

Department of Health (2001d) *The Essence of Care*. London: Department of Health.

General Medical Council (2001) *Good Medical Practice* (3rd edn). London: GMC. Available at www.gmc-uk.org/standards/good.htm.

Nursing and Midwifery Council (2002) *Code of Professional Conduct*. London: NMC. Available at www.nmc-uk.org/nmc/main/publications/CodeOfProfessionalConduct.pdf.

Royal College of Psychiatrists (2004) *Good Psychiatric Practice*, 2nd edn (Council Report CR125). London: Royal College of Psychiatrists. Available at www.rcpsych.ac.uk/publications/cr/cr125.htm.

Sackett, D. L., Straus S. E., Richardson, S., *et al* (2000) *Evidence-Based Medicine: How to Practise and Teach EBM* (2nd edn). London: Churchill Livingstone.

CHAPTER 19

Clinical governance and the role of the lead clinician

Tim Kendall and Katy Kendall

This chapter will:

- examine the role of the lead clinician in the implementation of clinical governance
- suggest that the lead clinician will need first to develop multi-disciplinary team working and an outcomes-oriented health service
- elaborate the main areas the lead clinician should focus on in implementing clinical governance
- identify the practical skills, experience and supports needed for the lead clinician to do their job in a modern health service.

Introduction

A First Class Service (Department of Health, 1998) proposed that, as an early key step in the development of clinical governance, the chief executives of trusts should identify a lead clinician to work closely with the trust board in leading staff into a 'new' National Health Service (NHS), whose primary concern would be the delivery of high-quality, cost-effective services focused on the needs of the population they serve. Although the trust board and the chief executive in particular were, for the first time in the NHS, accountable for the quality of clinical care provided by staff within the trust, the precise role of the lead clinician needed further elaboration.

Greater clarity appeared with the publication of the White Paper devoted to clinical governance (Department of Health, 1999). Although it was not prescriptive about the specific role of the lead clinician, it did suggest that lead clinicians should assemble a team to support the programme of clinical governance and it did identify some key characteristics, which serve as a guide to the principles underpinning the new role of lead clinicians and their teams:

- *Commitment*. The lead clinician, as a key player in the planning and implementation of clinical governance, must have full commitment from the top to ensure delivery of the new programme.

- *Inclusivity*. The lead clinician and their team should develop a local programme of changes that are properly inclusive, and ensure that all trust personnel are informed and involved wherever possible.
- *Good external relationships*. Other health organisations and agencies in the locality should be actively engaged to ensure the development of good external relationships with the community served by the trust.
- *Constancy of purpose*. The lead clinicians and their teams will be responsible for keeping the programme of radical change on course.
- *Accountable*. They should also be able, at all times, to account for the progress of the implementation programme.
- *Communication*. Underpinning these principles is the fundamental need for the lead clinician, the team and the trust board, actively and regularly to communicate with staff within the organisation and with external partners.

These principles place the new leadership arrangements at the heart of clinical governance, and make the lead clinician and their team, along with the trust board and the chief executive, the organisational leaders of change.

This chapter locates the role of the lead clinician and their team within the context of the modern and modernising mental health and social care trust. It clarifies their role in the implementation of clinical governance, highlights some of the problems and difficulties they face, and suggests some solutions.

Clinical governance

Within the broad framework of the 'new' NHS, clinical governance plays an overarching role in ensuring the dependable delivery of high-quality local services. This is not to say that the NHS has not, and does not, deliver high-quality services; it is rather that the delivery of health and social care has been highly variable, ranging from world-class through to extremely poor. The treatment and care provided by two adjacent trusts or services can differ to the extent that one provides excellent care, while its neighbour provides care that is barely acceptable. The aim of clinical governance is to introduce systems and mechanisms to monitor and continuously to improve the quality of treatment and care delivered by local services and to reduce variation between services.

A number of complementary national initiatives seek to reduce variation in the quality of services, and to help bring about improvements, such as the creation of the National Institute for Clinical Excellence (NICE) and its national collaborating centres (one of the six being specifically devoted to mental health) (see Chapter 6), the introduction of the Commission for Healthcare Audit and Inspection (the Healthcare Commission – see Chapter 5), and the development of the different National Service Frameworks (NSFs – see Chapter 8) and the NHS Plan (Department of Health, 2000). Their function is to provide local services with national clinical practice guidelines and other guidance produced by NICE, and to help trusts to participate in national multi-centre audits, to subject themselves to regular external review, to participate in the National Confidential Inquiries and to develop old and new types of service, in line with a range of national standards. Nevertheless, these national initiatives can bring about improvements only through the final and local common pathway of clinical governance.

The role of the lead clinician

Although the trust board and the chief executive are ultimately accountable for the quality of services, it is the lead clinician who has the responsibility for the local implementation of clinical governance (Box 19.1). It is the job of the lead clinician to develop effective local mechanisms to monitor and continuously improve the quality of healthcare provided by clinicians and social care staff, and to make these local mechanisms sensitive to national initiatives aimed at improving care and reducing variation in quality. It is also part of the lead clinician's role to work with other local health organisations to ensure that the range of local services available matches the needs of the local population, and that the services work harmoniously and seamlessly.

To achieve these ends, lead clinicians, with the support of their multidisciplinary implementation teams, need to work across the whole organisation and to link with the wider health community. They need the full support and backing of the trust board, as well as clearly agreed plans and a timetable for implementation. They need to work with, or lead, the clinical governance committee, and with all the departments within the trust, such as human resources, information technology and audit, which will need to realign themselves in line with plans for the implementation of clinical governance. And whatever their professional background, lead clinicians must be both willing and able to work with equanimity with leads from all the professions.

Box 19.1 The role of the lead clinician

It is the lead clinician's job:

- to lead the local implementation of clinical governance
- to ensure that local services are responsive to national quality initiatives
- to work with other health organisations to coordinate and integrate the local delivery of health and social care to match the needs of the local population.

Clinical governance involves cultural and organisational changes that run deep, throughout the whole organisation, and that concern all staff: changes in the way knowledge and information are managed; changes in clinical practice and service delivery to improve effectiveness; changes in the make-up and training of the workforce; changes in the way that risk is dealt with; and, finally, changes in the way the organisation works with other teams and organisations.

Since the aim of clinical governance is to improve the quality of health and social care delivered to its service users and carers, it is essential that the lead clinician works closely with those delivering care (health and social care teams) and with those receiving care (local service users and carers). Just as clinical governance is the final common pathway of the 'new' NHS, so the clinical and social care teams and their service users and carers are the final common pathway for the implementation of clinical governance. Before the changes necessary to put quality at the heart of the work of each NHS trust can be effected, the lead clinician will need to prepare the teams for the implementation process.

Preparing teams for clinical governance

In mental health and learning disability services, the multidisciplinary team is the indivisible unit for healthcare delivery, and the quality of the service it provides is the primary focus of clinical governance in practice. This means that the lead clinician should, either directly or indirectly, bring their influence to bear upon the delivery of care by multidisciplinary teams (Box 19.2). This can be partly brought about through the reorganisation and redeployment of departments, and partly through the development of team infrastructures that will allow a team to monitor and improve the quality of care it provides.

The lead clinician will need to be cognisant of the state of readiness of each team to begin the process of implementation. This is not an

---

Box 19.2 Preparing teams for clinical governance

Lead clinicians should:

- develop good working relations with all clinical and social care teams
- help teams to fully implement multidisciplinary working
- monitor team effectiveness, team leadership and team management
- ensure that all teams use appropriate clinical outcome measures at the start and end of each episode of care
- in conjunction with service users and carers, develop methods for monitoring their experiences of services.

---

easy matter: clinical and social care teams vary not only with regard to the quality of care they provide, but also in terms of the quality of management and leadership, and their degree of integration and multidisciplinary working. The lead clinician and the implementation team will need to work closely with team leaders and managers, and understand the differences between leadership and management; they will also need to be familiar with the principles and practice of multidisciplinary team working, and get to know the myriad influences upon each team and the way it works. Of course, it is not possible to know everything about all teams at all times, but it is essential to have a sufficient working knowledge of team functioning and team performance.

Multidisciplinary team working

A clinical and social care team, if fully staffed, will have representatives of all the disciplines involved in mental health: psychiatrists, nurses, social workers, psychologists, occupational therapists and sometimes others. Each discipline has its own professional hierarchy, its own supervisory structures, its own line management arrangements and usually its own training programmes. Over and above these influences, the team's activity and development are subject to team and service managers, the various trust departments (such as audit), its own particular team culture, and the requirements of the trust board, clinical governance committee and a number of external organisations. In addition, teams are influenced by the views and feedback of the patients and carers they serve, albeit to varying degrees. In short, when the lead clinician and the implementation team engage with a clinical and social care team, they are not entering a power vacuum.

Although mental health and social care teams are expected to be multidisciplinary, in practice they often operate as a collection of different clinicians competing for influence. This impairs team functioning and multidisciplinary working, and lessens their ability to provide the full range of care needed by patients and carers, which requires that individual clinicians and disciplines, managers and clinical leaders work cooperatively.

What does this involve? The team needs explicitly to agree a common clinical 'language' and to work to agreed standards of practice. Crucially, clinical team leaders must have the confidence and trust of those in other disciplines. Multidisciplinary team working involves formally adopting agreed referral protocols, using a common method of assessment and a single set of case-notes for each patient, routinely undertaking multidisciplinary care planning, discharge planning, care programming and multidisciplinary clinical reviews, and routinely employing commonly agreed outcome measures. Teams also need to monitor their own activity, audit their own practice, actively seek the involvement of patients and carers, and be able to communicate collectively with senior managers and other teams. Without proper multidisciplinary team working, the influence that a lead clinician and implementation team can usefully bring to bear upon the activity and function of a team will be limited. Clearly, where teams are not working in multidisciplinary ways, the first job of the lead clinician, the implementation team and the supporting trust departments will be to help teams to develop the necessary multidisciplinary structures and practices.

Outcomes in mental health and social care

Clinical governance has its roots in quality improvement models such as the 'business excellence' model of the European Foundation of Quality Management (see Chapter 7). Like these prior models, clinical governance is a systemic or organisational approach to quality. As with any quality management method, there must be clear measures of the successes and failures of the approach. Whatever changes lead clinicians introduce or foster, they must be able to demonstrate improvement in the 'outcomes' of mental health and social care, in terms of one or more of the following:

- the outcomes of healthcare (clinical, social and individual)
- the patients' and carers' experience of the treatment and care they receive
- the risks of harm to patients, carers and staff.

They will therefore also need to develop the means to measure, accurately and meaningfully, any or all of the above.

Service users and their carers must be confident that the health and social care provided will 'improve their lot', with as little risk as possible and delivered in a way with which they are pleased. The lead clinician will need to know how teams are monitoring these outcomes, and that the information generated is meaningful, and for this the recorded outcomes must be accurate, valid and reliable.

Implementing clinical governance

The full implementation of clinical governance will take some 5–10 years, depending on the state of readiness of services and the availability of adequate resources. However, as soon as a team has laid the foundations for the 'outcomes-oriented' delivery of multidisciplinary team-based care, it can begin the process of introducing the essential 'building blocks' of clinical governance. For ease of description, we have divided these building blocks into five key areas:

- knowledge and information management
- workforce development
- clinical effectiveness
- risk management
- interface issues.

It is the job of the lead clinician and the implementation team, in conjunction with departments, service managers and team managers, to help teams systematically address these five key areas. What follows is by no means exhaustive or prescriptive; it is intended to help in the organisation of the early implementation plans for teams.

Knowledge and information management

For them to be able to provide healthcare on the basis of need, teams and services need to have access to up-to-date information about the changing needs of the local population. Information of this kind has been generated by health authorities but is rarely used by services and teams. Teams and services also need integrated clinical information systems that are patient-focused, and generated by teams rather than by separate disciplines (i.e. they need single sets of individualised health records). To achieve this, information will need to be electronically recorded, safely stored, simply retrieved and accessible to the patient wherever possible. This raises important ethico-legal issues, such as confidentiality and data protection.

Clinical staff need access to up-to-date information about the effectiveness and risks of treatments, as do service users and carers. Service users and carers must also have accessible information about the health personnel involved in their care, and available services, including possible alternatives (see also Chapter 7).

Box 19.3 sets out the issues likely to be addressed first by the lead clinician in this area.

Box 19.3 First steps in the area of knowledge and information management

- Services should be based on accurate information about the needs of the local population (population-based healthcare needs analysis)
- Electronic clinical information systems are needed that are based on integrated health records
- Individualised patient and carer information packs are required
- User-focused service monitoring of both teams and services is required.

Workforce development

Teams need to be able to monitor their own performance, and need to have enough time for training and team development. This means that clinical staff work within a culture of lifelong learning and continuous professional development, in which staff develop the skills for evidence-based practice. Service managers and teams should have accurate and up-to-date knowledge of the skills of each team. Trust-wide training and recruitment strategies are also required for the development of new types of teams (such as those identified in the NHS Plan, for example crisis resolution and home treatment teams), as is a systematic approach to staff training, based on the needs of the population and the skill mix of teams (Audini *et al*, 2002). Appraisal and performance management, and for doctors revalidation, are central to developing an effective workforce and to reducing risk to patients.

Box 19.4 sets out the issues likely to be addressed first by the lead clinician in this area.

Clinical effectiveness

To minimise variation in the provision of healthcare, local protocols need to be derived from national, evidence-based, clinical practice guidelines, and these should be agreed across the whole mental health and social care community, including primary care. To monitor clinical effectiveness, good clinical information systems are required, as is support for targeted clinical audits. None of this is possible without valid and reliable outcome measures appropriate to the patient and the services provided; these must also be simple to use. It is also essential that we have accurate means of recording and analysing:

- the provision of care for all service users
- the support given to carers
- the use of specific treatments
- the incidence of side-effects.

Box 19.4 First steps in the area of workforce development

- Help teams to monitor their own performance
- Establish a register of skills for evidence-based interventions for all teams
- Develop appraisal mechanisms for all staff, linked to personal development plans
- Develop training plans based on the skill mix of teams
- Develop training and recruitment strategies for the development of new services and teams.

Box 19.5 First steps in the area of clinical effectiveness

- Train all staff in the use of appropriate outcome measures
- Develop local treatment protocols that are agreed with all relevant organisations
- Audit departments to help teams develop a rolling plan of clinical audits with agreed targets and timetables for delivery
- Help develop or join local, regional and national networks for self-review and peer review
- Help to develop or join local, regional and national networks for cascading information on clinical effectiveness.

Teams need help to develop an evaluation culture based on self-review and peer review.

Box 19.5 sets out the issues likely to be addressed first by the lead clinician in this area.

Risk management

To reduce the risks to patients, carers and staff, clinicians must be trained in agreed methods of risk assessment. Teams need time and the means to analyse untoward incidents, adverse health events, 'near misses' and complaints, within a 'no blame' culture. Poor performance is a matter for all the team as well as for each discipline: there must be established means for reporting poor performance, 'whistle-blowing' and responding to identified problems.

Box 19.6 sets out the issues likely to be addressed first by the lead clinician in this area.

Interface issues

Finally, trusts need to be part of an integrated mental health and social care community, and to have effective mechanisms to ensure that care between services and agencies is seamless and targeted to those in need.

Box 19.6 First steps in the area of risk management

- Train all staff to undertake and record agreed formal risk assessments
- Develop agreed systems for identifying, recording and analysing adverse health events, untoward incidents and complaints
- Ensure that teams have dedicated regular time to reflect upon, and respond to, identified problems, without fear of blame
- Establish mechanisms for 'whistle-blowing' at all levels of the organisation, from trust board to teams and individual practitioners.

Box 19.7 First steps in the area of interface issues

- Ensure that all staff are properly trained to use the care programme approach
- Establish effective partnerships with primary care trusts and the local authority through regular joint meetings
- Identify dedicated budgets for funding joint projects
- Establish joint programmes for the development of local referral protocols
- Establish a Mental Health Act monitoring group with representation from primary, secondary and tertiary care, social services, and service users and carers.

This involves developing good partnerships, undertaking joint planning, agreeing local referral protocols, sharing information and developing new services that stretch across the interfaces between primary care, secondary care and social care, and address mental health, learning disabilities and the physical health of those with mental health problems.

The lead clinician and implementation team can play an important role in ensuring that strategies are in place in order for these tasks to be undertaken and monitored. As a starting point, the care programme approach (CPA), case management and the coordination and monitoring of the use of the Mental Health Act are important means of monitoring and addressing a number of interface issues. Box 19.7 sets out the issues likely to be addressed first by the lead clinician in this area.

The skills and background of the lead clinician

It is clear from the above that the lead clinician must be a leader, with vision, drive and enthusiasm, and a will to implement radical change. Lead clinicians must work well with all disciplines, and have a good track record in multidisciplinary team working. As good communicators, they will be able to inspire others and to use clear and simple models of change and jargon-free language. As respected clinicians with good relations with service users, carers and managers, they will be well placed to win the confidence of other senior clinicians across the trust. They will, at least, be familiar with the potential clinical application of electronic information technologies.

The lead clinician will ideally have good working relations with other health organisations, such as primary care trusts, social services, the strategic health authority and the Workforce Development Confederation. A broad track record in management, including clinical management, line management and project management would be a considerable advantage. However, although it could be construed that the performance management of teams is the job of the lead clinician, it would be wrong to think of this role as primarily a management role. Skills in organisational development, and an ability to 'see the bigger picture' and to think both strategically and operationally, is more important. A background in research and development and reasonable skills in critical appraisal are likely to be advantageous.

Finally, lead clinicians must have a clear commitment to both the 'new' NHS and their own organisations. A person with this range and mix of skills and experience may not be easily available, and additional training and mentoring may well be necessary. It is important, nevertheless, to identify selection criteria relevant to the job in hand, and not to select on the basis of discipline rather than skills and experience.

Support for the lead clinician

We would like to end on a cautionary note. The job of lead clinician is a very important one, with great opportunities to influence the shape of services, the outcomes of care and the experience of patients. There is also great scope for personal development. But this is not a job to be taken on without a clear brief, adequate support and realistic resources (Box 19.8). Many lead clinicians act as 'associate' medical directors, recruiting and appointing medical staff and undertaking appraisal. Others are given a much broader brief, but with only one day a week to do the job and no cover arrangements. Many have no implementation team and have to work without effective organisational support, with little or no power to realign departments or to influence service managers – a situation that is not uncommonly compounded by a dysfunctional clinical governance committee, made up of all the great and the good but with no effective role except to receive reports and to pass them on to the trust board.

We are also aware that few, if any, trusts have properly 'taken the plunge' and created the post envisaged by the Department of Health. Indeed, in our own trust there are four lead clinicians, each with responsibility for an identifiable part of the trust, and each one a member of a multidisciplinary team. Other trusts have divided up the role of lead clinician in less clear-cut ways. In any event, the need for clinicians to take a leadership role in the development of services and the implementation of clinical governance, focused upon the needs of service users and carers, is, in our view, undeniable.

However the role of lead clinician is configured, those undertaking the work will still need full backing by the trust board, a close and direct working relationship with the chief executive, an implementation team and an effective, functional clinical governance committee. They need the power to make the necessary organisational rearrangements so as to influence the work of teams more directly. And they need enough time to

---

Box 19.8 Skills and support for the lead clinician

- Vision, enthusiasm and excellent communication skills
- Track record in multidisciplinary team-working
- Strategic, organisational and management skills
- Familiarity with research and development
- Practical support: time, resources
- Personal support: training, mentoring, supervision and direct access to the chief executive of the trust.

---

do the job properly. For a medium-size trust this will mean at least a half-time post with adequate clinical cover. A dedicated budget for personal training/mentoring and adequate resources to implement agreed plans are essential. Without the right tools, time and resources, the job will be a fruitless burden, and a sad reflection of a trust with no real commitment to the services it provides, or to the quality of care that service users receive.

Conclusions

The lead clinician is responsible for leading the local implementation of clinical governance and for ensuring that local services are sensitive to national quality initiatives and the development of other local health organisations. With the support of a multidisciplinary implementation team, and full backing from the chief executive and the trust board, lead clinicians will reorganise the trust departments, and develop systems and mechanisms able to support clinical and social care teams in the monitoring and improvement of the quality of care they provide. As a skilled leader with wide experience and the support of all the disciplines, the lead clinician will need time and sufficient resources to fulfil this role.

References

Audini, B., Cattermole, D. & Kendall, T. J. G. (2002) *Training Needs Analysis Pilot Project: Final Report*. London: Department of Health.

Department of Health (1998) *A First Class Service: Quality in the New NHS*. London: Department of Health.

Department of Health (1999) *Clinical Governance: Quality in the New NHS*, HSC 1999/065. London: Department of Health.

Department of Health (2000) *The NHS Plan: A Plan for Investment, a Plan for Reform*, cm 4818-I. London: TSO.

CHAPTER 20

Clinical governance and nurse leadership

Martin F. Ward

- Not all nurses have the appropriate roles to be able to make a full contribution to clinical governance
- Nurses are best suited for clinical governance activities where they have clear responsibility for clinical or professional outcomes
- Certain key nursing activities (i.e. special observation, control and restraint) are particularly susceptible to developments driven by clinical governance
- Consultant nurses are uniquely placed to represent nursing as participants in clinical governance activities because of the clear clinical and research focus of their role
- For an organisation's clinical governance to be totally representative, nursing knowledge has to be included as a component of available resources.

Introduction

While it is not known precisely how many psychiatric/mental health nurses are actually practising in the UK, some 56 000 are registered to do so with the UK Nursing and Midwifery Council. In 1999, a review of the mental health nursing membership of the Royal College of Nursing (Ward, 2000) indicated that at least 25 000 were members of that organisation; approximately 10% of them were in management or senior management positions, 5% were in academia and the remainder held clinical positions. Despite these large numbers, there was alarm at the time surrounding the ability of nursing to coordinate its own activities and concern that there was a missing cadre of senior clinical nurses able to act as both role models and clinical leaders. The origins of this situation are complex, but in part relate to the inability of mental health nursing to establish clear roles for itself within psychiatry and then develop specific educational and professional support programmes for those identified to lead it.

However, as mental health services themselves have become more focused, so too have nurses recognised that they have a significant part to play within these new developments. Indeed, over the past decade nurses have assumed many lead roles in the development of audit activities, coordination of the care programme approach (CPA), quality assurance procedures and the introduction of evidence-based mental healthcare. In addition, there has been an increase in graduate-level entry to the profession, and a greater emphasis upon the research orientation. Individual nurses have taken more active roles in both the local and national policy aspects of care provision. More recently, the introduction of clinical governance has provided nursing with the opportunity to formalise some of these activities (Department of Health, 1999a).

The case for clinical governance within nursing leadership

Clinical governance is important to mental health nurses because so much of what they have been developing as part of their professional portfolio is involved with the delivery of a quality service. True, clinical governance is not just about improving quality, but quality is at the heart of its intent (Rigby, 1995). Consider nursing against all the other core disciplines within psychiatry. All have responsibility for maintaining rigorous standards of quality control, not just within their own sphere of influence but also in every aspect of the service where they have some involvement. All have responsibility to 'govern' their respective professional domain (Scally & Donaldson, 1998) and are expected to manage their work for the good of the patient and the service. All have responsibility for identifying research agendas relevant to their practice focus, for seeking evidence to support change, for implementing change within their work and for evaluating performance against established benchmarks.

Genuine multidisciplinary and multi-agency working requires that each discipline contributes to interactive ways of working to provide continuity of patient care. Each has a responsibility for reflective teaching and learning, with each, in some way, responsible for developing discipline-specific education from its own definitions of clinical quality. Each uses its own definition to monitor leadership and clinical commitment. Finally, each is accountable both for its own professional actions as part of its input to the core team and as part of the feedback mechanism within the quality cycle, and to its patients, whose expectations of it demand that its conduct matches their purpose.

There are no differences here between disciplines. All have the same responsibility for care, for improving services, for reporting outcomes, for leading and acting as role models, and for maintaining and increasing quality. But differences there are. Nurses do not have the same responsibility in law as do their medical colleagues, nor do they have the same professional background as other colleagues on the team. Historically, many nurses have not been used to assuming lead roles within an organisational structure, nor even within clinical teams. Moreover, research from both the UK (Cioffi, 1997) and Belgium (Stordeur *et al*, 2000) suggests that senior nurses, more than other team members, are more prone to using heuristic or intuitive approaches to clinical decision-making, contrary to that expected of an evidence-based service.

These differences make it important to realise that while nurses have a commitment to clinical governance, they cannot be expected to undertake all the work that it entails. Conversely, as Gould *et al* (2001) point out, neither can they opt out of areas that are patently their responsibility, namely those that require nurses to undertake, manage, regulate and evaluate them. No one discipline would expect another to organise it, educate it and lead it in practice, and no one discipline in contemporary mental health practice has the time to 'govern' another (Goodman, 1998). It is therefore the responsibility of nursing to seek to apply the principles of clinical governance to its own actions and then to contribute, along with other disciplines, to the clinical governance of the core business of the service as a whole. Recognising and understanding this fact is central to appreciating how nurses may contribute to the clinical governance agenda.

For nurses to be involved in organisational clinical governance, they have to be in a position to understand how their employing organisation is managed, how its care philosophy is operationalised and how day-to-day management is negotiated and controlled. Nurse leaders have to take an active part in this, irrespective of whether they represent a clinical, managerial or academic function. For those nurses in a position to exert authority within an organisation, their role within clinical governance will be defined by their relationships with other members of the multidisciplinary team (MDT). As Goodman (1998) points out, clinical governance itself is based on effective relationships and will happen naturally where these exist. However, this means that nurses will have had to develop a reputation for being effective themselves, rather than being accepted simply because of the position they hold within an organisation. This may not always be the case for members of other disciplines.

Nurses will hold different levels of responsibility within an organisation, from junior clinical staff up to senior management. In some cases, it is the less senior nurses who are more clinically effective within the organisation, by reputation and performance, and it is to these individuals that other members of the MDT look rather than to those in more senior positions. Again, this is not always the case for other disciplines.

Nurses in these more junior positions may not have organisational authority and therefore decisions they make or advice they give is often dependent upon others to implement. This can lead to tension between disciplines and a sense of disempowerment for the nurses involved. Studies have shown that such situations often lead to professional disengagement and even to staff leaving an organisation because they feel abused (Barker & Walker, 2000).

The above observations are not cited as an excuse for nurses not to take an active part in clinical governance, but more to explain why it is that in some circumstances an organisation's expectations of them simply exceed their capabilities and may cause more harm than good. Goodman (1998) also sees a problem with the escalation of workloads as a consequence of increased quality measurement. This might be the case for a nurse who, in addition to clinical activities, was required to undertake exhaustive monitoring duties that interfered with his/her ability to carry out the clinical role effectively. A lack of primary resourcing and support for quality initiatives is short-sighted and shows a lack of understanding by senior service managers about the work of their staff (Richards, 1998).

It is simply not possible for many clinically based nurses to adopt wide-ranging generic monitoring or audit responsibilities. Their roles preclude them from taking an active part in organisational decision-making and, as such, their main area of concern has to be the clarification of their own areas of responsibility. Once the clinical governance activities for which they can have responsibility have been specified, they may be able to influence consequent change and development. Central to the success of this, however, is the organisation's ability to link the aspirations of these clinically based nurses with its own core strategy. This has to be achieved, in part, through linking the different levels of nurses themselves. Hence, the senior managerial nurses, and those in nursing leadership positions such as consultant nurses or nurse specialists, need to establish and maintain a dialogue with their more junior colleagues, each using the other to inform their own decisions.

Both Manley (2000) and Cunningham & Kitson (2000) show that nurse clinical leaders depend on effective working relationships, not just inter-disciplinary but also intra-disciplinary relationships, for a large part of their success. While it is the responsibility of those nurses to be aware of their communication parameters, it is not their responsibility alone. If an organisation wants its nurses to make a significant contribution to the clinical governance agenda, it has to do so in relation to their position and role within that organisation. Leaders should be expected to lead, but only where they have the authority to do so. An organisation needs to identify those who are invested with this authority and in the case of nurses this will invariably be the senior clinical grades and nurse managers. It should be through them alone that clinical governance activities are channelled, even though all nurses within an organisation may take part in the process.

In summary:

- nursing participation in clinical governance requires an understanding of the organisation in which they work
- adequate resourcing is necessary for nurses to participate in clinical governance and clinical work
- authority must be invested in those required to make clinical governance decisions.

Nursing representation within a multidisciplinary team

Multidisciplinary teams are usually made up of clinical leads within separate units of function. For example, an MDT on an acute admission unit may incorporate those responsible for primary nursing teams and specialist services (e.g. community, nurse therapies, etc.) as well as a senior nurse to represent nurses from the ward or unit, yet who may not have direct responsibility for all those nurses, particularly the specialists. Nevertheless, the other MDT members may expect that the senior nurse is responsible for nurses, just as the senior medical staff or the head occupational therapists are responsible for their own disciplines. However, within a ward or unit, even though the senior nurse will have overall responsibility for coordinating the junior nurses, primary nurses will be responsible for managing the patients within their teams and senior specialist nurses will have control over their own care activities (Ward, 1992). The lines of communication between the different nurse grades will determine the amount of information that each has about the working of the other, irrespective of their seniority. In many cases it may well be that ward-based clinical nurses have the same information about the work of another individual nurse as any other member of the team, because, like them, they meet with that nurse only at MDT meetings.

Expectations of a nurse by other members of the MDT may be at variance with that nurse's role or level of responsibility. To function effectively within an MDT, individuals have to be seen to know about their own skill, communicate that knowledge articulately to the other members of the team, and show that they are aware of options and alternatives. Their decisions must be seen to be based on evidence, or at least founded on critical thinking, and, above all else, they have to be able to defend those decisions appropriately in the face of debate and disagreement from other members of the MDT. Nurses participating in an MDT meeting may not have overall responsibility for the nursing package of care and therefore may not have the ability to fulfil all the expectations of other members at that meeting. Consequently, when asked to respond to questions outside their domain they may be seen as less capable because of that apparent lack of knowledge. Nursing is devalued in such circumstances. While it is not the purpose of this chapter to describe all the ways in which such a situation can be rectified, certainly the clinical governance agenda is one area where nurses can perform the work appropriate to their level of responsibility and make a positive contribution to the overall work of the MDT.

Consultant nurses and clinical governance

Since the introduction of consultant nurses in 1999, their contribution to clinical governance has been seen as a crucial part of their work (Manley, 2000). However, the appointment of this group has proved difficult. Nearly 20% of the first wave of consultant nurse appointments were within mental health, yet most of these were within specialist areas, such as eating disorders and self-harm. While this was good news for those areas, the main in-patient area of acute psychiatry was left without the opportunity to develop its nurse clinical leadership. Indeed, it could be argued that all the first appointments should have been within this particular area. Such a move would have provided nursing with a large core group of leaders who could have networked across the country to support each other in determining their roles and functions and provided a much-needed boost to the acute in-patient services (Department of Health, 1999b; Ward et al, 2000). As it is, by spreading this first batch of nurses throughout the different areas of psychiatry, their potential impact on nurse clinical leadership has been diluted.

The role of consultant nurses is firmly based in clinical practice. Their time is equally divided between practice and research and teaching. They have no management authority as such, but should be responsible for leading clinical teams and acting as a resource for other nurses. They are expected to hold their own case-load and this is presumably why so many trusts determined that the first group should work in areas where independent practice was routine. Research activities need to include the development of evidence-based mental health nursing, the coordination and collection of research and audit data, and the maintenance of outcome measures, to establish rigorous quality control (Sullivan, 1998). Because consultant nurses are free from the burden of direct management and are clearly focused on the clinical domain, their potential contribution to the clinical governance agenda is obvious.

Certainly, the consultant nurse is ideally positioned to fill the gap between the more junior clinical nurses and those in managerial positions, in as far as they represent a group of nurses whose main concern should be that of coordinating certain key features of clinical governance. For example, their roles are clearly defined and therefore it is much easier for them to be able to undertake clinical audit activities, establish research profiles and maintain continuity within a given area of practice. They have been appointed because of their proven ability to provide high levels of clinical input. They should be capable of communicating their skill to others, should have higher academic qualifications and should have additional post-registration qualifications, all enabling them to function at a senior clinical level. By definition, therefore, they are able to act as a role model for junior nursing staff while being considered by other MDT members as equals.

They differ from the nurse specialists as a group in that consultant nurses are employed to work full time within clinical practice, may have managerial responsibility for other members of their team and may also be the senior nurse for a service. In theory, consultant nurses are uniquely positioned to contribute to the clinical scene, the MDT consultative agenda and clinical governance activities. If the original guidance from the Department of Health (1999b) is to be adhered to, consultants nurse would appear to be of primary importance, as the guidance called on them to establish leadership, accountability and working relationships, conduct baseline assessments of capacity and capability, formulate clinical governance development plans, and clarify its reporting arrangements.

As already stated, no nurses should be put in a position where they are expected to make a contribution to clinical governance activities over which they do not have some degree of authority or for which they are not professionally accountable. In the case of consultant nurses working in acute in-patient settings, they are able to coordinate organisational or core clinical governance procedures, such as audit and quality control mechanisms for general service delivery. They are also in a position to develop activities related to the specific clinical function of the unit, even down to the work of individual practitioners. From this unique position, they can assess the introduction of protocols to shape or influence practice, provide outcome data for individualised care, and monitor change or practice development programmes, either generated from the organisation's core business or established strictly for their unit.

Nurses need new knowledge to be able to contribute to the changes in the NHS, but they also need to be able to consolidate what it is they already contribute to care. The overall intention of clinical governance as conceived by the Department of Health is to improve services, but the reality is that, in some cases, the best an organisation can do initially is to maintain what it already does, rather than strive, inappropriately, to improve or change it. Nursing's body of knowledge is all too often unknown to service managers and, consequently, cannot be included as an organisational resource nor contribute to assessing the competency of service delivery. As Hayward et al (1999) point out, some organisations' target areas for improvement are based on internal evidence of performance, but all too often organisations target everything without any real knowledge at all.

Consultant nurses are, in reality, the role models for nursing care, and it seems perfectly possible for them to produce registers of good practice, to lead the production of guidelines and standards, and to support others in their professional development. Moreover, while clinical governance itself is about organisations reaching optimum levels of performance, it is by assessing the care provided to individual patients that the real effects of the initiative are measured. The consultant nurse is able to link these two ends of the continuum by combining an understanding of the organisation's core business, through involvement in committee work and the MDT, with a first-hand knowledge of the aspirations of individual practitioners charged with operationalising that core business.

In summary:

- Because they have a clear clinical and research focus, consultant nurses are potentially an invaluable resource for the clinical governance agenda
- Consultant nurses are in a unique position to monitor the introduction of evidence-based practice
- As clinical leads, consultant nurses are able to link the care of individual patients to the overall process of clinical governance.

Clinical governance and special observation

To appreciate how the consultant nurse might make the contribution outlined in the previous section, it is necessary to consider an example where nurses have direct clinical responsibility for an individualised care procedure that in turn has significant consequences for an organisation as a whole. I have chosen the process of special, or close, observation of a patient who is deemed to be actively suicidal.

The purpose of nursing observations within psychiatry is to regard patients attentively and to prevent potentially suicidal, violent or vulnerable patients from harming themselves or others or from being harmed or exploited by others. The procedure is implemented according to different prescribed 'levels' of observation, which may vary in intensity according to the degree of perceived risk (Jones *et al*, 2000). Special observation, while being a multidisciplinary activity, is almost entirely the clinical responsibility of mental health nurses.

The activity is not without criticism. Duffy (1995) pointed to the excessive variation around the UK in terms of the quality of procedural standards and in role responsibilities. A review of 21 hospital trusts (Department of Health, 1999*b*) found little consensus regarding the principles, practice or procedures of special observation. Significantly, surveys of patient experiences of special observation show anomalies between what patients and nurses think is therapeutic (Ashaye *et al*, 1997; Conway, 1999; Fletcher, 1999; Jones *et al*, 2000). Special observation can use up to 50% of staff time during an average working day in acute admission areas (Ward *et al*, 1998), while reports indicate that there is a growing shortage of qualified nurses to work in acute psychiatry, where most special observation takes place (Sainsbury Centre for Mental Health, 1997, 1998). Estimates of the cost of this procedure vary, but a review undertaken by Ward & Wellman (1997) indicated that it costs the NHS in England upwards of £13 million a year in extra duty payments alone. Increasingly, trusts are attempting to rationalise the use of special observation, although as yet there is little or no consensus as to how this should be done. Moreover, some have criticised the whole procedure for being out of date, ineffective and custodial (Barker & Cutcliffe, 1999; Adams, 2000).

The above list of concerns about the procedure is by no means exhaustive. Evidence suggests that it is usually undertaken by the most junior members of staff (Sainsbury Centre for Mental Health, 1998), that its use relates more to organisational risk management than to patient care (Barker & Cutcliffe, 1999), and that its therapeutic value is devalued because nurses are untrained in the skills necessary to make it a positive activity, and because there is a lack of appropriate clinical supervision by senior nurses (Adams, 2000). Although there are any number of locally produced guidelines and standards for the procedure, the increasing amount of research on special observation is often absent from these documents. If Cioffi (1997) is to be believed, even if the evidence were incorporated into guidelines, a tension would exist between the junior staff who undertake the observations and the senior staff who should be supervising them. The former appear to use evidence to guide their practice, while the latter are more comfortable with their intuition and often ignore evidence to the contrary. Special observation, it would seem, is an ideal candidate for scrutiny within a clinical governance framework.

The clinical governance approach to developing a well-coordinated and quality-monitored special observation procedure should be no different to those for any other aspect of care:

- a review of local practice would identify shortfalls and areas to be developed
- a review of the current literature plus communication with other trusts and identification of areas of recognised good practice would reveal implementation options
- data on existing work practices, patient profiles and clinical decision-making would be gathered to establish a baseline for the work
- the chosen options would be implemented

305

- after a reasonable period (at least 6 months) the baseline measures would be re-evaluated
- a simple comparison of the baseline and follow-up measures would be made.

What is important here is not the approach itself, but the individuals who are charged with undertaking the work. First, a consultant nurse on an acute in-patient unit would be able to liaise with the MDT to establish the support for change among all the team members. Change affects everyone and unless all involved are satisfied with the options and their consequences, it is very easy for one or more individuals to jeopardise a whole development programme and, in so doing, alienate and frustrate those who wish to take responsibility for it. Second, the consultant nurse would have direct access to the clinical staff responsible for carrying out the procedure. They need to be directly involved in the decisions for change, the selection of options, their implementation and the data collection necessary to establish their effectiveness. Finally, the consultant nurse would be able to operationalise the development programme because of his/her unique position as a clinical lead and in holding the joint practice/research roles.

Conclusions

Selecting the right staff to undertake the right activities within clinical governance is crucial for its success. Mental health nurse clinical leadership is currently seeking ways to express itself and with the huge numbers of mental health nurses available to the service their value to change processes cannot be ignored. However, their involvement has to be commensurate with the level of their responsibility within an organisation. The consultant nurse group offers the opportunity to coordinate clinically oriented clinical governance areas of practice while liaising with both trust organisational structures and other members of the MDT. The example of special observation given above shows that such an activity, ripe for the clinical governance agenda, would best be served by employing this senior clinically based nurse both as a project manager and as the lead practitioner for the implementation of change.

The benefits to all concerned are obvious. Nurse clinical leadership and role modelling is enhanced by their involvement in appropriate clinical governance activities by using the right staff for the right job. Nurses are able to implement their skills to best effect when they manage their own clinical actions. The possible consequences in terms of an increase in professional confidence and a more competent nursing workforce cannot be undervalued. Patients benefit because the care offered during the delivery of an intimate and highly specialist procedure is more personalised. The MDT benefits because it recognises that one of its key representatives is developing its knowledge base and is able to make a far more constructive contribution to clinical decision-making. This, in turn, frees the MDT from having to make certain decisions which common sense would suggest are not really its responsibility. Finally, the organisation benefits because its nurses have undertaken rigorous practice development within their sphere of influence. Lines of responsibility and practice are clearly defined and patient care is improved. Thus the organisation's targeted commitment to the clinical governance mandate not only improves practice, but also develops staff.

References

Adams, B. (2000) Locked doors or sentinel nurses. *Psychiatric Bulletin*, **24**, 327–328.

Ashaye, O., Ikkos, G. & Rigby, E. (1997) Study of effects of constant observation of psychiatric in-patients. *Psychiatric Bulletin*, **21**, 145–147.

Barker, P. J. & Cutcliffe, J. (1999) Clinical risk: a need for engagement not observation. *Mental Health Practice*, **2**(8), 8–12.

Barker, P. J. & Walker, L. (2000) Nurse perceptions of multidisciplinary team working in acute psychiatric settings. *Journal of Psychiatric and Mental Health Nursing*, **7**, 539–546.

Cioffi, J. (1997) Heuristics, servants to intuition in clinical decision making. *Journal of Advanced Nursing*, **26**, 203–208.

Conway, E. A. (1999) *A Multi-dimensional Study of the Process of Observation in Acute Mental Health Wards, Involving Policy Documentation, Staff and User Views.* Newcastle upon Tyne: Newcastle City Health Trust.

Cunningham, G. & Kitson, A. (2000) An evaluation of the RCN Clinical Leadership Development Programme: Part 1. *Nursing Standard*, **15**(12), 34–37.

Department of Health (1999a) *Clinical Governance: Quality in the New NHS*, HSC 1999/065. London: Department of Health.

Department of Health (1999b) *Report by the Standing Nursing and Midwifery Advisory Committee (SNMAC). Mental Health Nursing: Addressing Acute Concerns.* London. HMSO.

Duffy, D. (1995) Out of the shadows: a study of special observation of suicidal inpatients. *Journal of Advanced Nursing*, **21**, 944–950.

Fletcher, R. F. (1999) The process of constant observation. Perceptions of staff and suicidal patients. *Journal of Psychiatric and Mental Health Nursing*, **6**, 9–14.

Goodman, N. W. (1998) Clinical governance. *BMJ*, **317**, 1725–1727.

Gould, D., Kelly, D. & Maidwell, A. (2001) Clinical nurse managers: perceptions of factors affecting role performance. *Nursing Standard*, **15**(16), 33–37.

Hayward, J., Rosen, R. & Dewar, S. (1999) Clinical governance. Thin on the ground. *Health Service Journal*, 26 August, 26–27.

Jones, J., Ward, M. F., Wellman, N., *et al* (2000) Psychiatric in-patients' experience of nursing observation. *Journal of Psychosocial Nursing*, **38**(12), 10–20.

Manley, K. (2000) Organisational culture and consultant nurse outcomes: Part 2. *Nursing Standard*, **14**(37), 34–38.

Richards, P. (1998) Professional self-respect: rights and responsibilities in the new NHS. *BMJ*, **317**, 1146–1148.

Rigby, B. (1995) A role fit for purpose? *Journal of the Association of Quality in Healthcare*, **3**, 3–15.

Sainsbury Centre for Mental Health (1997) *The National Visit.* London: Mental Health Act Commission and Sainsbury Centre for Mental Health.

Sainsbury Centre for Mental Health (1998) *Acute Problems: A Survey of the Quality of Care in Acute Psychiatric Wards.* London: Sainsbury Centre for Mental Health.

Scally, G. & Donaldson, L. J. (1998) Clinical governance and the drive for quality improvement in the new NHS in England. *BMJ*, **317**, 61–65.

Stordeur, S., Vandenberghe, C. & D'hoore, W. (2000) Leadership styles across hierarchical levels in nursing departments. *Nursing Research*, **49**, 37–43.

Sullivan, P. (1998) Developing evidence based care in mental health nursing. *Nursing Standard*, **12**(31), 35–38.

Ward, M. F. (1992) *The Nursing Process in Psychiatry* (2nd edn). Edinburgh: Churchill Livingstone.

Ward, M. F. (2000) *A Review of Mental Health Membership Within Forums of the RCN, 1999.* Unpublished internal review. London: Royal College of Nursing.

Ward, M. F. & Wellman, N. (1997) *A Review of the Observational Activities in Two English NHS Trusts.* Unpublished review. Oxford: Oxford Mental Health NHS Trust.

Ward, M. F., Gournay, K., Thornicroft, G., *et al* (1998) *The 1997 Census: A Survey of Inner London Acute Mental Health In-patient Services.* London: Royal College of Nursing.

Ward, M. F., Gournay, K. & Cutcliffe, J. (2000) *The Nursing and Midwifery and Health Visiting Contribution to the Continuing Care of People with Mental Health Problems.* London: United Kingdom Central Council for Nursing (UKCC).

CHAPTER 21

Managing change in mental health services

Jenny Firth-Cozens

- A reporting and learning culture is now required in the National Health Service, but it will be necessary for this change in culture to be managed
- Staff development will facilitate this change
- Clinical governance has the potential to increase staff stress and thereby to reduce the quality of care
- Resistance to change is normal and not necessarily a bad thing, but should not be ignored
- Poor performance must be analysed and tackled.

Introduction

Clinical governance involves change in a number of organisational arenas. First, it means the organisation itself needs to change, primarily in terms of its culture, towards one in which accountability and learning can coexist and develop. Second, it will involve change in terms of information, and this will require systematic reporting by individuals, teams and the organisation as a whole (Department of Health, 2000). Third, the organisation will have to tackle individual resistance to change: staff who may feel that they need not, cannot, will not, or even should not change. This chapter looks at these areas, and focuses on the role of teams in achieving these goals.

When clinical governance was first introduced, the words '"no blame" culture' featured in many discussions. Now these words are used less often, and we are more likely to hear about learning cultures, reporting cultures and just cultures (Department of Health, 2000). Marrying accountability and 'no blame' was perhaps too difficult for any health organisation to achieve; a more honest description of the approach – and words matter if you are trying to increase trust – is a learning culture that is 'open and fair'. This is a culture in which people know their individual and team responsibilities and those of other team members, but are able to admit error in the knowledge that this will be treated, within defined limits, as an opportunity to learn and improve patient care.

A reporting culture

Learning can occur only if both good and unsatisfactory behaviours are recognised and acknowledged in the first place. Although the recognition of good practice and the encouragement of its spread have always been an important part of the change that follows audit, it is the recognition and reporting of *error*, and change as a result of this, that is an important focus of the culture that allows clinical governance to work well. Nevertheless, a reporting system that allows creativity and learning is not always easy to achieve. Here are three true stories that provide a spectrum for what might occur:

- A large international airport was experiencing an unacceptably high level of ground accidents, and equipment, travellers' luggage and even some personnel were being damaged. This resulted in very high costs to the company. It brought in a genuine 'no blame' policy. Each error and near miss was reported and discussed in a 'quality' circle to see how things could be changed for the better in terms of practice, resources and training. The agreed changes were implemented as appropriate. Initially, accidents appeared to rise sharply as people began to report more freely, but then, as learning took place, they began to reduce until they were considerably lower than before the intervention.
- At a hospital in the United States, a 'three strikes and you're out' policy was introduced to reduce medication error. Staff were allowed to report two errors, but were expected to have learnt from that experience and would be dismissed if another error took place. Remarkably, the organisation found that this was successful, since no one ever reported more than two errors.
- A study of teamwork and medication error on the part of nurses showed that, contrary to expectations, teams that had reported good working relationships had higher error rates than those reporting poor ones. Following up this survey with an interview survey of team leaders, the authors discovered that poor teams were led by autocratic, punitive leaders, whereas good teams had democratic leaders who emphasised learning and genuine improvement (Edmondson, 1996).

These stories demonstrate the intimate links between reporting, trust, teamwork, leadership and change. Reporting is difficult because it is always directed to a particular end; for example, to show whether the care provided is good or not. Unless there is a belief that the reason for the reporting is to help staff produce better care rather than to punish them for mistakes, the reporting is likely to be inaccurate. There is a saying about this, illustrated by the second and third stories above: 'What gets measured gets manipulated'. However, the airport story shows that this is not inevitable. One way around this dilemma is to say 'We are judging the quality initially of your reporting systems alone: judged by a variety of studies you should be having x% of (say) medication errors in your team. If you are not having this percentage, please demonstrate why not.'

This shifts the emphasis both to the importance of reporting *per se* and to the explanation of good care, which is less threatening but equally effective in terms of learning. Another aid to this learning is to encourage the reporting of not only actual events but also near misses. Near misses have much less guilt and anger attached to them, and provide excellent material for encouraging cultural change (Department of Health, 2000; Firth-Cozens, 2000).

More accurate reporting and increased trust can also be engendered by taking an organisational systems approach to avoiding risk and producing better care (Reason, 1997). This takes the focus of problems away from the individual staff–patient dyad, and recognises and manages areas of concern throughout the system. It reduces the emotional debris that can occur when the focus is on the individual provider, and so learning can take place more widely (Firth-Cozens, 2000).

Key point

- Accurate reporting of error needs rewarding to encourage gains in staff trust.

The role of teams

Although an organisational approach to risk and learning is essential if the whole organisation is to understand the parts of its system that have failed, it is also true that healthcare organisations are usually too large to encourage this process on a day-to-day level. I have argued elsewhere (Firth-Cozens, 1995, 2000) that teams are the best place for both reporting and learning to take place: better than whole organisations and certainly better than at the individual level alone. On the one hand, failures in teamwork are apparent in the majority of internal inquiries (Reith, 1998). On the other hand, they provide a more supportive context for staff, who should know each other's roles and the demands that the job entails, and who understand the difficulties, risks and benefits for their patients of different types of practice. Good teams have lower stress levels than poor teams (Carter & West, 1999; Firth-Cozens & Rayner, 2000) and this is likely to be because members can offer support to one another. They may also produce better outcomes (Adorian *et al*, 1990). Importantly for clinical governance, studies from the military show that this does not always mean their *individual* members' error scores are lower than in teams that are less well formed; rather, it means that good teams can recognise, feedback and compensate for individual mistakes and so produce less *team* error (Fouchee & Helmreich, 1988).

However, not all teams are good teams, and even apparently good teams can become a law unto themselves unless they are linked appropriately into the management structure and are responsible for adhering to the strategic direction and demands of the organisation as a whole. Within this framework, teams can be self-managing (Shukla, 1997): it is for the team to design the way it achieves the organisation's goals and to be accountable for its day-to-day care. Leaders of such teams then need to report only poor care that continues despite the support and education that the team has been able to provide. In some cases reporting may come promptly (e.g. where abuse of patients is concerned); in others, it might come after a variety of ways to change practice have been offered to the individual.

All healthcare teams are multidisciplinary, and this offers not only a diversity of skills but also a variety of potential ways to support and develop fellow team members and patients alike. This diversity is a fundamental benefit of teamwork. However, health service teams are unusual in that their accountability is usually to their professional lead rather than to the nominal team leader, such as the consultant psychiatrist. Unless lines of authority and responsibility are made clear within the team, it becomes difficult for individuals to address causes for concern, and this affects both stress levels and patient care (Stokes, 1995).

Key point

- Teams are the primary unit for reporting and learning to occur.

Developing staff

This movement towards a culture of reporting and learning depends on good team leadership (Hogan *et al*, 1994) and ongoing team and individual development. It will also involve the recognition and management of risk, described above, rather than its simple monitoring. However, an early survey of developmental needs for clinical governance showed, among other things, that team leadership training for consultants and nurses was almost entirely missing, and few had any idea of how to take a more systemic approach to risk management (Firth-Cozens, 1999).

Although some people argue that leadership skills are innate (e.g. Nicholson, 1998), it is also clear that people benefit hugely from being helped to understand their own difficulties and strengths in leadership, the value of difference within teams, and ways to help individuals learn in a supportive environment (Fitzgerald & Kirby, 1997). It was clear from the survey that we have some way to go: one psychiatrist told me 'All my job entails is risk management', but when he described what he meant, it was to do with fire-fighting by himself rather than working out with staff how to tackle potential risks at every level.

Part of changing the culture towards clinical governance must involve training staff themselves to understand the elements of the process – leadership, patient involvement, audit, evidence-based healthcare, team-work, risk management and so on – and how these mesh together for better healthcare. With the development of the Modernisation Agency and the NHS University, there have been great developments in training since the survey took place. A useful website for free training is www.HealthcareSkills.nhs.uk, particularly for packages on patient safety and teamwork and leadership.

One way to judge the extent to which care is truly patient-centred in an organisation is to count the times that patient issues (as opposed to structural or professional concerns) appear on the agendas of board meetings.

Key point

- Culture will not change without investment in staff development and training, including leadership skills.

Leadership

A genuine learning culture requires leaders who:

- consistently demonstrate patient-centred care through their own behaviour
- can show that they trust their staff and are trustworthy themselves.

The importance of good leadership in *consistently* pushing forward any quality agenda cannot be emphasised too much. Binney & Williams (1997, p. 59) quote a senior manager from Nissan:

'To achieve real quality everyone in the organisation has to genuinely believe it and act on the belief. Management must mean what it says. As soon as a senior manager lets a car go through which is not the right quality level "because I have to meet the schedule" the battle is lost.'

Expediency and efficiency have been key top-down messages in health service management for many years, but they do not necessarily sit comfortably alongside quality; so, when there is a conflict between them, it is essential that leaders at senior and team levels consistently insist upon quality leading the way.

Staff will begin to trust their leader only when:

- this behaviour towards the promotion of patient-centred care is consistenly shown
- they are clearly trusted
- they participate at every level in the improvement of care.

It is clear from the third anecdote above what happens when a leader is not trusted: reporting becomes manipulated. Every organisation will need time for this trust to develop and chief executives and others may have to ride the waves of adverse publicity occasionally in supporting staff as much as possible, to engender this cultural change (Firth-Cozens, 2003).

Key point

- Leaders must value quality above expediency.
- Leaders must maintain consistency if trust and confidence in the changing culture are to grow.

Staff stress and quality of care

There is another aspect of human resources that often goes without acknowledgement and yet is one that crucially affects the quality of care delivered. This is the effect on care of staff stress. There is evidence of higher stress levels among health service staff than among the general working population (Wall *et al*, 1997) and in particular for doctors, including psychiatrists (Deary *et al*, 1996), and mental health nurses (Fagin *et al*, 1996). Various studies have shown psychiatrists to have higher levels of symptoms, of both stress and depression, and less job satisfaction than other groups (Deary *et al*, 1996; Firth-Cozens *et al*, 1999). This is likely to be due to various factors within the workplace, such as goal clarity (Thomsen *et al*, 1999) and team leadership (Thomsen *et al*, 1998), but there is also evidence that these differences between psychiatrists and other specialists are apparent even among medical students (Firth-Cozens *et al*, 1999). Mental health workers in general are likely to have experienced more childhood traumas than other health staff (Elliott & Guy, 1993) and this may need to be taken into account in terms of its potential effects upon patient care, and also upon organis-ational change.

We have evidence that links high levels of stress among health workers to poorer care (Firth-Cozens, 2001). High stress and low job satisfaction are almost always strongly correlated (up to around $r=0.6$) and job dissatisfaction has also been shown to be linked to factors

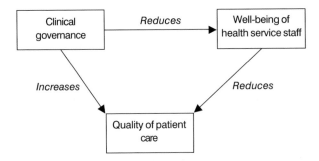

Figure 21.1 Links between clinical governance, staff well-being and quality of care.

indicative of poorer-quality patient care (Linn *et al*, 1985; DeMatteo *et al*, 1993).

Finally, we need to admit that healthcare nowadays takes place in an emotional context very different to that which occurred before 1980, and very different to those contexts from which other models of cultural change are gathered. This emotional context has been described accurately by Lucian Leape and colleagues (1998):

'patients and physicians ... live and interact in a culture characterised by anger, blame, guilt, fear, frustration and distrust regarding healthcare errors. The public has responded by escalating the punishment for error. Clinicians and some healthcare organisations generally have responded by suppression, stonewalling and cover-up.'

These three areas together – clinical governance, staff well-being and quality of care – provide us with a model which shows that clinical governance should have a beneficial effect on the quality of patient care, but that for staff it may at best involve extra work and at worst involve very real perceptions of threat – which is likely to raise stress levels. We also know that the quality of patient care is negatively affected by high stress. This process is illustrated in Fig. 21.1. Because of this, we need to include methods to reduce stress and increase job satisfaction as a major part of the cultural change towards clinical governance. Continuing to ignore it can lead only to failure. There are now many primary and secondary ways to tackle organisational stress, some of which have a reasonably good evidence base (Firth-Cozens, 2001). These will involve interventions at both the organisational (Murphy, 1999; Firth-Cozens & Rayner, 2000) and the individual level (Hale & Hudson, 1999).

Key point

- Initiatives towards clinical governance and quality in general will fail unless staff stress is tackled.

Resistance to change

In managing change, it has often been suggested that it is better to work with those keen to change – and perhaps also with those who are merely ambivalent – and leave aside those who are clearly resistant (Stocking, 1992). However, doing this is dangerous, for two reasons. First, it means that, because only those who are already more positive are engaged with, the variation in care is widened rather than narrowed – the very opposite of the purpose of initiatives such as the National Service Framework. Second, it means that only the more positive messages about the organisation and its abilities are heard, and it becomes possible to lose touch with the reality that those less-optimistic staff sometimes represent.

'Resistance' can have many meanings, even within and between dictionaries. It can be both a good thing and a bad thing, and both aspects of it need to be taken into account. For example:

'*Resistance* – Refusal to comply, hindrance; – a movement (especially of unconquered people in a conquered country).' *Oxford English Dictionary*

'*Resistance:* 1. The degree of immunity that the body possesses: a measure of its ability to withstand disease; 2. The degree to which a disease remains unaffected by antibiotics.' *Oxford Concise Medical Dictionary*

'I had long been puzzled by the notion of resistance in therapy .... I found it difficult to label as resistance when it seemed to be a message the clients were sending in an effort to help the therapist help them.' (de Shazer, 1985)

Organisational resistance should never be ignored. Its positive side is that it is an important message to leaders that things are not well, or are moving too fast for comfort or safety, or that people want to have their voices heard in deciding how change should come about. Its negative side is that people have dug in, perhaps because of high stress or dissatisfaction – dispositional or otherwise – or are afraid of what change might bring, or need further training to understand what is expected of them now. One way to understand these reactions to change is through a 'force field' analysis, where a team, or a 'diagonal slice' through the organisation, can have its say on what are the drivers for change (and how to increase them) and what are the barriers to change (and how to tackle them). This not only provides more understanding of the problems but it allows solutions to be generated by those who need to put them into practice – so long as they have the authority to do so.

This process encourages experience in adaptability and innovation, which is missing in a top-down hierarchical management structure, and provides the basis for a more radical, organic means of change (Binney & Williams, 1997). Old-style management depended on having an excess of seniors to oversee subordinates. This is no longer the case, and decision-making has to be passed down to the team as much as possible.

Job satisfaction appears to counteract resistance. Since healthcare workers in general, and mental health workers in particular, come into their profession largely in order to 'do good', it is often difficult for them to stop doing something on the grounds of evidence-based disinvestment. Therefore, if this is necessary, it can help to offer them another means of providing help: 'You shouldn't do this because ...; but you can do more of this because ...'. Similarly, the current emphasis on serious mental illness within psychiatry leaves little obvious scope for a sense of achievement. Managing this difficult area will involve both making other aspects of the work rewarding – for example, through improvements in service delivery – and including other types of work that will provide more obvious satisfaction; for example, further training in and delivery of therapy for neurotic illnesses, or development of a mentoring role as consultants and nurses grow older.

Finally, the provision of good support and supervision is essential within mental health services. While most of this can be provided by good teamwork, access to one-to-one support and supervision is also important.

Key point

- Resistance to change is normal and not always a bad thing. It should not be ignored but should be dealt with both in teams and by management.

Tackling poor performance

Clinical governance requires the introduction of systems to recognise poor performance and of a range of ways to address it (Department of Health, 2000). Wherever possible, this should be done at the team level (Firth-Cozens, 2000), but speaking up about problems concerning a colleague's performance, even in terms of feeding back to him/her within the safety of a team, is still not culturally acceptable in healthcare in the UK. As I have discussed earlier, focusing on near misses is likely to be easier for staff, and may lead to a culture where sharing and feeding back on marginal performance or errors is the norm. London & Mone (1994) have set out a flow chart to deal with problem staff which begins with problem analysis (whether the problem is characterised by: high ability, low effort; low ability, high effort; or low ability, low effort) and leads on to a range of interventions for change. For example, high ability and low effort require rewards, role models and management; low ability and high effort might require goal setting, delegation or job redesign; while low ability and low effort might require transfer or demotion.

Key point

- Poor performance should not be tackled by a hasty or ill-considered reaction.
- A system of analysing performance and providing remedies is an essential part of change.

Conclusions

Most of the management of change is, luckily, not involved with marginal performance, but with staff who are working hard and well to bring about good patient care. Change towards something even better than this is brought about most successfully by leaders who have the attention of their peers and the respect of staff – staff who feel fully involved in the process. In the National Health Service the management of this process is undoubtedly difficult and slow, but recognising this will help to stop you, the change-maker, becoming cynical and demoralised. The recipe for success includes setting yourself realistic goals over a 5-year period – what do you hope to achieve in 6 months, 1 year, 3 years, 5 years – and then doubling these intervals. Add to this list clear operational definitions of how you will recognise that each step has been achieved, and do not forget to plan for your own succession, so that someone equally committed can take over when you move on. Having such a long-term plan, which needs to incorporate flexibility to address the unforeseen, will enable you to see the progress you have made – and what still needs to be done.

Key points

- Health service staff want to provide even better care.
- Cultural change is necessarily slow, so it is important to set realistic goals and to recognise and celebrate small steps on the way.
- Plan your succession.

References

Adorian, D., Silverberg, D. S., Tomer, D., *et al* (1990) Group discussions with the healthcare team: a method of improving care of hypertension in general practice. *Journal of Human Hypertension*, 4, 265–268.

Binney, G. & Williams, C. (1997) *Leaning into the Future: Changing the Way People Change Organizations*. London: Nicholas Brealey.

Carter, A. J. & West, M. A. (1999) Sharing the burden – team work in health care setting. In *Stress in Health Professionals: Psychological and Organizational Causes and Interventions* (eds J. Firth-Cozens & R. L. Payne), pp. 191–202. Chichester: Wiley.

de Shazer, S. (1985) *Keys to Solution in Brief Therapy*. London: Norton.

Deary, I., Agius, R. & Sadler, A. (1996) Personality and stress in consultant psychiatrists. *International Journal of Social Psychiatry*, **42**, 112–123.

DeMatteo, M. R., Sherbourne, C. D., Hays, R. D., *et al.* (1993) Physicians' characteristics influence patients' adherence to medical treatment: results from the Medical Outcomes Study. *Health Psychology*, **12**, 93–102.

Department of Health (2000) *An Organisation with a Memory. Report of an Expert Group on Learning from Adverse Events in the NHS.* London: TSO.

Edmondson, A. C. (1996) Learning from mistakes is easier said than done: group and organizational influences on the detection and correction of human error. *Journal of Applied Behavioural Science*, **32**, 5–28.

Elliott, D. M. & Guy, J D. (1993) Mental health professionals versus non-mental health professionals: childhood trauma and adult functioning. *Professional Psychology: Research and Practice*, **24**, 83–90.

Fagin, L., Carson, J., Leary, J., *et al* (1996) Stress, coping and burnout in mental health nurses: findings from three research studies. *International Journal of Social Psychiatry*, **42**, 102–111.

Firth-Cozens, J. (1995) Tackling risk by changing behaviour. *Quality in Health Care*, **4**, 97–101.

Firth-Cozens, J. (1999) *Clinical Governance Training Needs in Health Service Staff.* Durham: NHS Executive Northern & Yorkshire.

Firth-Cozens, J. (2000) Teams, culture and managing risk. In *Clinical Risk Management* (ed. C. Vincent). London: BMJ Books.

Firth-Cozens, J. (2003) Organisational trust: the keystone to patient safety. *Quality and Safety in Healthcare*, **13**, 56–61.

Firth-Cozens, J. & Rayner, K. (2000) *Report of the Training Experiences of Pre-registration House Officers and Comparing Two Systems.* London: North Thames Postgraduate Deanery.

Firth-Cozens, J., Lema, V. C. & Firth, R. A. (1999) Speciality choice, stress and personality: their relationships over time. *Hospital Medicine*, **60**, 751–755.

Firth-Cozens, J., Moss, F., Rayne, C., *et al* (2000) The effect of 1-year rotations on stress in preregistration house officers. *Hospital Medicine*, **61**, 859–860.

Fitzgerald, C. & Kirby, L. K. (eds) (1997) *Developing Leaders: Research and Applications in Psychological Type and Leadership Development.* Palo Alto, CA: Davies-Black.

Fouchee, H. C. & Helmreich, R. L. (1988) Group interaction and flight crew performance. In *Human Factors in Aviation* (eds E. L. Weiner & D. C. Hagel), pp. 189–227. San Diego, CA: Academic Press.

Hale, R. & Hudson, L. (1999) Doctors in trouble. In *Stress in Health Professionals: Psychological and Organisational Causes and Interventions* (eds J. Firth-Cozens & R. L. Payne), pp. 219–230. Chichester: Wiley.

Hogan, R., Curphy, G. J. & Hogan, J. (1994) What we know about leadership. *American Psychologist*, **49**, 493–504.

Leape, L. L., Woods, D. D., Hatlie, M. H., *et al* (1998) Promoting patient safety by preventing medical error. *Journal of the American Medical Association*, **280**, 1444.

Linn, L. S., Brook, R. H., Clark, V. A., *et al* (1985) Physician and patient satisfaction as factors related to the organization of internal medicine group practices. *Medical Care*, **23**, 1171–1178.

London, M. & Mone, E. M. (1994) Managing marginal performance in an organization striving for excellence. In *Human Dilemmas in Work Organizations: Strategies for Resolution* (eds A. K. Korman *et al*), pp. 95–124. New York: Guilford Press.

Murphy, L. (1999) Organisational interventions to reduce stress in health care professionals. In *Stress in Health Professionals: Psychological and Organisational Causes and Interventions* (eds J. Firth-Cozens & R. L. Payne), pp. 149–162. Chichester: Wiley.

Nicholson, N. (1998) How hardwired is human behavior? *Harvard Business Review*, July–August, 135–147.

Reason, J. (1997) *Managing the Risk of Organizational Accidents*. Aldershot: Ashgate.

Reith, M. (1998) Risk assessment and management: lessons from mental health inquiry reports. *Medicine, Science and the Law*, **38**, 221–226.

Shukla, M. (1997) *Competing Through Knowledge*. New Delhi: Response Books.

Stocking, B. (1992) Promoting change in clinical behaviour. *Quality in Health Care*, **1**, 56–60.

Stokes, J. (1995) Institutional chaos and personal stress. In *The Unconscious at Work: Individual and Organizational Stress in the Human Services* (eds A. Obholzer & V. Zagier Roberts), pp. 121–128. London: Routledge.

Thomsen, S., Dallender, J., Soares, J., *et al* (1998) Predictors of a health workplace for Swedish and English psychiatrists. *British Journal of Psychiatry*, **173**, 80–84.

Thomsen, S., Soares, J., Nolan, P., *et al* (1999) Feelings of professional fulfilment and exhaustion in mental health personnel: the importance of organisational and individual factors. *Psychotherapy and Psychosomatics*, **68**, 157–164.

Wall, T. D., Bolden, R. I., Borril, C. S., *et al* (1997) Minor psychiatric disorder in NHS trust staff: occupational and gender differences. *British Journal of Psychiatry*, **171**, 519–523.

CHAPTER 22

Vulnerable people in care: person-centred values and clinical governance

Errol Cocks

- People with learning disabilities experience heightened vulnerabilities as a consequence of their dependence on formal care
- Safeguards consist of preventive strategies and measures that address this vulnerability
- Person-centred values provide a necessary foundation for service reforms such as clincial governance.

Introduction

This chapter focuses on people who are in continuing care in formal human services, some of whom may have been in formal care for most of their lives. They include people with psychiatric, learning and physical disabilities, and older people. This group may share characteristics of clinical need similar to those of people in forms of acute health services; however, they have *fundamental* needs that arise from their life experiences and the fact that their entire lives are lived in formal settings such as hospitals, nursing homes and other forms of congregate care. These are needs for social valuation, belonging, personal development, relationships, good health and social inclusion. They are basic human needs, captured clearly in a survey of older persons in regard to sheltered housing, cited by the Department of the Environment, Transport and the Regions (2001, ch. 5, p. 7):

'Having a flat that is one's home; having control over one's financial affairs; choice over lifestyle; the potential to live a life focusing on what one can do, not on what one can't; the potential to learn new things and to have fun and maintain old friendships and relationships with kin in the privacy of one's own home.'

The extent to which service users' needs are addressed is directly and inextricably linked to the quality of the formal services in which they are so firmly embedded. In addition, the service setting is, in effect, their home, although it may bear little resemblance to culturally valued expressions of 'home'. Quality approaches must be sufficiently broadly conceived to take this into account. A sole emphasis on clinical issues, acute health settings and a technocratic approach will result in further neglect of this group. Attention must be given to both the conceptualisation and the operationalisation of governance if it is to improve the life conditions of vulnerable people in continuing care.

Clinical governance is conceived as a 'statutory duty of quality' aimed at shifting quality towards exemplary performance (Department of Health, 1999a). It has a strong organisational and systemic focus, supporting leadership development, structural and organisational change, and the incorporation of clinical decision-making into a management and organisational framework (Donaldson & Muir Gray, 1998). It is both service and politically driven, utilising service user involvement and professional development (Hall & Firth-Cozens, 2000). Clinical governance is a major strategy in the reform of health services in the UK. Arguably, what clinical governance lacks is a base of person-centredness.

Consideration of the needs of vulnerable people whose lives are virtually completely shaped and dependent upon formal human services presents a challenge to the technological and technocratic nature of modern formal human services. This challenge is how to make human services more 'humanised' – more person-centred and less system-serving. Reform in this direction is not new in human services; however, at the beginning of the 21st century, formal human services have never been so large, complex or formal, and dealt with so many crises. Reform attempts in fact are dominated by the very system characteristics that can be diagnosed as part of the problem! If it is acknowledged that a major problem is the formalism and complexity of human service systems, technical measures will be insufficient without consideration of humanist cultural and values issues. The major thesis of this chapter is the need for person-centred values to feature more prominently and to underpin and shape more technical measures.

There are major quality issues in formal services for people with learning disabilities; these include poor quality (Flynn, 1999), substantial variations in quality and outcomes (Department of Health, 1999b) and abuse (Sobsey, 1994; Conway et al, 1996). Reflecting a person-centred notion of risk, Emerson et al (1999), in a major study of the quality and costs of residential services, described the relationship between certain characteristics of people with learning disabilities and outcomes. For example, people with more severe levels of intellectual disability were more likely to experience:

- less choice
- less social integration
- fewer chances of employment

- a less active lifestyle
- an increased chance of being underweight
- less engagement in leisure and community-based activities.

If service users also had a mental health problem, they were at greater risk for poor outcomes overall and for accidents.

This chapter adopts the concept of *human services*. This term is inclusive in the sense that it recognises that some characteristics are shared by the full range of formal helping services for the full range of service user groups. Some of these universal characteristics are identified and explored below.

The safeguards concept

Safeguards are measures taken within or outside formal human services, the purposes of which are to ensure the personal integrity, well-being and rights of people who are perceived to be vulnerable and to protect them from harm. In contrast to the contemporary discourse of risk in human services, which is concerned primarily with risk to the system and to society, safeguards are focused on the vulnerable person. This entails recognition that some of the characteristics of the system itself increase vulnerability and risk for vulnerable service users. There are three rationales that underpin safeguards:

- heightened personal and social vulnerability
- the characteristics of modern formal human services
- the nature of the reform and change process.

Heightened personal and social vulnerability

Vulnerability provides the most important rationale for the need for safeguards. *Intrinsic* vulnerability refers to the shared experiences of all human beings in childhood through 'the miserable, extended, helpless state in which we are born and remain for so long' (Gaylin *et al*, 1981, p. 3). It also includes the adventitious vulnerability that comes from various occurrences common in life, such as loss of loved ones or illness. The notion of *heightened* vulnerability refers to a different experience in which, for some people, 'the likelihood of negative consequences is much higher, and the depth and extent of those negative consequences is much greater than for other people' (Cocks & Duffy, 1993, p. 17). Personal risk includes the presence of one or more of three conditions in a person's life (Ferguson, 1978):

- endangerment through exploitation or abuse by another person
- personal vulnerability through a lack of capacity to care for oneself
- social vulnerability through insufficient or inappropriate support.

In social role valorisation (SRV) theory (Wolfensberger, 1998, 2000), heightened vulnerability is associated with people who are members of certain groups held in low social value in society. Such groups typically include people who use human services, especially those who are in long-term formal care. Heightened vulnerability can also result from certain life experiences such as living in deprived, institutional environments or experiencing a lack of continuous, close, personal relationships. SRV links heightened vulnerability with the likelihood of a person having certain *wounding* experiences, which include rejection and social exclusion, loss, deprivation and abuse. These real human experiences may be redefined as symptomatic of pathology by formal services or seen as beyond their remit or capacity to address.

Heightened vulnerability also includes vulnerability that comes from reliance or dependence upon services that are dysfunctional and impose further harm on their users. Examination of the nature of system failures in this sense requires that the limitations and inadequacies of formal human services are clearly understood and measures put in place to counter them. The social model of disability (Oliver, 1990), which is relevant to other groups of service users, also draws attention to the contribution made by social policies and institutions to the social exclusion and disempowerment of people with a disability. In a very real sense, many of the people who are in continuing formal care experience heightened vulnerability and wounding. Safeguards measures are necessary in order to ensure that human services, among other social institutions, do not impose further wounding.

Key points

- Intrinsic vulnerability may be heightened by complex factors such as use of formal human services.
- Safeguards are necessary in order to protect people from further harm.

The characteristics of modern formal human services

The paradigm of modern formal human services is underpinned by a set of dominant assumptions which gained sway during the 19th century about a wide range of human and social problems (Cocks, 1994). The most prominent assumption was the acceptance that many unfortunate human conditions are illnesses and that formal health systems can provide the solution. The tremendous growth of human services after the Second World War, and the social, economic and political dependency of Western societies on them, are unprecedented (McKnight, 1996). Within the substantial critical literature, some 30 years ago Ivan Illich wrote prophetically:

'The disabling impact of professional control over medicine has reached the proportions of an epidemic .... Limits to professional healthcare are a rapidly growing political issue. In whose interests these limits will work will depend to a large extent on who takes the initiative in formulating the need for them: people organised for political action that challenges status-quo professional power, or the health professions intent on expanding their monopoly even further.' (Illich, 1976, pp. 3–4)

Seven key dimensions provide an opportunity for reflection on the direction of needed reforms of human services.

- *Leadership* – from a proliferation of hierarchical leadership *positions* that emphasise technical, managerial competence and portability of those skills, to charismatic and visionary leadership which is focused on people and their causes
- *Involvement* – from high levels of professionalisation and the disengagement of both ordinary citizens and informal systems, to high levels of access, involvement and influence from key constituents
- *Orientation* – from massive goal displacement towards system needs, organisational restructuring, growth and power, to high goal orientation towards people
- *Complexity* – from high levels of complexity, reductionism and fragmentation, to focused, purposeful and relatively simple structures
- *Workers* – from rigid specialism within complex industrial and professional constraints and high levels of discontinuity for workers, to flexible division of labour and high levels of continuity for workers
- *Culture* – from high levels of staff confusion and uncertainty of purpose, dissatisfaction and low morale, to interpersonal climates of enthusiasm and commitment to people
- *Values* – from the managerial ethos of value-free or content-free *management* of human and social problems, to a vision of the dignity and potentialities of people within person-centred ideologies.

Key point
- Modern formal human services require reform in the direction of person-centredness.

The nature of the reform and change process

Change in human services is certainly about structure and function, but success depends upon *cultural* shift. Human services are so dependent upon people that no reform will succeed without winning the 'hearts and minds' of the key stakeholders. Because human services are *complex social systems* (Forrester, 1969), they have certain character-istics that engender resistance to planned reform, and many of these characteristics reflect human tendencies. For example:

- Complex social systems are so replete with counterintuitive influen-ces that intuitive strategies are unlikely to succeed. This is illustrated in what appear to be causes and effects –

'Much statistical and correlation analysis is fussily pursuing this will-o'-the-wisp. In a situation where coincidental symptoms appear to be causes, a person acts to dispel the symptoms. But the underlying causes remain. The treatment is either ineffective or actually detrimental.' (Forrester, 1969, p. 110)

- Human behaviour is very resilient and 'social systems are dom-inated by natural and psychological factors that change very little' (Forrester, 1969, p. 110).
- Much reform is counteracted by the system –

'Probably no active, externally imposed program is superior to a system modification that changes internal incentives and leaves the burden of system improvement to internal processes.' (Forrester, 1969, p. 111)

- The short-term responses to change on the part of complex social systems are commonly in the opposite direction from the long-term effect. Forrester (1969) called this the 'worse before better effect'. Since the time perspective of much political and bureaucrat-ically inspired change is short term and reactive, this characteristic of systems creates considerable problems.

Key point
- Human services possess characteristics that resist reform in the direction of person-centredness.

Social influence

At the heart of any reform process is social influence, whereby the behaviour of a person changes as a result of an influencing agent who offers or makes available to the person 'a specific new behaviour, attitude, or belief – or perhaps a new pattern of responding or a different way of interpreting events that challenges habitual reactions and existing beliefs' (Kelman & Hamilton, 1989, p. 78). Kelman & Hamilton (1989) described three processes of social influence:

- *Compliance* means that people do what the influencing agent wants them to do, or what they think the agent wants, in order to gain a reward or avoid a sanction. People learn to behave in a particular way regardless of their personal beliefs. Occurrence of the behaviour requires that it is observable in some way by the influencing agent (e.g. monitoring) and the behaviour is usually of short duration.

- *Identification* involves people behaving in a way consistent with a satisfying, self-defining relationship to another person or group. This occurs through the adoption of all or part of a *role* (e.g. a professional) and may not be a fully conscious process. In order for the behaviour to occur, it requires the activation of the appropriate role and thus, like compliance, is dependent upon an external influencing agent.

- *Internalisation* means that people behave in particular ways because the behaviour fits with their value system –

'One of the functions of a value system is to generate a set of personal standards by which the person accepts or rejects induced behaviour. When we speak of internalisation, then, we refer to the acceptance of influence because the induced behaviour meets such personal standards. In the case of internalisation, in contrast to compliance and identification, the content of the induced behaviour is intrinsically rewarding.' (Kelman & Hamilton, 1989, p. 108)

Compliance, identification and internalisation correspond to rules, roles and values, respectively. Deviations from the standards set by these three processes may be thought of as *violations*, each of which has particular consequences for the person. Rule violations correspond to fear of social consequences; role violations correspond to guilt or shame; and values violations correspond to regret, remorse or self-disappointment (Kelman & Hamilton, 1989, p. 113).

These categories represent ideal states and an effective reform strategy would engage all three appropriately. The importance of incorporating a values strategy is that it takes account of the person's own relationship to the influence process rather than the process being largely externally driven. In addition, exposure to the personal and social vulnerability of the service users with whom this chapter is concerned inescapably engages people in values issues. This analysis suggests that reform that is largely dependent upon a technical, command-and-control approach, without calling upon deeper motivations, is unlikely to succeed.

A further reflection on compliance was provided by Walsh's (1991) description of two concepts of quality. The first defines quality as the degree to which a particular service or product conforms technically to its specification. The more dynamic view of quality examines the extent to which the product is fit for the intended purpose. This requires consultation with the user. Walsh reflected further:

'A definition of quality in terms of conformance becomes less useful the more the nature of requirements changes. Organisations must look outward as the key determinant of success changes from the control of internal production systems to the relationship with the consumer.' (Walsh, 1991, p. 504)

Key point

- Reform in the direction of person-centredness requires that the value systems of the workforce must be addressed.

The nature of person-centredness

The concept of person-centredness in human services refers to aspects of service quality that are primarily concerned with directly addressing the needs of *service users* in contrast to the needs of other stakeholders. At the heart of person-centredness are processes of identifying the needs of individual service users and planning based on those needs (O'Brien & O'Brien, 2000). Some of the key characteristics of person-centred approaches are:

- having a good knowledge of the service users that goes beyond objective facts or diagnoses and includes an understanding of their life experiences, aspirations and identities
- understanding them in a wide social context, not just the service setting
- understanding that there are universal and fundamental needs shared by all human beings, specific needs that may be unique to the person, and urgent needs that may have to be addressed before other needs
- using processes that are participatory, that involve the person and other people important to that person
- being flexible and process-oriented rather than relying solely upon regulated or mandated events, such as formal case meetings
- having a picture of optimal life conditions for service users that provides a vision for the future.

The concept of *model coherency* addresses these issues at a more organisational level (Wolfensberger & Glenn, 1973), by posing the question 'Are the right people working with the right clients, who are properly grouped, doing the right thing, using the right methods, and consistently so?' This approach uses a framework of four elements to describe and analyse a human service:

- First, there are the key assumptions that underpin a service, especially those that are concerned with what is believed to be the nature of the problem the service is addressing, likely solutions and the outcomes sought.
- Who are the service users? This element of the framework contains a description of the service users' needs that reflects a holistic and existential approach (as described above).

- The content of a service is essentially which needs of the service users the service is addressing (e.g. health needs, developmental needs).
- Service processes describe how the service content is delivered and include aspects such as the methods and technologies used, the physical characteristics of the service setting, and the manner in which the service groups users.

Model coherency defines quality as being directly related to the extent of the *coherency* or *fit* between what a human service does, how it does it and the needs of the service recipients. *Incoherency* may come from:

- incorrect key assumptions (e.g. assuming that people with learning disabilities are sick)
- lack of acknowledgement of fundamental needs of service users (e.g. addressing specialised needs in deprived physical and psychological environments)
- choosing a service content that is more about what the service is able to do, or perhaps has always done, rather than what service users need (e.g. providing play therapy for people who need meaningful work)
- service processes that congregate and segregate service users (for example, by placing them in hospitals located on the edge of a town).

Key point

- Key elements of person-centred models of services are a broad knowledge and understanding of service users, and a good fit between the needs of service users and what the service provides.

Examples of person-centred safeguards

In the context of formal human services, safeguards can be operationalised at four levels (Wolfensberger & Zauha, 1973; Wolfensberger, 1977; Kendrick, 1994; Cocks, 1997):

- basic assumptions or precepts
- the individual service user
- the human service organisation
- the human service system.

As you consider safeguards within this framework, note the extent to which safeguards are drawn from aspects of systems and decision theory as outlined above with reference to the work of Forrester.

Basic assumptions or precepts underpinning safeguards thinking and practice

- A mindset is required that acknowledges the reality of heightened vulnerability and that it is possible through safeguards to minimise or prevent either the vulnerability itself or the harmful consequences of that vulnerability.
- There are desirable aspects of human services that should be safeguarded and enhanced and undesirable aspects against which there should be safeguards.
- A mindset is required that acknowledges that things will go wrong, usually when least expected. All human activities, whether expressed in personal behaviour or in social structures, systems and institutions, are vulnerable to failure through entropy and goal displacement. This is an expression of human frailty aptly captured by Janis & Mann (1977, p. 15):

'Like Lewin, we see man not as a cold fish but as a warm-blooded mammal, not as a rational calculator always ready to work out the best solution but as a reluctant decision-maker – beset by conflict, doubts, and worry, struggling with incongruous longings, antipathies, and loyalties, and seeking relief by procrastinating, rationalising, or denying the responsibility for his own choices.'

- Because safeguards themselves can fail, there is a need for multiple and redundant safeguards (i.e. back-up measures).
- Safeguards can be specialised according to: the stages of effort in human services, from initial planning through to implementation; the level of focus, which may be on individuals, groups, human service organisations, or systems; whether they are carried out within or by formal systems and informal systems.
- Those making decisions should utilise multiple pathways in doing so, prefer multiple options and assume that there will always be another, probably better way of doing something than the chosen way.

Safeguards focused on the individual service user

These include:

- the presence and influence of key people in the person's life (e.g. family members, friends, neighbours)
- the availability of a range of types of advocacy and support (including advocacy that is independent of the service) such as individual advocacy, self-advocacy, peer group support and legal advocacy
- service users' involvement in and influence over the services they receive
- the selection of staff who have the appropriate person-centred values and commitments

- transparent, written individual objectives and grievance procedures for service users and their advocates.

Safeguards focused on the human service organisation

These include:

- organisational renewal – that is, maintaining low internal and external barriers to enhance a self-critical culture that is person-centred (measures include internal rotation of staff, opportunities for critical reflection, internal and external service reviews and evaluations, the recruitment of diverse staff, staff exchanges with other services, and external study tours by staff – Wolfensberger, 1977)
- service users' participation in governance
- regular feedback from service users
- clear roles and goals for service users and providers
- education and training that are values-based and person-centred and that involve service users.

Safeguards focused on the human service system

These include:

- an unambiguous fixed point of responsibility for services
- legal specification of rights to services and to service quality
- small, specialised service providers that are closely connected to local communities
- service users' and public participation and influence in service planning and provision
- external consultancy, advice and assessment
- funding contingent upon external assessment
- independent research focused on service quality and service users' outcomes.

Key points

Person-centredness to improve service quality can be safeguarded through a variety of measures taken at different levels, including:

- the key assumptions underpinning the service
- the service users
- the organisation
- the broad human service system.

Conclusions

This chapter has argued for the importance of person-centred values and processes as the driving force and yardstick for reform and quality enhancement in human services, especially for vulnerable people in formal systems of care. Clinical governance measures need to have a clearer connection with a humanistic values base. Person-centredness provides many opportunities for the engagement of human values.

This chapter suggested five strategies to promote person-centred services:

- connecting responses to risk and the understanding of human vulnerability
- being clear about the needed directions of reform in order to move away from major reliance on formal, technological measures and to move towards the human dimensions
- using social influence strategies that do not depend largely on coercion and compliance but which engage the values and commitments of stakeholders
- ensuring that planning for and evaluating quality incorporate the concept of coherency (i.e. the match between what a service does, how it does it and the needs of service users)
- using the framework of safeguards in order to develop person-centred measures in a systematic way at the levels of assumptions, individuals, organisations and systems.

References

Cocks, E. (1994) *Encouraging a Paradigm Shift in Services for People with Disabilities*. *Social Research and Development* monograph no. 9. Perth: Centre for the Development of Human Resources, Edith Cowan University.

Cocks, E. (1997) Building safeguards into the development of services. In *Human Services. Towards Partnership and Support* (eds P. O'Brien & R. Murray), pp. 165–180. Aukland: Dunmore Press.

Cocks, E. & Duffy, G. (1993) *The Nature and Purposes of Advocacy for People with Disabilities*. *Social Research and Development* monograph no. 4. Perth: Centre for the Development of Human Resources, Edith Cowan University.

Conway, R. N. F., Bergin, L. & Thornton, K. (1996) *Abuse and Adults with Intellectual Disability Living in Residential Services*. Mawson: National Council on Intellectual Disability.

Department of the Environment, Transport and the Regions (2001) *Quality and Choice for Older People's Housing – A Strategic Framework*. London: DETR.

Department of Health (1999a) *Clinical Governance: Quality in the New NHS*, HSC 1999/065. London: Department of Health.

Department of Health (1999b) *Facing the Facts. Services for People with Learning Disabilities: A Policy Impact Study of Social Care and Health Services*. London: Department of Health.

Donaldson, L. J. & Muir Gray, J. A. (1998) Clinical governance: a quality duty for health organisations. *Quality in Health Care*, **7** (suppl.), S37–S44.

Emerson, E., Robertson, J., Gregory, N., *et al* (1999) *Quality and Costs of Residential Supports for People with Learning Disabilities. A Comparative Analysis of Quality and Costs in Village Communities, Residential Campuses and Dispersed Housing Schemes*. Manchester: Hester Adrian Research Centre, University of Manchester.

Ferguson, E. (1978) *Protecting the Vulnerable Adult: A Perspective on Policy and Program Issues in Adult Protective Services*. Ann Arbor, MI: Institute of Gerontology.

Flynn, R. J. (1999) A comprehensive review of research conducted with the program evaluation instruments PASS and PASSING. In *A Quarter-Century of Normalisation and Social Role Valorisation: Evolution and Impact* (eds R. J. Flynn & R. A. Lemay), pp. 317–349. Ottawa: University of Ottawa Press.

Forrester, J. (1969) *Urban Dynamics*. Cambridge, MA: MIT Press.

Gaylin, I., Glasser, S., Marcus, S., *et al* (eds) (1981) *Doing Good: The Limits of Benevolence*. New York: Pantheon Books.

Hall, J. & Firth-Cozens, J. (2000) *Clinical Governance in the NHS: A Briefing*. Leicester: British Psychological Society.

Illich, I. (1976) *Limits to Medicine*. London: Marion Boyars.

Janis, I. L. & Mann, L. (1977) *Decision Making. A Psychological Analysis of Conflict, Choice, and Commitment*. New York: Free Press.

Kelman, H. C. & Hamilton, V. L. (1989) *Crimes of Obedience. Toward a Social Psychology of Authority and Responsibility*. New Haven, CT: Yale University Press.

Kendrick, M. (1994) Some significant ethical issues in residential services. In *Choice and Responsibility. Legal and Ethical Dilemmas in Services for Persons with Mental Disabilities* (ed. C. J. Sundrum), pp. 101–115. Albany, NY: New York State Commission on Quality of Care for the Mentally Retarded.

McKnight, J. (1996) *The Careless Society: Community and its Counterfeits*. New York: Basic Books.

O'Brien, J. & O'Brien, C. L. (2000) *The Origins of Person-Centred-Planning. A Community of Practice Perspective*. Lithonia, GA: Responsive Systems Associates, Inc.

Oliver, M. (1990) *The Politics of Disablement*. Basingstoke: Macmillan.

Sobsey, D. (1994) *Violence and Abuse in the Lives of People with Disabilities: The End of Silent Acceptance*. Baltimore, MD: Paul Brookes.

Walsh, K. (1991) Quality and public services. *Public Administration*, **69**, 503–514.

Wolfensberger, W. (1977) *A Balanced Multi-component Advocacy/Protection Schema*. Ontario: Canadian Association for the Mentally Retarded.

Wolfensberger, W. (1998) *A Brief Introduction to Social Role Valorization: A High-Order Concept for Addressing the Plight of Societally Devalued People, and for Structuring Human Services* (3rd edn). Syracuse, NY: Training Institute for Human Service Planning, Leadership and Change Agentry, Syracuse University.

Wolfensberger, W. (2000) A brief overview of social role valorization. *Mental Retardation*, **38**, 105–123.

Wolfensberger, W. & Glenn, L. (1973) *Program Analysis of Service Systems (PASS): A Method for the Quantitative Evaluation of Human Services. Vol. 1: Handbook. Vol. 2: Field Manual* (2nd edn). Toronto: National Institute on Mental Retardation.

Wolfensberger, W. & Zauha, H. (1973) *Citizen Advocacy and Protective Services for the Impaired and Handicapped*. Toronto: National Institute on Mental Retardation.

Clinical governance standards – Structures and strategies

CLINICAL GOVERNANCE STANDARDS
for Mental Health and Learning Disability Services
Structures and Strategies

Foreword
Development of the standards
The Standards
1. Clinical Governance Strategy and Structures
2. Service User and Carer Involvement and Experience
3. Clinical Audit
4. Clinical Risk Management
5. Evidence Based Practice
6. Staffing and Staff Management
7. Education, Training and Continuing Personal and Professional Development
8. Information Management

Foreword

It was a happy day when we within the NHS were instructed to place clinical governance – the necessity of assuring constant improvement in the quality of our services – at the head of the agenda for mental health and learning disability services. I believed, like many others, that important though fiscal issues are, too great an emphasis had been placed on the financial, as opposed to the clinical, aspects of the services.

Trusts now have a clear responsibility constantly to improve the quality of their services. Many have already achieved much, but some have found it more difficult and still have some way to go.

These new standards, carefully and comprehensively set out, will help both trusts which have already made considerable progress and those still grappling with the impact of the clinical governance process, critically examine their services and identify areas for further development. This document should be of value to commissioners, managers and practitioners.

The Royal College of Psychiatrists is extremely pleased that the Clinical Governance Support Service, based at the College Research Unit, is so successfully supported by participative trusts. It is the only national body with a specific remit for supporting clinical governance in mental health and learning disability services.

August 2001, CRU no. 017. Edited by Adrian Worrall.

Feedback, both from review policies and legislation and from use of these standards in CGSS reviews, will be incorporated in an annual revision of these standards. In the meantime, I hope that all concerned with clinical governance – which means all of us – will find these of interest and value.

Dr Sheila Mann
Clinical Governance Lead
Royal College of Psychiatrists

The Development of Clinical Governance Standards

Background

These standards cover key aspects of clinical governance relevant to trusts providing mental health and learning disability services. This is the first version of an evolving set of standards that will annually incorporate trust feedback and new policy and legislation.

The standards are the basis for the CGSS self and external peer reviews. The aim of the reviews is to gradually improve the quality of services using the principles of the clinical audit cycle. The standards represent ideal practice and as such the level of service they describe is not expected to be found universally.

Methods

The development involved three main processes: a review of key documents; consultation with CGSS members; and editing. We used the information from members to supplement the standards derived from the literature review. This ensured that the standards were up-to-date and that they took account of the views of relevant staff.

i. Review of key documents

These included standards and information from the Health Advisory Service, the Commission for Health Improvement, the Clinical Governance Support Service, the Royal College of Psychiatrists, the Clinical Negligence Scheme for Trusts, the Clinical Standards Board for Scotland and a range of documents from regional and local trusts. The CHI's *Acute clinical governance reviews: review issues* was particularly relevant. Generic standards were selected rather than standards specific to acute services or other specialty areas. We derived about 350 statements that formed the basis of the first draft of the standards.

General statements are classified as standards, and more specific statements as criteria within these. Each standard has typically four or five criterion statements. In this document standards are in bold text and relevant criteria are given in plain text below these.

ii. Consultation

Members were asked to rate each standard as "very important", "important" or "not important". They were also asked to suggest new standards. More general feedback was also obtained during an induction event.

iii. Editing

Low rated standards were removed. Other editing criteria included: ease of measurement; achievability, e.g. how achievable statements were; and local adaptability, e.g. how adaptable statements were to variations in local practice. These reduced standards will be adapted into data collection tools for use on self and external peer reviews.

The standards will now be further developed and updated annually as part of their use in service reviews.

Important note and disclaimer

Mental health and learning disability services are organised and provided in many different ways. These standards attempt to be generic but may not apply well to all services. We have classified the standards to describe various topics within clinical governance, but they could be classified in other equally appropriate ways. Each section begins with a higher order standard and then continues with more specific standards, in bold text, and relevant criteria below these. Criteria are not comprehensive, but are generally given as examples of good practice relating to the standard.

These are best practice statements and consequently we would not expect services to meet every standard. There are some statements that are based upon legal requirements. This document is not intended to act as a legal guide in any way.

If you have any questions about these standards, please contact Adrian Worrall at the Royal College of Psychiatrists' Research Unit; Email: aworrall@cru.rcpsych.ac.uk

1. Clinical Governance Strategy and Structures

1   The trust is committed to implementing clinical governance to improve care and the service users' experience

1.1   The trust has the structures and accountabilities to lead this

1.1.1   The trust has a multidisciplinary clinical governance committee with service user and carer representation

1.1.2   The trust has appointed a person to lead clinical governance

1.1.3   The chair of the clinical governance committee is a member of the trust board

1.1.4   There is a clear line of accountability from the chief executive level

1.1.5   Clinical governance is a standing item on the trust board agenda

1.2   The clinical governance committee regularly reports to the trust board

1.2.1   The clinical governance committee provides an annual clinical governance report to the trust board

1.2.2   The report identifies progress and development needs in each component area of clinical governance

1.3   The trust has an up-to-date written clinical governance strategy. This specifies:

1.3.1   Roles and responsibilities of staff

1.3.2   Timescales for implementation of clinical governance objectives

1.3.3   Cross organisation arrangements and inter-agency issues, including with primary care and social services

1.3.4   The skills and knowledge necessary to implement clinical governance, training needs and ways to address these

1.3.5   Dedicated staff time and budgets to support clinical governance

1.3.6   Arrangements for reviewing clinical governance progress

1.3.7   Expected outcomes for the implementation of clinical governance, e.g. service user care and experience, improved safety, etc.

1.3.8   Systems for quality improvement, e.g. service development is informed by an annual evaluation of clinical governance activities

1.3.9   The strategy relates to and specifies other service development priorities including: the health improvement programme; the National Service Frameworks for mental health and older adults; the learning disabilities white paper, Valuing People; the NHS Plan

1.3.10   Each clinical directorate has a clinical governance plan which links to the clinical governance strategy

1.4   Clinical team members understand their roles and responsibilities in relation to clinical governance

1.4.1   Clinical teams meet regularly to discuss clinical governance issues and review progress

2. Service User and Carer Involvement and Experience

2   **The trust is committed to communicating with service users and carers and understanding their needs and priorities**

2.1   **The trust has the structures and accountabilities to lead consultation and service user and carer involvement**

2.1.1   The trust has established a committee dedicated to service user and carer consultation and involvement or this is an explicit duty of other management committees

2.1.2   The trust has appointed a person to lead service user and carer consultation and involvement

2.1.3   The committee reports regularly to the clinical governance committee

2.2   **The trust has mechanisms to involve a range of service users and carers, or their representative organisations, in the planning and monitoring of services. These include:**

2.2.1   Consultation with service user representatives or groups

2.2.2   Lay/citizen representation on the trust board and clinical governance committee

2.2.3   Service user and carer surveys

2.2.4   Use of validated instruments to find out service users' views, e.g. Carers' and Users' Expectations of Services (CUES)

2.2.5   Patient councils or panels

2.2.6   Complaints procedures and suggestion boxes

2.3   **The trust has an up-to-date written strategy for service user consultation and the provision of information for service users**

2.3.1   The strategy describes ways to meet the information needs of service users, relatives and carers

2.3.2   The strategy describes links with local user/community groups

2.3.3   The strategy describes mechanisms for incorporating service user feedback

2.3.4   The strategy was developed in consultation with service users and carers

2.4   **Service users, and carers with appropriate consent, are provided with information about their care. For example this includes information about:**

2.4.1   Diagnosis and condition

2.4.2   Treatment alternatives, including drug and psychotherapy treatments and side effects

2.4.3   Services and expected waiting times

2.4.4   Facilities

2.4.5   Advocacy services

2.5   **Information materials are easily understood, e.g. they are jargon-free and in translation where necessary**

2.5.1   Information for service users and carers is presented in a variety of formats, e.g. verbally; or using leaflets, posters and videos; and in computer-based formats

2.5.2   Service users and carers are involved in preparing and reviewing information materials

2.6 **All service users have up-to-date written care plans as part of their care management programme, e.g. care programme approach or care planning in Wales**

2.6.1 Service users are given copies of their care plans

2.6.2 Service users' health and social care needs are routinely recorded in the care plan

2.7 **The trust has processes for effectively dealing with complaints**

2.7.1 The trust has a multidisciplinary complaints committee with service user and carer representation

2.7.2 The complaints committee reports to the trust board

2.7.3 The complaints procedure is clearly advertised

2.7.4 Staff are made aware of complaints that are relevant to their work and the outcome of the complaints process

2.7.5 Complaints are monitored and used to inform service development, e.g. records of complaints are referred to in management meetings

2.7.6 There is a joint complaints policy between social care and mental health services

2.8 **There are arrangements to find out about, and meet, service users' needs**

2.8.1 These include cultural, spiritual, disability and dietary needs

2.8.2 Questions are asked about expectations of friends and family

2.8.3 An interpreter is used when necessary who understands the signs and symptoms of major diagnoses and needs of different groups

2.9 **Service users' rights to privacy and dignity are respected**

2.9.1 The trust ensures that in-patients may sleep, bathe and wash in privacy and in areas separate from the opposite sex

2.9.2 The trust provides in-patients with access to a telephone in a private area

2.9.3 There are arrangements for the safe-keeping of in-patient's property including their money

2.9.4 Single sex wards are provided for in-patients, or there are plans to replace any mixed sex wards with single sex wards in line with NHS Plan requirements. (This is not specified in the Welsh plan but is considered good practice.)

2.9.5 Hospital and community-based facilities are clean and comfortable

3. Clinical Audit

3   **The trust is committed to the management and direction of the clinical audit programme**

3.1   **The trust has the structures and accountabilities to lead the clinical audit programme**

3.1.1   The trust has established a clinical audit committee

3.1.2   This committee is multidisciplinary (e.g. it has representatives from the medical, nursing, therapeutic and other relevant professions) and has service user representation

3.1.3   This committee meets regularly

3.1.4   The trust has appointed a clinical audit lead

3.1.5   The committee reports regularly to the clinical governance committee

3.2   **The trust has an up-to-date written clinical audit strategy**

3.2.1   This audit strategy includes reference to locally agreed clinical audit procedures, e.g. regarding consultation on standards

3.2.2   The audit strategy is referred to in the trust's mental health strategy

3.2.3   The audit strategy includes national and local priority topics for clinical audit

3.2.4   Audit topics are identified from complaints procedures and adverse events, e.g. complaints about lack of privacy lead to an audit of service user rights as described in the Patients Charter

3.3   **A range of audits is conducted. These include:**

3.3.1   The use and side effects of major treatments, e.g. the diagnosis and dose for antipsychotic and antidepressant drugs

3.3.2   Aspects of the care programme approach care plan or, in Wales, aspects of the written management plan or care plan

3.3.3   Rates of emergency readmission to psychiatric units (required nationally as a high level performance indicator, NHSE 1996b)

3.3.4   Implementation of the Mental Health Act, e.g. Section 5(2) required by the Mental Health Act Commission

3.3.5   NICE guidelines, e.g. attention deficit disorder

3.3.6   Delivery of electro-convulsive therapy (national guidance is available)

3.3.7   Use of procedures for the management of violence

3.3.8   Risk management procedures in accordance with Clinical Negligence Scheme for Trusts' standards

3.4   **Audit has been carried out in each directorate/service over the last year in line with trust priorities**

3.5   **The clinical audit committee or lead reports audit results and recommendations, e.g. using verbal presentations and in a written report**

3.5.1   Audit findings and recommendations are reported to the trust board, clinical teams, the clinical governance committee and other interested parties

3.5.2   Audit findings are used to inform service planning

3.6   **Clinical teams and other relevant staff develop action plans in response to audit reports and recommendations**

3.6.1   The area is re-audited to monitor improvements, e.g. audits are continued for 2 or more cycles

3.7   The trust participates in national audits, e.g. the trust funds practitioners' participation in multi-centre audits

3.8   Clinical audit work cuts across organisational boundaries, e.g. some audit projects involve primary care, social services or voluntary services

3.9   Staff and service users are involved in clinical audit

3.9.1   Service users and carers help identify audit topics and agree standards

3.9.2   Managers and practitioners help identify audit topics, agree standards and action plans

3.9.3   Clinical teams, rather than individual members only, are involved in clinical audit

3.10   All senior managers and practitioners have received training in clinical audit

3.11   Clinical audit is sufficiently resourced

3.11.1 The trust has dedicated funds to support clinical audit

3.11.2 Dedicated clinical audit personnel are available centrally

4. Clinical Risk Management

4   **The trust is committed to the management and direction of the clinical risk management programme**

4.1   The trust has the structures and accountabilities to lead the clinical risk management programme

4.1.1   The trust has established a risk management group or committee

4.1.2   This committee is multidisciplinary (e.g. it has representatives from the medical, nursing, therapeutic and other relevant professions) and has service user representation

4.1.3   The committee meets regularly

4.1.4   The trust has appointed a risk management lead

4.1.5   The trust has appointed risk management leads within directorates/ services

4.1.6   There is a named executive director of the trust board charged with responsibility for clinical risk management

4.1.7   The committee reports regularly to the clinical governance committee

4.2   **The trust has an up-to-date written strategy and procedures for clinical risk management**

4.2.1   This strategy has been agreed with the local authority and other relevant partner organisations

4.2.2   There are systems for reporting clinical incidents including "near misses"

4.2.3   The trust has written procedures for assessing clinical risks

4.2.4   The trust has written procedures for the identification, monitoring, assessment and management of serious incidents and clinical risk

4.2.5   Guidance and protocols have been developed in consultation with clinical staff for dealing with specific incidents and identified clinical risks

4.3   The trust promotes an open, blame-free culture for reporting incidents

4.3.1   Critical incident analyses use a systems approach, i.e. the trust looks for systems improvements rather than scapegoats

4.3.2   The trust has provided information to staff regarding anonymous reporting of adverse events and "near misses" (this information may also relate to "whistle-blowing" and reporting unsafe practice)

4.4   **Staff understand their requirements in relation to clinical risk management**

4.4.1   This includes staff requirements to report risks and adverse events

4.4.2   Staff requirements for clinical risk management are included in the induction training

4.5   **Partner organisations are involved in clinical risk management for individual service users whose care is provided by a number of services, e.g. social services attend discharge planning meetings for service users at risk**

4.6   **Trust managers and clinicians learn from information collected on clinical risks**

4.6.1   Incident reviews and other information on clinical risks informs action plans and service planning

4.6.2   Information systems help managers identify trends in incidents

4.7 **The risk management committee or lead provides reports on risks and incidents, e.g. using verbal presentations and in a written report**

4.7.1 Findings and recommendations are reported to the trust board, clinical teams, the clinical governance committee and other interested parties

4.7.2 Findings are used to inform service planning

4.8 **The trust participates in the National Reporting Scheme. The Regional Office is notified of specific serious clinical incidents**

4.9 **External risk management standards (e.g. CNST) are used for service evaluation or audit**

5. Evidence Based Practice

5   **The trust is committed to the management and direction of an evidence based practice programme**

5.1   **The trust has the structures and accountabilities to lead the evidence based practice programme**

5.1.1   The trust has established an evidence based practice committee

5.1.2   This committee is multidisciplinary (e.g. this includes medical, nursing, therapeutic and other relevant staff) and has service user representation

5.1.3   The committee meets regularly

5.1.4   The trust has appointed a person to lead evidence based practice

5.1.5   The committee reports regularly to the clinical governance committee

5.2   **The trust has an up-to-date written strategy for implementing and monitoring evidence based practice**

5.2.1   The research strategy and evidence based practice strategy are referred to in the trust's mental health strategy

5.3   **The committee reviews national information on evidence based practice, such as NICE guidelines, NSFs and other agreed national guidelines, and adapts this where necessary to suit the local population and service**

5.3.1   The committee has led the development of local guidelines on the management of schizophrenia and the management of depression

5.3.2   The committee has led the development of integrated care pathways for the management of schizophrenia and depression

5.3.3   The committee involves clinical staff in the development of guidelines and care pathways

5.3.4   The committee has disseminated information on evidence based practice to local staff, e.g. local guidelines for the management of schizophrenia and depression have been disseminated to practitioners

5.4   **Evidence based practice is monitored, e.g. the prescribing of anti-psychotic drugs is audited against local guidelines and protocols**

5.4.1   Where practice is found not to be evidence based, and good evidence exists, training and information are quickly provided

5.5   **The committee co-ordinates local research**

5.5.1   The committee has a local research strategy that includes national and local research priorities

5.6   **The findings of local research projects are effectively disseminated using a range of methods, e.g. via an R&D newsletter, notice boards, intranet and internet**

5.7   **Staff have received the necessary training in evidence based practice**

5.7.1   Staff have received training in evidence based practice, the use of the specific clinical guidelines and protocols used by the trust

5.7.2   Staff have received training in critical appraisal

5.7.3   Staff have received training in the use of library and database facilities and search techniques

5.8 **Staff have good access to up-to-date information about the evidence behind the treatments they provide**

5.8.1 Staff have good access to clinical journals and books

5.8.2 Staff have access to the internet and know how to use the key sources of information, e.g. Cochrane database and NeLMH

6. Staffing and Staff Management

6   **The trust is committed to the management and direction of staff**

6.1   **The trust has the structures and committees to lead this**

6.1.1   The trust has appointed a person to lead staffing and staff management

6.1.2   The committee reports regularly to the clinical governance committee

6.2   **There is an up-to-date written human resource strategy which includes local and national priorities**

6.2.1   The strategy is referred to in the clinical governance strategy

6.2.2   The strategy addresses Working Together targets

6.2.3   The strategy addresses Improving Working Lives targets

6.2.4   The strategy specifically promotes equality of opportunity, e.g. in terms of gender, race, religion and disability

6.2.5   The strategy addresses the retention of staff

6.3   **There is an active recruitment policy to ensure vacant posts are filled quickly with well qualified candidates**

6.4   **External human resource standards are attained (e.g. Investors in People)**

6.5   **Workforce planning is linked to service planning**

6.5.1   The clinical skill requirements within clinical teams are determined by the local health and social care needs assessment

6.5.2   The skill mix of clinical teams is reviewed at least annually

6.6   **All staff receive annual appraisal and personal development planning**

6.7   **All clinical staff receive clinical supervision**

6.8   **The trust has procedures for dealing with poor performance**

6.8.1   Staff know procedures for reporting concerns about poor performance

6.8.2   Staff are encouraged to report cases of poor performance and understand their obligations to do this. Trusts encourage this by promoting a blame-free culture where system faults are identified rather than individual scapegoats

6.8.3   There is a forum where staff are able to express concerns about service users' care and these concerns are taken seriously

6.8.4   Agencies are informed of poorly performing locums, bank and agency staff

6.8.5   There are mechanisms for dealing with poor performance, e.g. retraining, shadowing, and other remedial action

6.9   **The trust has a mechanism for formally recognising good performance**

6.10   **There are sufficient numbers of skilled staff to safely meet the needs of service users at all times, e.g. each shift always has an agreed minimum number of qualified staff**

6.10.1   Minimum 'safe' numbers and staff mix have been locally agreed for all service areas

6.10.2   There are suitable schemes of delegation and supervision operating at night

6.10.3   There are protocols for staff working in extended roles (e.g. nurse prescribing)

6.11   **There are strategies to protect staff and maintain safety**

6.11.1   The risk management strategy includes reference to reducing violence affecting staff

6.11.2   The trust complies with relevant health and safety legislation

6.11.3   The trust complies with directives on working time

6.12   There is a system to ensure that clinical staff are registered and qualified. This requires that:

6.12.1   Clinical staff registration and qualifications are checked on appointment

6.12.2   Clinical staff registration and qualifications are checked on revalidation

6.13   Good staff morale is recognised as important and efforts to improve morale are made when necessary

6.13.1   There is a forum in which staff can discuss morale issues with senior management

6.13.2   There are clear procedures for managing complaints from staff

6.13.3   There are employee support services e.g. occupational health services, grievance procedures, pastoral staff support

6.13.4   Staff sickness rates, vacancies and turnover are monitored and acted upon when necessary

7. Education, Training and Continuing Personal and Professional Development

7	**The trust is committed to educating, training and the continuing personal and professional development of its staff**
7.1	**The trust has the structures and accountabilities to lead education, training and the continuing personal and professional development of its staff**
7.1.1	The trust has established an education or "CPD" committee
7.1.2	The committee meets regularly
7.1.3	The trust has appointed an education or "CPD" lead
7.1.4	The committee reports regularly to the clinical governance committee
7.2	**The trust has an up-to-date written strategy for education, training and the continuing personal and professional development of its staff**
7.2.1	This strategy includes details for individual directorates
7.3	**The trust is involved with partner organisations in education, training and "CPD"**
7.3.1	There are partnerships with academic institutions
7.4	**Joint training is organised with staff from other health and social care organisations where there is partnership working**
7.5	**The training needs of staff have been formally assessed**
7.5.1	The training needs assessment informs, and is referred to in, the training or workforce development strategy
7.5.2	The training needs to implement clinical governance are specifically addressed
7.5.3	Training needs are identified from clinical audit and risk management reports, a skills audit, staff appraisal, individual development plans and support and supervision systems
7.5.4	Training needs have been assessed in the last year
7.6	**Staff and multidisciplinary teams participate in effective work-based training**
7.6.1	All clinical staff participate in programmes that support continuing personal and professional development
7.6.2	There are dedicated "CPD" budgets for all clinical staff
7.7	**The trust provides support for staff looking to gain further and professional qualifications**
7.8	**Basic skills and mandatory training requirements for clinicians are met, these include:**
7.8.1	Basic life support
7.8.2	Handling and moving
7.8.3	Dealing with fire
7.8.4	General health and safety
7.8.5	The management of violence, e.g. control and restraint techniques, breakaway techniques
7.8.6	Risk management
7.8.7	Clinical audit
7.8.8	Using service user feedback and complaints handling

7.8.9   Evidence based practice, including use of guidelines, and searching for effectiveness information

7.8.10   Performance appraisal

7.8.11   Care planning as part of their care management programme, e.g. care programme approach or care planning in Wales

7.8.12   Use of service user outcome measures such as HoNOS

7.8.13   All clinical staff and managers receive training in clinical governance and its component activities

7.9   A record of training is kept to ensure that basic training has been provided to all clinicians

7.9.1   Training is provided to clinicians where training needs have been identified

7.10   Appropriate training methods are used to ensure staff training is effective

7.10.1   Whenever appropriate staff training is multidisciplinary and multi-agency

7.10.2   Induction training is provided for temporary, locum and permanent staff before they have unsupervised access to service users

7.11   The trust attains external standards and accreditation

7.11.1   Standards are maintained in line with guidance from professional organisations and other relevant bodies, e.g. Investors in People (IIP), Royal Colleges, etc.

8. Information Management

8   **The trust is committed to the development and use of information to improve care and service users' experience**

8.1   **The trust has the structures and accountabilities to lead this**

8.1.1   The trust has a multidisciplinary clinical information/health record committee with service user representation

8.1.2   The trust has appointed a person to lead clinical information management and technology

8.1.3   The trust has appointed a qualified librarian or information specialist to manage library and information facilities

8.2   **The trust has an up-to-date written strategy for information management and technology**

8.2.1   The trust has an agreed plan for the development of electronic clinical information systems

8.2.2   Clinical governance needs are prioritised within the information management and technology strategy, e.g. systems to support clinical audit and risk management

8.2.3   The strategy has been agreed with social services, primary care and other relevant partner organisations

8.3   **The information technology infrastructure offers good access to high quality and helpful information**

8.3.1   This information directly informs service strategies and plans

8.3.2   This information is used to support performance review and improvement

8.4   **Staff have access to training and support in access to and use of information**

8.5   **Staff have access to a well equipped library and quiet study area**

8.6   **The trust has systems for assuring data quality**

8.6.1   Quality indicators have been developed and are monitored and used to improve the quality of information

8.6.2   Clinical staff receive feedback on the quality of the information they provide

8.7   **The trust complies with NHS data collection requirements, e.g. data are collected for:**

8.7.1   National patient surveys

8.7.2   Patient charter monitoring

8.7.3   Common information core

8.7.4   National Service Frameworks

8.7.5   Our Healthier Nation targets for mental health

8.7.6   Mental health national performance indicators

8.7.7   Outcome measures, e.g. HoNOS

8.7.8   Risk indicators are collected as part of a clinical information system

8.7.9   Progress has been made toward completing the mental health minimum data set

8.8   **The trust complies with requirements to keep service user information confidential**

8.8.1   A Caldicott Guardian has been identified

8.8.2   Managers and practitioners are aware of trust guidelines on confidentiality, e.g. a written guideline has been disseminated

8.8.3   There are locally agreed protocols for the sharing of service user information with other agencies and services, e.g. social services, voluntary organisations and the private sector

8.9   Information management and technology reports are presented to the trust board

Clinical governance standards – Enabling front-line staff

CLINICAL GOVERNANCE STANDARDS
for Mental Health and Learning Disability Services
Enabling Front-Line Staff:
Turning clinical governance strategies into practice

Foreword
Development of the standards
The standards
1. Environment and Facilities
2. Staffing and Recruitment
3. Monitoring and Management of Performance
4. Staff Training and Development
5. Services and Resources to Support Staff
6. Involving Staff and Keeping them Informed
7. Organisational Culture

Foreword

Policy-makers are more explicit now about what is required than they have been at any other time during my 20 years working in mental health services. The National Service Framework and NHS Plan list the service components that should be put in place and define the values that should be adhered to. Guidance about the CPA, and from NICE about clinical practice, describe the process of care that should be followed, sometimes in minute detail. Performance indicators are being piloted that the Commission for Health Improvement will use to ensure that the desired outcomes are achieved.

Last year's CGSS reviews confirmed that managers in mental health services have responded to these top-down demands and have translated national requirements into local policies and procedures, usually under the broad umbrella of clinical governance. However, one consistent theme to emerge from peer-review visits was doubt amongst trust managers about whether their ambitious plans had been translated into improvement at grass-roots level.

The mechanisms by which clinical teams can be influenced to adopt new or changed practices are complex to the extent that these teams can appear to be "black boxes". Inputs in the form of new policies and procedures sometimes do not result in outputs that demonstrate change in the direction desired.

November 2002, CRU no. 025. Edited by Adrian Worrall.

In our view, this black box must be the focus of this year's work for CGSS. We have therefore reformatted the standards and now present them from the perspective of front-line staff. The standards and criteria continue to represent all of the components of clinical governance but they are written in language that will resonate with practitioners. The central question they address is *does this service have a culture and practices that enable its staff to work in a way consistent with the principles of clinical governance?*

Professor Paul Lelliott
Director
College Research Unit

The Development of the Standards

Background

These standards aim to help trusts that provide mental health and learning disability services turn clinical governance strategies into practice. They describe the actions managers can take to enable front-line staff's clinical governance work.

The standards are the basis for the CGSS self- and external peer-reviews. The aim of the reviews is to gradually improve the quality of services using the principles of the clinical audit cycle. The standards represent ideal practice and as such the level of service they describe is not expected to be found universally.

These standards do not replace CGSS' preceding set of standards, *Clinical Governance Standards for Mental Health and Learning Disability Services (August 2001, CRU No. 017)*, but rather specify clinical governance work at a different service level.

Methods

The development involved three main processes: a review of key documents; consultation with CGSS members; and editing. We used the information from members to supplement the standards derived from the literature review. This ensured that the standards were up-to-date and that they took account of the views of relevant staff.

i. Review of key documents

Many standards were adapted from CGSS' preceding set of standards (*CRU No. 017*). These focus on structures and strategies but have implications for management support for front-line staff. The review also included standards and information from the Health Advisory Service (HAS); the Commission for Health Improvement (CHI); the Royal College of Psychiatrists; and Clinical Accountability, Service Planning and Evaluation (CASPE). The CHI's Clinical Team Self-Assessment tools were particularly relevant. Some local trust documents were very useful including South London and Maudsley NHS Trust's modular workbook, *Clinical Governance and the Clinical Team*.

In particular, some standards on staffing levels were derived from the Royal College of Psychiatrists' report of the working group on the size, staffing, structure, siting and security of new acute adult psychiatric in-patient units, *Not Just Bricks and Mortar* (CR62, 1998), and the Department of Health's Mental Health Policy Implementation guidance covering adult acute inpatient care (http://www.doh.gov.uk/mentalhealth/inpatientcp.pdf) and community mental health teams (http://www.doh.gov.uk/mentalhealth/cmht.pdf). We derived about 320 statements that formed the basis of the first draft of the standards.

ii. Consultation

Feedback from CGSS members was particularly valuable to this set of standards. Members were asked to rate each standard as "very important", "important" or "not important". They were also asked to suggest new standards.

iii. Editing

Low rated standards were removed. Other editing criteria included: ease of measurement; achievability, e.g. how achievable statements were; and local adaptability, e.g. how adaptable statements were to variations in local practice. These reduced standards have been adapted into data collection tools for use on self- and external peer-reviews.

Format

Section headings have been chosen to reflect the action managers can take to support front-line staff. General statements are classified as standards, and more specific statements as criteria within these. Each standard has typically four or five criterion statements. In this document standards are in bold text and relevant criteria are given in plain text below these.

Many of these standards directly refer to managers' responsibilities and their actions to enable front-line staff. It would be a mistake, however, to think of managers and front-line staff as two distinct groups. There are managers at many levels of the service from clinical and administrative team managers to service managers and medical directors. Then, of course, there are many staff who have both clinical and managerial roles. It would probably be more helpful to think of "management" as a function rather than "managers" as a distinct group. Good standards, however, specify the person/people responsible for the action described, and for this reason and for the sake of simplicity we have decided refer to "managers" rather than the "management" function.

Important note and disclaimer

Mental health and learning disability services are organised and provided in many different ways. These standards attempt to be generic but may not apply well to all services. We have classified the standards to describe various topics within clinical governance, but they could be classified in other equally appropriate ways. Criteria are not comprehensive, but are generally given as examples of good practice relating to the standard.

These are best practice statements and consequently we would not expect services to meet every standard. There are some statements that are based upon legal requirements. This document is not intended to act as a legal guide in any way.

354

If you have any questions about these standards, please contact Adrian Worrall at the Royal College of Psychiatrists' Research Unit; Email: aworrall@cru.rcpsych.ac.uk

1. Environment and Facilities

1.1   **Premises are well designed and maintained**

1.1.1   Premises are clean, well decorated, and have a welcoming atmosphere

1.1.2   There is a waiting area with appropriate reading material, e.g. information sheets and magazines

1.1.3   The service entrance and key clinical areas are clearly sign-posted

1.1.4   There is sufficient car parking space for staff, service users and visitors

1.1.5   Ward-based staff have access to a separate staff room

1.2   **Premises are designed and managed so that service users' rights, privacy and dignity are respected**

1.2.1   In-patients and other residential clients have the option of a single bedroom

1.2.2   In-patients and other residential clients may sleep, bathe and wash in privacy and in areas separate from the opposite sex

1.2.3   Wards have a specific room for physical examination and minor medical procedures

1.2.4   There are private rooms for in-patients to meet with relatives and friends

1.2.5   In-patients have access to quiet rooms

1.2.6   In-patients and other residential clients may choose to eat in a communal dining area or in a smaller alternative area

1.2.7   In-patients and other residential clients have a choice of well prepared meals and special options are available for vegetarians and those from certain religious groups

1.2.8   There are facilities for in-patients and other residential clients to make their own hot and cold drinks and snacks

1.2.9   Front-line staff encourage in-patients and other residential clients to personalise their bedroom spaces

1.2.10   Wards and residential settings have a telephone for service users in a private area

1.2.11   All confidential case material, e.g. notes, is kept in locked cabinets or locked offices

1.2.12   The environment meets the needs of people with physical disabilities

1.3   **The trust provides facilities to enable practitioners to provide good clinical care**

1.3.1   There are sufficient numbers of large and small rooms for individual and group work when needed

1.3.2   There are identified interview rooms

1.3.3   There are rooms in community settings which service users can use for formal meetings

1.3.4   Drugs are kept in a secure place with the dispensary book

1.3.5   The facilities for ECT are provided according to the standards set by the Royal College of Psychiatrists

1.4   **Service users have the opportunity to engage in a range of activities which are interesting, sociable, recreational and therapeutic**

1.4.1   There is a timetabled programme of activities for the day, evenings and weekends

1.4.2   There is sufficient space inside and outside for service users' recreation

1.4.3   Books and magazines are provided in recreation areas for service users

1.4.4   There are facilities for playing games appropriate to the client group, e.g. a pool table and board games are provided

1.4.5   A television, video and audio system are provided

1.5   The trust provides a working environment that is safe for staff and service users

1.5.1   There is an alarm system or quick way for service users or staff to raise an alarm in an emergency

1.5.2   Exits and entrances have clear lines of sight to enable staff to see who is entering or leaving

1.5.3   Equipment for communication and personal safety is available to all community staff, e.g. mobile phones and/or personal alarms are provided

1.5.4   There are areas with clear lines of sight to enable staff to monitor service users who require a high level of observation

1.5.5   There are appropriate facilities for security within hospital wards and residential settings, e.g. certain doors may be locked if needed

1.5.6   Security staff are available to support front-line staff in the event of a violent incident

1.5.7   Resuscitation equipment which staff are able to use is easily accessible and its location is clearly identified

1.5.8   Clinical settings provide minimal environmental risk, e.g. possible ligature points have been identified and dealt with

1.5.9   Wards and residential settings have facilities for the safe-keeping of in-patients' property including their money

1.5.10   Wards, residential settings and community settings have facilities for the safe-keeping of staff property including their money

2. Staffing and Recruitment

2.1 **There are sufficient numbers of skilled staff to safely meet the needs of service users**

2.1.1 Clinical staff and managers have agreed minimum 'safe' numbers and staff mix for all service areas, e.g. each shift always has an agreed minimum number of qualified staff

2.1.2 A system of case load management and support is available for staff

2.1.3 A typical CMHT includes 1.0 consultant psychiatrist, 1–1.5 non-consultant medical staff, 1–3 mental health support workers, 1–1.5 administrative assistant or secretary and additional reception staff

2.1.4 A typical CMHT has 8 care co-ordinators including: 3–4 community mental health nurses; 2–3 social workers, including ASWs; and 1–1.5 occupational therapists (the care programme approach does not operate in Wales, although similar arrangements may be found as part of care planning)

2.1.5 In a typical CMHT, care co-ordinators have a maximum caseload of 35

2.1.6 A typical CMHT has a maximum caseload of between 300–350 service users (This may be considerably less and will depend on case mix and availability of other staff such as assertive outreach teams)

2.1.7 Clinical teams based in wards or day units include mental health nurses, support workers, ward/day unit managers and psychiatrists as a minimum, and there is access to other practitioners as appropriate to the needs of the client group

2.1.8 A typical three ward unit (e.g. 30–45 beds in total) has a minimum staffing during the day of three registered nurses per shift

2.1.9 One junior doctor is provided per ward of 15 places when community and out-patient work is allowed for

2.1.10 In-patient services and day units have input from psychological therapies staff (art, drama, music, psychology, psychotherapy) and occupational therapists

2.1.11 There is an identified duty doctor available at all times

2.1.12 Ward shifts are managed so that each has sufficient staff trained in behaviour management techniques according to the needs of the client group, e.g. control and restraint or other de-escalation techniques

2.1.13 Staff operate a lone worker procedure for staff operating alone in community settings

2.1.14 Staff whereabouts are logged and missing staff are followed up

2.2 **Staff work effectively as a multidisciplinary team**

2.2.1 There are regular multidisciplinary clinical team meetings

2.2.2 Community teams have integrated health and social care staff, e.g. the team uses one set of notes

2.2.3 CMHT's have fully integrated consultant staff, e.g. consultants attend team meetings

2.3 **There is sufficient flexibility in staffing numbers to accommodate services' changing needs**

2.3.1 Staff receive help from surrounding hospital-based services in the event of untoward incidents, e.g. If staff need to escort a service user to an accident and emergency department, then staff from other services help provide cover

2.3.2 Extra staff are available to services with unusually high numbers of high dependency service users, e.g. bank staff are available to support teams that are caring for a particularly high risk in-patient

2.4 There is a clear management structure which works effectively to support services

2.4.1 There are clear lines of accountability

2.4.2 There is clear clinical and managerial leadership

2.4.3 The roles and responsibilities of front-line staff are clearly defined, e.g. in job descriptions and in operational policy

2.4.4 Front-line staff are aware of their level of authority and what decisions they can and cannot take

2.5 Recruitment practice ensures that the full staffing complement is maintained

2.5.1 Staff vacancies are advertised promptly, i.e. as soon as resignation is accepted, rather than when the post becomes vacant

2.5.2 When posts are vacant or in the event of long-term sickness, prompt arrangements are made for temporary staff cover

2.5.3 Reasons for staff leaving are established, particularly for positions where there is a high staff turnover, e.g. exit questionnaires or interviews are used

2.5.4 Managers and front-line staff have identified critical posts which must be immediately filled should positions become vacant

2.5.5 Service users and carers are involved in interviewing candidates where appropriate

2.6 Staffing budgets are devolved, e.g. team leaders manage staffing budgets

3. Monitoring and Management of Performance

3.1   Staff performance is monitored and managed within the trust

3.1.1   All staff receive annual appraisal and personal development planning

3.1.2   Managers and front-line staff have agreed clear and realistic clinical performance targets

3.1.3   Managers have informed staff of their obligation to report cases of poor performance

3.1.4   Retraining, shadowing and supervision are provided to address any poor performance identified

3.1.5   Each service area (e.g. CAMHS, AMH and EMI) has a dedicated human resources advisor

3.1.6   There are clear procedures for managing complaints from staff

3.2   Good performance, e.g. innovative practice or sustained high levels of patient safety, is recognised and rewarded

3.2.1   Managers have a mechanism for formally recognising good performance, e.g. at events, in newsletters and with achievement awards

3.3   The use of clinical outcome measures and other clinical data is promoted and supported. These measures include:

3.3.1   Outcome measures, e.g. HoNOS

3.3.2   Risk indicators

3.3.3   Measures of team performance, e.g. percentage of known carers present at review meetings, hours of face to face clinical supervision, attendance at whole team clinical reviews

3.3.4   Measures of service user satisfaction and experience

3.3.5   Discharge questionnaires to collect service user feedback

4. Staff Training and Development

4.1 **Training needs are systematically identified, e.g. from clinical audit and risk management reports, a skills audit, staff appraisal, individual development plans and support and supervision systems**

4.2 **Effective staff training methods are used**

4.2.1 There is an induction training programme for all new staff

4.2.2 Wherever appropriate staff training is multidisciplinary and multi-agency

4.2.3 Service users and carers are directly involved in training, both as participants and as trainers when appropriate

4.2.4 Community team induction training includes a primary care placement

4.3 **Managers support practitioners' continuing professional development and those looking to gain further relevant professional qualifications**

4.3.1 Training budgets enable front-line staff to meet requirements for their continuing professional development

4.3.2 There are arrangements for staff cover to allow staff to attend training

4.3.3 All clinical staff participate in programmes that support continuing personal and professional development

4.3.4 There is equity of access to training for all staff groups

4.3.5 There are established links with higher education institutions

4.4 **Staff are trained in components of clinical governance that are relevant to their work**

4.4.1 Basic training is provided and updated to meet mandatory requirements. This includes basic life support, handling and moving, dealing with fire, general health and safety, and the management of violence

4.4.2 Practitioners have been trained in evidence-based practice, e.g. how to make use of library and database facilities, search techniques, critical appraisal and specific clinical guidelines

4.4.3 Practitioners have been trained in how to conduct and participate in clinical audit

4.4.4 Practitioners have been trained in risk management and risk assessment

4.4.5 Practitioners have been trained in suicide awareness and prevention techniques

4.4.6 Practitioners are trained in, and informed about, how to involve service users and carers

4.4.7 Practitioners have been trained in care planning as part of their care management programme, e.g. care programme approach (or care planning in Wales) including discharge planning

4.4.8 Practitioners have been trained in the use of appropriate service user outcome measures such as HoNOS or HoNOS-LD

4.4.9 All relevant staff receive regular updates on the Mental Health Act and its Code of Practice

4.4.10 Front-line staff, and particularly administration staff, are provided with training to manage distressed, angry, demanding or otherwise challenging people

4.4.11 Performance appraisal is provided by trained appraisers

4.4.12 Clinical supervisors are provided with training on clinical supervision

4.4.13   All staff have been trained in the use of clinical information and confidentiality and receive regular updates

4.4.14   Practitioners have been trained in procedures for assessing carers' needs

4.4.15   There is a training programme for the development of staff in clinical leadership

4.4.16   Training and support is provided in budget management for key front-line staff

4.4.17   Training is provided on trust policy, procedure and guidelines

5. Services and Resources to Support Staff

5.1   **All clinical staff receive clinical supervision in line with trust policy, e.g. for specified amounts of time and from approved supervisors**

5.2   **The trust provides front-line staff with appropriate information technology**

5.2.1   All practitioners have access to the trust's intranet including "out of hours" access

5.2.2   All practitioners have access to the Internet including "out of hours" access

5.3   **The trust provides front-line staff with study facilities**

5.3.1   Front-line staff have access to a trust library staffed by librarians or trained information officers

5.3.2   Facilities are provided for study, seminars and training events

5.4   **Front-line staff have protected time to engage in clinical governance activity relevant to their work, e.g. time for clinical audit and researching clinical guidelines**

5.5   **The trust supports clinical audit**

5.5.1   Audit support staff are available to provide practical help to clinical teams engaged in audit

5.5.2   Managers support clinical teams' participation in national audits, e.g. managers fund teams' participation in multi-centre audits

5.5.3   A specialist clinical effectiveness worker is available to support clinical teams and specific clinical audit projects

5.5.4   There is a commitment to support changes identified by audit work

5.6   **The trust supplies a range of written material that staff can give to service users, e.g. booklets and leaflets**

5.6.1   Information is up to date and regularly supplied to all relevant service areas in sufficient quantity

5.6.2   Information materials are easily understood, e.g. they are jargon-free and in translation where necessary

5.6.3   The material includes information about diagnosis and condition, treatment alternatives, services and expected waiting times, facilities, advocacy services, and local support organisations

5.6.4   A "welcome pack" or introductory booklet is provided when people first use the service

5.6.5   Relevant posters are displayed in appropriate places in community and hospital-based services

5.6.6   The complaints procedure is clearly advertised, e.g. in posters and leaflets

5.7   **Administrative support is provided to meet the needs of each service**

5.7.1   Front-line staff have sufficient administrative support to discharge their responsibilities under the care programme approach (care planning in Wales)

5.7.2   Administrative support is provided to copy and disseminate care plans and to arrange review meetings

5.8   **Service users and front-line staff have access to interpreters**

5.8.1 Interpreters understand basic signs and symptoms of major diagnoses and needs of different groups

5.9 Service users can access general primary and secondary care and they are informed how to do this if required

5.10 A range of written policies and procedures is available to guide and support staff. These include documents that cover:

5.10.1 Prescribed medication

5.10.2 Medication errors

5.10.3 Care programme approach, including clinical risk assessment and management and discharge planning

5.10.4 Prevention and management of violence

5.10.5 Use of illicit substances by patients

5.10.6 Health and safety

5.10.7 The reporting of poor performance or "whistle-blowing"

5.10.8 Clinical supervision

5.10.9 Staff appraisal

5.10.10 Bullying, harassment and discrimination

5.10.11 Reporting and learning from accidents and untoward incidents

5.10.12 Medical emergencies, such as cardiac arrest

5.10.13 Complaints from staff

5.10.14 Complaints from service users and carers

5.10.15 Child protection roles and responsibilities of staff

5.11 A range of written policies and procedures is available to guide and support hospital-based staff. These include documents that cover:

5.11.1 Implementation of the Mental Health Act

5.11.2 Admission

5.11.3 Visitors

5.11.4 Searches of service users and their property

5.11.5 Absence without leave

5.11.6 Transfer of service users between services

5.11.7 Service user use of the telephone

5.11.8 Close observation

5.11.9 Discharge against medical advice

5.12 A range of written policies and procedures is available to guide and support community-based staff. These include documents that cover:

5.12.1 Patients in the community causing concern

5.12.2 Lone worker procedure for staff operating alone in community settings

5.12.3 Caring for service users that are difficult to engage or make contact with

6. Involving Staff and Keeping them Informed

6.1 **Front-line staff are consulted in the development of policies, procedures and guidelines that relate to their practice**

6.1.1 Managers and practitioners have agreed treatment guidelines, e.g. for the management of service users with schizophrenia and depression

6.1.2 Managers and practitioners have agreed standards for elements of the main care pathways, e.g. admission process, elements of ongoing care and treatment, and discharge

6.2 **Middle managers relay information in both directions between senior management and front-line staff**

6.2.1 Managers represent the needs of front-line staff to senior trust management, e.g. there are regular opportunities for front-line staff to raise concerns and express opinions and these are relayed to senior management meetings

6.2.2 Front-line staff clearly state their support needs and contribute to local debate about service development

6.3 **Policies, procedures and guidelines are formatted, disseminated and stored in ways front-line staff find accessible and easy to use**

6.3.1 Staff in community-based services have access to all relevant policies and procedures, e.g. relating to Care in the Community

6.4 **Staff have access to up to date information about evidence-based practice**

6.4.1 Current relevant professional and technical journals are available to staff

6.4.2 All staff have access to information about clinical effectiveness and evidence-based practice from dedicated staff, and through online facilities, e.g. NeLMH, Cochrane and NICE databases

6.4.3 Staff have access to national information and resource centres, e.g. NeLMH

6.4.4 Staff have access to information about relevant standards and results of projects completed within the organisation

6.4.5 Local guidelines have been disseminated, e.g. on the management of schizophrenia and depression

6.4.6 Information has been disseminated on integrated care pathways, e.g. for the management of schizophrenia and depression

6.5 **The trust routinely gives feedback to front-line staff about issues that can inform their practice**

6.5.1 Managers feedback relevant complaints and the outcome of the complaints process to front-line staff

6.5.2 The findings of local audit and research projects are disseminated in an easy-to-read format using a range of methods, e.g. via an R&D newsletter, notice boards, intranet and Internet

6.5.3 Managers feedback the findings of incident reviews and other information on clinical risk to front-line staff

6.5.4 Managers monitor uptake of training, and feedback this information to front-line staff

6.5.5   Managers regularly generate summary reports of key measures for practitioners to discuss at team meetings including referrals, admissions, emergency re-admissions, length of stay, DNA's, caseloads and outcome measures

6.5.6   Service user satisfaction is monitored and the findings of surveys, focus groups and other exercises are fedback to front-line staff

6.5.7   Managers monitor the implementation of policies and procedures and provide feedback to front-line staff

6.5.8   The implementation of clinical guidelines is monitored and feedback is provided to front-line staff

6.6   **Practitioners are involved in identifying priority audit topics in line with national and local priorities, and agree standards. The clinical audit programme includes:**

6.6.1   The use and side effects of major treatments, e.g. the dose for antipsychotic and antidepressant drugs

6.6.2   Aspects of the care programme approach care plan or, in Wales, aspects of the written management plan or care plan

6.6.3   Rates of emergency readmission to psychiatric units

6.6.4   Implementation of the Mental Health Act, e.g. Section 5(2) required by the Mental Health Act Commission

6.6.5   NICE guidance

6.6.6   Delivery of electro-convulsive therapy

6.6.7   Use of procedures for the management of violence

6.6.8   Priorities from the National Service Frameworks and NHS Plan

6.7   **The findings of clinical audit projects are used to develop action plans**

6.7.1   Practitioners and managers agree action plans in response to audit reports and recommendations

6.7.2   Topics are re-audited to monitor improvements, e.g. audits are continued for 2 or more cycles

7 Organisational Culture

7.1 The trust promotes a "service user-friendly" culture

7.1.1 Service users are told the name of their key worker, care co-ordinator, primary nurse or named nurse, e.g. this is written down and given to service users when they first use the service

7.1.2 Service users can meet with members of staff, particularly their key worker and/or care co-ordinator, and are told how to do this

7.1.3 Service users can make themselves at home, e.g. they can make drinks, watch television etc. without asking staff first

7.2 There is an open, blame-free culture for reporting incidents

7.2.1 Managers use a systems approach to critical incident analyses, i.e. managers look for opportunities for system improvements rather than scapegoats

7.2.2 Managers have provided information to staff regarding anonymous reporting of adverse events and "near misses" (this information may also relate to "whistle-blowing" and reporting unsafe practice)

7.3 The trust promotes a learning culture

7.3.1 Staff meet to critically reflect on their practice and identify and support each others' learning needs

7.4 Managers recognise staff morale as important and make efforts to improve morale when necessary

7.5 Trust leaders at all levels support clinical governance

7.5.1 Leaders develop and communicate clear values and priorities for the trust, e.g. in meetings, at events and in newsletters

7.5.2 Leaders ensure service and staff development work is sufficiently resourced

7.5.3 Leaders promote training and provide training according to their area of expertise

7.5.4 Leaders make themselves accessible to trust staff

7.5.5 Leaders actively participate in quality improvement initiatives

7.5.6 Leaders use appraisal and promotion systems to support improvement and involvement

7.6 Responsibility is devolved to enable front-line staff to make key decisions about the service they provide

7.6.1 Managers are "results orientated" and do not dictate how front-line staff should achieve targets

7.7 The trust provides an equitable and non-discriminatory environment for staff and service users

7.7.1 The trust has an equal opportunities policy

7.7.2 The trust has a policy and procedure for dealing with bullying and harassment

Index

Compiled by Caroline Sheard